FIFTY INCREDIBLE CRICKET MATCHES

FIFTY INCREDIBLE CRICKET MATCHES

Patrick Murphy

Stanley Paul
London Melbourne Auckland Johannesburg

Stanley Paul & Co. Ltd
An imprint of Century Hutchinson Ltd
62–65 Chandos Place, London WC2N 4NW
Century Hutchinson Australia (Pty) Ltd
PO Box 496, 16–22 Church Street, Hawthorn, Melbourne,
Victoria 3122
Century Hutchinson New Zealand Limited
PO Box 40–086, Glenfield, Auckland 10
Century Hutchinson South Africa (Pty) Ltd
PO Box 337, Bergvlei 2012, South Africa

First published 1987
© Patrick Murphy 1987

Set in Linotron Sabon by Input Typesetting Ltd, London SW19 8DR
Printed in Great Britain by Anchor Brendon Ltd, Tiptree, Essex

British Library Cataloguing in Publication Data
Murphy, Patrick, 1947–
Fifty incredible cricket matches.
1. Cricket——History
I. Title
796.35'87   GV913
ISBN 0 09 166470 5

Photographic aknowledgement
For permission to use copyright photographs in this book, the author and
publishers would like to thank BBC Hulton Picture Library, Photo Source,
Patrick Eagar, All-Sport and Sport and General Press Agency.

Contents

Foreword
by Bob Willis

It is ten years now since Pat Murphy pressed the doorbell of my bachelor flat in Birmingham and suggested that we write a cricket book together. Since then we have penned four literary works and become the firmest of good friends. It is therefore a special thrill for me to introduce his latest offering to you. Having worked with Pat producing about a quarter of a million words on cricket, one can only sit back in amazement at his unique knowledge of the subject involved. Obviously his job as Midland Region Sports Producer for BBC Radio has given him rare access to many of the great personalities of the game, and his prowess as an opening bowler with the Pebble Mill XI will have shown him some of the problems the professionals face at a rather higher level; but his greatest attribute as a cricket writer is an incredible memory for facts, figures and dates of the great moments in the sport. This uncanny gift that Pat possesses is perfectly suited to this superb collection of memories of fifty of the more unlikely matches that the game of cricket has produced.

The book covers over one hundred years in the game's illustrious history. Apart from the incredible goings-on across the Irish Sea in 1969 when the mighty West Indians were humbled by the local part-timers, all the matches are first-class in status. From the Varsity Match of 1870, the collection comes right up to date with the 1986 visit to Pakistan by Viv Richards' side. The scorecards of the matches themselves are interesting in their own right, but are brought to life by Pat's very readable interpretations. As usual Pat has done his homework with meticulous detail: he has covered the length and breadth of the country in his search for interviews with the survivors of the chosen games and has spent many a long day poring over the match reports of the day in Birmingham

University library. Research is the key to a book of this type, and once again he has left no stone unturned.

There is an even spread of matches across the broad spectrum of cricket's history. There are accounts of contests in the last century, either side of the Great War, and the joyous matches after the Second World War which signalled the beginning of the end for the Gentlemen *v*. Players games. But freakish results were not confined to the good old days, and the eighties have already had more than their share of upside-down finishes. I took part in two of the recent matches featured – the Headingley Test of 1981 and the Melbourne nail-biter of the 1982–3 series. As usual, Pat's memory of even these games is better than my own, and it was great fun reliving those magic moments.

The author's insight into the inner workings of a cricket match is really very special. He is aware that some finishes are caused not by brilliant captaincy or one great performance, but more often than not by dear old Lady Luck. Both the Tests in which I feature had more than their share of fortune about them. At Headingley it was a last desperate bid for my Test-match career that prompted me to persuade Mike Brearley to bowl me down the hill that fateful Tuesday afternoon. No tactical genius at Melbourne either by yours truly when I tossed the ball to the resident miracle-worker Botham to take the last wicket with the Aussies within four runs of victory. More and more these days, the international player believes in the wheel of fortune. With the Tests coming so thick and fast it is far more likely that freakish results will be thrown up. Who would have dreamt of another tied Test? But I bet the next comes in less than a quarter of a century.

The Press-box pundits and waffling commentators so often forget the human element of the matches that they are covering, but Pat goes behind the scenes to find out what the people involved were actually saying, thinking and feeling at the vital moments when a particular game changed course. The players of this and past generations have an unusually close relationship with Pat and, because they have absolute trust in him, they are far more willing to bare their innermost thoughts than to a fly-by-night hack who's out for a quick scoop. Pat's BBC training has stood him in good stead for waiting patiently until the subject is relaxed and ready to chat one to one about his feelings. His patience has been well rewarded here in this unique collection.

Introduction

The word 'incredible' is, of course, a judgement of value. What fascinates me in a cricket match could easily induce heavy eyelids in anyone else. For me the acid test is: Do I want to know more about the particular game, rather than content myself with the scorecard? Robert Brooke and I have waded through 300 matches to whittle down the total to just fifty. We have given scope to the bizarre, the heroic, the ridiculous and the close-run thing. We hope we have got the balance right between gripping finishes, romantic revivals, towering individual achievements and outstanding examples of captaincy – but the fingers are crossed as I write.

So many remarkable matches are missing. No Tied Test. None from the Bodyline Series. Nothing of Bradman's largesse, nor Hutton's at the Oval in the year of Neville Chamberlain's piece of paper. I am fully aware that a cricket buff could sit down and come up with a list of fifty amazing games that bear no relation to mine. It is an arbitrary selection. All the games are first class, with the exception of Ireland's humiliation of the West Indies in 1969; with a name like mine, I owed it to Hibernia to include that one. I feel that one-day matches are essentially artificial, that the equation of runs per overs is mechanical and no longer yields many surprises. In contrast a game lasting at least three days is organic: there is more scope for all the human quirks and tactical niceties that make cricket so fascinating.

Looking back on the list of matches, I am struck by the regular presence of Somerset and Warwickshire. It is a complete fluke, with no intent of partiality. It simply seems that both counties have had a long and honourable proclivity towards the daft and the unpredictable. The consistent Northern counties of Yorkshire,

Lancashire and Nottinghamshire appear less inclined to the spectacular. Perhaps they were too busy winning cricket matches.

I hope that some flavour of cricket's varied history will come through from this book. In my opinion modern cricket as we know it started in 1864, with the legalisation of round-arm bowling and the emergence of W. G. Grace. We thus started looking at matches from that date onwards and, with luck, the reader will get at least an impression of the trends in cricket over the decades.

This book would not have been possible without the tremendous statistical authority of Robert Brooke. His ability to ferret out data is uncanny; he always seems to be able to put his hand on an interesting piece of information. With Robert at the statistical helm, I was free to indulge in recreating history. My thanks also to Steve Bates for assistance on Major R. M. Poore and Captain E. G. Wynyard's varied careers (chapter 7), to Brian Croudy for research into the overseas matches, to Tony Woodhouse for matches involving Yorkshire, to L. T. Newell for matters Northamptonshire, and to John Mace for looking after Gloucestershire's details. The reference library at Birmingham University was a treasure trove for myself, while Birmingham's Central Library kept Robert Brooke busy in the newspaper archives.

Many first-class cricketers from past and present were only too happy to furnish me with their reminiscences. I was pleasantly surprised at their sure grasp of detail, bearing in mind the effect that nostalgia can have. A gentle prompt or two, an open Wisden and a glass of amber fluid were usually enough to stir the memory cells.

Finally, my thanks to that persistent publisher Roddy Bloomfield. He kept nagging me to do this book and I hope he is satisfied with it.

Patrick Murphy
NOVEMBER 1986

I
Oxford *v.* Cambridge
1870

It falls to few cricketers to be associated eternally with one cricket
match, to be the man whose performance transcended the efforts
of the other twenty-one players. Such a man was Frank Carroll
Cobden. He was an Old Harrovian who bowled right-arm fast
and straight: during one sunlit evening in June 1870, he touched
greatness. At the age of twenty, Cobden ended the Oxford *v.*
Cambridge in sensational fashion. With Oxford needing just four
runs to win and three wickets still standing, Cobden realized his
twenty-seventh over of the innings would be decisive. It was – he
performed the hat-trick and Cambridge won by two runs. That
single over ensured Cobden's name would forever live in cricket
history, while the climactic final stages of the match galvanized
interest in first-class cricket and, in particular, Oxbridge cricket.

Oxford had played Cambridge annually at Lord's since 1851,
but interest in the fixture was spasmodic and parochial. The deeds
of the professionals and the emerging genius of W. G. Grace excited
greater attention up and down the land. On the first morning of
the 1870 match, *The Times* ignored it and concentrated on the
Henley Royal Regatta and a preview of a pigeon-shooting contest
at Hurlingham between representatives from the House of Lords
and the Commons. The following day's edition carried the result
of that stirring pigeon shoot and the odds for the Goodwood Stakes
ahead of a report on the first day at Lord's. Cobden's *tour de force*
changed the emphasis – next day the match report led the sport
column, and later that week *The Field* magazine's account polished
up a cliché that was hoary and old even in those understated days:
'How true is the adage "a match is never lost till won".'

In dull weather, the first day's play made great inroads into the
match. Twenty wickets fell and Oxford obtained a lead of 28 that

OXFORD UNIVERSITY *v* CAMBRIDGE UNIVERSITY
At Lord's, 27 and 28 June 1870

CAMBRIDGE UNIVERSITY

Mr J. W. Dale b Francis	15	– c Ottaway b Francis	67
Mr F. Tobin b Francis	13	– b Belcher	2
*Mr W. B. Money b Belcher	10	– b Francis	6
†Mr W. Yardley c Butler b Francis	2	– (7) c and b Francis	100
Mr F. E. R. Fryer c Stewart b Hadow	8	– (4) b Francis	0
Mr A. T. Scott b Belcher	45	– c Tylecote b Francis	0
Mr C. I. Thornton b Belcher	17	– (5)c Hadow b Butler	11
Mr F. A. Mackinnon not out	17	– b Belcher	2
Mr F. C. Cobden b Francis	7	– c Hadow b Francis	7
Mr L. A. Bourne b Belcher	3	– b Francis	0
Mr E. E. Ward st Stewart b Francis	2	– not out	3
B 3, l-b 4, w 1	8	– B 4, l-b 3, w 1	8
	147		**206**

1/20 2/40 3/40 4/46 5/65 6/93 7/126
8/137 9/144

1/6 2/19 3/19 4/40 5/40
6/156 7/189 8/135 9/195

Bowling: *First Innings* – Belcher 45–25–52–4; Francis 42.2–16–59–5; Butler 11–4–16–0; Hadow 7–2–12–1. *Second Innings* – Belcher 29–10–38–2; Francis 42.3–12–102–7; Butler 2–0–8–1; Hadow 4–1–11–0; Hill 13–6–27–0; Pauncefote 4–2–5–0; Fortescue 3–1–7–0.

OXFORD UNIVERSITY

Mr A. T. Fortescue b Money	35	– (2)b Ward	44
Mr W. H. Hadow b Cobden	17	– (1)c Scott b Cobden	0
Mr C. J. Ottaway b Bourne	16	– c Fryer b Ward	69
*Mr B. Pauncefote c Dale b Ward	15	– b Ward	5
Mr E. F. S. Tylecote c Thornton b Ward	25	– b Ward	29
Mr W. Townshend st Yardley b Money	0	– c Money b Ward	1
Mr F. H. Hill b Ward	23	– not out	13
Mr C. K. Francis b Cobden	12	– lbw b Ward	1
Mr S. E. Butler b Cobden	18	– c Bourne b Cobden	0
†Mr W. A. Stewart b Cobden	0	– (11)b Cobden	0
Mr T. H. Belcher not out	0	– (10)b Cobden	0
B 10, lb 2, w 1, nb 1	14	– B 7, lb 3, w 3, nb 1	14
	175		**176**

1/28 2/66 3/82 4/110 5/111 6/124
7/144 8/166 9/166

1/0 2/72 3/86 4/153 5/160
6/165 7/175 8/176 9/176

Bowling: *First Innings* – Bourne 21–11–36–1; Cobden 19–6–41–4; Money 17–4–37–2; Ward 16–8–33–3; Fryer 14–5–14–0. *Second Innings* – Bourne 30–15–41–0; Cobden 27–10–35–4; Money 7–0–24–0; Ward 32–16–29–6; Fryer 7–1–15–0; Thornton 10–4–13–0; Dale 3–1–5–0.

Umpires: J. Grandy and T. Hearne.

Cambridge won by 2 runs.

* captain
† wicket-keeper

would probably prove invaluable in a low-scoring game where the wicket assisted the faster bowlers. Cobden gave a portent of things to come by cleaning up the Oxford tail, and his fast bowling appeared as impressive as his physique. At six feet and twelve stone he was stronger and more athletic than many of his contemporaries, and his ability to bowl long spells would enable him to make his name the following day.

Tuesday, 28 June began rather dull in London, but in the afternoon the sun came out and the excellent light allowed the match to proceed to its breathless climax at 7.35 p.m. Cambridge were soon in trouble when they batted again – 19 for 3, then 40 for 5, a lead of only twelve. Then the elegant Dale and the powerful Yardley turned the game with a stand of 128. Yardley played brilliantly to record the first hundred ever hit in the University match (stark testimony to the quality of the Lord's pitches in those days), and he underlined his reputation as the best batsman in the country, apart from the redoubtable W. G. Grace. Despite this heroic partnership, Cambridge could only manage 206, with the last five wickets falling for eleven runs. Oxford needed just 179 to win.

Cobden secured an early breakthrough, when he had his fellow-Harrovian Hadow caught at mid-on before a run was on the board. Then Fortescue and Ottaway added 72, and although Fortescue and Pauncefote were both out within a few minutes of each other, the initiative soon passed back to Oxford. Ottaway and Tylecote (one of the best wicket-keeper/batsmen of the Victorian age) batted splendidly. The hundred was posted after 135 minutes and the score advanced to 153 for 3, with just 26 needed. Ward and Cobden had bowled many overs, and although five more bowlers were used, they all looked spent and inconsolable as the runs trickled away. Then Tylecote fell to Ward: 153 for 4. At the stroke of seven o'clock, Townshend walked in to bat and it was decided to carry on for an extra half-hour, so that Oxford could clinch their deserved victory, instead of returning on the morrow for a handful of runs. Townshend, with a massive batting reputation from Rossall School, was caught at slip almost immediately. In his later years, Canon William Townshend would muse philosophically about his scores of 0 and 1 in Cobden's Match and ponder the irrelevance of huge scores at school before facing the pressure of a tight Varsity game.

Ottaway's three-hour vigil had ended in the over before Townshend's dismissal, and when Ward trapped Francis lbw the score was now 175 for 7. Four runs needed, three wickets left. Ward, left-arm medium pace with a slingy action, bowled to the massive, hard-hitting Butler. He swung lustily and all eyes looked to the mid-wicket boundary for the winning runs. They were mistaken. Bourne had made an astonishing stop at short-leg, taking the pace off a fierce hit and no run was taken.

Ward's over ended at 7.28 with Oxford still 175 for 7. He did not know it, but his part in the game was over. Cobden started an over that changed his life. The first ball was played by Hill to mid-off and a single was taken. Two to tie, three to win, and three wickets left. Butler smashed the next ball to cover-point, where the ubiquitous Bourne held on to a catch that a lesser man would have avoided. Enter Thomas Belcher, later Vicar of Basingstoke and emphatically a bowler; he was bowled off his right pad first ball. The last man, Stewart, walked in, deathly pale, with the crowd eerily silent. Cobden crammed his cap firmly on his head, rushed up to the crease and bowled a long hop. Luckily for Cambridge it was a fast long hop and Stewart was beaten for pace and bowled. Cambridge – and Cobden – had won by two runs, a few minutes after odds of a hundred to one against them had been offered and accepted in the pavilion. Seven wickets had fallen for 23 runs, six of them in the extra half-hour that had been blithely claimed by Oxford.

The crowd surged round the pavilion and called for Cobden. They might also have singled out several others – Yardley for a wonderful 100 out of 152 while at the wicket, Bourne for his two brilliant efforts in the field in the space of a few deliveries and, above all, Ward for his excellent bowling. The Rev. Edward Ewer Harrison Ward gave fifty-nine years' service to the Church of England and lived to his ninety-second year – yet he maintained he was never robust as a cricketer. After taking the second and third Oxford wickets on that last day, he asked to be taken off because he was tired. After gathering his strength he came back and took four wickets, ending with 6 for 29 off 32 overs. Five of those wickets were certainly the best batsmen in the Oxford team, and some good judges considered that Cobden's four wickets were those of the four worst batsmen. Ward took 9 for 62 in the match – compared with Cobden's 8 for 76 – and it seems his contribution was overshadowed by three deliveries at the other end.

Yet those three balls ended the game in the grand manner. It is hard to begrudge credit to a man who finishes off a tense, desperately close match by performing the hat-trick, and Cobden could savour the memory for another sixty-two years before he died in Wales, where he ran a hotel business. He could also reflect happily that three deliveries at furious pace had helped the University Match to move centre stage in public interest. For an Oxbridge Blue, that remained the crucial factor.

2
Hampshire *v.* Derbyshire
1876

If ever a man deserved to win a cricket match, it was William Mycroft. Over two scorching days in July 1876 he did everything that was humanly possible to beat Hampshire. He took seventeen of the nineteen wickets to fall, caught the eighteenth and took part in the largest stand of Derbyshire's first innings – yet Derbyshire lost agonizingly by one wicket. Mycroft became the first bowler to take seventeen wickets in a first-class match, but he failed to get the vital victim, as Hampshire's last-wicket pair scrambled nine precious runs. In a more sophisticated age, Mycroft would have qualified for a generous productivity bonus; instead he had to be happy with a few pints and a gallant part in a great match.

Mycroft was thirty-five when he entered the record books. He had come to the first-class game comparatively late. He was a miner, and nothing had been heard of him until 1873, but he quickly established himself as one of the best left-arm bowlers in the country. He mixed spin with swerve and pace and for a time looked the complete bowler, able to adapt to any wicket. His fast yorker was devastating, although serious doubts were often expressed about the legality of the delivery. Whatever the merits of his action – and he was not unique in this respect during that period – Mycroft performed wonders for a Derbyshire side that was little more than a chopping block for the big guns during its formative years in first-class cricket. There is little doubt that Mycroft would have played for England if Test cricket had existed in the mid–1870s; by the time Australia had become regular visitors to these shores a decade later he was past his best.

He was certainly at his best at the Antelope Ground when he bowled his county back into the game after a poor start. On an excellent wicket in tropical heat, Derbyshire had made a meagre

HAMPSHIRE v DERBYSHIRE
At Southampton, 24 and 25 July 1876

DERBYSHIRE

W. Rigley b Ridley	8	– b Ridley	22
Mr J. Smith c and b Galpin	17	– b Galpin	1
*Mr R. P. Smith c Tate b Galpin	1	– (4)c Tate b Ridley	6
Mr S. Richardson b Galpin	0	– (8)c Hargreaves b Ridley	0
J. T. B. D. Platts st Hyslop b Ridley	28	– (3)c Tate b Galpin	26
A. Hind b Ridley	13	– (6)st Hyslop b Ridley	3
T. Foster b Galpin	15	– (5)c Foster b Ridley	11
Mr W. G. Curgenven b Galpin	10	– (7)b Galpin	8
†A. Smith b Ridley	0	– (11) not out	0
G. Hay not out	9	– (9)st Hyslop b Ridley	8
W. Mycroft c Tate b Ridley	11	– (10)b Galpin	4
Extras leg byes	3	– leg byes	2
	115		**91**

1/15 2/18 3/19 4/40 5/61 6/78 7/91
8/91 9/94

1/5 57 3/63 4/68 5/78 6/81
7/87 8/91 9/91

Bowling: *First Innings* – Galpin 34–16–42–5; Ridley 33.2–10–70–5. *Second Innings* – Galpin 26.1–11–39–4; Ridley 22–7–42–6; Holmes 3–1–8–0.

HAMPSHIRE

G. Carter b Mycroft	0	– b Mycroft	30
†H. H. Hyslop b Mycroft	0	– c Hind b Platts	8
Mr G. H. Longman c A. Smith b Mycroft	0	– b Mycroft	19
Mr A. W. Ridley b Mycroft	24	– b Mycroft	13
*Mr C. Booth b. Mycroft	14	– b Mycroft	12
Mr R. G. Hargreaves b Mycroft	4	– not out	35
Mr A. F. Jeffreys b Mycroft	4	– b Mycroft	3
H. Holmes b Mycroft	3	– c Richardson b Mycroft	8
H. W. Tate c Mycroft b Hay	0	– (10)c Richardson b Mycroft	1
Mr F. G. Foster b Mycroft	10	– (9)c sub b Mycroft	2
J. G. Galpin not out	4	– not out	1
Extras	0	– B 5, l-b 8	13
	63	**(9 wickets)**	**145**

1/0 2/0 3/5 4/38 5/39 6/43 7/49
8/52 9/53

1/16 2/51 3/68 4/89 5/92
6/96 7/122 8/130 9/135

Bowling: *First Innings* – Mycroft 21.3–13–25–9; Platts 7–3–19–0; Hay 14–6–19–1. *Second Innings* – Mycroft 38.1–11–78–8; Platts 11–4–22–1; Hind 26–9–32–0.

Hampshire won by one wicket.

115. It would have been less than a hundred if Mycroft had not
helped George Hay add 21 for the last wicket, until Mycroft was
caught at slip. He then showed he was more than just an obdurate
bat: in his first over, Hyslop played on to the second delivery and
next ball Longman was superbly caught at the wicket. In Mycroft's
third over, Carter was clean bowled, making the score 5 for 3.
Ridley and Booth then added 33, but Mycroft eventually got them
both. Indeed he took the first eight wickets, and only interrupted
the sequence when he caught Tate at slip at 53. Ten runs later a
typical fast yorker undid Foster, and Hampshire were all out after
just an hour and a half. Derbyshire led by 52, and they increased
that by another 56 for the loss of their captain, Smith, who was
bowled by a shooter – one of the few dismissals in the day that
stemmed from misfortune rather than excellent bowling.

The following day play began at eleven, an hour and three
quarters earlier than the previous day. Playing regulations were
much laxer in the 1870s! By 12.20 p.m. Derbyshire were all out
for 91. Brilliant Hampshire fielding and a deteriorating pitch led
to the collapse and, although Ridley's cunning lob bowling had
lured six Derbyshire batsmen to self-destruction, there seemed
every prospect that Mycroft would prove even more devastating.
A target of 143 was surely beyond Hampshire, even if Ridley, last
year's Oxford captain and a century-maker for the Gentlemen
against the Players in 1876, was in such impressive batting form.
Yet Hampshire set off with gusto – Hyslop and Carter hit the first
twelve balls for thirteen and the innings was launched. The score
was 16 when Derbyshire picked up a fortuitous wicket. Hyslop
cut Platts hard to point where the captain, R. P. Smith, was hit
hard on the head; the ball rebounded twenty yards to cover point
where the catch was held. Smith was led off dazed and took no
part in the game. Hardly the captain's match – bowled by a shooter
the previous evening and now a sore head. Ten years later his luck
changed dramatically. He inherited a large fortune, eased himself
into the life of a country squire in rural Nottinghamshire and
changed his name to Stevens; after all Smith was a rather common
surname for a gentleman!

Back to events at the Antelope Ground. By 1.30 p.m. Hampshire
had put on fifty for the loss of that one freakish wicket. Then
Mycroft dismissed Carter at 51 and seventeen runs later, the prized
wicket – Ridley bowled in the same way as the first innings, by a
ball that pitched middle stump and hit leg. Lunch was taken at 75

for 3, with the sound Booth and the elegant Longman together. They proceeded calmly for a time afterwards (perhaps the interval of an hour had soothed their nerves!), and in one Mycroft over, he was driven to long-off for a total of nine runs. Was Mycroft at the end of his tether? No one would blame him if his labours had drained even his massive stamina. Somehow he hauled his team back in contention: after switching ends he bowled Booth off-stump, took out Longman's leg-stump and forced Jeffreys to play on. Within a few minutes 89 for 3 had become 96 for 6. For a time Holmes suggested permanence, with one cut to the boundary off Mycroft impressing everyone, but then he was held at point: 122 for 7. When Foster was caught at short leg by Hyslop, the substitute fielder, the score had reached 130 for 8 – thirteen to win and just two wickets left. By now Mycroft scented victory, and the wicket was helping his spin. Hampshire's nerve ends were twanging and Tate almost ran himself out. At 135 he was caught at point: eight runs or one wicket needed for victory. Galpin came in to join Hargreaves and the number eleven decided to leave the boldness to his partner. He did not disappoint. Hargreaves late cut Mycroft for a precious three runs. Then Mycroft gambled. He switched ends with just three runs needed. Hargreaves was equal to the task, and at 4.15 p.m. he drove a rare half-volley from Mycroft to the cover-point boundary and Hampshire were home. *Bell's Life in London* reports that the winning hit came 'amidst the loud shouts and hurrahs of the Hampshire folks', and gave this tribute to Mycroft's great effort: 'The way in which he mowed down the Hampshire wicket was a caution.' A caution indeed: 17 for 103 in the match and still he finished on the losing side. The only wicket he did not secure in the second innings was the bizarre catch off his captain's head, yet the lucky bowler, John Platts, deserved that slice of luck. He had been a shadow of the fast bowler who had impressed so many players a few seasons earlier, and the reason was simple. In 1870 Platts bowled the ball that leapt from a rough Lord's pitch and killed poor George Summers. Platts was inconsolable and dropped his pace thereafter. He hated playing at Lord's after the tragedy and was never the same bowler again.

Another Derbyshire player from this Hampshire game made a significant contribution away from the playing arena. Samuel Richardson was a mediocre cricketer (he made a 'pair' against Hampshire), but he led a colourful life. At this time he combined playing with the duties of assistant secretary to the county and that of secretary to Derby County Football Club. After sixteen years in the post he disappeared suddenly to Europe. The reason was simple: he had been caught with his finger in the till. He was found out by no less a personage than the great F. R. Spofforth, the Australian fast bowler. Spofforth had married a Derby girl and had come to live in the area, playing occasionally for the county and running a local business. He was asked to scrutinize the club's accounts and discovered that one Samuel Richardson had been pocketing money on a regular, profitable basis. The assistant secretary of Derbyshire CCC soon metamorphosised into the court tailor to the King of Spain, and he lived till he was ninety-three before dying in Madrid. Presumably Richardson changed the subject adroitly whenever the King asked about his early sporting career.

Hargreaves, the batsman who guided Hampshire to victory with such aplomb, also has an honourable mention in the 'I'm Nearly Famous' contest. He married Alice Pleasance Liddell, the girl on whom Lewis Carroll based the character of Alice in Wonderland. Perhaps Hargreaves occasionally fell asleep by the side of a stream in a meadow, and instead of seeing the White Rabbit he encountered the vision of William Mycroft – bowling on and on, switching ends whenever the batsmen looked comfortable and cursing his luck to play for a poor county team.

3
MCC *v.* the Australians
1878

One cold, damp Maytime day in 1878 stands out as a seminal event in the history of Anglo-Australian conflict. On that day the bubble of English cricketing invincibility was pricked. In conditions ideally suited to the English, the Australians bowled them out twice for a paltry fifty-two runs. No less than thirty-one wickets fell for 105 runs in under a full day, and the English cracks were outplayed in every department.

There had been hints that the Australian nation was about to become a cricket power before this first tour of England in 1878. They had won the first-ever Test a year earlier at Melbourne, and although England soon gained revenge, their players had returned from the Antipodes with a new respect for their natural, uncoached abilities. This change of emphasis had not yet percolated the complacent corridors of the English sporting press. When the Australians landed on the *City of Berlin* steamship in Liverpool on 13 May, the press referred to them as 'the Colonials' and patronizingly commented on their stout efforts in the first match at Trent Bridge. With Nottinghamshire winning by an innings, bowling out the tourists for 63 and 76, it was appropriate to encourage the welcome visitors to these shores in case their heads dipped too early in the tour. They would need all the luck in the world for their next game, against a very strong MCC side.

The team which opposed the Australians was more or less an England X1. It contained W. G. Grace, and his opening partner was A. N. Hornby, an outstanding amateur batsman of that era. The batsmen included A. J. Webbe, one of the best schoolboy cricketers of the Victorian age, who was to give great service to Middlesex after captaining Oxford. G. F. Vernon was a clean, natural hitter with a very good eye, George Hearne a capable bat

MCC v AUSTRALIANS
At Lord's, 27 May 1878

MCC

*Mr W. G. Grace c Midwinter b Allan	4	– b Spofforth	0
Mr A. N. Hornby b Spofforth	19	– b Boyle	1
Mr C. Booth b Boyle	0	– b Boyle	0
Mr A. W. Ridley c A. C. Bannerman b Boyle	7	– b Boyle	0
Mr A. J. Webbe b Spofforth	1	– b Spofforth	0
†F. Wild b Boyle	0	– b Spofforth	5
W. Flowers c and b Spofforth	0	– b Boyle	11
G. G. Hearne b Spofforth	0	– b Spofforth	0
Alfred Shaw st Murdoch b Spofforth	0	– (10) not out	2
Mr G. F. Vernon st Murdoch b Spofforth	0	– (9)b Spofforth	0
F. Morley not out	1	– c Horan b Boyle	0
Extras leg bye	1	–	0
	33		**19**

1/4 2/5 3/27 4/29 5/30 6/31 7/31
8/31 9/31

1/0 2/0 3/1 4/1 5/16 6/17
7/17 8/17 9/17

Bowling: First Innings – Boyle 14–7–14–3; Allan 9–4–14–1; Spofforth 5.3–3–4–6. Second Innings – Boyle 8.1–6–3–5; Spofforth 9–2–16–5.

AUSTRALIANS

C. Bannerman c Hearne b Morley	0	– b Shaw	1
W. E. Midwinter c Wild b Shaw	10	– not out	4
Mr T. P. Horan c Grace b Morley	4	– not out	7
A. C. Bannerman c Booth b Morley	0	–	
Mr T. W. Garrett c Ridley b Morley	6	–	
Mr F. R. Spofforth b Shaw	1	–	
*Mr D. W. Gregory b Shaw	0	–	
Mr H. F. Boyle c Wild b Morley	2	–	
†Mr W. L Murdoch b Shaw	9	–	
Mr F. E. Allan c and b Shaw	6	–	
Mr G. H. Bailey not out	3	–	
Extras	0	– (1 wicket)	0
	41		**12**

1/0 2/11 3/11 4/19 5/20 6/20 7/23
8/23 9/34

1/1

Bowling: First Innings – A. Shaw 33.2–25–10–5; Morley 33–19–31–5. Second Innings – A. Shaw 8–6–4–1; Morley 8–4–8–0.

Umpires: A. Rylott and M. Sherwin.

Australians won by 10 wickets.

and very good left-arm fast medium bowler, Wilfred Flowers was to perform the 'double' five years later and play for England as late as 1893, and the wicket-keeper Fred Wild was the first Nottinghamshire batsman to score a hundred at Trent Bridge, in 1872. The bowling was excellent: Alfred Shaw, the best medium-pace bowler in the country over a decade, and Fred Morley, the outstanding left-arm fast bowler. Against that array of talent the tourists could only hope for damage limitation, especially as they were so short of match practice and the weather was so unfavourable.

Grace won the toss for the MCC and elected to bat. The initial problem for the 4742 spectators lay in identifying the Australians. Billy Murdoch was easy – he was the wicket-keeper – and the graceful left-arm bowling style of Frank Allan marked him out. Pre-tour publicity had dubbed him 'the Bowler of a Century' after some prodigious deeds in domestic cricket, and the cognoscenti were keen to see how he measured up against his English counterparts. He started well enough against W. G. Grace: the great man smacked his first ball to the square leg boundary, but had him caught at short leg next ball, trying the same shot. Then Booth was bowled off-stump by Boyle. With the score 5 for 2, some retrenchment was necessary before the Colonials ran out of steam. Hornby and Ridley battled away for a time until they forced a bowling change at 25 for 2. One Frederick R. Spofforth was called up, and in the next half-hour he forged a new chapter in cricket history. Born in Sydney of Yorkshire stock Spofforth was twenty-five years of age and an impressive physical specimen. At six feet three, he delivered the ball from a great height that was aided by a spectacular final leap in the delivery stride. His run-up was no more than eight yards, yet he generated great speed from a powerful follow-through. He was to learn bewildering variations in speed and a devastating break-back, but for the moment he undid the flower of English batting by sheer pace. In his second over he bowled Hornby leg-stump, and when Webbe went the same way the score was 29 for 4. Boyle bowled Wild and had Ridley held at long-on: 31 for 6. At the same total Spofforth caught and bowled Flowers. In his next over, he performed the hat-trick with his first three balls, taking the impressive scalps of Hearne, Shaw and Vernon. Remarkably the innings was over in just seventy minutes. The last eight wickets had gone for six runs, and Spofforth had taken 6 for 4 in twenty-three balls.

The crowd sportingly cheered the Australians into the pavilion, and then set to wondering how their batsmen would fare on a damp wicket ideally suited to the likes of Shaw, Morley and Flowers. By lunch they were 17 for 3, and although Midwinter was grafting solidly away they looked no more impressive than their alleged superiors. After lunch five wickets fell for a mere six runs, while Shaw wheeled away at one end: at one stage he took 2 for 1 in seventeen overs! Allan and Murdoch added eleven precious runs – Murdoch with some style and Allan by bucolic, fortuitous methods that amused the crowd. Then Bailey, born of English parents, batted through nine overs for three runs before the innings closed at 3.40 p.m. It took the Australians sixty-six four-ball overs to scrape together forty-one runs, and their unfamiliarity with the conditions was writ large in every stroke they attempted. Surely it would now settle down into a normal game of cricket, with the upstarts duly punished for their effrontery?

At four o'clock, Grace and Hornby went in again. Ten minutes later the MCC score stood at 1 for 4. Gregory wisely opted for Spofforth to open with Boyle, and in his first over he yorked both Grace and Webbe. At the other end Boyle's deceptive flight accounted for Booth and Ridley in successive balls, and the innings lay in ruins. Worse was to follow – Hornby was hit by Spofforth in the next over and had to retire. Flowers hit a defiant legside boundary, but then he, Hearne and Wild fell in quick succession. At 17 for 7, Hornby limped in with Grace as his runner – at that stage in his career Grace's torso had not yet thickened out to its famous Falstaffian proportions. He stayed long enough to see Vernon collect a 'pair', courtesy of a Spofforth yorker, then he was bowled by Boyle after a feeble few minutes at the crease. The innings ended when Morley was out to a low catch at mid-on off his second ball. In fifty-five minutes a very strong batting side had been dismissed for 19. Spofforth had claimed four of his five wickets with the yorker, the ball that was to become associated with his name. No bowler of first-class standard ever clean bowled such a high proportion of his victims. Once he broadened his repertoire, he was to become the perfect bowler. This day in May 1878 marked out his credentials.

Although the Australians needed a mere eleven runs to win, they took their time. It took eight overs to get the last four runs and the match ended at 6.20 p.m. The chastened MCC side wanted to play a return match the following day, but the tourists rightly decided to rest on their laurels and watch with amusement as the shockwaves reverberated through the cricket establishment. The press debated long and painfully on the humiliating defeat, preferring to dwell on English inadequacies rather than Australian brilliance. *The Field* magazine seemed to think it was simply an act of God: 'The word "extraordinary" is nowadays so frequently misapplied that it loses much of its original force and meaning. No instance can be recollected of a match like that which occurred on Monday last at Lord's, to which the polysyllable more fitly belongs.'

Never again would the Colonials be dismissed so patronizingly. Their athletic fielding was a revelation, their bowling hostile and varied and although the batting seemed ill-equipped for the stern rigours of English surfaces, there was enough natural talent on hand to augur well. Although Frank Allan failed to be the bowler of the month never mind of the century, the performances of Boyle and Spofforth more than compensated. Boyle proved to be the Australian version of Alfred Shaw, a line and length bowler of patience and variety, with the knack of making the ball get up disconcertingly. Spofforth was simply a revelation – in all cricket on the 1878 tour he took 391 wickets, while two years later his tally stood at 326, in each case at a cost of six runs. He was to plague England for another decade, playing a decisive part in the Test at the Oval that led to the inauguration of the Ashes.

More than a century later, the battle for the Ashes is still the pre-eminent cricket contest, whatever the standing of the respective countries in any unofficial world league. On the eve of each Ashes series, the old chestnuts are raked over again and great moments relived as the anticipatory pulse quickens. We must be grateful to eleven Australians in blue and white caps for jolting English cricket out of its complacency. They managed that considerable feat in less than six hours of play in May 1878, in the process opening out the windows of English cricket to a brasher, more competitive world.

4
Gents *v*. Players
1881

Many superb matches evolve because the sides are evenly matched and it takes a great player to tip the scales decisively. Every nerve and sinew is tested to the full when each run and wicket is crucial, and it is a test of cricketing greatness to be able to prosper in that crucible of temperament. Alfred Shaw thrived on such a challenge throughout a career lasting thirty-three years, and he was seen at his best at Brighton in August 1881. The scores were amazingly close, yet the Players triumphed because Shaw took 6 for 19 in the climactic tense stages – and for good measure held a blinding catch off his own bowling to win the game by the narrowest of margins.

Around this time the games between the best amateurs of the day and their professional counterparts were tremendous contests. There was talent in abundance and invariably an engrossing encounter. Four years earlier the Gents had triumphed by one run after slumping to 97 for 9, with 46 needed. Amid great tension, W. G. Grace's brother, Fred, and W. S. Patterson hit off the required runs and the stolid denizens of the Lord's pavilion went wild with delight. By August 1881, poor Fred Grace had been dead for almost a year – he had caught a chill from sleeping in damp sheets – but his memory was honoured in another stirring battle.

Alfred Shaw, the pivotal figure in the Brighton game, was one of the more interesting cricketers of that age. He was cricket's first trade unionist, and the summer of 1881 saw him plying his professional wares up and down the land because of his principles. Following a complete breakdown in communication between the Nottinghamshire committee, Shaw and his great friend Arthur Shrewsbury simply downed metaphorical tools and refused to play for their county. They were cushioned slightly by the fact that they had just opened a sports shop in Nottingham and therefore the

GENTLEMEN v PLAYERS
At Hove, 8, 9 and 10 August 1881

THE PLAYERS

G. Ulyett b Appleby	0	– b Steel	14
A. Shrewsbury b Appleby	14	– (3)b Appleby	0
W. Barnes b Bettesworth	36	– (4)c Steel b Appleby	5
J. Selby c Tylecote b Appleby	12	– (5)c Tylecote b Steel	46
R. G. Barlow not out	54	– (2)c Appleby b Steel	9
W. Bates c Whitfield b Appleby	50	– st Tylecote b Bettesworth	23
T. Emmett b Appleby	0	– b Steel	3
H. R. J. Charlwood run out	3	– c Bettesworth b Steel	0
†A. Payne st Tylecote b Steel	0	– b Steel	1
*Alfred Shaw b Steel	18	– not out	8
F. Morley b Appleby	13	– c Vernon b Steel	2
Extras leg byes	4	– leg bye	1
	204		**112**

1/0 2/43 3/63 4/65 5/134 6/136
7/145 8/145 9/171

1/21 2/22 3/24 4/32 5/86 6/89 7/91 8/99 9/108

Bowling: *First Innings* – Appleby 51.1–22–92–6; Bettesworth 41–25–40–1; Steel 32–11–54–2; Lucas 10–4–14–0. *Second Innings* – Appleby 30–17–35–2; Bettesworth 20–8–22–1; Steel 51–26–54–7.

THE GENTLEMEN

Mr T. S. Pearson st Payne b Bates	24	– b Shaw	34
Mr R. T. Ellis b Bates	8	– (9)c Selby b Bates	0
Mr A. H. Trevor b Bates	12	– (4)b Emmett	4
Mr H. Whitfeld not out	34	– (7)b Bates	4
Mr A. G. Steel b Bates	0	– (2)b Shaw	22
Mr G. F. Vernon b Morley	13	– (5)b Shaw	4
*Mr A.·N. Hornby b Barnes	69	– (8)c and b Bates	15
†Mr E. F. S. Tylecote c Payne b Barnes	4	– (6) lbw b Shaw	0
Mr M. P. Lucas c Barnes b Bates	20	– (3)c Payne b Shaw	10
Mr W. A. Bettesworth c Emmett b Barnes	4	– not out	5
Mr A. Appleby c Emmett b Barnes	8	– c and b Shaw	3
Extras byes	8	– B 7, l-b 2, w 1	10
	204		**111**

1/8 2/28 3/47 4/47 5/60 6/150 7/160
8/187 9/193

1/55 2/64 3/69 4/78 5/78 6/78 7/99 8/99 9/108

Bowling: *First Innings* – Bates 39–12–73–5; Morley 26–10–28–1; Shaw 7–2–14–0; Emmett 5–1–17–0; Barnes 28–12–36–4; Barlow 13–2–28–0. *Second Innings* – Bates 27–17–16–3; Morley 5–3–10–0; Shaw 26.1–15–19–6; Emmett 19–8–26–1; Barnes 14–7–13–0; Barlow 5–2–17–0.

Umpires: C. Payne and H. Stubberfield.

Players won by one run.

lost match fees would not be too onerous a burden, but in fairness the two great cricketers were acting on behalf of their team-mates as well. They resented being employed on a match basis, rather than for a season, requested a benefit for every player of ten years' playing experience and politely suggested to the committee that the days of serfdom were over. The Notts committee reacted with the kind of high-handed moral indignation so typical of Victorian institutions and, as a result, seven players were lost to Nottingham-shire for most of the 1881 season. Shaw and Shrewsbury did not play a game for the county after May.

By the time the Brighton match came around, Alfred Shaw was in the kind of self-justificatory mood that occasionally spurs on most top sportsmen. He wanted to show his county what they were missing, and what better arena than the Gents v. Players match? This one was staged for the benefit of James Lillywhite, the famous Sussex slow bowler who also arranged the fixture lists for the first two Australian tours. The subscription list was headed by £100 from Lord Sheffield, the famous cricket benefactor and entrepreneur who enjoyed a solid business relationship with Alfred Shaw. On the first two days a couple of thousand spectators attended, and around fifteen hundred on the final day, so James Lillywhite had no complaints. Just for good measure he received another benefit in 1889, when North played South.

Play on the first day followed a fairly low-key pattern, with the Players all out for 204 by 5.30 p.m. and the Gents 13 for 1 when heavy rain forced a closure. *The Times* hardly pulled out all the literary stops to describe the play – the following morning a report on MCC Club and Ground v. Hertfordshire was as comprehensive as the account from Brighton. The odds for the Ebor Handicap and St Leger received larger prominence over both cricket games. Two days later the Brighton game would be treated with greater interest in that august organ.

The second day (dull in the morning, sunlit by evening) was illuminated by a typically audacious 69 by A. N. Hornby. He even essayed a reverse sweep off Tom Emmett; he missed and the ball went for four byes. One wonders if Ian Botham and Mike Gatting, those current practitioners of the impudent stroke, have heard of the man who played it with impunity a century earlier. Once Botham learned of Hornby's pugilistic instincts and his fondness for the hunting field, he would no doubt recognize a soul-mate!

Other notable moments in the Gents innings were a superb catch at mid-off by Tom Emmett to get Appleby ('a catch almost worth the journey to Brighton to see', according to *The Field*) and an innings of 34 not out in three hours by Herbert Whitfeld. Now Whitfeld was an Old Etonian, who played four times for Oxford in the Varsity match and established a reputation for barn-door defence that makes Trevor Bailey look positively skittish. He once made six in an hour and a half for Sussex against the MCC, and stands as a cogent reminder that not every amateur batsman of Victorian times was imbued with a quixotic desire to hit the ball straight back past the bowler.

The Players were left with ninety minutes' batting on the second day, and they closed on 45 for 4. With the scores level on the first innings, it did not need a senior wrangler to work out the lead. The state of the wicket was harder to fathom: Hornby only gave one difficult chance and looked comfortable, and yet the big-hitting Vernon had been undone by a shooter before lunch. When it rained hard on the third morning, the game was even more open. Once play resumed at 12.30, A. G. Steel took five of the last six wickets and the Players were all out by 2 p.m. Steel had an impressive bowling record in these matches, but he could not be measured in the same breath as Alfred Shaw, the master of line and length. If anyone could win this one for the professionals, it was the portly, bearded medium-pace bowler who was never seen without a small cap perched on his head. He was at his peak, having taken a hundred wickets nine times in the previous ten seasons and 186 at only 8.54 the summer before. He claimed he never bowled a wide in his first-class career, and he sent down more overs than he had runs scored off him – 25,699 overs, compared with 24,873 runs. When Shaw was bowling, no two deliveries were the same, even though they looked so similar. It was up to Alfred Shaw to confirm that his absence from county cricket in 1881 had not diluted his effectiveness.

He had made a significant contribution on that final day before he delivered one ball. He came in as last man with the score 99 for 9 and every run vital. Shaw, a cool sensible batsman, was immediately dropped at point by Pearson; he then hit Steel for a four and a two to the onside. Shaw finished on eight not out, and three hours later those runs would prove to be crucial.

Steel and Pearson opened for the Gents, with the target 113. They put on 55 for the first wicket, although progress was slow. At one stage Billy Bates bowled seventeen overs for just eight runs.

Poor Bates! Eighteen months later he lost an eye at net practice on the Melbourne ground when he failed to get out of the way of a fast-travelling ball. At the age of thirty-three a fine England career was over, and on the return sea voyage he tried to commit suicide. He was thwarted, but died at the age of forty-four, broken-hearted that he could no longer play the game he loved.

While Bates wheeled away, Alfred Shaw must have wondered if he would ever get a bowl. At 55 he came on – and bowled Pearson in his first over. Soon it was 69 for 3, with Steel and Lucas gone. Trevor and Vernon each cut deliveries to the third man boundary, but they were both bowled at 78. When Tylecote was lbw at the same score, Shaw had taken 5 for 9. For a time Hornby and Whitfeld ran their singles well and hinted at a recovery, but when Bates took over from Emmett, he caught and bowled Hornby: 99 for 7, and 14 still needed. Ellis was taken at point with the score still on 99, and then the hundred came up at 5.40. Shaw was the ideal bowler for such a crisis; the batsmen knew they would get nothing loose from him, that he would simply nag away at them until their concentration snapped. Whitfeld was joined by Bettesworth, a slow bowler and good enough batsman to top the Sussex averages that year. Both picked up two runs from on-drives. With five runs needed, Bettesworth was dropped at point off Shaw. At the same total Whitfeld was bowled: 108 for 9, five to win. Enter Arthur Appleby, a fine fast bowler who played twelve times for the Gentlemen, but with no claims to batting prowess. Yet he snicked three runs off his second ball to bring the sides almost level. Would the Gents sneak another last-wicket win? Alfred Shaw had other ideas. The first ball he delivered to Appleby was smashed straight back at the bowler, so hard that it must go to the boundary unless a brave man intervened. Shaw did not flinch – he stuck out both hands and clung to the ball. Victory to the Players by one run, and in the words of *The Field*, 'loud and long were the cheers which greeted the victorious players on their return from the ground'. The loudest cheers were reserved for the squat slow bowler with the avuncular beard.

Shaw had proved his point to the Nottinghamshire committee. The following season he was back in the team as captain, and for the next five seasons they won the county championship under his leadership. Shaw's business acumen remained undiminished, and he took three English sides out to Australia. He met with mixed financial fortunes on those trips, but he continued to travel the world – he once played cricket by the light of the midnight sun on the ice at Spitzbergen! He had as many entrepreneurial schemes as Phil Edmonds among modern players, yet he never lost sight of his cricketing goals. At the age of fifty-three he played for Sussex after an absence from the first-class game of seven years, and although heavy and with a very low bowling arm, he proceeded to show a new generation what all the fuss was about two decades earlier. As long as his legs could stand the strain, Alfred Shaw could still bowl all day. Such self-confidence and concentration served him well on an August day in 1881.

5
England *v*. Australia
OVAL 1882

This was the game that led to the creation of the historic struggle for the Ashes. The famous announcement about the soul of English cricket being cremated appeared in Saturday's *Times*, four days after the shattering defeat; English supporters still could not believe it. How could such a talented side lose by seven runs after being 51 for 3, just thirty-four short of victory? The answer is complex. There was a fatal lack of nerve and backbone about the later English batting, the Australians bowled superbly and fielded demonically, the toss and the elements favoured Australia, and the England captain messed up the batting order in the final, desperate innings. The cock-up theory should never be dismissed when cricketing post-mortems rage.

Scores of cricket books have dealt with the latter stages of the match, describing in infinite detail how unbelievably tense the proceedings became. I have read many times that in the closing stages a spectator gnawed through the handle of his umbrella and another dropped dead. I cannot vouch for the umbrella eater, but I can rule out a death at the ground when the game was approaching its gripping climax. Page ten of *The Times* for Wednesday, 30 August features a short report at the bottom of the right-hand page, headlined 'Sudden Death at the Oval'. We learn that one George Eder Spendlen of 191 Brook Street, Kennington complained of feeling unwell immediately after the end of the Australian innings, left his seat and fell over. By the time he was carried to the Oval pavilion, he was dead. The Australian innings ended at 3.25 p.m., the game was over at 5.46 – so England's lamentable failure amid great hysteria did not claim a life. That anecdote is a classic example of the Neville Cardus approach to

ENGLAND v AUSTRALIA
At the Oval, 28–29 August 1882

AUSTRALIA

A. C. Bannerman c Grace b Peate	9	– c Studd b Barnes	13
H. H. Massie b Ulyett	1	– b Steel	55
*W. L. Murdoch b Peate	13	– (4) run out	29
G. J. Bonnor b Barlow	1	– (3) b Ulyett	2
T. P. Horan b Barlow	3	– c Grace b Peate	2
G. Giffen b Peate	2	– c Grace b Peate	0
†J. M. Blackham c Grace b Barlow	17	– c Lyttelton b Peate	7
T. W. Garrett c Read b Peate	10	– (10) not out	2
H. F. Boyle b Barlow	2	– (11) b Steel	0
S. P. Jones c Barnes b Barlow	0	– (8) run out	6
F. R. Spofforth not out	4	– (9) b Peate	0
B 1	1	– B 6	6
	63		122

1/6 2/21 3/22 4/26 5/30 6/30 7/48
8/53 9/59 10/63

1/66 2/70 3/70 4/79 5/79
6/99 7/114 8/117 9/122

Bowling: *first Innings* – Peate 38–24–31–4; Ulyett 9–5–11–1; Barlow 31–22–19–5; Steel 2–1–1–0. *Second Innings* – Peate 21–9–40–4; Ulyett 6–2–10–1; Barlow 13–5–27–0; Steel 7–0–15–2; Barnes 12–5–15–1; Studd 4–1–9–0.

ENGLAND

R. G. Barlow c Bannerman b Spofforth	11	– (3) b Spofforth	0
W. G. Grace b Spofforth	4	– (1) c Bannerman b Boyle	32
G. Ulyett st Blackham b Spofforth	26	– (4) c Blackham b Spofforth	11
A. P. Lucas c Blackham b Boyle	9	– (5) b Spofforth	5
†Hon. A. Lyttelton c Blackham b Spofforth	2	– (6) b Spofforth	12
C. T. Studd b Spofforth	0	– (10) not out	0
J. M. Read not out	19	– (8) b Spofforth	0
W. Barnes b Boyle	5	– (9) c Murdoch b Boyle	2
A. G. Steel b Garrett	14	– (7) c and b Spofforth	0
*A. N. Hornby b Spofforth	2	– (2) b Spofforth	9
E. Peate c Boyle b Spofforth	0	– b Boyle	2
B 6, l-b 2, n-b 1	9	– B 3, n-b 1	4
	101		77

1/13 2/18 3/57 4/59 5/60 6/63 7/70
8/96 9/101 10/101

1/15 2/15 3/51 4/53 5/66
6/70 7/70 8/75 9/75 10/77

Bowling: *First Innings* – Spofforth 36.3–18–46–7; Garrett 16–7–22–1; Boyle 19–7–24–2. *Second Innings* – Spofforth 28–15–44–7; Garrett 7–2–10–0; Boyle 20–11–19–3.

Umpires: L. Greenwood and R. Thoms.

Australia won by 7 runs.

moulding a legend whereby a good story should not be spoiled by the facts.

There were enough remarkable facts about this game to keep any raconteur awash with reminiscences by the fire in his dotage. It seems amazing that the England team should be chosen by three leading amateurs and a Surrey committee man who simply sent in their lists to Surrey County Cricket Club. Lord Harris, V. E. Walker, F. Burbridge and I. D. Walker were asked for their opinions, and they made three serious errors. On the grounds of experience Lord Harris should have been chosen, while E. M. Grace's battle-hardened approach would have been ideal on that final afternoon. Moreover A. N. Hornby should not have been picked as captain or player. Since Spofforth had worked him over at Lord's in 1878 (see chapter 3), Hornby had never played well against the Australians. After 1878 his top score against them was 94, hardly representative of his abilities, and the hold that Spofforth exerted on him was similar to that of Dennis Lillee on Dennis Amiss a century later. The captain ought to have been W. G. Grace; he would not have fiddled around so crassly with the batting order.

It rained a great deal over the weekend in southeast London, par for the course in that appallingly wet summer when just one fortnight in May proved to be dry. The wicket on the Monday was slow and treacherous and likely to get worse, so Australia had no hesitation in batting first. Within two and a quarter hours they were all out for 63, with Barlow's left-arm medium pace proving particularly deadly. At one stage fourteen successive maidens were bowled, and just three singles trickled out in twenty overs. When England batted the light was appalling, and in the circumstances a lead of 38 would seem invaluable. Spofforth again proved redoubtable, but Steel and Read batted with spirit. George Ulyett, that happy cavalier Yorkshireman, was the day's top scorer with 26, but he was criticized for being stumped playing a rash shot. The following day the Englishmen would be lambasted for not attempting to play positively. Whatever the era, the sporting press has always been ready to wear the hat of convenient omniscience. One worrying feature for the English supporters – a slump from 57 for 3 to 70 for 7, a foretaste of some pusillanimous batting on the morrow.

Tuesday, 29 August dawned wet and miserable after another overnight downpour. Play was delayed forty minutes until 12.10

p.m., and the heavy roller that was used meant the pitch would play a good deal worse in the afternoon. Spofforth would need little encouragement to display his greatness, so quick runs were the order of the day for the tourists. Their opener Massie proceeded to play a great innings for his side. A naturally free, hard-driving batsman, he prospered on the sodden turf, hitting 55 out of 66 for the first wicket. He was dropped by Lucas at long-on off Barnes when the score was 48 (Massie on 38), but when he was bowled leg-stump he had not made another mistake, hitting nine superb boundaries. When Massie went, it was soon clear that the wicket was deteriorating. A score of 66 for 0 became 79 for 5, but then Murdoch and Blackham inched them up to 99. Then it rained – short and sharp but heavy – and the wicket became even more tricky. By 3.25 Australia were all out. Murdoch had made 29 of the last 56 runs, displaying fine, sound technique while Blackham's 7 took seventy minutes. At least Massie, Murdoch and Blackham had given their side a glimmer of hope, even if the strong English batting was expected to win with a fair degree of comfort.

At 3.45 Grace and Hornby walked out to bat, enveloped by hearty cheers from the crowd of 20,000. After a careful start, they lost two wickets at 15 – Hornby bowled off-stump and then Barlow played on first ball. It was a blow to lose Barlow; one of the most obdurate batsmen in history (5 in 150 minutes and a nought that took eighty minutes, for example), he was an ideal man for this type of situation, where runs would have to be chiselled out. For a time England prospered. Grace on-drove Spofforth for a three and a four, and the fifty came up after fifty-five minutes. Then Spofforth changed ends coming on at the pavilion end while Boyle started to bowl steadily and craftily from the gasometer end. At 51, Ulyett was splendidly caught low down at the wicket. At 53, Grace checked his stroke and was easily caught at mid-off. This was disconcerting because Grace had looked in great form; it would have been pleasing to see the great man guide England to victory and secure a 'not out'. Never mind, somebody else would have the honour of making the winning hit against these colonial upstarts. Only twenty-eight runs were needed after all. This was the period when England effectively lost the match. Lyttelton and Lucas were so paralysed by nerves that they played through twelve successive maidens. Only one run came off seventeen overs from Spofforth and Boyle and in the eighteenth over Lyttelton was bowled by one that hit the top of the middle stump. Five wickets in hand and only 19 to win. Lucas late cut Boyle to the boundary, amid hysterical applause. Spofforth took the next over and Steel was meekly caught and bowled off the first delivery; from the third, Read was bowled middle and off stumps. It was now 70 for 7, with fifteen needed: high time we saw the appearance of C. T. Studd, one of the best batsmen in the country that year. He had already scored two centuries against the Australians in 1882 as well as a hundred for the Gents against the Players at Lord's. A classical, upright batsman, a fine medium-pace bowler, he was one of the great all-rounders of the time – yet Hornby kept him back. Billy Barnes went in ahead of him and added five tentative runs with Lucas, three of them byes. Finally, Lucas, after deftly keeping out so many of Spofforth's break-backs, played one onto his stumps. Ten runs needed, two wickets in hand and at last we saw the arrival of C. T. Studd. He could hardly have come in any lower – the last man, Edmund Peate, was a genuine tail-ender, even though he was a marvellous slow bowler. As soon as Studd joined Barnes, the Nottinghamshire all-rounder was caught at point. Enter Peate, a droll man with an idiosyncratic view of the world who never really took himself seriously and abused his talent amid trays of beer. Peate had surveyed the timorous efforts of the best amateur batsmen of the day and decided that a son of true Yorkshire stock would put to shame the Oxbridge dilettantes. Off his first ball he clubbed two runs past square leg. He played a loose shot at the next and somehow survived. He was less lucky with the fourth ball of Boyle's over – clean bowled. Australia had won improbably by seven runs. C. T. Studd, the very apotheosis of majestic batsmanship, had not faced one ball.

In the second hour of the innings, England had lost six wickets for 24 runs and Spofforth had taken 5 for 12 in eleven overs after switching ends. He had bowled throughout the innings, and again proved himself the greatest bowler in the world. As the hapless Hornby shared a drink with the victors in the Australian dressing-room, we were treated to our first exclusive interview with a cricket superstar. The intrepid correspondent of *Bell's Life in London* managed to penetrate the security cordon a good deal more easily than his successors in the press a century later, and he sat down beside Spofforth to record that worthy's thoughts. He admitted that he could not have bowled on a wicket that was more suitable to his style of bowling, and he praised the Englishmen for their sporting acceptance of defeat. End of interview. How would the tabloids of the Murdoch and Maxwell age have treated such a gilt-edged opportunity to clean up on their rivals?

Meanwhile in the England dressing-room, Edmund Peate was telling his fellow-professionals, 'Ah couldn't troost Maister Stood!' It is not known whether he dared to mention that in front of Hornby or the other amateurs, but Peate's whimsies apart, the captain deserves censure for keeping back such a fine batsman as Studd. No wonder Studd left first-class cricket two years later at the age of twenty-four. He took himself off to China for missionary work, and in an admirably selfless life he spent much of his later years as a missionary in the Belgian Congo. Perhaps his experience at the hands of Peate had convinced him of man's inherent frailty and drove him towards saving souls!

The Australians had been desperately keen to beat England before the match started – the press had made sneering remarks about their standard after twice losing to the Players and once to Cambridge University – but two events during the game hardened their resolve even more. In the first innings, Bannerman was given out caught by Grace, low down at point. The batsman stood his ground until the umpire ruled he was out, an unusual sight in those days. Then Grace was involved in another controversy in their second innings when he ran out S. P. Jones. After completing a run, Jones strayed out of the crease to look at the pitch. Grace broke the wicket from point and Thoms, the umpire, who ruled the ball was not dead, said, 'If you claim it, sir, out!' W. G. Grace was never bashful about claiming anything and Murdoch, the other batsman, was furious. When Grace batted for the second time it was clear that Garrett and Blackham were trying to do the same to him. *The Field*, ever mindful of Grace's place in the affections of the people, called it 'an amusing incident', but the Australians did not think so. As we bewail the coarsening values of cricket in the 1980s we should remember that the bearded doctor with the massive girth and ego remains the Uri Geller of cricket rules and conventions.

The Australians did not drop one catch, or give away a single run in the field. They were driven on by their great team spirit, the conviction that they would make their own luck, or at least capitalize on whatever came their way. Above all they had F. R. Spofforth. His deeds undoubtedly shaped cricket history, in the process moulding a self-regard of W. G. Grace proportions. Years later, after settling into the English business community, he would regale his cronies with tall tales, maintaining that he was the fastest bowler ever, that no one could rival him as a varied performer. We can perhaps forgive Spofforth his conceits – genius is not always circumscribed by diffident conventions – but there is no doubt that his influence helped make Test cricket vibrant and remarkably popular. Although the game was watched by 40,000 over two days, you could treble the number to accommodate all those who swore to their grandchildren that they witnessed the moment when C. T. Studd realized that God's calling was preferable to that of a cheerful Yorkshireman who loved his pint.

6
England *v.* Australia
SYDNEY 1894

'There'll be a good deal said about this match.' The words were uttered by Andrew Stoddart, the England captain, at a dinner after the sixth and final day of one of the most remarkable Tests of all times. It was an observation full of typical Victorian understatement; almost a century later, Sydney 1894 still stands out as one of the great Test matches, full of towering individual achievements, a dramatic change in fortune, a crucial failure of nerve and a breathlessly close finish. For the first time a side made to follow on had triumphed – it was to be another eighty-seven years before Ian Botham and Bob Willis inspired a sequel at Leeds.

Like Leeds 1981, the Sydney Test of 1894 galvanized the series. By the fifth Test at Melbourne the score was two-all in the series, and it seemed the whole Australian nation was beside itself with excitement. Record crowds thronged the grounds, reaching the destination by horseback and foot as well as train and steamer. For the first time there was a massive press interest, not just among the specialist newspapers. Test cricket was inching towards the front pages. The *Pall Mall Gazette* spent a small fortune on sending back to London the tour details, and it is rumoured that even Queen Victoria asked for regular updates. Yet the gripping events at Sydney were kept from English breakfast tables for two days, due to a cable failure. Not until Friday, 21 December could the nation read of the last three days' play which culminated in Thursday's momentous victory. There was much to savour.

Friday, 14 December was a day of tropical heat in Sydney although, portentously, there was a threat of thunder. When Andrew Stoddart watched Jack Blackham toss the coin, he said, 'Someone will be swearing directly, Jack. I hope it's you!' Stoddart was unlucky. Australia batted first on a dry pitch and lightning

AUSTRALIA v ENGLAND
(First Test)
At Sydney Cricket Ground, 14–20 December 1894

AUSTRALIA

J. J. Lyons b Richardson	1	– b Richardson	25
G. H. S. Trott b Richardson	12	– c Gay b Peel	8
G. Giffen c Ford b Brockwell	161	– lbw b Briggs	41
J. Darling b Richardson	0	– c Brockwell b Peel	53
F. A. Iredale c Stoddart b Ford	81	– (6) c and b Briggs	5
S. E. Gregory c Peel b Stoddart	201	– (5) c Gay b Peel	16
J. C. Reedman c Ford b Peel	17	– st Gay b Peel	4
C. E. McLeod b Richardson	15	– not out	2
C. T. B. Turner c Gay b Peel	1	– c Briggs b Peel	2
*†J. M. Blackham b Richardson	74	– (11) c and b Peel	2
E. Jones not out	11	– (10) c MacLaren b Briggs	1
B 8, l-b 3, w 1	12	– B 2, l-b 1, n-b 4	7
	586		**166**

1/10 2/21 3/21 4/192 5/331 6/379
7/400 8/409 9/563 10/586

1/26 2/45 3/130 4/135 5/147
6/158 7/159 8/161 9/162 10/166

Bowling: *First Innings* – Richardson 55.3–13–181–5; Peel 53–14–140–2; Briggs 25–4–96–0; Brockwell 22–7–78–1; Lockwood 3–2–1–0; Ford 11–2–47–1; Stoddart 3–0–31–1. *Second Innings* – Richardson 11–3–27–1; Peel 30–9–67–6; Briggs 11–2–25–3; Lockwood 16–3–40–0.

ENGLAND

A. C. MacLaren c Reedman b Turner	4	– b Giffen	20
A. Ward c Iredale b Turner	75	– b Giffen	117
*A. E. Stoddart c Jones b Giffen	12	– c Giffen b Turner	36
J. T. Brown run out	22	– c Jones b Giffen	53
W. Brockwell c Blackham b Jones	49	– b Jones	37
R. Peel c Gregory b Giffen	4	– b Giffen	17
F. G. J. Ford st Blackham b Giffen	30	– c and b McLeod	48
J. Briggs b Giffen	57	– b McLeod	42
W. H. Lockwood c Giffen b Trot	18	– b Trott	29
†L. H. Gay c Gregory b Reedman	33	– b Trott	4
T. Richardson not out	0	– not out	12
B 17, l-b 3, w 1	21	– B 14, l-b 8	22
	325		**437**

1/14 2/43 3/78 4/149 5/155 6/211
7/211 8/409 9/563 10/566

1/44 2/115 3/217 4/245
5/290 6/296 7/385 8/398
9/420 10/437

Bowling: *First Innings* – Turner 44–16–89–2; Jones 18–6–44–1; Giffen 43–17–75–4; McLeod 14–2–25–0; Trott 15–4–59–1; Reedman 3.3–1–12–1; Lyons 2–2–0–0. *Second Innings* – Turner 35–14–78–1; Jones 19–0–57–1; Giffen 75–25–164–4; McLeod 30–6–67–2; Trott 12.4–3–22–2; Reedman 6–1–12–0; Lyons 2–0–12–0; Iredale 2–1–3–0.

Umpires: C. Bannerman and J. Phillips.

England won by 10 runs.

outfield. Yet within half an hour, Australia's score stood at 21 for 3, with all the wickets going to Tom Richardson, that great, indomitable fast bowler. Then, as the bowlers tired in the broiling heat, Frank Iredale and George Giffen took toll. They added 171 for the fourth wicket, then Giffen added another 139 with Syd Gregory. Just before the close Giffen was caught at slip for 161, and Australia finished on 346 for 5.

It had been a demoralizing day for Stoddart. From such a dynamic start, he had seen his team wilt under the positive approach of the Australians. Richardson and Bobby Peel had been over-bowled, but with Bill Lockwood retiring in mid-afternoon with a shoulder strain, he had little option but to persevere with his two best bowlers. In the dressing-room, Leslie Gay tried hard not to catch his captain's eye. Gay had kept goal for England at soccer the previous winter, and he had been preferred to Hylton Philipson for this first Test. He proceeded to drop Giffen twice when he was 75, fumble a return when Giffen and Iredale were both at the bowler's end, drop Giffen at 90 and generally did nothing to arrest the slump in fielding standards. This was to be Leslie Gay's one and only Test, and from a distance of almost a century, his status as England's worst wicket-keeper seems imperishable.

The following day, Stoddart had more on his mind than Gay's impersonation of a penguin with gloves and pads. Syd Gregory made 201 (his home crowd collected £103 for him in honour of the feat) and Australia posted a new record total of 586. A crowd of 26,000 (another record for Sydney) loved the carnage, only pausing to admire the astonishing stamina of Tom Richardson. Clearly all the luck was with Australia: when England batted, the clouds rolled up and conditions were far from easy. At the close England were 130 for 3, and approaching that part of a game where experienced players know there is little else to fight for but self-respect.

After heavy rain on the Sunday, England resumed in sunshine and batted stolidly throughout Monday until they were dismissed just before the close for 325. The wicket was affected by the combination of sun and rain, and Albert Ward's 75 deserved the highest praise. Although he was well supported by the later battings, the deficit remained 261. There was no doubt that an innings defeat loomed. The only worry for Australia was the cracked thumb suffered by Blackham, their captain and great wicket-keeper. It happened when he took a ball from Lyons and he had to give up the gloves to Charlie McLeod. Blackham's injury proved to be the first straw in the wind that blew England to victory.

First England had to bat for at least two whole days to give themselves even an outside chance. When they followed on first thing on Tuesday morning, they were dismayed to find that the outfield was remarkably thick because of the recent rain. Every run would have to be worked for, there would be no prospect of simply leaning on the ball and watching it flash away to the distant boundary. Truly the gods were favouring Australia! After an understandably slow start, England found themselves 115 for 2, with MacLaren and Stoddart gone. Then Brown and Ward joined in a thrilling counter-attack that at least showed there was still some spirit left in the England camp. Albert Ward's hundred proved to be one of the most valuable innings in Test cricket at that time, while Jack Brown did not give a chance until he was astonishingly caught on the run in the outfield by the fast bowler, Ernie Jones. Bobby Peel and Billy Brockwell played out the last few tense overs in drizzle, leaving England just seven runs ahead with six wickets left. The threat of rain did little to reassure Stoddart and his men, but at least they had battled hard throughout the day.

Under leaden skies England lost Peel and Brockwell early on Wednesday: 296 for 6, only thirty-five ahead. As the crowd grew after lunch, Francis Ford chanced his luck and hammered a swift 48. Johnny Briggs, useful bat and wonderful slow bowler, kept his natural instincts in check and helped Ford add 89 precious runs. Then Bill Lockwood, a man good enough to do the 'double', at last made his mark in the game by chipping an invaluable 29. The Australian fielding grew rather ragged as the tail wagged; both Ford and Briggs were badly missed. Giffen, leading the side in Blackham's absence, over-bowled himself, not for the first time – when he was once asked about a change of bowling after he had put in a long stint, Giffen replied, 'Good idea, I'll go on at the other end!' His rival captain was seen applauding every run as England passed 400. Only the hapless Gay failed to reach double figures (to sum up his fortunes, he was bowled off his pads by a full toss), and Australia eventually needed 177 to win. Of course, there was still no question about the victory, simply the margin, but the pluck and durability of the English batting were in the finest traditions of the Ashes battles.

At four o'clock Jack Lyons and Harry Trott walked out to start the formalities. Another significant phase of this enthralling match lay in store, as the bulk of the batting froze under pressure. Jack Lyons was never one to bother about pressure – he had rattled up 25 to Trott's single in a quarter of an hour before Richardson bowled him off his pad. Giffen came in and made it clear he was playing for tomorrow. Trott seized up completely, and at 45 he was caught behind. Joe Darling escaped a 'pair' in his first Test, and when he was dropped by Stoddart he decided to chance his arm. At the close, Australia needed only 64 to win with eight wickets left. Darling was 44 not out, Giffen 30, made in an hour and three quarters. The wicket was still playing well, and although Giffen's all-round qualities were admired, the uneasy feeling among the Australians was that he should have finished the job that night.

That thought struck Giffen like a sledgehammer the following morning when he looked out of his hotel window. It had rained heavily in the night, but now the sun was beating down. As he walked downstairs he met Jack Blackham with, in Giffen's words, 'a face as long as a coffee pot'. As they rode to the ground, the furrows in the damp ground made Blackham's face even longer.

Over in the England hotel, Bobby Peel was yawning and scratching himself after a convivial evening. The bonhomous Bobby had decided to unwind with a few convivial beers the night before: after all, the Test was well and truly lost and there would be other times for revenge. When he got to the ground and saw the brownish colour of the pitch, he spluttered, 'Give me t'ball, Mr Stoddart and Ah'll get t'boogers out before loonch!' Not before the captain put his trump card under a cold shower to sober him up!

Within twenty minutes of the resumption of play the wicket was unplayable. Left open to the elements, it was a classic 'sticky' with the hot sun beating down. Joe Darling realized the desperate straits and tried to hit his way to glory – but at 130 he was marvellously caught in the deep by Brockwell. In his first over, Briggs trapped Giffen lbw: 135 for 4, 42 needed. As the ground rapidly filled up (only fifteen hundred saw the start of play), Briggs and Peel tightened the screw. They had seen countless 'sticky' wickets in their time in England, and this offering would not be spurned. Iredale was caught and bowled. Gregory was caught behind and Reedman stumped after charging at Peel. Eighteen to win, three wickets left. Turner was caught at cover point and Jones held in the deep. One wicket left, fifteen runs to win. Enter Jack Blackham, a man who made 74 in the first innings, his highest Test score, but now cruelly incommoded by his cracked thumb. Blackham would sell his wicket dearly, but it was up to Charlie McLeod at the other end to win it for his side. A useful all-rounder, an effective if ungainly batsman, McLeod nudges a single here and there, but he is powerless to protect completely the wincing Blackham. Eventually the pressure tells on Blackham and he prods back a catch to Peel. England have won by ten runs, just two minutes before lunch – as promised by a genial Yorkshire slow bowler with a hangover.

At the post-match dinner, Stoddart graciously acknowledged Australia's ill-fortune with the weather. If Blackham had been fit, England might have garnered less runs in their second innings revival and his experienced batting would have been invaluable against Peel and Briggs. Yet Australia helped to lose it as well. Giffen over-bowled himself and missed a tactical trick by sitting on the splice near the end of the fifth day. In the end England pulled the game around by a supreme team effort and gleefully accepted the huge slice of luck that came their way.

Good luck proved to be a transient commodity for several of that famous England side. Poor Johnny Briggs suffered a seizure during the Leeds Test of 1899. It was learned that he suffered from a form of epilepsy for which there was no known cure. One of the most popular cricketers of the age died in a Cheshire asylum in 1902, aged thirty-nine. As for Bobby Peel, his fondness for ale led to his expulsion from first-class cricket in 1897. Lord Hawke, his captain, sent him off the field at Bramall Lane, after Peel was spotted bowling at the sightscreen and urinating on the outfield. He never played again for Yorkshire, and Wilfred Rhodes's impressive debut in 1898 forged another link in the chain of great Yorkshire slow left-arm bowlers. Peel's team-mate Jack Brown died of heart failure at the age of thirty-six while Tom Richardson suffered the same fate at the age of forty-one. Their beloved captain Andrew Stoddart was also blighted. In 1915, besieged by financial worries, he shot himself.

It is hard to contemplate that list of tragedies within the context of such a great sporting performance. The dark side of life was never far from the surface in Victorian times, with the adult male life expectancy no more than forty-six. We can merely give thanks to Andrew Stoddart and his men for living long enough to ignite a wonderful Test series and for underlining the glorious uncertainty of cricket.

7
Somerset *v.* Hampshire
1899

From this distance, the year 1899 would seem one of the outstanding seasons in the Golden Age of cricket. The sun shone regularly, the Australians were popular visitors, Victor Trumper and Wilfred Rhodes began their great Test careers and there seemed a galaxy of talent on display, with the positive intent to match it. Yet *Cricket, a Weekly Record of the Game* was carrying articles on 'Is English Cricket Decaying?' and the great Arthur Shrewsbury replied in an article, 'Yes, For the Moment, English Cricket is Under a Cloud.' Well, if ever there was proof that the English cricket zealot can be a *laudator temporis acti*, there you have it. In July of that year, two distinguished army officers gave the cricket world something to chatter about, rather than look back in anger.

In the space of four hours and twenty minutes, Major Robert Montagu Poore and Captain Edward George Wynyard added a little matter of 411 runs against a demoralized Somerset attack. At the time it was the second best stand for any wicket in a first-class match, and it remains the best partnership for the sixth wicket in England. The stand transformed a game that seemed to be going Somerset's way; all out for 315, they had reduced Hampshire to 38 for 3, then 62 for 4 on the first day. Yet Somerset lost by an innings.

Poore and Wynyard were a remarkable pair, the very embodiment of the Victorian ethos of muscular, uncomplicated sports prowess combined with daring, style and a deep commitment to public service. Major Wynyard was a Carthusian; commissioned in 1883, he served in the Burma campaigns and, after twice being mentioned in despatches, he was awarded the DSO in 1887. He was later awarded the Royal Humane Society's bronze medal for rescuing a Swiss peasant from drowning. For good measure, he

SOMERSET *v* HAMPSHIRE
At Taunton, 20–22 July 1899

SOMERSET

Mr. H. T. Stanley b Soar	28	– c Steele b Heseltine....	9
Mr. C. A. Bernard c Robson b Heseltine	42	– c Steele b Baldwin	7
E. Robson b Soar	74	– run out	19
Mr. R. C. N. Palairet c Robson b Soar	29	– run out	27
Mr. J. Daniell c Robson b Baldwin	0	– c Lee b Baldwin	57
G. B. Nichols b Baldwin	64	– c Lee b Wynyard	13
G. C. Gill c Steele b Heseltine	8	– c Webb b Wynyard ...	6
*Mr. A. E. Newton c Robson b Wynyard	46	– c Steele b Baldwin	33
E. J. Tyler not out	15	– c English b Baldwin...	10
†Rev. A. P. Wickham b Wynyard	1	– not out	0
B. Cranfield absent	0	– b Wynyard	3
L-b 7, n-b 1	8	B 19, l-b 1, w 2..	22
	315		**206**

1/63 2/81 3/159 4/164 5/194 6/204
7/290 8/309 9/315

1/16 2/26 3/63 4/78 5/98
6/114 7/189 8/199 9/206

Bowling: *First Innings* – Heseltine 26–4–80–2; Baldwin 39–13–84–2; Lee 6–1–15–0; Steel 7–1–34–0; Soar 19–4–74–3; Wynyard 11.3–3–20–2. *Second Innings* – Heseltine 19–2–58–1; Baldwin 25.4–13–53–4; Lee 3–1–10–0; Soar 15–5–31–0; Wynyard 10–3–18–3; Steele 4–0–14–0.

HAMPSHIRE

†Mr. C. Robson c and b Tyler	15
V. A. Barton lbw, b Tyler	12
Major R. M. Poore st Wickham b Tyler	304
Mr E. A. English b Gill	0
Mr. E. C. Lee c Nichols b Cranfield	11
T. Soar c Cranfield b Gill	95
*Capt. E. G. Wynyard c Bernard b Tyler	225
H. Baldwin not out	1
A. S. Webb not out	2
Mr. C. Heseltine .... did not bat	
Mr. D. A. Steele .... did not bat	
L-b 3, w 4	7
	*672

*Innings declared closed.

1/26 2/31 3/38 4/62 5/258 6/669 7/670

Bowling: *First Innings* – Gill 44–8–127–2; Tyler 63–6–201–4; Cranfield 22–3–113–1; Robson 22–4–75–0; Nichols 21–2–104–0; Stanley 3–0–26–0; Daniell 4–0–19–0.

Umpires: G. Burton and H. Pickett.

Hampshire won by an innings and 151 runs.

was Europe's top tobogganer in 1894, and played soccer in the FA Cup Final of 1881. As a batsman, he was a good enough player to keep illustrious company in the England team which clinched the Ashes in 1896, finding himself alongside Grace, Ranji, Jackson, Hayward and MacLaren. He could not spare the time to go with England to Australia in 1897/8, and ten years later refused the invitation to captain the side out there. How the selectors could imagine that a forty-six-year-old retired Army captain should skipper the side in Australia defies comprehension – yet the offer underlines Wynyard's considerable credentials.

Wynyard's first-class career extended thirty-five years, and in his mellow old age he reckoned he had hit 150 hundreds in all forms of cricket. When he batted for Hampshire, he would wear the I Zingari cap, polo shaped with a strap under his chin. His attacking shots were devastating: he was one of the first batsmen to play 'inside out', stepping back to hit the bowler over cover point, a stroke common to the 1980s. He would regularly drop onto his right knee and pull a half-volley over mid-on. Wynyard had a reputation for irascibility – he once fell out with the gentle Ranji over his claim to a bunch of grapes – and the professionals in the Hampshire side recognized his unerring ability to count to six, when he wanted to keep the bowling. As befits a man of action he never wore a box – his son said it was 'because he never got hit there'.

Captain Wynyard was the superior player, but Major Poore was a remarkable character and batsman. He did not take to cricket at all until his mid-twenties, and then it was only to ward off boredom while in India with the 7th Hussars. He read the *Badminton Book of Cricket*, practised the mechanics of batting in front of a mirror and decided he would be a batsman. In the early 1890s he was ADC to Lord Harris, the Governor of Bombay, and he started to pile up massive scores. When Poore went to South Africa on military duties, he again scored prolifically and soon found himself playing three Tests for his adopted country against England (the qualifications for Tests were a good deal more tolerant in those days!). By the time he was thirty-two, Poore fancied trying his luck at county cricket; he wanted to see if his stiffly effective style would be successful against the superior English bowlers. He treated the whole exercise as a military operation, planning his leave and dissecting his performances back in South Africa. Poore averaged 34 in 1898, and although he had difficulty adjusting to the English wickets, he expressed himself satisfied. He determined to have one more spell of extended leave the following season – better get it out of the system, old boy, before I have to address myself to sterner matters like these damned Boers. That spell of leave made cricket history.

Poore's performances in two months of the 1899 season were simply phenomenal. From 12 June to 12 August he made 1399 runs for Hampshire at an average of 116.58, with seven hundreds. In all first-class matches he averaged 91.23 (1551 runs), an average not exceeded till Sutcliffe and Bradman during the acquisitive 1930s. For good measure he displayed his sporting versatility during one fortnight in June – he was on the winning side in the Inter Regimental Polo Tournament, won the best 'man-at-arms' mounted event at the Royal Tournament and scored three consecutive hundreds for Hampshire. The man was a marvel, surely? The press flocked to him, wondering how they had failed to spot the wonder of the age. Major Poore could not understand all the fuss. All he had done was read a good coaching book a decade ago and put its precepts into practice. Military men invariably grasp the simplicities earlier than journalists.

What was Poore's secret? Hard to categorize: he was 6 feet 4 inches tall, massively built and a ferocious driver off the front foot. He believed in hammering a ball straight back over the bowler's head and peppering the area between mid-off and cover point. In 1899 the bowlers usually attacked, relying on changes of flight and expecting catches in the deep. In a more pragmatic cricket age Major Poore would have been curtailed, but he thrived on the good wickets of his golden summer.

By the time Poore walked in to bat at 5.45 p.m. on Thursday, 20 July, the Somerset bowlers were already sick of the sight of his massive presence. At Portsmouth he had smashed them for two centuries and, as the Manchester *Sunday Chronicle* remarked, 'The opinion the Somerset bowlers have of Major Poore is not on record. Maybe it is not for publication in a family newspaper.' Poore's average of 81.37 at the start of the match at Taunton presaged an innings from a man in form, and when the Hampshire professionals presented him with an engraved matchbox on the first morning it looked as if nothing could stop the Major's inexorable progress towards batting greatness. The omens were propitious for this game at least: the great Sammy Woods was absent following the death of his sister and Somerset's bowling looked distinctly threadbare, apart from their excellent slow left-arm spinners, Beaumont Cranfield and Edwin Tyler. Tyler was so slow that his dubious action did not concern the vigilant activists who were determined to stamp out throwing in the first-class game. When you were as slow as Tyler, you hardly posed much of a physical threat; pity the same tolerance was not extended to Geoff Cope eighty years later.

On the first day Somerset batted in a heatwave. For some unknown reason Cranfield arrived late, and his team batted a man short. No matter; Ernie Robson, enjoying his best season, stroked twelve boundaries and anchored the Somerset innings. Hampshire started their innings at 5.25 on the first day and, when Charles Robson was out after twenty minutes, the impressive figure of Robert Poore marched to the wicket. Immediately afterwards Victor Barton was lbw to the persevering Tyler. At 31 for 2 Poore was dropped by the wicket-keeper when he had only scored four, and at 38 English was yorked for a 'duck'. At 62 Lee was caught in the slips, and although Hampshire had scored quickly they ended the day perilously placed on 65 for 4, with Poore 24 not out and Tom Soar, fast bowler-cum-batsman, on two.

Friday was distressingly warm if you were a bowler or fielder. The temperature neared the nineties and the newspapers were full of warnings on behalf of old folk and animals. Crops were drying up and weather experts were invoking the summer of 1876 for a similar drought. It must have reminded Major Poore of high summer on the Veld; he had no intention of yielding his wicket to the perspiring bowlers, his education needed completion. Tom Soar kept him company for another 115 minutes, until he was out for the best score of his career. They had added 196 in 115 minutes, with Soar making his last 45 in thirty minutes. Half an hour before lunch, the tall, commanding figure of Teddy Wynyard made its way to the shimmering heat of the wicket. The score was 258 for 5, still 57 adrift, with Poore 120 not out, and the Somerset bowlers trying to persuade the rapacious Major to have mercy on them. By lunch at 1.20, the Hampshire score was 306 for 5, with Poore on 146 and Wynyard 22 not out. In two hours twenty minutes, no less than 241 runs had been scored.

Lunch in this relaxed era lasted an hour, but the delay did not affect Poore. He passed 150 in the first over, and within seventy minutes the stand was worth a hundred. Poore passed his previous best of 175 by cutting Cranfield to the boundary, and soon the

Somerset bowlers realized they were up against the worst kind of amateur batsmen – men who knew how to play on a good wicket and saw no reason at all why they should not accumulate greedily like a professional with a bonus in mind. Wynyard employed his favourite pull shot by depositing Cranfield onto a cottage roof adjoining the grounds, and he even tried a reverse sweep to Tyler. He reached his hundred in 145 minutes, and at tea Poore was 216 not out, Wynyard 106 not out and the score 461 for 5.

After tea Wynyard tired and offered several chances – at 146 to Bernard in the deep, then a caught and bowled chance to Cranfield on 158, and he was dropped again when the score was 620. After four hours, Wynyard passed his double century. At one stage Wynyard hit 39 off eighteen balls, and he seemed to be game for more slaughter as Poore tired. Finally, a merciful release: at 6.25, Wynyard was out after hitting 36 fours and two fives. As so often happens with a major stand, the surviving partner did not last very long. Poore was out in the same over, stumped by Wickham, exactly three hundred runs after he had missed the massive Major. Poore had hit 45 fours in the seventh highest innings up to that time. Later he attributed his stamina in the enervating heat to the fact that his father had sent him out on five mile runs at an early age. *The Times* said it was 'an extraordinary display of batting', while the *Taunton Mail* admitted that 'the rate of scoring was not slow'. It seems that understatement was the *sine qua non* of Victorian cricket: 606 runs in a day's play was emphatically not slow, nor was a total of 152 five-ball overs, or twenty-one overs an hour in modern parlance.

The final day was anti-climactic. Somerset needed 358 to avoid an innings defeat, but the openers went for 25 and the rest subsided gently, apart from a stand of 75 in an hour by Daniell and Newton. At lunch the score was 137 for 6, and it was all over by 3.15. The Army officers had knocked the stuffing out of Somerset, and no one could blame them unduly. Wynyard took three wickets with his lobs, and one wonders what pleased him more – the world-record stand or those wickets? He was idiosyncratic enough to prefer the wickets. . . .

As for Major Poore, he returned to South Africa within three weeks of his triple hundred. He was content to have proved himself at county level, and expected nothing else out of the game. Seven of his ten first-class hundreds were scored within that two-month period in 1899, and he could never understand why others could not reduce batting to its simplicities. In his later years he was a familiar figure at Bournemouth, coaching youngsters with great verve and sincerity. When he was asked how he would play Body-line in 1933 he replied, 'I'd charge them, sir!' That must remain the fitting epitaph of a glorious Victorian and the prevailing atmosphere that allowed him to realize his flights of fancy.

8
Gents *v*. Players
1900

As Queen Victoria's reign drew peacefully to a close, English cricket relished its high summer. The game has never seen such a concentration of talent to match that between 1890 and 1914 in England. There was a depth and variety about the bowling, the batting was generally dashing while the pitches encouraged the strokemaker as well as the bowler who would buy his wickets. Offside play flourished against bowling that usually opted to attack, rather than contain. The Gents *v*. Players match at Lord's in 1900 epitomized the flair and brilliance of the Golden Age. Played in blistering sunshine throughout, it contained wonderful batting, resourceful bowling and a marvellous finish against all odds. After being dismissed for 136 on first innings, the professionals reached their target of 501 in just over seven hours. *The Times* match report called it 'a fourth innings almost unique in cricket of any standing' and concluded, 'Cricket is inexplicable.' Only two sides have surpassed such a total in winning a first-class match, but it is the manner in which it was won that burns so brightly down the ages.

With no Australian visit in 1900, the Gents *v*. Players game was the fixture of the year. With the papers full of the sombre news of men killed or missing in the Boer War, with troops being shipped out daily from Southampton, Woolwich and Colchester, the nation needed a sporting diversion or two. These two brilliant sides provided it for three days. The available quality was so high that four teams of equal merit could have been selected from the first-class game that year. Among those left out of the Players side were George Hirst, Schofield Haigh and Johnny Tyldesley. The Gents were lacking the services of W. G. Grace for the first time at Lord's in thirty-five years, while Archie MacLaren and K. S. Ranjitsinhji

GENTLEMEN *v* PLAYERS
At Lord's, 16–18 July 1900

GENTLEMEN

Mr. A. O. Jones c Ward b Trott	9	– b Rhodes	5
Mr. C. B. Fry b Rhodes	68	– hit wkt. b Ward	72
Mr. C. L. Townsend run out	30	– b Rhodes	22
Mr. R. E. Foster not out	102	– c Brown b Trott	136
Mr. J. R. Mason b Trott	2	– c Lilley b Trott	27
Mr. D. L. A. Jephson lbw b Rhodes	9	– not out	18
Mr. G. L. Jessop c Lilley b Rhodes	18	– b Trott	18
*Mr. S. M. J. Woods c Lilley b Rhodes	7	– c Carpenter b Ward	0
Mr. E. Smith c Rhodes b Gunn	26	– c Brown b Trott	16
Mr. C. J. Kortright b Gunn	4	– c sub., b Trott	12
†Mr. H. Martyn c Brown b Gunn	3	– c Quaife b Trott	4
B 15, 1-b 4	19	B 5, 1-b 4	9
	297		**339**

1/26 2/99 3/127 4/131 5/177 6/ 7/216 8/273 9/277

1/10 2/43 3/228 4/ 5/ 6/ 7/ 8/ 9/

Bowling: *First Innings* – Rhodes 30–4–93–4; Trott 27–11–66–2; Mead 21–5–58–0; Gunn 17.3–3–61–3. *Second Innings* – Rhodes 15–2–51–2; Trott 20.2–0–142–6; Mead 14–1–57–0; Gunn 7–3–23–0; Ward 10–3–39–2; Quaife 1–0–18–0.

PLAYERS

*R. Abel b Jessop	30	– c Jones b Jessop	98
A. Ward c Jones b Mason	16	– c Martyn b Jessop	4
T. W. Hayward b Jessop	8	– c Martyn b Kortright	111
W. G. Quaife b Jessop	9	– lbw, b Jones	29
J. T. Brown, sen. c Foster b Mason	18	– c Jones b Smith	163
H. A. Carpenter run out	14	– b Woods	9
†A. F. A. Lilley b Mason	10	– b Mason	30
A. E. Trott c Foster b Mason	9	– not out	22
J. R. Gunn c Martyn b Kortright	4	– b Kortright	3
W. Rhodes not out	1	– not out	7
W. Mead b Kortright	4	B 13, 1-b 8, w1, n-b 4...	26
B 9, 1-b 4	13		
	136		**502**

1/48 2/61 3/ 4/ 5/ 6/ 7/ 8/ 9/

1/ 2/81 3/246 4/348 5/399 6/448 7/469 8/485

Bowling: *First Innings* – Kortright 12.4–4–30–2; Jephson 4–0–9–0; Mason 17–7–40–4; Jessop 14–5–28–3; Jones 5–0–16–0. *Second Innings* – Kortright 18–4–60–2; Jephson 14–2–46–0; Mason 34–11–92–1; Jessop 28–8–74–2; Jones 23–4–69–1; Woods 19.5–3–70–1; Smith 18–3–57–1; Townsend 2–0–8–0.

Umpires: J. Wheeler and J. Phillips.

The Players won by 2 wickets.

were also absent. The fact that Ranji was able to turn out on the same day for Sussex against Hampshire remains one of cricket's more baffling scenarios! Whatever the reasons for Ranji's absence, he would have been just one more dazzling batsman on display amid a cornucopia of flair. A study of the cricketers on either side is rewarding: both possessed batsmen of verve and imagination, two great wicket-keepers were on hand, the bowling was rich in quality and variety and top-class all-rounders seemed everywhere the eye turned. Of the eight bowlers used by the amateurs, seven of them were authentic batsmen, while the two men who won the match for the professionals in the closing stages were or became great all-rounders – Albert Trott and Wilfred Rhodes. Add the sublime slow bowling of Rhodes to the hostile fast attack of Charles Kortright and Sammy Woods, mix in the presence of the fabulous Gilbert Jessop, and you have a heady brew.

Even the weather applied its genial benediction to the proceedings: twelve hours of sunshine every day in London and an average temperature of 83 degrees. The heat would prove a decisive factor on the final afternoon as the Players' batsmen launched their assault, but the prolonged sunshine meant a hard, fast pitch, the ideal conditions for any cricketer with enough confidence in his ability. Such men were plentiful at Lord's in July 1900.

The first cricketer to stamp himself on the match was a tall, willowy batsman named Reginald Foster. At the age of twenty-two, he had already scored 171 that summer for Oxford in the Varsity match; now, in his first appearance for the Gentlemen, he scored two hundreds in the match. This had never been achieved before. After this match, C. B. Fry, an exacting judge of batting standards, said only Ranji had ever wielded a bat with greater speed and fluency – praise indeed for a young player. Foster seemed to relish the big occasion: in his first Test he scored 287 against Australia in 1903, and his brilliant offside driving and deft cutting bore the hallmark of class. One of seven brothers who played for Worcestershire, R. E. Foster adorned the Golden Age of cricket, but sadly he died of diabetes just as the last summer before the Great War began. He was just thirty-six.

Although Foster took twenty-five minutes to get off the mark, his century in the first innings took just two and a half hours. He was indebted to the last man, Harry Martyn, for seeing him to his hundred. Martyn had been in the same side as Foster in the Varsity match earlier in the summer – to underline the batting depth of the Gents side, Martyn had scored 94 and 35 for Oxford. He was one of the great wicket-keepers of the Golden Age: tall, with long arms and a superb pair of hands, he usually stood up to the fastest bowlers and rarely let through a bye. It is a measure of Dick Lilley's quality behind the stumps that Martyn never played for England.

The Players were left with an hour and three quarters batting on the first day and they had a torrid time. Albert Ward, that natural opener, was caught at slip and the imperturbable Tom Hayward was bowled by Jessop. Bobby Abel and Billy Quaife, both short in stature and long in courage, held out against some torrid overs from Kortright and Jessop. They bowled frighteningly fast, and Jessop hit each batsman about the body. Somehow they held out in one of the rare defensive partnerships of the match.

On the second morning the Players lost eight wickets for just seventy runs, and it must be said they did not relish the fast bowlers. Sammy Woods, one of the best of the breed, did not even need to put himself on as Kortright, Mason and Jessop did the damage. The dry, fast wicket assisted the bowler who bent his back, and one or two of the professionals seemed happy just to get out of the way. In contrast, their medium-pace and spin bowlers seemed innocuous as the amateurs built up a huge lead. Their second innings of 339 lasted just three hours, with only C. B. Fry playing circumspectly, making 72 in two-and-a-half hours – even then, no less than 260 runs were scored during that time. Foster's second hundred came out of 195 in just a hundred minutes, and Jessop contributed a delightful cameo of eighteen in six balls. It was intoxicating stuff, and when the Players started their long haul towards 501 with three quarters of an hour left on the second day, they could only hope to do themselves justice in getting a reasonable score. Nevertheless they scored at a run a minute and ended on 44 for 1.

The wicket was still perfect on the final day and Billy Quaife and Jack Brown played the bowling on its merits until Quaife fell leg before at 81. Then Brown and Abel shared an exhilarating stand of 165 in two hours. It was a surprise to see both batsmen playing so freely: Brown had been struggling for form all season, while Abel, at the age of forty-three, played his best innings in Gents v. Players cricket. It had always been a mystery why someone of Abel's class had never succeeded in these games at Lord's (in his career he only averaged 26.77 for the Players at Lord's), but this time he showed much of his Surrey form. Although limping from the attentions of Jessop's bowling in the first innings, he thrashed the short stuff away on the leg side and cut like a rapier on the offside. Brown was equally devastating off the back foot as the amateurs persisted in bowling short on the fiery wicket. When Abel was caught at square leg just before lunch, Tom Hayward came in and kept the momentum going. He added 102 with Brown, until the Yorkshireman was caught at slip after an innings that was as brilliant as anything from his impressive, attractive career. In four and three quarter hours he gave just one chance and batted with immense bravery against great intimidation. Of his 163, 112 came in boundaries.

At Brown's dismissal, the Players still needed 153 with six wickets left. Carpenter did not last long, but Dick Lilley made some fine drives in company with Hayward before cutting a ball into his stumps: 448 for 6. While Hayward was there, playing his usual well-balanced game, the professionals still had a chance, but at 469 he was superbly caught low down at the wicket. He had been the rock on which the innings had been built, playing the support role to Brown's pyrotechnics, then unfurling his masterful driving as senior partner. At least he had ensured that the Players would go down gallantly. When John Gunn was bowled, the score was 485 for 8, still sixteen short. The men charged with the professionals' fortunes were contrasting characters: Albert Trott, the ebullient Australian who spent the rest of his career trying to emulate his six over the pavilion at Lord's in 1899, and the reserved, shrewd Wilfred Rhodes. Although Rhodes was just beginning his wonderful career as a slow bowler he was also starting to work at his batting: that season he averaged 21 (as well as taking 261 wickets!) and the following year he scored his first century. For his part Trott was ridiculously placed so low in the order: that summer he scored 1337 runs and took 211 wickets. He was the best all-rounder in the country at that time, and the Players were fortunate to have a man of his calibre on hand to shepherd Rhodes to a historic victory. The match ended on the stroke of 6.30, with Lord's still bathed in sunshine. It was a fitting end to a glittering game played by a marvellous collection of players for whom counter-challenge was second nature. In another, more passive era, a side facing a victory target of 501 would have settled for crease occupation, and polishing up of averages, courtesy of a not out. The spirit of 1900 demanded a daring riposte, and more than 1200 runs over three days underlines the prevailing philosophy.

Eight bowlers were used by the Gents, some of them tremendous performers. By common consent, Charles Kortright was the fastest of his age and, for all we know, the quickest of all time. Jessop and Woods were not far behind. The Kent captain J. R. Mason was a high-class bowler at fast-medium pace, while the remarkable Digby Jephson had taken 6 for 21 against the Players a year earlier with his baffling lob bowling. Charles Townsend was the best leg-spinner in England as well as a good enough batsman to score 2440 runs the season before. It is true that some of the Gents' bowlers wilted in the broiling heat, that they overdid the short stuff against small men like Abel, Quaife and Brown, but it was a tremendous effort to keep going on such a daunting run chase against such a testing attack. The manner of victory stands as fitting memorial to a great cricketing epoch.

9
Yorkshire *v*. Somerset
1901

The shock upset is part of the attraction of sport, whether it is the early exit of the champion at Wimbledon at the hands of an unseeded teenager, the demise of the FA cupholders in the third round by an unfashionable Fourth Division side – or the humbling of a great cricket team. Yorkshire experienced that demoralizing feeling in July 1901 after dominating the first day's play and looking certain to record their forty-eighth championship match without defeat. That the highly entertaining and popular Somerset side managed to lower the White Rose colours was doubly pleasing to everyone outside Yorkshire.

Although capable of individual brilliance, Somerset were far from a cohesive unit at the start of the twentieth century. They rarely managed to get their best team on to the field because their amateurs were often otherwise engaged. On the morning of the Yorkshire match, Somerset had lost six of their eight championship games, languishing fourth from the bottom of the table. In contrast, Yorkshire were heading for yet another title. In the first three years of the twentieth century they carried off the championship, losing just two matches – to Somerset. Game after game was dominated by three great Yorkshire bowlers – George Hirst, Wilfred Rhodes and Schofield Haigh. This trio combined all the qualities of pace, swerve, left-arm spin and flight, and off-breaks if the pitch turned 'sticky' after rain. They also had Edward Wainwright, who did the 'double' twice in the 1890s, and a great captain in Lord Hawke, a man with the rare gift of inspiration and popularity with the professionals in the side. The batting was very deep – six players scored over 1200 runs for Yorkshire that season and the fielding (particularly Hirst, Denton and Tunnicliffe) was the best in the country. Above all Yorkshire expected to win every game, like all

YORKSHIRE v SOMERSET
At Leeds, 15–17 July 1901

SOMERSET

Mr L. C. H. Palairet b Hirst	0	– c and b Brown 173
L. C. Braund b Rhodes	0	– b Haigh 107
A. E. Lewis c Tunnicliffe b Rhodes	10	– b Rhodes 12
Mr F. A. Phillips b Hirst	12	– b Wainwright 122
*Mr S. M. J. Woods c Hunter b Haigh	46	– c Tunnicliffe b Hirst 66
Mr V. T. Hill run out	0	– c Hirst b Rhodes 53
E. Robson c Hunter b Rhodes	0	– c Tunnicliffe b Rhodes.... 40
G. C. Gill c Hunter b Rhodes	4	– st Hunter b Rhodes 14
†Mr A. E. Newton b Haigh	0	– c Taylor b Rhodes 4
Mr G. Barrington c Brown b Rhodes	11	– st Hunter b Rhodes 15
B. Cranfield not out	1	– not out 5
B 2, 1-b 1	3	B 16, n-b 3 19
	87	630

1/0 2/0 3/16 4/32 5/38 6/38 7/64 8/65 9/86

1/222 2/244 3/341 4/466
5/522 6/570 7/597 8/604
9/609

Bowling: *First Innings* – Hirst 12–5–36–2; Rhodes 16–8–39–5; Haigh
4–0–9–2. *Second Innings* – Hirst 37–1–189–1; Rhodes 46.5–12–145–6; Haigh
20–4–78–1; Wainwright 34–3–107–1; Brown 18–1–92–1.

YORKSHIRE

J. T. Brown c Braund b Cranfield	21	– c sub, b Gill 5
J. Tunnicliffe c Newton b Gill	9	– c Palairet b Braund 44
D. Denton c Wood b Gill	12	– b Braund 16
Mr T. L. Taylor b Cranfield	1	– absent hurt....................... 0
Mr F. Mitchell b Gill	4	– b Braund 21
G. H. Hirst c Robson b Cranfield	61	– lbw b Braund 6
E. Wainwright b Gill	0	– c Lewis b Cranfield 1
*Lord Hawke b Robson	37	– c Barrington b Cranfield . 4
S. Haigh c Robson b Cranfield	96	– not out 2
W. Rhodes c Lewis b Robson	44	– st Newton b Cranfield 0
†D. Hunter not out	10	– c Woods b Cranfield....... 0
B 18, w 5	18	B 12, n-b 2 14
	325	113

1/13 2/33 3/44 4/51 5/55 6/86 7/142 8/167
9/285

1/14 2/57 3/91 4/99 5/104
6/109 7/109 8/109 9/113

Bowling: *First Innings* – Cranfield 27–5–113–4; Gill 23–2–105–4; Braund
5–0–33–0; Robson 10–1–35–2; Woods 5–1–21–0; Palairet 1–1–0–0. *Second
Innings* – Cranfield 18–5–85–4; Gill 4–1–23–1; Braund 15–3–41–4.

Umpires: W. Wright and T. Mycroft.

Somerset won by 279 runs.

the best county sides, and they made a pretty good fist of that: they had not lost a championship match since August 1899. Somerset had come closer than anyone earlier in the 1901 season, when Yorkshire scraped home by one wicket, thanks to the cool head of Rhodes, but there seemed little hope of a repeat performance at Leeds.

The first day's play more or less suited the exacting demands of 10,000 partisan souls packed into the Headingley ground. Somerset won the toss, decided to bat and promptly lost both their openers before a run was scored. Within fifty minutes, six men were out and Hirst, Rhodes and Haigh were vying with each other for cheap wickets. Sammy Woods, the Somerset captain, decided to attack in his customary breezy fashion, opening those muscular shoulders for several massive pulls. It could not last against such bowling quality, and he was caught behind trying one exotic pull too many. Within ninety minutes, Somerset were all out for 87, and the Yorkshire crowd were preening as only they can.

They had to rein back a shade on the complacency after an hour's bowling from Somerset. Cranfield, slow left arm and Gill, right-arm fast, gave them a few early shocks and half the side was out for 55. Yorkshire lost another wicket before passing the visitors' score, but then the game changed character. George Hirst came in and smashed eleven boundaries in just over an hour; he was helped in a stand of 56 by Lord Hawke, the captain again demonstrating his sound temperament when his side really needed him. When they were both out, Yorkshire led by only eighty with two wickets left, but then Haigh and Rhodes showed they knew a bit about batting as well as bowling. They added 118 in 55 minutes, then David Hunter kept Haigh company as he advanced to his hundred. He missed it by four runs, but the best score of his career to date only took him a hundred minutes. Once again Yorkshire had shown their resilience, with the last four men piling up 239 runs. They had scored them at a great pace, which allowed enough time to bowl Somerset out again – one of the hallmarks of every outstanding county team. With two days left, there seemed every prospect of a free Wednesday.

Lionel Palairet and Len Braund had other ideas. Next morning they opened for Somerset, and put together a little matter of 222 in only 140 minutes. This facing a deficit of 238 against great bowlers; the counter-attack was typical of the age. Palairet, one of the game's great stylists, made a hundred before lunch, one of five such occasions in the summer of 1901 – a record that has never been equalled. Among Somerset batsmen he was the forerunner to Arthur Wellard and Ian Botham in his fondness for huge, booming drives that landed in the river or the churchyard at Taunton. Stylish, graceful and dazzling, Palairet exemplified the advantages of learning how to bat on public school and Oxbridge wickets. His partner Len Braund was less fortunate; he had to serve a two-year residential qualification after playing three seasons for Surrey. At last he qualified in 1901, and he quickly became a marvellous all-rounder: solid, attractive batsman, clever leg-spinner and wonderful slip fielder. He developed a reputation as a man for the big occasion, and his performance in the Leeds game helped establish his reliability.

Yet Len Braund was lucky during this tremendous first-wicket stand. He was dropped twice off Hirst, and then at 55 he was caught at slip by Tunnicliffe. However umpire Mycroft could not give a decision because his view had been obscured. Walter Wright, the square-leg umpire, ruled in Braund's favour, to the consternation of the fielders. Several of them swore in later years that Braund was out and they were convinced that Wright's decision marked the turning point of the match. Braund added another 52 before he was out, and the bowling began to get uncharacteristically ragged. After Lewis went at 244 for 2, Palairet was joined by Frank Phillips, an Oxford blue with a penchant for attack, as befits a man just back from winning the DSO in the Boer War. Phillips was never defensively solid, so he rightly opted to play the game that suited him. He and Palairet added 97 in an hour, until Palairet's sumptuous innings ended at 341. He gave just one chance and made his runs in 220 minutes. There was to be no respite for Yorkshire as Phillips added a merry 125 in 74 minutes with his captain Sammy Woods. Then Vernon Hill, another Oxford blue and strong driver, plundered 56 in half an hour with Phillips, until Phillips was out after a thrilling three-hour stay. At the close, Yorkshire tottered back to the pavilion, reeling under an onslaught that had yielded 549 for 5 in only five and three quarter hours. It had been a devastating reminder of the venerable parable about eggs and chickens.

In the first hour of the third day, Somerset continued chasing runs and added another 81. In the face of a scoring rate of a hundred an hour, only Rhodes could claim any honour among the bowlers. For George Hirst it was to prove one of the biggest thrashings of his great career. Five men who had failed to score a run between them in the Somerset first innings had contributed 377 at the second time of asking. It was the manner of the revival that shattered the Yorkshiremen: Why else would they proceed to collapse so abjectly?

They needed 393 to win in just under five hours and, although that was a tall order for a tired side, they should have offered sterner resistance. Yet they were all out forty minutes after lunch, as Braund and Cranfield exploited a wearing pitch with their spin. Yorkshire had got to 98 for 3 at lunch and, although Taylor would not be able to bat because of an injured hand, they had demonstrated their impressive batting depth two days earlier and they ought to have come near to saving the match. Six wickets went down for just fifteen runs, with Cranfield taking four for two in six overs after lunch. Yorkshire's feeble collapse was not in the best traditions of that illustrious county, yet the crowd of 6000 gave a marvellous reception to Sammy Woods and his side. The colours had been lowered at last and in astonishing fashion. Cricket lovers up and down the land had become bored by Yorkshire's hegemony. This was not to belittle their talents, merely a reflection on sport's need to provide the element of surprise. When the upset is caused by brave, attacking play after the odds had seemed insuperable, then you have the justification for Somerset's nation-wide popularity in 1901.

No cricketer was more loved at that time than Sammy Woods, the Australian who settled in the West Country and played cricket and lived his life with such unaffected gusto. Sammy was so delighted by the result that he strode into the team's hotel after the match and, with a beam, spoke one word: 'Magnum.' The bubbly flowed generously, and the side was welcomed back at Taunton station as if they were conquering heroes from the Boer War. The match captured the imagination so much that one evening newspaper in London put out a bill on the streets containing nothing but a cartoon of Somerset's captain with the single word 'Sammy' printed underneath.

Just to underline Somerset's flair for the unexpected, they beat Yorkshire in the next two seasons as well, to complete a memorable hat-trick. Lord Hawke and his men must have been delighted that lightning could only strike twice a season: with a man like Sammy Woods leading a side of such flair and daring, Somerset were always dangerous.

10

England *v.* Australia
OLD TRAFFORD 1902

For sheer unrelenting drama the Old Trafford Test of 1902 would be hard to beat. A fortnight later, England squeezed home by one wicket at the Oval after looking well beaten, but the heart-stopping tension only took over on the final afternoon. At Old Trafford, the twists and turns of fortune over three days emulated anything that had gone before in Test cricket. It will always be remembered as Fred Tate's Match for the most poignant reasons. Tate, a good county bowler with Sussex, played his one and only game for England here and to say he failed to stake a permanent claim to a place ranks as the euphemism of all time. At a vital stage of the Australian second innings, he dropped Joe Darling and then watched the stand add 48, the biggest of the innings. Worse was to follow when Tate batted. With England needing just four to win, he was bowled fourth ball and the Australians scrambled home. Tate sobbed his heart out in the England dressing-room, and later left for the station, alone in a hansom cab, with the blinds pulled down. No player has ever made a more heartbroken exit from the Test arena than Fred Tate. Yet it seems unfair to saddle him with all the blame for this historic defeat: the cock-up theory rears its awkward head again.

First, the England selectors should be pilloried. In the summer of 1902 they had at their disposal the most brilliant collection of players ever available, yet they contrived to hand the series to Australia, even though the appalling summer did not favour the visitors. Australia had already won at Sheffield, after escaping at Birmingham through bad weather, following a first innings dismissal for 36. Now at Old Trafford, England left out C. B. Fry, Gilbert Jessop and George Hirst, three of the great figures in the current game. Fred Tate, a slow medium bowler, was brought in

ENGLAND v AUSTRALIA
(Fourth Test)
At Old Trafford, Manchester, 24–26 July 1902

AUSTRALIA

V. T. Trumper c Lilley b Rhodes	104	– c Braund b Lockwood	4
R. A. Duff c Lilley b Lockwood	54	– b Lockwood	3
C. Hill c Rhodes b Lockwood	65	– b Lockwood	0
M. A. Noble c and b Rhodes	2	– (6) c Lilley b Lockwood	4
S. E. Gregory c Lilley b Rhodes	3	– lbw b Tate	24
*J. Darling c MacLaren b Rhodes	51	– (4) c Palairet b Rhodes	37
A. J. Y. Hopkins c Palairet b Lockwood	0	– c Tate b Lockwood	2
W. W. Armstrong b Lockwood	5	– b Rhodes	3
†J. J. Kelly not out	4	– not out	2
H. Trumble c Tate b Lockwood	0	– lbw b Tate	4
J. V. Saunders b Lockwood	3	– c Tyldesley b Rhodes	0
B 5, l-b 2, w 1	8	– B 1, l-b 1, n-b 1	3
	299		**86**

1/135 2/175 3/179 4/183 5/256 6/256 7/288
8/292 9/292 10/299

1/7 2/9 3/10 4/64 5/74 6/76
7/77 8/79 9/85 10/86

Bowling: *First Innings* – Rhodes 25–3–104–4; Jackson 11–0–58–0; Tate
11–1–44–0; Braund 9–0–37–0; Lockwood 20.1–5–48–6. *Second Innings* –
Rhodes 14.4–5–26–3; Tate 5–3–7–2; Braund 11–3–22–0; Lockwood
17–5–28–5.

ENGLAND

L. C. H. Palairet c Noble b Saunders	6	– b Saunders	17
R. Abel c Armstrong b Saunders	6	– (5) b Trumble	21
J. T. Tydesley c Hopkins b Saunders	22	– c Armstrong b Saunders	16
*A. C. MacLaren b Trumble	1	– (2) c Duff b Trumble	35
K. S. Ranjitsinhji lbw b Trumble	2	– (4) lbw b Trumble	4
Hon. F. S. Jackson c Duff b Trumble	128	– c Gregory b Saunders	7
L. C. Braund b Noble	65	– st Kelly b Trumble	3
†A. F. A. Lilley b Noble	7	– c Hill b Trumble	4
W. H. Lockwood run out	7	– b Trumble	0
W. Rhodes c and b Trumble	5	– not out	4
F. W. Tate not out	5	– b Saunders	4
B 6, l-b 2	8	– B 5	5
	262		**120**

1/12 2/13 3/14 4/30 5/44 6/185 7/203 8/214
9/235 10/262

1/44 2/68 3/72 4/92 5/97
6/107 7/109 8/109 9/116
10/120

Bowling: *First Innings* – Trumble 43–16–75–4; Saunders 34–5–104–3; Noble
24–8–47–2; Trumper 6–4–6–0; Armstrong 5–2–19–0; Hopkins 2–0–3–0.
Second Innings – Trumble 25–9–53–6; Saunders 19.4–4–52–4; Noble
5–3–10–0.

Umpires: J. Moss and T. Mycroft.

Australia won by 3 runs.

for Hirst on the strength of 130 wickets for Sussex. Only Rhodes had taken more, but Hirst was averaging thirty with the bat in a wet summer and he had taken 62 wickets. Apart from that, his indomitable spirit and marvellous fielding were values that could not be easily tossed aside. They were. . . .

On the first day, in front of a crowd of 20,000, Australia had all the luck. They won the toss and batted in conditions that were so damp that Bill Lockwood could not be risked until just before lunch, even though the pitch was tailor-made for his fast-medium bowling. When England batted in the evening the sun came out, and Hugh Trumble's off-spin caused havoc. At one stage, England were 44 for 5, and although Stanley Jackson and Len Braund stopped the rot, the follow-on still loomed at 70 for 5 when play ended. Yet though Australia enjoyed good fortune, they had the good sense to capitalize on it. In Victor Trumper and Reggie Duff they had just the opening pair to exploit the discomfiture of England's bowlers. Trumper, in particular, was breathtaking; throughout this dreadful summer he made 2570 runs with eleven hundreds, more than the rest of the tour party put together and in the process establishing himself as the most exciting batsman in the world. This day at Old Trafford saw Trumper become the first man to score a Test hundred before lunch. He cut Tate for thirteen in one over, he lofted Rhodes into the vacant leg-side area and his placement through the covers was uncanny. Reggie Duff, too, was a very punishing player – few opening partnerships have rivalled these two for glamour – but he was content to give Trumper his head and marvel at the other end. A hundred came up in an hour, and then Lockwood at last risked himself on the damp footholds. He almost got Duff caught at slip in his first over, but then he had him held at the wicket five minutes later: 135 for 1 in seventy-eight minutes. Trumper sailed to his dazzling century out of 168 in a hundred and eight minutes, and at lunch Australia's score stood at 173 for 1. They had played resourcefully and disrespect-fully, as if they knew that the bowlers would regain the upper hand soon. They were right. After lunch the ball started to turn, and Rhodes picked up three wickets in four overs – Trumper caught behind, Noble caught and bowled inches from the ground and another catch to Lilley got Syd Gregory. It was now 183 for 4 and no one would have bet against a score of 225. Then Joe Darling, the Australian captain, made the first of his decisive contri-butions. He decided to attack Rhodes before the bowler nailed

him. It worked – he hit him out of the ground twice for six, and
rattled up 51 in ninety minutes. Clem Hill, another great left-
hander, helped him add 73 in forty-five minutes and the bowlers
were wilting, especially as they were now expected to run through
the Australians with the wicket getting more difficult. Darling's
positive attitude enabled the Australians to get near 300 by the
time they were out at 5 p.m. They should have gone for much less,
but it was an object lesson in making your own luck by playing
positively. Yet on the final afternoon it was abundantly clear that
the English batsmen had not assimilated the lesson.

The second day was another wonderful exhibition of cricket.
England began it deep in trouble but a masterful stand of 141
between Jackson and Braund revived them, and then Lockwood
bowled superbly to reduce the Australians to 85 for 9, a lead of
only 122. It was fine and sunny and a heavy dew meant the ball
did not misbehave as it did the previous evening, when the sun
had baked the damp pitch. Trumble was never less than taxing,
however: he wheeled away for two-and-a-quarter hours in a spell
of 2 for 24 off thirty overs. The other bowlers were not so
demanding – even Trumper turned his arm over – and Darling
resorted to rotating them, hoping for a false stroke. Jackson's late
cutting was faultless and he gave no chance in a stay of four-and-
a-quarter hours. Braund, again proving his excellent temperament,
kept him company until just before lunch when he was beaten for
pace off the pitch. At 185 for 6 some retrenchment was still needed,
and Lockwood and Rhodes supported Jackson admirably. Jackson
reached his hundred with a quick single at 214 for 8, and when
he was last out to a splendid running catch in the deep the crowd
of 25,000 cheered him lustily as if he were a Lancastrian. The lead
was a handy 37 and England needed to strike hard in the remaining
two hours of play that evening.

They opened with Lockwood's pace and Braund's leg-spin. Can
you imagine a modern Test captain trusting a legspinner with every
run vital? Lockwood achieved the early breakthroughs – Trumper
caught cleverly at slip, and when Hill and Duff went in his third
over, the score was 10 for 3. It should have been 16 for 4 when
Darling lofted Braund to deep square leg: Tate, standing almost
on the boundary edge, judged the ball well but dropped it. Darling
and Gregory advanced the score to 62 until Tate made partial
amends when he had Gregory mistiming a pull. At 74 Darling's
adventurous innings was ended by a wonderful catch by Palairet,

who took a low, raking drive running backwards. Lockwood had Hopkins caught at mid-on and Noble was taken at the wicket, and when Rhodes bowled Armstrong with an unplayable delivery, it was 79 for 8. Trumble and Kelly held on for dear life to the close. With so many imponderables, it was impossible to predict which way the match would go.

For a time on Saturday morning it looked as if the weather would have the final word. It rained heavily in the night and the umpires would not permit a start until midday. Australia could only manage one run in twenty minutes for their last two wickets – time enough for a display of petulance by Trumble after umpire Moss gave him out lbw, and then a beautifully judged catch in the deep by Johnny Tyldesley to get Saunders. England needed 124 to win in conditions that favoured the bowlers. Yet England possessed great batting depth: even Tate, the last man, was averaging 18 for the season. . . .

It was soon apparent that the English batsmen were having one of their occasional seizures, where ordinary deliveries remain unpunished. It had happened in 1882 at the Oval where they collapsed under pressure, and now it looked as if they were determined to scrape home the hard way. It was so uncharacteristic of MacLaren and Palairet to crawl to 36 for 0 at lunch, even though the Australian fielding and bowling had been impressive. Yet no more than 88 was now needed and it should be wrapped up by tea. Then the elements again influenced the match. MacLaren, the captain, watched anxiously as the heavy clouds banked up over Manchester and he resolved to increase the tempo after lunch. Within twenty five minutes they had lost three wickets – Palairet bowled by a break-back, Tyldesley caught at slip when he should have played back, and MacLaren out to a fine catch at long-on. When the captain returned to the dressing-room he threw down his bat in disgust and told William Howard, the attendant, 'William, I've lost the match and the rubber.' Several of MacLaren's team-mates contrived to vie with him in self-destruction over the next two hours.

As Bobby Abel and Ranjitsinjhi tried to bat calmly, a shower interrupted them and drove them off the field for fifteen minutes. When they returned the break had clearly done nothing for Ranji; he poked about like a novice, and it was no surprise that he was lbw at 92. F. S. Jackson walked in to a great reception – surely this man of steel, this veteran of the Boer War, would be able to see the situation in perspective? Before he could settle, Abel, who had played with fine judgement, hit across one from Trumble and was bowled: 97 for 5. Braund snicked a three through the slips and hopes rose that they would repeat their indomitable effort of the first innings. Then at 107, a bodyblow: Jackson hit a full toss to Gregory at cover and he brought off a great catch, leaping up. Dick Lilley came in, with 27 needed and four wickets left. Braund was beautifully stumped two runs later. Enter Bill Lockwood, a good enough all-rounder to have done the 'double' twice and hit fifteen centuries in his first-class career. Off his first ball, Trumble appealed for lbw, but it was turned down; off the third ball, Lockwood was bowled by a vicious break-back. At 109 for 8, it was time for stern resolve and clear judgement. In Dick Lilley, a vastly experienced wicket-keeper/batsman, and Wilfred Rhodes, the unflappable young Yorkshireman, England surely had the men of the hour. They gathered a single here and there and Rhodes pulled Saunders over the ropes. Eight years later, when the regulations were altered, that would have been a six, but now Rhodes had to settle for a four. Then Clem Hill brought off the catch of a lifetime. Lilley pulled a ball towards the deep mid-wicket boundary, and Hill set off from long-on in the hope of at least stopping the ball from going over the boundary. After sprinting thirty yards, he threw himself sideways and caught the ball inches from the ground. To everyone's amazement the ball stuck. Years later Hill admitted it was a fluke, that he gave chase to save runs, not in any hope of getting a catch.

At 116 for 9, Fred Tate walked out to join Rhodes. Immediately a heavy shower sent the players racing to the pavilion. They stayed there for three quarters of an hour, contemplating the equation of eight runs and one wicket. The Australians knew that the wet ball would not favour them on the resumption, that a couple of loose deliveries would cost them the match. They knew that Rhodes was a cool customer, a man who had already made a name for himself in tight finishes with Yorkshire. Tate had to be the vulnerable batsman; it was his first Test, even if, at thirty-five, he was an experienced county cricketer. The strategy was to keep Rhodes away from the strike wherever possible and attack Tate.

Hugh Trumble accomplished the first aim by bowling a tight over at Rhodes. So Tate had to face the slow left-arm spin of Jack Saunders. The first ball grazed Tate's stumps. The second was nicked down to fine leg off the inside edge and it went for four, despite a vain pursuit by Armstrong. Tate missed the third ball. Three deliveries to survive, just one boundary from Rhodes would do it. Then Saunders bowled a ball that ruined Fred Tate's career: it came on with the arm, kept fiendishly low and took out the off-stump. It was a good enough delivery for any England batsman, but it gave Australia victory by three runs. No one dared mention that Jack Saunders' action always looked highly suspicious when he bowled the quicker one; when needed he had come up with the match-winning delivery.

In the England dressing-room, Fred Tate was inconsolable. He did not move until Len Braund looked at his red-eyed face and said, 'It's only a game, Fred, now go upstairs and get your money.' In his misery, Tate blurted out that he had a son at home who would make the Australian's pay for this day – he was called Maurice and for once, there was a happy ending. Maurice became one of the greatest fast-medium bowlers of all time and played an instrumental part in restoring England's self-respect after the Great War. Maurice was a proud member of the side that regained the Ashes at the Oval in 1926, and mercifully his father was alive to see it. Fred played just three more seasons after the Old Trafford nightmare; he seemed to lose heart for the game.

Is it fair to saddle Fred Tate with the responsibility for losing the match? The role of Archie MacLaren should be examined. According to C. B. Fry, MacLaren wanted Schofield Haigh to play, but the Yorkshire captain Lord Hawke refused. In a fit of pique MacLaren dropped Hirst, another great Yorkshireman, and opted for Tate. The Sussex bowler was never in the same class as Hirst or for that matter Haigh, who finished top of the national averages that season. MacLaren also blundered when Darling was crucially dropped by Tate. With Len Braund bowling, he asked to have Lionel Palairet fielding at square leg for both Gregory (right hand) and Darling (left hand). Palairet always fielded at square leg for Braund when they played together for Somerset, and he took some great catches in that position. When Gregory took a single off Braund and Darling took the strike, MacLaren haughtily refused to move Palairet over. Instead he summoned Tate, who did most of his fielding in the slips or close to the bat – never at deep square leg. In that same over Darling lofted the ball out to Tate, with historic consequences. One more brickbat for MacLaren: why did he bat so feebly in the second innings when his characteristic style was one of lordly disdain for the wicket's vagaries? His nerves clearly percolated through to the others – Ranji, in particular, was a bag of nerves and looked ill at ease when he walked out to bat.

Years later, Stanley Jackson blamed himself for his vital dismissal; he could have placed that full toss anywhere for an easy two, but he chose to smash it to Gregory. It is true that the Australians were luckier with the weather, but Trumper's wonderful hundred, Hill's thrilling catch to get Lilley and Trumble's inspiring bowling owed nothing to good fortune. Within a week or two it was England's turn for a favourable spin on the wheel of fortune – but Fred Tate was not there to see it.

11
England *v.* Australia
OVAL 1902

Revenge was a rare emotion to enter the genial natures of George Hirst and Gilbert Jessop, but the Oval Test of 1902 must have given them cause for at least a wry smile or two. After being dropped from the Old Trafford Test, they were reinstated and played decisive roles in a pulsating win by one wicket.

Hirst displayed his rugged all-round qualities by taking the first five Australian wickets on the opening day, by steering England away from the threat of the follow-on as the sun dried out a wet pitch, and then sharing in a historic unbroken stand of fifteen with Wilfred Rhodes to claim victory with the last pair together. Jessop played what can be fairly described as the most famous of all Test innings. England were 48 for 5 – still 215 short of victory – when Jessop came in, forty-five minutes before lunch on the final day. He made 104 in seventy-seven minutes out of 139 against top-class bowling and fielding on a difficult wicket. Jessop was missed twice (one of them desperately hard), but his certainty of strokeplay off just eighty balls was astonishing. It was an innings that helped confirm Jessop's status as the most consistent hitter of a cricket ball that the game has seen.

Jessop had always been a law unto himself. Over the previous decade, he had played so many remarkable knocks at speed that few doubted his talent. His footwork was bewildering, his keen eye enabled him to see the ball early and charge the fastest bowlers. He could manipulate the ball anywhere with steely wrists and an innate sense of timing. Throughout most of his career, a batsman had to hit the ball clean out of the ground for it to count as six, otherwise Jessop's record would have been even more phenomenal. It was pretty remarkable in any event: fifty-three centuries, yet he only batted twice for three hours, and ten times for two hours.

ENGLAND v AUSTRALIA
(Fifth Test)
At the Oval, 11–13 August 1902

AUSTRALIA

V. T. Trumper b Hirst	42	– run out	2
R. A. Duff c Lilley b Hirst	23	– b Lockwood	6
C. Hill b Hirst	11	– c MacLaren b Hirst	34
*J. Darling c Lilley b Hirst	3	– c MacLaren b Lockwood	15
M. A. Noble c and b Jackson	52	– b Braund	13
S. E. Gregory b Hirst	23	– b Braund	9
W. W. Armstrong b Jackson	17	– b Lockwood	21
A. J. Y. Hopkins c MacLaren b Lockwood	40	– c Lilley b Lockwood	3
H. Trumble not out	64	– (10) not out	7
†J. J. Kelly c Rhodes b Braund	39	– (11) lbw b Lockwood	0
J. V. Saunders lbw b Braund	0	– (9) c Tyldesley b Rhodes	2
B 5, l-b 3, n-b 2	10	– B 7, l-b 2	9
	324		**121**

1/47 2/63 3/69 4/82 5/126 6/174   1/6 2/9 3/31 4/71 5/75 6/91 7/99
7/175 8/256 9/324 10/324   8/114 9/115 10/121

Bowling: *First Innings* – Lockwood 24–2–85–1; Rhodes 28–9–46–0; Hirst 29–5–77–5; Braund 16.5–5–29–2; Jackson 20–4–66–2; Jessop 6–2–11–0. *Second Innings* – Lockwood 20–6–45–5; Rhodes 22–7–38–1; Hirst 5–1–7–1; Braund 9–1–15–2; Jackson 4–3–7–0.

ENGLAND

*A. C. MacLaren c Armstrong b Trumble	10	– b Saunders	2
L. C. H. Palairet b Trumble	20	– b Saunders	6
J. T. Tyldesley b Trumble	33	– b Saunders	0
T. W. Hayward b Trumble	0	– c Kelly b Saunders	7
Hon F. S. Jackson c Armstrong b Saunders	2	– c and b Trumble	49
L. C. Braund c Hill b Trumble	22	– c Kelly b Trumble	2
G. L. Jessop b Trumble	13	– c Noble b Armstrong	104
G. H. Hirst c and b Trumble	43	– not out	58
W. H. Lockwood c Noble b Saunders	25	– lbw b Trumble	2
†A. F. A. Lilley c Trumper b Trumble	0	– c Darling b Trumble..	16
W. Rhodes not out	0	– not out	6
B 13, l-b 2	15	– B 5, l-b 6	11
	183	(9 wickets)	**263**

1/31 2/36 3/62 4/67 5/67 6/83 7/137 8/179   1/5 2/5 3/10 4/31 5/48
9/183 10/183   6/157 7/187 8/214 9/248

Bowling: *First Innings* – Trumble 31–13–65–8; Saunders 23–7–79–2; Noble 7–3–24–0. *Second Innings* – Trumble 33.5–4–108–4; Saunders 24–3–105–4; Noble 5–0–11–0; Armstrong 4–0–28–1.

Umpires: C. E. Richardson and A. A. White.

England won by one wicket.

This out of 855 innings. His scoring rate was around eighty runs an hour over a career that lasted twenty years. Truly he could score off every ball on any of his frequent days of inspiration and he often changed the course of a match within half an hour. If ever a cricketer deserved the adjective 'fabulous' it was Gilbert Jessop: his intelligent fast bowling and dazzling fielding added to the lustre of a player who was fêted on every ground.

When the teams assembled at the Oval on Monday, 11 August, the atmosphere was celebratory and jingoistic. King Edward VII had been crowned two days earlier and London was *en fête* to the world. *The Times* devoted twelve pages to the Coronation on the Monday, and not even the cold threatening weather could dilute the fervent enthusiasm. Many uniformed Australian volunteer soldiers were to be seen in the crowd of 20,000 as a reminder that the Boer War was in its third year, and their presence only served to cement the bond of Dominion interdependence that had been confirmed on Coronation Day. A narrow win for England after the Old Trafford trauma would satisfy Anglo/Australian honour for another Ashes series, even if the tourists would then come away 2/1 winners.

Australia made it clear on the first day that there would be no consolation prizes. On an easy wicket, deadened by so much recent rain, the ball came through halfway up the stumps and the bowlers were emasculated. Hirst was his usual optimistic, bounding self but even he could not penetrate the iron defence of Noble (two hours for 52) and Trumble (64 not out in two-and-a-half hours). In the first hour after lunch, just thirty-eight runs were scored and only Trumper and Kelly looked to force the pace throughout the day. The fielding was keen – particularly the restored Jessop and Hirst – and only one chance was missed, when Lilley dropped Trumble off Jackson. With Australia all out on the stroke of time, few could dispute the forecast by *The Times:* 'If there is no change in the weather and the England batting does not completely break down, there is every possibility of a draw.'

The weather did change and alter the course of the match. More heavy rain in the night meant a torrid morning for the English batsmen. In cold, gloomy conditions, Hugh Trumble was devastating: from his great height he managed to get the ball to rise up sharply and his command of line and length was faultless. At 83 for 6, the threat of the follow-on was very real. George Hirst had other ideas – he decided to chance his arm, pulling Saunders from off to leg with impunity. He made 43 of the 54 runs added when he was at the crease. As the sun came out, England still looked certain to follow-on, but Lockwood and Braund hung on and eked out some priceless runs. Lockwood was missed in the deep by Hill early on; by Hill's standards as a fielder it was not a difficult chance and if he had taken it the follow-on would have been almost certain.

A lead by Australia of 141 was hardly comforting for England, but at least they now had the chance to grab some wickets with the light deteriorating. Lockwood followed up his valuable batting with five wickets, and Jessop's fast reactions at cover point accounted for the invaluable wicket of Trumper. He made a marvellous stop to a Trumper drive, and Duff sent Trumper back when he saw the ball had not penetrated the offside cordon; Trumper slipped in trying to get back and Jessop ran him out. That was just the start England needed, and afterwards nobody batted with any authority. The overnight lead was 255, with two wickets left – still more than enough for an Australian victory, especially if it rained again overnight.

It did rain, and the pitter-patter of drops led Gilbert Jessop into a wager that would cost him a few pounds. He was staying at the Great Central Hotel during the Test, and after a convivial dinner with his fellow-amateurs he heard the sound of rain with dismay. Recalling Trumble's dominance earlier in the day, he offered odds of 10 to 1 that he would get fifty, and 20 to 1 he would make a century. Bets were struck – a tribute to the respect his colleagues had for Jessop's genius – and the rest is history. Jessop later admitted that he had supped a goodly measure of bubbly when he offered those odds, but such a gloomy prognostication of the match's outcome from a normally confident cricketer simply underlines how heavily the odds were stacked in Australia's favour.

The Australians added only seven runs in the morning and were doubtless glad to be bowling as soon as possible. At 11.35 England started batting on a wicket that Hugh Trumble would have wanted to carry around with him. Soon England were 10 for 3, then 48 for 5 and there was an air of inevitability about the proceedings. Once more, England had the worst of the luck and the wicket, and a 3/0 series result seemed only a matter of time. F. S. Jackson was the only batsman to resist in the first hour, playing his cultured drives with serene confidence and defending resolutely. Three quarters of an hour before lunch he was joined by Jessop, a man who needed a decent score for England if he were not to be dismissed as simply a destroyer of county bowling. This was his tenth Test, and he had only one half-century to his name. Some of Jessop's brilliance would at least entertain the crowd before the inevitable. Before lunch he was comparatively circumspect, scoring twenty-nine; any other player would have been delighted with such a score in forty-five minutes, but Jessop was not conventional. After lunch his genius bloomed for a momentous half hour. He took seventeen off one Saunders over, taking toll of three full tosses and one long-hop. Jackson was content to support his brilliant partner, admiring the sensible way that Jessop attacked the off-spin of Trumble – he refused to sweep him, but drove him straight or through the offside with the full face of the bat. Despite his unorthodox methods, Jessop watched the ball as closely as anyone.

Jackson was caught and bowled after contributing just 18 to the stand of 109, but his polished effort over a hundred minutes had kept England in the game when the wicket was at its worst. They were now 106 short of a famous victory with four wickets left. The new batsman was George Hirst, and Jessop could have wished for no sturdier a partner. Trumble was twice deposited into the pavilion in one over by Jessop, and the pair added thirty in just eight minutes. Jessop roared to his hundred, but then he fell in anti-climactic fashion spooning up an easy catch to short leg off Armstrong's leg-break. As Jessop turned towards the pavilion Jack Kelly, the Australian wicket-keeper, patted him consolingly on the shoulder and every one of his team-mates applauded the batsman all the way back. For a moment, the exigencies of the match were transcended by the realization that those present had watched an awesome performance.

As Bill Lockwood made his way out to join Hirst, the Australians regrouped and considered the permutations. England needed another 76 with three wickets left, and there seemed little hope. Trumble was still bowling wonderfully, Armstrong was tucking up the batsmen on the leg-stump and the pitch remained far from easy. Now Hirst took over the responsibility for winning the game. He was too equable a man to bear grudges for very long, but he must have felt he had a score to settle after being dropped at Old Trafford. Lockwood helped him add 27, then Lilley stayed for another 34 before he was excellently taken at mid-off. All the while Hirst had played with the utmost good sense, punching the ball away with those powerful forearms and dropping his wrists whenever Trumble made one rise sharply. With fifteen needed the last man, Wilfred Rhodes, walked calmly out to the middle. Legend (or more pertinently Neville Cardus) had it that the two Yorkshiremen agreed 'we'll get 'em in singles' but both men denied this in later life. Like the sensible pragmatists they were, Hirst and Rhodes played each ball on its merits, attempting an attacking shot to any loose deliveries and blocking the straight ones. They had one close shave at 259, when Trumble appealed loudly for lbw against Hirst. For the remaining thirty-six years of his life, the sporting, chivalrous Trumble swore that Hirst was 'plumb' out: it would have meant another three-run win for Australia if the verdict had gone his way.

Finally Rhodes ended the torment by pushing Trumble for a single past mid-on's left hand and then bolted for the pavilion. Ever the canny cricketer, Rhodes had seen the crowd massing by the boundary edge and felt the hysteria welling up. A crowd invasion in those days was as likely as the sun setting on the British Empire, but the frenzied reaction of the spectators was surely understandable after the events since lunch. One can only shudder at the antics of a modern crowd in similar circumstances.

So England gained their impossible victory and Joe Darling was left rueing his decision to persevere with Jack Saunders. Jessop had pulverized Saunders, pulling him brutally and crashing him away through the offside. Saunders had taken the first three England wickets, but Jackson, Jessop and Hirst clearly had his measure, and Monty Noble should have been brought on earlier. If Lockwood had been caught by Clem Hill when the follow-on loomed, if Trumble had won that close lbw decision against Hirst, if Kelly had brought off a difficult stumping when Jessop was just beginning to master his onslaught, if Trumble's wonderful sixty-five over stint in the match had been rewarded at the other end by unyielding accuracy and unflinching concentration in the face of 'Hurricane' Jessop. The 'ifs' are as plentiful as Jessop boundaries – and there were seventeen of them.

With the scores level, and Hirst taking an eternity to prepare himself for each ball – he was a great gardener of the pitch and pad fiddler – a parson ran onto the outfield in a state of foaming excitement. Mercifully he was hauled back, but such a display from a pillar of the church hints at the way the nerve ends were being shredded. Many fainted, and when Hirst hit one away for two the roar that rocked the Oval must have been heard for miles around. Yet it seemed the coolest men on the ground were the two Yorkshire batsmen who had grown up together in the same village of Kirkheaton. After all Rhodes finished top of the batting averages that series, with 67, being dismissed just once in seven innings. A handy man to come in last: the following season he opened for Yorkshire and performed the first of his sixteen 'doubles'.

As for Jessop, he was cheered all the way to the crease the following day at Cheltenham and proceeded to make 42 out of 46 in forty minutes, slightly under his usual rate of scoring. He never scored another hundred for England, and ended up with an average of 21 from eighteen Tests. No matter; if he had never made another run after 13 August, 1902 his fame would have been imperishable.

One final thought: Lionel Palairet played just twice for England during his attractive career. They were at Old Trafford and the Oval in 1902 – more than enough memories there to warm his anecdotalist years by the fireside.

12
Derbyshire *v.* Essex
1904

If ever a distinguished cricketer could be deemed unlucky, it was Percy Perrin. In a career that stretched over thirty-two seasons, he made almost 30,000 runs at the respectable average of 35.96, he scored sixty-six hundreds and eighteen times topped a thousand runs in a season. Perrin was one of the most powerful front-foot drivers in an age when the game was stacked with such batsmen – yet few of them could match Perrin's terrifying threat that invariably forced a fast bowler to place three or four men in the deep for the drive. Over six feet tall, Perrin was a handsome, prolific batsman. Yet he never played for England, nor even gained one consolatory appearance for the Gents against the Players. Partly this was due to the scintillating standard of amateur batsmen during Perrin's pomp, partly because he was such a poor fielder. He was laughably slow to get to the ball – he would resemble an ocean-going liner as he turned massively to intercept or chase the ball. There was always a run to Perrin wherever he was hidden in the field. Yet his record was so impressive that he deserved at least a trial at a higher level.

The game at Chesterfield in 1904 just about sums up Perrin's frustrating career. In five hours and forty-five minutes he made what remains the highest score in a losing side. Somehow, after scoring almost 600, Essex contrived to lose handsomely. Perhaps they scored their first innings runs too quickly – the innings only lasted six hours – but Derbyshire's comeback ranks with any of the great revivals. At that time the only comparison was with Stoddart's victory at Sydney in 1894 (see chapter 6), but Derbyshire had none of Stoddart's advantages: they did not follow on and tire out the opposition bowlers, rain did not come to their aid and they managed to win in under three days, whereas England did it in six

DERBYSHIRE *v* ESSEX
At Chesterfield, 18–20 July 1904

ESSEX

*Mr. F. L. Fane, lbw b Curgenven	63	– b Warren		2
H. A. Carpenter, b Bestwick	5	– c Warren b Bestwick		2
Mr. P. A. Perrin, not out	343	– c & b Warren		8
Mr. C. P. McGahey, b Bestwick	32	– c Cadman b Bestwick		5
Rev. F. H. Gillingham, c & b Warren	43	– absent ill		0
E. H. D. Sewell, b Warren	10	– c Cadman b Curgenven		41
W. Reeves b Warren	0	– b Bestwick		0
Mr. R. P. Keigwin lbw b Ashcroft	14	– c Needham b Warren		0
Mr. J. W. H. T. Douglas b Ollivierre	47	– not out		27
†A. E. Russell c Humphries b Cadman	23	– b Curgenven		0
C. P. Buckenham lbw b Bestwick	3	– b Warren		8
B 2, l-b 5, w 3, n-b 4	14	– W 2, n-b 2		4
	597			97

1/12 2/132 3/179 4/300 5/314 6/314
7/383 8/513 9/586 10/597

1/4 2/4 3/17 4/21 5/21 6/26 7/83
8/83 9/97

Bowling: *First Innings* – Warren 29–3–143–3; Bestwick 42.1–8–160–3; Cadman 22–3–65–1; Storer 7–0–41–0; Curgenven 16–1–67–1; Ashcroft 7–1–38–1; Morton 8–1–39–0; Wright 4–0–15–0; Ollivierre 3–0–15–1. *Second Innings* – Warren 16.1–5–42–4; Bestwick 16–4–34–3; Cadman 2–0–10–0; Curgenven 5–2–7–2.

DERBYSHIRE

Mr. L. G. Wright c Fane b Reeves	68	– c Carpenter b Buckenham	1
Mr. C. A. Ollivierre b Reeves	229	– not out	92
W. Storer b Buckenham	44	– not out	48
*Mr. E. M. Ashcroft b Sewell	34		
E. Needham b Reeves	47		
Mr. G. Curgenven b Buckenham	31		
A. Morton b Reeves	16		
A. R. Warren b Douglas	18		
S. W. A. Cadman c Douglas b Reeves	34		
†J. Humphries not out	2		
W. Bestwick lbw b Douglas	0		
B 6, l-b 18, w 1	25	B 4, l-b 2, w 1, nb 1	8
	548	(For 1 wkt.)	149

1/191 2/319 3/378 4/401 5/462 6/478
7/499 8/530 9/544 10/548

1/11

Bowling: *First Innings* – Buckenham 43–5–176–2; Keigwin 7–1–36–0; Reeves 51–7–192–5; Douglas 15.3–1–54–2; McGahey 11–2–34–0; Sewell 7–0–31–1. *Second Innings* – Buckenham 13–0–78–1; Reeves 13–1–43–0; Douglas 2–0–14–0; McGahey 2–1–6–0.

Umpires: W. Wright and S. Brown.

Derbyshire won by 9 wickets.

days a decade earlier. Truly it was a remarkable performance by Derbyshire in a match that threw up many heroes – but the biggest was the heavy-footed man whose tally of sixty-eight boundaries in a single innings remains a record to this day.

In sapping heat and with the wicket looking blameless, the decision to bat first was simplicity itself for the Essex captain, Freddie Fane, the only Irishman ever to captain England at cricket. Fane went in first, and when Carpenter was bowled after a quarter of an hour, Perrin strode in to launch the slaughter. He added 120 in seventy minutes with Fane, then simply decimated the Derbyshire attack. He was helped in a stand of 126 in seventy minutes by the Reverend Frank Gillingham, who later became the second cricket broadcaster to be heard on radio after Sir Pelham Warner and eventually was appointed chaplain to King George VI. By the time the reverend gentleman was out, the bowlers were praying for divine assistance. The blinding heat slowed Perrin for a time and he started to make mistakes: Bill Bestwick dropped an absolute sitter off Arnold Warren at mid-off when Perrin had made 152, and as he began to loft his drives he was missed three more times in the outfield. It did not deter Perrin; after a second wind, he realized this was his lucky day and he finished with 295 not out from an Essex score of 524 for 8.

It was thought that Essex might have declared overnight to give themselves enough time to bowl out Derbyshire twice, but not a bit of it. Perrin reached his triple hundred in the day's first over, and he eventually carried out his bat. The *Derby Evening Telegraph* commented: 'His leg placing and on-driving were singularly clean and perfect and his effort will long be remembered by any real devotee of cricket who was privileged to watch it.' The fact that Derbyshire managed to bowl 138.1 overs in six hours when a fair amount of time was lost retrieving the ball from the boundary serves to exemplify the attacking spirit of the era. Soon Derbyshire's batsmen were displaying a similar approach.

When Derbyshire went in just before one o'clock they needed a little matter of 448 to avoid the follow-on: by close of play, they were just two runs short with only four wickets down. By lunch they were 144 without loss, with the Derby schoolmaster Levi Wright 44 not out and Charles Ollivierre 91 not out. Now Ollivierre was an interesting character. He came to England in 1900 with the first West Indies touring side. He was twenty-three and looked a talented, if erratic, batsman. He remained so, but once he had qualified for Derbyshire he gave rich entertainment for a short while. Ollivierre was the first West Indian batsman to show English cricket the type of exotic, daring brilliance that was emulated by the likes of Constantine, Headley, Weekes, Kanhai, Sobers and Richards. On this day at Chesterfield, he was irresistible.

No less than 217 runs had been scored in the morning session, and the mayhem continued after lunch. When Wright was easily caught at mid-on, the first wicket had added 191 in a hundred minutes. Billy Storer helped him put on 128 in seventy-five minutes, although he ought to have been caught first ball at mid-off if the man there had been anyone other than that shire horse of a fielder, Percy Perrin. After tea, Ollivierre raced to his double century in 190 minutes before he was third out at 378 after 225 minutes of exhilarating unorthodoxy. The Essex attack was far from negligible: Claude Buckenham was one of the fastest bowlers of the age and good enough to play four times for England, the genial Billy Reeves took a hundred wickets at medium pace that season and the young Johnny Douglas was learning the arts that turned him into the best new ball bowler of his time, in the opinion of Jack Hobbs. They all came alike to Ollivierre. What entertainment that beautiful Chesterfield ground had seen over the first two days! So far 1043 runs, many of them magnificently compiled against two good bowling sides. It would no doubt peter into a high-scoring draw the next day, but the fare had been sumptuous so far.

For some reason, play started fifteen minutes early next morning – one of those charming cricketing idiosyncracies that the game tolerated in those Corinthian days. Despite the early start, there seemed little prospect of a positive result, especially as Derbyshire batted a further eighty-five minutes before they were all out, just 49 behind the Essex total. Essex had forty-five minutes batting before lunch, and the main interest lay in whether Perrin would carry on the carnage. Two splendid fast bowlers had other ideas. Arnold Warren and Billy Bestwick were an excellent opening pair, and when their collective dander was up they were a handful on and off the field. Both were over-fond of their ale and they had erratic lifestyles: Bestwick once found himself on a manslaughter charge after a drunken brawl but the case was dropped, and Warren walked out on his county and family for a time, living rough and on his wits before he returned to first-class cricket. They were hard to handle, but turned in great performances – Bestwick's splendid physique stemmed from his winter occupation as a miner and that strength and stamina gave him genuine pace off a short run, while Warren played for England against Australia the following year. He took 5 for 57 at Leeds, including the wicket of Trumper twice in the match, and never played again for England. No wonder the professional fast bowlers of that period were occasionally temperamental!

In the Essex first innings, Warren and Bestwick had conceded over three hundred runs, so we may safely assume they had a score to settle. By lunch they had reduced Essex to 27 for 6, with Bestwick in particular making the ball fly off the rock-hard pitch. Perrin was superbly caught and bowled, Charlie McGahey brilliantly taken at mid-off and, in the same position, Keigwin was acrobatically held by 'Nudger' Needham, better known as the soccer half-back who played sixteen times for England. Then Billy Reeves collected his 'king pair' – out first ball in each innings. By lunchtime urgent messages were being relayed to Nottingham for the Reverend Gillingham, not for a suitable prayer but to get out of his sick bed. The Reverend had been told not to move because of lumbago, but when the dire tidings came through he answered the call. Unfortunately he missed the appropriate train by three minutes, and by the time he arrived at Chesterfield the match was all over. Essex were bowled out in just 110 minutes; the pitch was still perfect but the bowling had been excellent, the fielding faultless and the batting feeble.

So Derbyshire needed 147 to win in 125 minutes – chicken feed judged by the phenomenal rate of scoring in this game so far. Charles Ollivierre again went off like an express train, and within an hour Derbyshire had made a hundred. The West Indian was just as devastating as the previous day, as he cut mercilessly and missed nothing off his legs in traditional Caribbean style. It was his twenty-eighth birthday, and every Derbyshire supporter must have wished he would seal victory with his second wonderful hundred of the match. Billy Storer had other ideas, however. Storer had been a good enough player to represent England six times, but he was now nearing the end of his career and dogged by the financial uncertainty most professionals experienced at that time. Talent money was available to any professional who reached fifty, and the prospect of a guinea exercised Storer's canny mind far more than playing second fiddle to a West Indian amateur who had been found a clerical job by the county while qualifying. So

Storer started to pinch the strike to get his fifty, with the result that both batsmen missed out on their individual targets. Ted Sewell, one of the Essex players and later a cricket journalist, firmly believed that they each tried to run the other out in the closing stages, but they were less proficient at that than picking off the demoralized bowlers.

So at 5.30 on a sunlit evening, Storer cut a ball away to the boundary and a remarkable game was over. Around 8000 people had watched 1391 runs scored over three days, with the winning runs coming in just eighty minutes. No one would have bet against an Essex victory after the first day, but audacious batting and relentless fast bowling pulled the game around. Any batsman who scores a total of 321 in 280 minutes for once out deserves to be a winner.

Perrin was left to rue the illogicalities of a sport where he could compile the fifth highest individual score in the game's history, yet finish on the beaten side. He needed a philosophical streak as his sterling career continued to miss out on international recognition, and he must have enjoyed the irony that saw him appointed chairman of the England selectors in 1939. Good enough to be chairman, but not good enough ever to play for England: not even one solitary appearance, even though many an England player has rivalled Perrin's slowness in the field.

At least Perrin was more fortunate than Charles Ollivierre. He only played another three years of county cricket before having to retire with serious eye trouble at the early age of thirty-one. The dashing West Indian made only three hundreds for Derbyshire, but one of them (and a near-miss) placed him forever in the annals.

13
Somerset *v.* Yorkshire
1906

We have seen earlier how Somerset enjoyed some titanic battles with Yorkshire in the early years of the twentieth century. The game at Bath in 1906 does not belong in that category: Somerset's resistance was too spineless for that. Its only distinction lies in the performance of George Hirst. In cricket history, no one has emulated his feat of two hundreds and eleven wickets in the same match. Indeed that feat at Bath serves as a microcosm of a unique season for Hirst. That year he became the first cricketer to score two thousand runs and take two hundred wickets and that record still stands alone. Nor is it ever likely to be equalled, with the decrease in first-class matches over the past twenty years or so.

It seems strange that two centuries and ten wickets in a match still stands alone. One would have thought that a Hammond, a Woolley, a Botham or a Sobers might have got there, but no. No wonder many good judges consider George Hirst to be the greatest county cricketer of all time. This is not to gainsay his occasional splendid efforts for England over twenty-four appearances, but for Yorkshire, Hirst was outstanding throughout three decades. He performed the 'double' fourteen times (only his team-mate, Wilfred Rhodes beats that with sixteen), and his fielding at mid-off was for long the talk of the land. Hirst's marvellous temperament, his fighting qualities and his unfailing cheerfulness all contributed to his reputation as one of the most popular cricketers of any age.

He was very fit and he needed to be. How else could he have performed such monumental deeds season after season, and specifically in the summer of 1906? It was certainly not the fault of George Hirst that Kent pipped Yorkshire to the county championships that year, because no man has ever done more for his side in a season. By the time Yorkshire came to Bath at the end of

SOMERSET v YORKSHIRE
At Bath, 27–29 August, 1906

YORKSHIRE

J. Tunnicliffe c and b Braund	4	– c Braund b Bailey	38
W. Rhodes c Johnson b Bailey	64	– not out	115
D. Denton c Martyn b Braund	67		
Mr. T. L. Taylor c Poyntz b Mordaunt	41		
G. H. Hirst c and b Merchant	111	– not out	117
H. Rudston c Poyntz b Braund	21		
*Mr E. Smith c Mordaunt b Braund	34		
S. Haigh b Braund	1		
H. Myers lbw, b Braund	6		
†D. Hunter b Mordaunt	8		
W. Ringrose not out	2		
L-b 7, w 1, n-b 1	9	B 2, l-b 6, w 2	10
	368		***280**

* Innings declared closed.

1/24 2/126 3/161 4/225 5/308 6/318   1/38
7/323 8/339 9/356

Bowling: *First Innings* – Braund 38.3–3–125–6; Lewis 11–3–43–0; Bailey 19–2–81–1; Robson 14–2–37–0; Mordaunt 36–10–71–3. *Second Innings* – Braund 6–0–44–0; Lewis 10–2–52–0; Bailey 10–2–36–1; Robson 4–0–39–0; Mordaunt 9–0–54–0; Phillips 2–0–19–0; Palairet 2–0–9–0; Martin 2–0–17–0.

SOMERSET

†Mr. H. Martyn b Ringrose	2	– c Rhodes b Hirst	23
Mr. P. R. Johnson b Rhodes	29	– b Hirst	5
A. E. Lewis b Hirst	3	– b Hirst	0
L. C. Braund b Hirst	28	– b Ringrose	12
*Mr. L. C. H. Palairet b Hirst	31	– c Hunter b Hirst	42
Mr. F. A. Phillips lbw, b Rhodes	2	– b Hirst	2
E. Robson c Hunter b Hirst	3	– b Haigh	26
Mr. H. S. Poyntz c Hirst b Rhodes	14	– b Haigh	10
Mr. F. M. Lee not out	6	– not out	6
Mr. O. C. Mordaunt b Hirst	3	– lbw, b Haigh	0
A. E. Bailey b Hirst	0	– b Haigh	2
B 3, l-b 1	4	B 2, l-b 1, w 1, n-b 2	6
	125		**134**

1/7 2/18 3/62 4/84 5/87 6/100 7/103   1/9 2/9 3/28 4/40 5/87 6/90 7/121
8/107 9/125   8/132 9/132

Bowling: *First Innings* – Hirst 26–3–70–6; Ringrose 12–5–21–1; Rhodes 14–4–28–3; Haigh 1–0–2–0. *Second Innings* – Hirst 15–2–45–5; Ringrose 9–1–38–1; Rhodes 10–1–34–0; Haigh 5–1–11–4.

Umpires: W. A. J. West and A. Millward.

Yorkshire won by 389 runs.

August, Hirst was a tired man and a disappointed man. In the previous game, Yorkshire had lost by a single run to Gloucestershire; it was the first time Gloucestershire had beaten them since 1897 and it had come at a bad stage in the season, with Kent and Yorkshire going for the title. Somerset, that scourge of the White Rose, had to be beaten or else the championship would be lost.

It was not a vintage eleven that year. Stanley Jackson, the hero of the Ashes battle the previous summer, did not play one game, while John Tunnicliffe (sound opener and superb slip fielder) was in decline. Too much depended on the batting of the quicksilver David Denton and the all-round excellence of Hirst and Rhodes. For the last three seasons, Rhodes had performed the 'double' after he had worked his determined way up the batting order, while Hirst was at his peak. With the bat, his speed of eye-to-hand co-ordination was breathtaking, so that many class bowlers felt they could only keep him quiet with a yorker; everything else he seemed to treat as a long hop. He loved to hook, and his pulling on the leg-side was prolifically faultless. As a bowler, Hirst could well be termed the father of modern swing bowling. Before he showed what could be achieved with a new ball, fast bowlers used to rub it in the ground to lose the shine and get a better grip on it. Hirst, in contrast, would shine the ball to ensure it swung around. He could make the new ball swerve and dip in so late that many a batsman used to say that being bowled by Hirst was akin to being thrown out by cover point!

Somerset proved no match at all for Hirst's all-round excellence. They were a moderate side in 1906, with just four victories. Lionel Palairet, their best batsman, only made his debut for the season in the Yorkshire match, and the captain, Sammy Woods, was sadly past his effervescent best. On the first day Yorkshire concentrated on building a big score. *The Times* described the cricket as 'colourless', reporting that T. L. Taylor 'laboured' an hour and a half for 41, an acceptable scoring rate at any stage after the Great War. A score of 347 for 8 at the close hardly indicates slothful progress, and a stand of 102 in fifty-five minutes between Rhodes and Denton was an attractive cornerstone of the innings. Hirst came in just before lunch at 161 for 3 (it must have been a 'colourless' morning's play!) and after a suspicious opening, he proceeded to enjoy himself. In just over two and a half hours, he made his fifth hundred of the season and finished with 111 out of 157, without giving a chance.

Yorkshire batted on for a quarter of an hour on the second day, and then bowled out Somerset in two hours forty minutes. Johnson, Braund and Palairet all batted stylishly, but after lunch the last seven wickets went down for just 63 runs. The ball produced by Hirst to bowl Palairet was typical of his late swerve: Palairet thought it was passing way outside leg-stump, but when he missed his shot it swung in late and clipped the leg-stump low down. It is hard to legislate for such a delivery and with Hirst hitting the stumps eight times in the match the Somerset batsmen were regularly bemused.

With Somerset 243 runs behind, the follow-on could have been invoked, but Yorkshire opted to pile up the runs instead. The batsmen obeyed the precept of quick runs and at the close, after just two hours' batting, Yorkshire had made 280 for 1, a lead of 523. Rhodes was freer than usual, but it was Hirst who really forced the pace. He came in at 78 for 1 (after forty minutes), and in the next seventy-five minutes he and Rhodes added 202 runs. It was rather different from the hysterical atmosphere of their famous partnership four years earlier at the Oval, but these two shrewd professionals knew when to look a gift horse in the mouth. Towards the end, wicket-keeper Martyn bowled a couple of very slow overs, while Palairet tried some lobs. The two Yorkshiremen had no intention of showing mercy; they had not forgotten the drubbing handed out by Palairet at Leeds in 1901 (see chapter 9). Hirst roared to his hundred in sixty-six minutes, while Rhodes took half an hour longer. Only one chance was given – by Hirst, on 93, when Johnson split his hand trying to catch him at long-on. During his innings Hirst completed 2000 runs for the season for the third time in a row; it had been a shrewd idea to promote him up the order to garner some quick runs.

Even Yorkshiremen sometimes show mercy to a demoralized opponent, so the overnight declaration left Somerset with two options: either bat out the final day or lose. They chose the latter. Hirst was more than helpful in the decision: in his second over he bowled both Johnson and Lewis. With the score at 40, he did the same to Frank Phillips, another of the 1901 heroes. Palairet batted with his customary polish for an hour and a quarter, but at 90 for 6, with Hirst taking five of them, Somerset were in disarray. At 104 for 6, Hirst was taken off; he would just about have worked up a sweat after fifteen overs but his captain, Ernest Smith, felt he knew best. This time he was right – Schofield Haigh polished off the innings and picked up some cheap wickets. If Hirst had stayed on, his haul of wickets would have been even more impressive, but he was always a man to put the team first, and a victory by 389 runs was handsome reward for his versatility.

Hirst's *annus mirabilis* did not end happily for his side. On the day that he completed his remarkable match double at Bath, Kent beat Middlesex by seven wickets. They went on to take the title and Yorkshire had to make do with the consolation of having beaten and drawn with the county champions that summer. There was another consolation from the 1906 season that proved to be historic – the astonishing all-round feats of George Hirst.

14
Middlesex *v.* Somerset
1907

During his benefit season the modern cricketer usually approaches the cricket-playing aspect of the year with a certain amount of trepidation and resignation. All those hours spent on the telephone, playing in celebrity golf matches and ingratiating himself with the public inevitably take their toll. It is rare for a beneficiary to have a successful playing year in these commercially-minded days, rarer still if he dominates his benefit match by his cricket skills. Eighty years ago it was different. The appropriate beneficiary relied exclusively on proceeds from his benefit match: he needed three fine days, attractive opposition and an outstanding performance from himself, to swell the coffers from a collection around the ground. Albert Trott only got the last part of the equation right when he took his benefit in 1907. He finished off his own benefit match at ten minutes past one on the final day by a remarkable piece of bowling. Within the space of half an hour, he performed the hat-trick twice. More specifically he took four wickets in four balls – and only a coat of varnish robbed him of five in five – and then he wrapped up the Somerset innings with three in three. No beneficiary has ever approached such a feat, but it was typical of Albert Trott that he should at once demonstrate his cricketing brilliance and his lack of financial acumen. If he had somehow contrived to reserve his historic bowling until later in the day, the crowd would have been larger and the takings correspondingly generous. With no cricket after lunch, the crowd on the final day was small, so Trott was directly responsible for ending up with a meagre benefit.

Somehow Albert Trott remained one of life's losers, despite his great cricketing gifts and a whimsical, attractive personality that brought him deserved popularity. He was an Australian, and at the age of twenty-one he made an excellent Test debut against

MIDDLESEX v SOMERSET
At Lord's, 20–22 May 1907

MIDDLESEX

Mr. P. F. Warner b Mordaunt	46	– b Lewis	11
F. A. Tarrant c Lee b Lewis	52	– c Palairet b Mordaunt	28
Mr. G. W. Beldam lbw, b Mordaunt	12	– lbw, b Lewis	0
Mr. B. J. T. Bosanquet c Johnson b Mordaunt	32	– b Balley	29
Mr. E. S. Litteljohn c Braund b Lewis	44	– b Mordaunt	52
A. E. Trott b Lewis	1	– c Wickham b Robson	35
Mr. H. A. Milton b Lewis	3	– b Mordaunt	0
*†Mr. G. MacGregor c Woods b Bailey	39	– c Poyntz b Robson	39
H. R. Murrell b Robson	33	– c and b Braund	9
J. T. Hearne not out	3	– not out	4
E. Mignon b Bailey	1	– c Wickham b Braund	0
B 15, l-b 4, n-b 1	20	B 8, l-b 2, n-b 1	6
	286		**213**

1/89 2/117 3/117 4/163 5/165   1/20 2/20 3/54 4/110 5/
6/171 7/223 8/280 9/285   6/ 7/ 8/ 9/

Bowling: *First Innings* – Lewis 32–14–88–4; Bailey 16–5–33–2; Braund 13–1–33–0; Mordaunt 30–6–97–3; Robson 7–1–15–1. *Second Innings* – Lewis 7–2–17–2; Bailey 16–3–58–1; Braund 13.4–1–55–2; Mordaunt 15–1–47–3; Robson 6–2–30–2.

SOMERSET

*Mr. L. C. H. Palairet c MacGregor b Mignon	6	– c Bosanquet b Tarrant	35
L. C. Braund c MacGregor b Bosanquet	59	– not out	28
Mr. P. R. Johnson b Tarrant	57	– c Trott b Tarrant	14
A. E. Lewis c Tarrant b Mignon	31	– lbw, b Trott	1
Mr. E. S. M. Poyntz lbw, b Tarrant	9	– b Trott	0
Mr. S. M. J. Woods c Bosanquet b Tarrant	17	– b Trott	0
E. Robson not out	20	– b Trott	0
Mr. F. M. Lee b Hearne	18	– c Trott b Tarrant	7
Mr. O. C. Mordaunt c Baldam b Tarrant	1	– c Mignon b Trott	4
†Rev. A. P. Wickham c Trott b Tarrant	0	– b Trott	0
A. E. Bailey c Litteljohn b Tarrant	3	– c Mignon b Trott	0
l-b 14, w 1	15	B 4, l-b 4	8
	236		**97**

1/12 2/131 3/137 4/154 5/194   1/56 2/74 3/75 4/75 5/75
6/194 7/ 8/ 9/   6/75 7/90 8/97 9/97

Bowling: *First Innings* – Beldam 4–1–15–0; Mignon 24–6–88–2; Trott 5–1–10–0; Hearne 8–1–22–1; Bosanquet 8–0–39–1; Tarrant 15–4–47–6. *Second Innings* – Beldam 3–1–10–0; Mignon 5–1–24–0; Trott 8–2–20–7; Tarrant 14–4–35–3.

Umpires: F. W. Marlow and S. Brown.

Middlesex won by 166 runs.

England in the 1894/5 series. At Adelaide he made 38 and 72 – both undefeated – and took 8 for 43 in the second innings. After making 85 not out at Sydney, he appeared the best all-rounder in Australia and a certainty to go on the 1896 tour to England, not least of all because his brother Harry was to captain the side. For some unaccountable reason Albert was not picked; the atmosphere must have been tense in the Trott household at Melbourne and Albert was so disappointed that he upped and left for England. He would qualify and play county cricket and show Australia what they had missed. If England selected him for a Test, he would accept with alacrity. That rebuff in 1896 was the first of many for a man who had seemed to have been sprinkled by the gods with greatness.

For a time all went well in England for Alberto, as he came to be known. He qualified for Middlesex and played two Tests for England in South Africa in 1898. When the Australians came over the following year, he was keen to show them what they had missed. He had developed a reputation for hard, spectacularly long hitting – he was the first to use a heavy bat of around three pounds in weight – and he vowed to come up with something special when he batted against the Australians. In July of that year, he played for the MCC at Lord's and he hit Monty Noble clean over the pavilion. The ball cleared the roof, struck a chimney and finished up in the garden of a dressing-room attendant. It was a monstrous hit and no one has managed a similar feat apart from the same Albert Trott, in a mood of revenge against his fellow-Australians.

By the turn of the century, Alberto was a great all-rounder. For two seasons in a row he scored a thousand runs and took two hundred wickets, with his varied bowling which encompassed generous spin, changes of pace from a lowish arm, and a fast yorker that brought him a stack of victims. In addition, his fielding and catching were both brilliant. The Lord's crowd loved Alberto: something always seemed to be happening when he was involved. At last he seemed to have found himself after the disappointments back home.

Unfortunately Alberto shared a fault with another droll icono-clast of that time, Oscar Wilde – he could resist everything except temptation. He continually tried to emulate that massive blow over the Lord's pavilion, with the result that his batting fell away. There were still some notable displays of hitting, but he never scored a thousand runs again after his second great season of 1900. He

became a wild, rash slogger – remaining convinced that one day
the luck would turn for him and he would then demoralize attack
after attack. It seemed odd that such an intelligent bowler could
not spot his own frailties as a batsman, yet percipience remained
a quality foreign to him. He took to drink, became rather heavy
and muscle-bound and looked a sad sight after the glories of recent
seasons. His weakness for bookmakers and three-legged horses left
him perpetually broke. If ever a man needed a prosperous benefit
match it was Albert Trott.

It was typical of his luck that the game should have been played
in miserably cold weather during one of the wettest summers in
living memory. Yet why was he given a game so early in the
summer: whoever heard of a benefit match in the third week of
May? Surely high summer was the time to pack in the crowds,
during the holiday period? That decision was one more riddle in
the tragic life of Albert Trott. His astonishing bowling in his benefit
game was another, because he had looked a shadow of his former
self in the previous season, when he took just sixty-two wickets at
a cost of 25.67 – in stark contrast to the earlier tally of 626 wickets
in three successive seasons. It seems strange to choose Somerset for
a benefit game: they were talented but very brittle and heavily
dependent on amateurs who could not always spare the time to
play. Their batting had been very weak for some seasons now, and
they were not the sort of side you could guarantee would sell their
wickets dearly to prolong a game for a grateful beneficiary. The
hard heads of Lancashire, Yorkshire and Nottinghamshire were
the ideal choice for that, while the dazzling men of Kent would
have been the most attractive opposition, the team to persuade the
waverers to part with their money, given poor weather. Almost
any side but the Somerset of 1907. . . .

Over the first two days the contest was fairly even, although the
bitterly cold, rainy conditions hardly encouraged cavalier cricket
or bottoms on seats. Rain and bad light halted play for fifty minutes
on the first day, and Middlesex were all out just before the early
close. Trott managed the traditional 'one off the mark' accorded
to all beneficiaries, but he then suffered his customary fate. On
Tuesday it was still cold and cheerless as Middlesex built a useful
lead of fifty. Trott looked as innocuous as usual during five routine
overs, but he batted more sensibly second time around. He and his
captain Gregor MacGregor forged a valuable partnership after
the loss of early wickets and, although Trott could not resist the

occasional waft or smear, he played with uncharacteristic discretion.

Somerset thus began the final day needing 264 to win on a wicket that seemed to be holding up well enough. Much depended on the early batsmen, and Braund and Palairet added 56 for the first wicket in a manner that indicated the pitch had not become infested by demons. Certainly there was no hint of the shocks to come. Palairet was caught at cover point with the score at 56, but then Johnson and Braund looked unruffled as they came to 74. Then Middlesex tried a double bowling change with the two Australians, Trott and Tarrant, replacing Mignon and Beldam. Immediately Trott caught Johnson – 74 for 2. Then Trott started a momentous over.

He had Lewis lbw off the first ball. In came Massy Poyntz, an amateur batting way out of his class, with little to recommend him except direct ancestry to a Roundhead general from the Civil War. He shaped up like Oliver Cromwell to his first ball, which deceived him in the flight and bowled him. Sammy Woods came in to face the hat-trick ball. Dear old Sammy may have been forty years of age now, but he could be relied upon for a positive response to a crisis. He did not fail us – trying an ambitious chop through the slip area, he lost his off-stump. The hat-trick to Trott, but he was not done yet. Ernie Robson, a good sound professional all-rounder, came in next and was bowled first ball. Four in four. To the next ball, Lee missed the ball and somehow it avoided the off-stump. MacGregor, the wicket-keeper, was so sure it was about to hit the wicket that he dropped his hands and the ball went for four byes.

Soon Trott saw off Lee, catching him at slip off Tarrant. It was 97 for 7 at the start of Trott's eighth over, and at the the end of it Somerset were 97 all out. Off the fourth ball, Mordaunt played Trott tamely to mid-off. The Rev. A. P. Wickham, aged fifty-two and sporting a battered Harlequin cap, completed a 'pair' in the briefest possible time when Trott bowled him. Then Bailey essayed a forcing stroke, but simply spooned another easy catch to mid-off. Another hat-trick for Trott, all watched at the bowler's end by Len Braund, who had carried out his bat.

How did Trott manage to reach back into his halcyon years and pull out such a performance? It would have been understandable if it had happened between 1899 and 1901, but not in 1907. He had looked a spent force before his benefit match and again afterwards. Until he retired in 1910, he was only ever dangerous on a wet wicket, and he seemed completely to lose his fizz and that productive yorker. What happened to him over half an hour on a dank, dismal May morning? Well, the light was very bad and he did a few of his seven victims in the flight. The Somerset batting was appalling: it included a venerable clergyman who had played in the Varsity match of 1878, while E. S. M. Poyntz (batting average 4.66 for the season) was ludicrously placed at number five. For both hat-trick balls Woods and Bailey played airy shots that most first-class cricketers of later vintage would not have attempted in a similar situation. Having said that, Trott put the ball in the right spot and he made history. If it ruined the last day of his benefit match, so be it; the money lost would only have been frittered away on a horse that simply refused to raise a gallop.

The Somerset game was the last memorable signpost of Albert Trott's career. He was not inspired to great heights after his benefit match and he drifted sadly out of the game, unfulfilled and chronically broke. He tried first-class umpiring for a time, but the effort of concentration was too much for a butterfly mind that was beginning to crack. In the summer of 1914, as Europe embarked on a war of self-destruction, Albert Trott followed suit. He had been a patient at St Mary's Hospital in the hope that his morose fatalism would improve, but he discharged himself after just a week, complaining about the boredom and dreariness of hospital life. Nobody wanted a wager or a chat about old times with Alberto, the demon hitter. Three days after leaving hospital, he shot himself through the head in his lodgings at Harlesden. All he left was sixpence. He was just forty-two. The tributes rolled in, but too late to save Albert Trott. When he needed admiration, reassurance and a few pounds, nobody was there.

Ironically, brother Harry died three years later, after he too had suffered from mental illness. What would have happened to Albert Trott if fraternal feelings had followed cricketing logic back in 1896? He might have become Australia's greatest all-rounder. Few players of such talent have fallen away so rapidly. When he remarked wryly that his benefit match performance was tantamount to bowling himself into the workhouse, he was tragically close to the truth.

15
Northamptonshire *v.* Gloucestershire
1907

It must be hard for a side to settle for a draw after bowling out the opposition for twelve, then reducing them to 40 for 7 at the second time of asking. It must be even more galling for a bowler to take 15 wickets in a day for just 21 runs and not pick up a win bonus. That was the fate of Gloucestershire and George Dennett in the soggy summer of 1907. Inevitably it was rain that saved Northants as they faced a final day with just three wickets saving them from a thrashing. While the players were changing on that final morning the rain started and did not relent all day. As George Dennett sat in the pavilion, flexing his deadly left hand, he needed all the philosophical reserves that every cricketer needs to draw on at some stage.

Devotees of uncovered wickets will note that in a match that contained play for only five hours and five minutes, a total of 37 wickets fell for just 200 runs. On Tuesday alone, 33 wickets were taken for 180 runs in four hours and twenty-five minutes. Northants' score of twelve remains the lowest total in a county match, and in all first-class cricket it is only equalled by Oxford University's twelve against MCC in 1877 – although Oxford batted a man short. So it is fair to say that no first-class team has been so humiliated, yet escaped with a draw. On Tuesday evening their prospects of getting another 96 for victory were nil, but the element of luck that is crucial for sporting success told against Gloucestershire.

It was the kind of anti-climax that littered the career of George Dennett. Over twenty years he took more than two thousand wickets, picked up a hundred wickets in a season twelve times –

GLOUCESTERSHIRE *v* NORTHAMPTONSHIRE

At Gloucester, 10–12 June 1907

GLOUCESTERSHIRE

H. Wrathall b Thompson	4	– b Thompson	7
Mr. E. P. Barnett lbw, b Thompson	3	– b East	0
†J. H. Board b Thompson	3	– lbw, b Thompson	5
Mr. M. G. Salter c Buswell b East	3	– c and b East	3
*Mr. G. L. Jessop b East	22	– c Hawtin b East	24
Mr. R. T. H. Mackenzie b East	0	– c King b East	21
T. Langdon b East	4	– lbw, b Thompson	4
J. H. Huggins c Crosse b East	8	– c Buswell b East	3
E. J. Spry lbw, b Thompson	6	– b East	4
C. W. L. Parker not out	2	– not out	8
E. G. Dennett c Pool b Thompson	0	– b East	0
B 2, l-b 3	5	B 9	9
	60	(for 7 wickets)	88

1/5 2/13 3/14 4/20 5/20 6/32 7/45
8/58 9/60

1/17 2/ 3/ 4/52 5/57 6/57 7/77
8/ 9/88

Bowling: *First Innings* – Thompson 16.5–7–29–5; East 16–5–26–5. *Second Innings* – Thompson 15–2–43–3; East 14.2–4–36–7.

NORTHAMPTONSHIRE

*Mr. E. M. Crosse c Board b Dennett	4	– c and b Dennett	0
M. Cox lbw, b Dennett	2	– c Barnett b Dennett	12
Mr. C. J. T. Pool c Spry b Dennett	4	– st Board b Dennett	9
†W. A. Buswell st Board b Dennett	1	– c Langdon b Dennett	0
Mr. L. T. Driffied b Dennett	0		
G. J. Thompson b Dennett	0	– not out	5
Mr. R. W. R. Hawtin lbw, b Dennett	0	– lbw, b Dennett	8
W. East st Board b Dennett	0	– lbw, b Dennett	2
Mr. R. N. Beasley b Jessop	1	– b Dennett	0
Mr. S. King not out	0	– not out	1
W. Wells c Parker b Jessop	0	B 2, l-b 1	3
	12		40

1/5 2/10 3/11 4/11 5/11 6/11 7/11
8/12 9/12

1/0 2/17 3/ 4/31 5/31 6/31
7/33

Bowling: *First Innings* – Dennett 6–1–9–8; Jessop 5.3–4–3–2. *Second Innings* – Dennett 15–8–12–7; Jessop 10–3–20–0; Parker 5–2–5–0.

Umpires: A. Millward and J. E. West.

The game was a draw.

and never played for England. Yet season after season he was a deadly proposition on wickets that gave him any assistance, while he was accurate and guileful enough to keep batsmen guessing on plumb pitches. During his time with Gloucestershire they were never very strong, and he and his fellow-spinner Charlie Parker carried the attack for many seasons. Yet they managed one England cap between them, despite taking nearly 5500 wickets. Among slow left-arm bowlers of their vintage, the likes of Wilfred Rhodes, Colin Blythe, Frank Woolley and Roy Kilner were preferred for very good reasons, but there is a strong case for casting George Dennett as the Percy Perrin of bowlers, the best never to have played for England.

Dennett was discovered in Bristol club cricket by that sincere encourager of young players, Gilbert Jessop. The great man was not just a genius, he believed passionately in the welfare of Gloucestershire cricket and he guided young Dennett in his early years. For his part, Dennett remained earnest, hard-working and thoroughly professional and he did not let Jessop down. For a time, before Parker blossomed, Dennet *was* the Gloucestershire attack and he relished the hard work and the responsibility.

When Northants came to the Spa ground at Gloucester in June 1907, George Dennett was already in a rich seam of form that was to see him become the only bowler to take two hundred wickets that season. For their part, Northants were starting to dread the presence of a class slow left-arm bowler – ten days earlier Colin Blythe had taken 17 for 48 to hustle them to a heavy defeat. Confidence among their batsmen was very low and they knew that if Dennett trapped them on a wet wicket (and in the prevailing damp spell that was very likely), they would not be boosting their batting averages. Northants were a very poor side in those days; they had attained first-class status in 1905, largely through the sterling all-round qualities of Bill East and George Thompson, two seam bowlers of endless stamina and high skill. Thompson became the first Northants player to represent England in 1909, and he took a hundred wickets eight times and did the 'double' twice. In a sense he was the father of modern cricket in that county, and only Bill East's support at the other end approached the same class. In 1907 they won just two out of twenty championship games, and were a soft touch for any outstanding cricketer. That year George Dennett was certainly in that category.

Only forty minutes' play was possible on the first day of the

Gloucestershire match and in that time the home side lost four wickets for twenty, with three of the wickets going to Thompson. Conditions were difficult and likely to get worse as the rain affected the clay subsoil. When play resumed an hour later on the following day, it was clearly going to be a bowler's wicket. Gloucestershire lasted another hour for forty runs, and if Jessop had not played with such resource they would have been humiliated. Jessop showed what could be done with a good eye and judicious hitting: he made 22 out of 31 in half an hour, an innings every bit as valuable as some of his spectacular efforts.

The wicket was at its worst when Northants went in to bat, and Dennett opened the bowling with a steely resolution. He had to wait until the openers put on six runs before his first success, when he had Crosse taken at the wicket. Pool was beaten by three successive deliveries from Dennett, and he and Cox took the score to ten. They were in desperate straits as Dennett turned the ball square at speed and Jessop bowled fast and tightly at the other end. When Pool was caught low down at point, it was 10 for 2. Buswell took a single, then Dennett took three wickets in four balls – Cox, Driffield and Thompson. The score was 11 for 5, and the demoralized batsmen were ripe for plucking. When Hawtin was lbw and East charged his first ball to be stumped, Dennett was again on a hat-trick, but Beasley, in his first county match, played him away for a single. Then Buswell was stumped off the next delivery, so Dennett had again taken three wickets in four balls. He had now taken 8 for 9 and was looking for the cheapest 'all ten' in cricket history. The next over from Jessop ruined that – he beat Beasley for pace and had Wells taken at cover point. So Dennett missed the record, but his figures were still remarkable: after being hit for six runs he then took eight wickets for just three runs. Just one boundary had been scored, by Crosse, and it was all over in forty minutes. Back in Northampton, the news was greeted with incredulity. The club secretary sent a telegram to the scorer at the Gloucester ground: 'Your message says Gloucestershire 60, Northamptonshire all out 12. Surely this is incorrect.' A more waggish, anonymous wire came through to the Northants captain: 'Bring the boys home at once – Mother.'

Well, E.M. Crosse resisted such temptation and looked to Thompson and East to salvage some self-respect for his side. That was a role the opening bowlers had grown accustomed to and they did their best, although the pitch was now easier and not as conducive to seam as it was to spin bowling. Mackenzie, on his debut, hit pluckily but only one other batsman reached double figures – the inevitable Jessop. In half an hour he made 24 out of 33, with some booming drives and swift running between the wickets. Once again he looked a class apart from anyone else, and he perished in the grand manner to a catch at long-off.

So Northants were left with 137 to win, and with the sun now disappeared there seemed hope that they would get somewhere near the total, given luck, a degree of application and a broken left arm for Dennett. The pitch was not quite so fearsome as in the morning, so Northants enjoyed the comparative prosperity of 28 for 3, as Jessop lost control of line and length. When Charlie Parker came on to partner Dennett, the senior member of the spinning duo ensured he would not be sharing any cheap wickets. Only Cox and Thompson seemed to have an inkling of where the ball was going to break after it pitched. Thompson hung on gallantly, then watched Dennett keep his appointment with a hat-trick that had been denied him twice earlier in the day. Hawtin, Beasley and Buswell succumbed meekly, and Dennett had then taken all seven. Given the feckless nature of the batting, there seemed every prospect that the game would not last another Dennett over.

With the score at 40 for 7, Jessop sent one of his fielders over to where the Northants captain was sitting. He asked Crosse if he would mind allowing Gloucestershire to claim the extra half-hour to finish off the match that night. Crosse had been sitting alongside H.V. Page, a fine bat for Oxford and Gloucestershire in his day and Crosse's cricket master when he had studied at Cheltenham College. On being asked his opinion by his erstwhile pupil, Page said, 'Don't ask me – I'm on the Gloucester committee!' In the end Crosse decided to exercise his prerogative – probably because the unyielding Thompson was still battling away out there – and he opted to return the next day. The rest was in the hands of Jupiter Pluvius.

For Dennett, it was particularly frustrating to watch the rain sweep across the ground on that final day. He would have preferred an outright victory rather than further personal glory, but why could he not have both? He had taken a match analysis so far of 15 for 21, and with three wickets still to fall, he was on course to beat Colin Blythe's record match aggregate of 17 for 48 set up ten days earlier against the hapless Northamptonshire. Dennett's control was so mesmerizing that he must have been fancied to end up with eighteen wickets – but it was not to be. His only consolation came later that season in the return match at Northampton, when he bowled his side to an innings victory. Dennett's aggregate against them in two matches stood at thirty wickets for 118, with just seven wickets going elsewhere. Perhaps the Northants players should have gone home to mother after all. And stayed there.

16
Australia *v.* England
MELBOURNE 1908

It may seem a harsh assessment on a young cricketer, but at the age of nineteen Gerry Hazlitt lost a Test for Australia. If he had kept his head and lobbed the ball to his wicket-keeper over a distance of twenty yards, the Melbourne Test of 1908 would have been the first tie in Test cricket. Instead we had to wait another fifty-two years and eleven months before Joe Solomon showed how to react under pressure when he threw down Ian Meckiff's wicket.

Hazlitt's supporters could say that a teenager can be excused a *folie de jeunesse* in just his second Test match. True – but he had already shown his capabilities on his debut a few weeks earlier, when a calm innings of 34 had guided Australia to an exciting victory by two wickets at Sydney. Now at Melbourne, with the last England pair together and the scores level, he had the chance to confirm he had the big-match temperament. Sydney Barnes played Warwick Armstrong to point and called his partner, Arthur Fielder, for a run. Fielder, realizing that he would be running to the danger end, hesitated, then shouted 'No!' but Barnes – never a man to brook contradiction – kept on running. His partner, a large burly fast bowler who lacked speed off the mark, put his head down and did his best to get down the other end, yet the odds were very much on Hazlitt. He had the ball in his hand at point with Fielder still yards adrift, and every coaching manual ever printed has the same instruction in a similar circumstance: throw the ball calmly and accurately to the gloves of the wicket-keeper. Hanson Carter stood at the stumps, waiting for just that, but Hazlitt panicked. He threw wildly at the stumps and the ball evaded both timber and expostulating wicket-keeper. Fielder scrambled home and England had won a great match by one wicket, after the last pair had added 39 runs.

AUSTRALIA *v* ENGLAND
(Second Test)
At Melbourne Cricket Ground, 1–7 January 1908

AUSTRALIA

V. T. Trumper c Humphries b Crawford	49	– lbw b Crawford	63
C. G. Macartney b Crawford	37	– (6) c Humphries b Barnes	54
C. Hill b Fielder	16	– b Fielder	3
*M. A. Noble c Braund b Rhodes	61	– (2) b Crawford	64
W. W. Armstrong c Hutchings b Crawford	31	– b Barnes	77
P. A. McAlister run out	10	– (4) run out	15
V. B. Ransford run out	27	– c Hutchings b Barnes	18
A Cotter b Crawford	17	– (9) lbw b Crawford	27
†H. Carter not out	15	– (8) c Fane b Barnes	53
G. R. Hazlitt b Crawford	1	– b Barnes	3
J. V. Saunders b Fielder	0	– not out	0
L-b 1, w 1	2	B 12, l-b 8	20
	266		397

1/84 2/93 3/111 4/168 5/197
6/214 7/240 8/261 9/265 10/266

1/126 2/131 3/135 4/162 5/268
6/303 7/312 8/361 9/392 10/397

Bowling: *First Innings* – Fielder 27.5–4–77–2; Barnes 17–7–30–0; Rhodes 11–0–37–1; Braund 16–5–41–0; Crawford 29–1–79–5. *Second Innings* – Fielder 27–6–74–1; Barnes 27.4–4–72–5; Rhodes 16–6–38–0; Braund 18–2–68–0; Crawford 33–6–125–3.

ENGLAND

*F. L. Fane b Armstrong	13	– b Armstrong	50
J. B. Hobbs b Cotter	83	– b Noble	28
G. Gunn lbw b Cotter	15	– lbw b Noble	0
K. L. Hutchings b Cotter	126	– c Cotter b Macartney	39
L. C. Braund b Cotter	49	– b Armstrong	30
J. Hardstaff st b Saunders	12	– c Ransford b Cotter	19
W. Rhodes b Saunders	32	– run out	15
J. N. Crawford c Ransford b Saunders	16	– c Armstrong b Saunders	10
S. F. Barnes c Hill b Armstrong	14	– not out	38
†J. Humphries b Cotter	6	– lbw b Armstrong	16
A. Fielder not out	6	– not out	18
B 3, l-b 3, w 1, n-b 3	10	B 9, l-b 7, w 1, n-b 2	19
	382		282

1/27 2/61 3/160 4/268 5/287
6/325 7/353 8/360 9/369 10/382

1/54 2/54 3/121 4/131 5/162
6/196 7/198 8/209 9/243

Bowling: *First Innings* – Cotter 33–4–142–5; Saunders 34–7–100–3; Noble 9–3–26–0; Armstrong 34.2–15–36–2; Hazlitt 13–1–34–0; Macartney 12–2–34–0. *Second Innings* – Cotter 28–3–82–1; Saunders 30–9–58–1; Noble 22–7–41–2; Armstrong 30.4–10–53–3; Hazlitt 2–1–8–0; Macartney 9–3–21–1.

Umpires: P. Argall and R. W. Crockett.

England won by one wicket.

It was an absorbing Test throughout. Two men who were to die in the Great War played leading roles – Kenneth Hutchings with a dashing hundred for England, and 'Tibby' Cotter with some tremendous fast bowling in searing heat. Another ill-fated cricketer, Victor Trumper, played two innings of great charm, while Warwick Armstrong and Monty Noble showed their all-round qualities. For England, Jack Hobbs marked his Test debut with a composed 83, while Syd Barnes again looked the world's greatest bowler. We had almost come to take Barnes's bowling qualities for granted at this stage – there seemed nothing he could not do with a cricket ball, he was almost impossible to classify – but it was his batting that really shone. His friends and team-mates always maintained he was a far better bat than many judges realized, but it was typical of this difficult man that he would not exercise himself unduly at the crease. He was being paid – and handsomely paid – by his various masters to bowl sides out and he saw no reason why he should tire himself out in another sphere of the game. Leave that fancy stuff to others. Yet Syd Barnes was the kind of man who could achieve anything if he applied his considerable mind to the challenge; on a hot afternoon on the Melbourne ground, with the ladies in the pavilion hysterically squealing at each precious run, Barnes decided he was going to win the match for England. Sheer bloody-mindedness, rather than patriotism was his lode star – he had not been impressed by several umpiring decisions in the game – and he was just the man to thwart Australia when all seemed lost. Any side that garners 73 from their last two wickets to win a Test in such a pressure-cooker atmosphere deserves the spoils.

England needed the victory. It had not been an easy tour so far. The captain, A.O. Jones, had fallen ill and was to miss the first three Tests; he was to die of consumption six years later. Some strange selections had hampered England at Sydney in the first Test, where Gerry Hazlitt's auspicious debut helped secure a match that Australia ought to have lost. Incredibly, Jack Hobbs was not picked at Sydney, even though he was now fit after a debilitating bout of seasickness on the trip over from England. The selectors turned to George Gunn, who was not even in the tour party, but recuperating in the sunshine for health reasons. Gunn made a hundred, but it seems odd that players like Freddie Fane and R.A. Young should keep out Hobbs. It seems even odder that Young should be preferred as wicket-keeper to Joe Humphries, who had kept so well for Derbyshire in recent seasons. Young, who wore spectacles, had a nightmare at Sydney and Humphries was rightly preferred at Melbourne with an immediate improvement in the all-round fielding. He also batted bravely on the last day, adding 34 with Barnes for the last wicket.

This was hardly a representative England tour party. MacLaren, R.E. Foster, Fry, Jessop and Jackson were not available for various reasons while the professionals, Hirst, Lilley, Tyldesley and Hayward had refused the terms offered by the MCC. The captain was fifth choice behind Fry, Foster, Jackson and Warner and not worth his place in the side as a batsman. It is a tribute to the depth of talent in England at that time that a side was sent to Australia and actually managed to win one Test.

On the first day of 1908, Australia won the toss and batted in glorious weather in front of 27,000 people. Barnes and Fielder opened the bowling to Trumper and Macartney, a challenging joust that would grace the Elysian Fields of cricket. England bowled superbly on a good wicket, fielded magnificently and did well to contain Australia to 255 for 7 at the close. The press complained about the slow scoring – yet the openers put on 84 in eighty-three minutes, and 150 came up in 170 minutes and Noble's fine 61 took two and a half hours. Clearly the press had been spoiled by the dynamic spirit of the age; they seemed unable to appreciate a tense struggle.

On the second day, the English batting was more impressive than Australia's. Hobbs, aware that he owed his place to the advocacy of Wilfred Rhodes and Len Braund, batted serenely in his first Test innings, taking an hour and three quarters for his fifty, and his partnership with Kenneth Hutchings was a joy. At that time Hutchings was one of the great sights of the English game. He was twenty-five and his brilliant driving and dashing approach epitomized Kent cricket. Even the great George Hirst would retreat a yard or two at mid-off when Hutchings came in to bat, and when the Muse of inspiration was with him he was wonderfully entertaining. So it was at Melbourne: he made 92 between tea and the close, finishing on 117 not out in a score of 246 for 3. In three quarters of an hour he doubled his score, reaching his century in two hours and eight minutes, and the Australian experts said it was the best innings by an English batsman since the great days of Ranji a decade earlier.

Hutchings did not last very long on the third day and, in his absence, England opted to bat soundly to secure a big lead.

Braund's 49 took 144 minutes while Rhodes batted almost two and a half hours for 32, until, horror of horrors, the obdurate Wilfred was bowled having a wild smear across the line – tantamount to Syd Barnes ever agreeing with another's opinion! Eventually England gained a lead of 116, handy enough but rather disappointing after the glories of Hobbs and Hutchings on the previous day. Trumper and Noble made 96 without being parted in the last eighty minutes of the day, so the game was again wide open.

Australia ended the fourth day on 360 for 7, a lead of 244, after another absorbing, keenly contested contest. They lost Trumper and Noble fairly early, but a stand of 106 in a hundred minutes between Armstrong and Macartney pulled them round. Just as they looked to be taking control, Barnes broke through twice and he also had Ransford caught in the slips. So Cotter and Carter needed to retrench and consolidate. They managed that and, with the rest day approaching and the wicket still holding firm, it was anybody's game now.

On the fifth morning Carter valuably guided his team to 397, leaving England 282 to win with five sessions ahead of them. It was unbelievably hot – 90.5° in the shade and 140.5° in the sun – and Hobbs and Fane naturally took no chances, hoping to wear down the bowling in such equatorial conditions. After an hour, they had got to 54 without any alarms, but then Hobbs and Gunn were out at the same total. Fane and Hutchings then batted with great self-restraint as Armstrong bowled six overs for just nine runs, and Noble was also steadiness itself. At 121 Fane played on, the ball gently kissing the leg-stump. Ten runs later Hutchings could contain himself no more after an uncharacteristic vigil of ninety minutes. He launched himself into one of his booming drives only to be caught at mid-off. Now England had to play in the same vein as Carter and Cotter on the Saturday night. They must hold firm and regroup the following morning. Braund and Hardstaff managed that, adding 28 in the last fifty-five minutes. At 159 for 4 England needed 123 and Australia six wickets. It looked like being a momentous finish. It was.

For a time on the final morning it went Australia's way. In muggy weather, Hardstaff was caught at long leg, mishooking with only three runs added. These were testing times for England, with Cotter bowling very fast with the wind behind him and Noble swinging the ball in an ideal atmosphere. Rhodes was dropped at slip by McAlister off Cotter when he had made two; next ball

Braund was given the benefit of the doubt over an lbw appeal and Cotter looked very disappointed at the decision. Noble shuffled his bowling, bringing on Saunders and Armstrong. Off his fifth ball Armstrong bowled Braund, whose valiant innings had lasted an hour and a half. That was 196 for 6, and two runs later Rhodes made his second batting misjudgement of the match. He played a ball to Armstrong at third man, and was run out by a lightning return. Even the imperturbable Rhodes seemed affected by the tension that had permeated all six days of the game.

The two hundred came up in four hours and forty minutes as Jack Crawford decided to counter-attack and break the shackles of tight bowling. He hit one superb shot over square leg off Armstrong, then was badly missed by Saunders at mid-on. The crowd groaned in their disappointment: would that miss prove crucial? Crawford was a fine player (he had performed the 'double' in England in 1907) and he had the attacking inclinations that were dangerous for a fielding captain in a tight situation. Monty Noble need not have worried – one run later Crawford was caught at third man from an over-ambitious stroke. At 209 for 8, with just the tail to come, England had little hope.

By lunch Barnes and Humphries had gathered twelve runs without any problems. Cotter and Saunders took up the bowling after the interval, and they found the two Northerners in cussed mood. Armstrong replaced Cotter at 231, and every ball was followed with rapt attention by the crowd. At 241 Humphries was adjudged lbw and he took the decision very badly indeed. At one stage it looked as if he was refusing to leave the crease, and he eventually walked back very slowly. Not every first-class cricketer of that chivalrous age believed in the umpire's infallibility! Sydney Barnes was never one to trust an umpire unless his right finger was raised at the great man's bidding, so he resolved to play every ball with his bat from now on. The lbw decisions had gone against England in this match – George Gunn was livid with the two he suffered, and now this one with Joe Humphries. Barnes was lucky with his choice of partner, with 39 needed. Arthur Fielder was no mug with the bat, unlike many fast bowlers of the time who loved to wind up their arms and try to hit the ball out of sight. Fielder could bat, a fact he proved a year later when adding 235 for the last wicket against Worcestershire in the company of Frank Woolley. He would give Barnes all the support he needed and, if they managed to get somewhere near the target of 282, it would be the Australians' turn to worry.

They ran superbly between the wickets and, although Noble alternated between himself, Cotter and then Armstrong, the swift bowling changes did not disturb the batsmen. With seven needed, Noble brought on Charlie Macartney to bowl left-arm spin. Can you imagine many modern captains trusting a spinner in such a situation? Barnes and Fielder were not disturbed, nor did they ever look like getting out until the final over. Fielder played Armstrong to mid-on; Saunders threw to the wicket-keeper's end and Carter fell over trying to gather in the ball. If he had done so, Barnes would probably have been run out. Then in the same over, Gerry Hazlitt blew his chance of immortality and England were home. Barnes had batted an hour and a half for his 38 not out, an innings of aplomb and nerve that made many wonder why he did not bat like that more often.

The two Englishmen were given a great reception by the partisan crowd when they returned to the pavilion, and the president of the Melbourne Club, Mr Justice Cussen, told them it had been the most exciting finish ever seen on the ground. Civic dignitaries went in for such windbaggery in those days, while the animated spectators had to listen with something approximating interest. They did not need Mr Justice Cussen to tell them that a great cricket match does not have to consist of breakneck scoring or demon bowling; it needs character, tension, fluctuating fortunes and a dramatic finish. Heroes and villains are also preferable. England had two of the former – Barnes and Fielder – while Hazlitt was cast in the role of villain. Poor Hazlitt: he had done little in the match and was dropped for the next Test. He missed the 1909 tour to England, but bowled well on the 1912 tour and impressed with his fielding. He died young, aged twenty-seven, just a few months after the immortal Victor Trumper. For many good reasons, Trumper's sad passing overshadowed that of Hazlitt: after all, the great Victor never lost a Test match to the old enemy with one moment of rashness.

17
Northamptonshire *v.* Yorkshire
1908

A year after being shredded by George Dennett (chapter 15), Northamptonshire suffered an even more demoralizing experience. After three embarrassing seasons in the county championship, the club felt sufficiently emboldened to offer a home match to Yorkshire – that perennial test of strength, the yardstick with which they could measure progress. They must have regretted the offer: on the second day they were bowled out twice in just 140 minutes. The Northants batsmen made a very creditable attempt at compiling the lowest-ever total in first-class cricket, but they finished four runs short and had to be content with the third worst score in history. For their part, Schofield Haigh and George Hirst bowled unchanged throughout both innings and resisted any efforts by their team-mates to get the ball off them. England bowlers who have sweated buckets on pluperfect wickets against great batsmen know how to cash in when the opposition is feeble.

Northants were feeble in that match. A fledgling county always has difficulty in adjusting to the rarified atmosphere in county cricket and around this time, Northants were noted for a grinding mediocrity at best and at worst, a hapless inability to master the basics. In 1908 they won just three of their twenty-two championship matches, finished second bottom and tried thirty-one players. Only George Thompson and 'Bumper' Wells looked like competent bowlers, as Bill East's health failed. No one made a thousand runs and their captain, Thomas Manning, was hardly the man to inspire the troops: this product of Wellingborough School and Cambridge University was such a docile personality that when he was once given out lbw after the ball hit his elbow, he smiled pleasantly at

NORTHAMPTONSHIRE *v* YORKSHIRE
At Northampton, 7–8 May 1908

YORKSHIRE

W. Rhodes b R. Hawtin	40
J. W. Rothery b R. Hawtin	27
D. Denton b Wells	110
W. H. Wilkinson c A. R. Thompson b R. Hawtin	36
G. H. Hirst c A. R. Thompson b R. Hawtin	44
W. E. Bates b Cox	12
*Mr. H. S. Kaye c A. Hawtin b R. Hawtin	15
S. Haigh b Falconer	13
H. Myers not out	14
J. T. Newstead not out	19
B 17, l-b 5, w 1, n-b 3	26
	*356

†D. Hunter did not bat *Innings declared closed.

1/63 2/96 3/187 4/265 5/286 6/308 7/312 8/322

Bowling: *First Innings* – G. J. Thompson 26–6–77–0; Wells 31–10–86–1; R. Hawtin 25–3–78–5; Falconer 21–4–62–1; Cox 18–5–27–1.

NORTHAMPTONSHIRE

Mr. W. H. Kingston b Hirst	8	– b Hirst	3
M. Cox b Hirst	0	– b Hirst	2
Mr. A. P. R. Hawtin lbw, b Hirst	2	– lbw, b Hirst	0
Mr. G. A. T. Vials b Haigh	0	– c Myers b Hirst	5
Mr. R. W. R. Hawtin b Hirst	1	– lbw, b Hirst	2
Mr. A. R. Thompson b Haigh	1	– b Haigh	1
*Mr. T. E. Manning b Hirst	0	– lbw, b Haigh	2
†W. A. Buswell b Haigh	4	– b Haigh	0
W. Wells not out	5	– not out	0
R. Falconer b Hirst	2	– b Hirst	0
G. J. Thompson absent, ill	0	– absent, ill	0
B 3, l-b 1	4		
	27		15

1/0 2/8 3/9 4/11 5/12 6/16 7/18 8/22 9/27

1/3 2/3 3/9 4/10 5/13 6/15 7/15 8/15 9/15

Bowling: *First Innings* – Hirst 8.5–4–12–6; Haigh 8–1–11–3. *Second Innings* – 11.2–8–7–6; Haigh 11–6–8–3.

Umpires: W. Flowers and H. Bagshaw.

Yorkshire won by an innings and 314 runs.

the umpire, thanked him and walked off! Their wicket-keeper Walter Buswell had come late to the job at the age of thirty-one. This stout son of farming stock justified his position in the side thus: 'I went there because no one else would go.' He also caused great amusement in some late-order partnerships with Manning and 'Bumper' Wells, a genial fast bowler whose predilection for strong ale led him to the early grave occupied by many uncompli- cated fast bowlers of that age.

In contrast, Yorkshire were county champions in 1908, and they did not lose a game. It was not a vintage Yorkshire eleven, but Rhodes and Hirst again did the 'double', Newstead took a hundred wickets, Denton batted with consistent brilliance and Wilkinson topped a thousand runs. Their strength was varied bowling, superb fielding and a matchless team spirit. Rather more than enough for the Northamptonshire of 1908, especially as they lacked the services of Charles Pool, their classiest batsman, and Bill East's fast bowling for the Yorkshire game.

On the first day, Denton made a glittering hundred in about the same time as Herbert Asquith took to deliver his Budget speech in the House of Commons on that very day. After lunch the wicket became appreciably faster as the sun came out, and Denton advanced to his century with nineteen runs from five consecutive deliveries from Thompson. He had been troubled earlier by Thompson, whose figures were as false as Roger Hawtin's, but as the day wore on it was clear that Yorkshire were set for a big total. They finished on 333 for 8, following the established pattern of quick runs to leave the bowlers time to dismiss the opposition twice.

They did not need much time. After a morning's drizzle, play did not start till 2.30, yet the game was over by 5.40. In the first half-hour, Yorkshire slogged a few more runs, then declared. Northants began their innings at three o'clock; at 4.20 they were all out. Hirst got Cox without a run on the board, and after thirty- five minutes, they were 12 for 5. The wicket was not unplayable – it was soft after so much recent rain, but fairly dead – yet Hirst and Haigh cut, seamed and swung the ball at will. Thompson could not bat after an attack of lumbago, but it seems unlikely that he could have done much more than offer dogged resistance.

Northants followed on 339 runs behind, and soon Kingston was yorked by Hirst. After forty minutes they were ten for 4, with Hawtin, on his first-class debut, totalling two runs in his two innings. Half the side were out for 13, and they were then polished off for the addition of just two runs. Thompson was again absent, so Northants had lost eighteen wickets for forty-two runs. That combined total lasted as a record for fifty-one years. There was just one boundary – a hit to leg off Hirst by Vials – and the stumps were disturbed thirteen times. There seemed to be a few things awry with the home team's batting technique. . . .

Despite the freakish nature of the match, *The Times* did not deem it worthy of too much space in its august columns. The game between Surrey and Hampshire received four times the coverage, while the Freshmen's match at Oxford enjoyed double the space of Northants *v.* Yorkshire. Perhaps *The Times* realized that it was simply a case of men against boys, despite the first-class status.

Life among the big boys could only get better for Northants. It did. The club started to look outside the narrow confines of a small county for players, and the trawling policy slowly paid dividends. By 1909 the West Indian slow left-arm spinner S. G. Smith had qualified; he did the 'double' in his first season and he gave Thompson valuable support until the outbreak of war in 1914. In 1909 Northants finished seventh, and the next year they were ninth; they actually ended up second in the championship table of 1912 and fourth the following season. Out of the darkness of that Yorkshire game, light began to flood into Northants' cricket.

18
Gloucestershire *v.* Middlesex
1908

When a game is as close at this one, the quality of fielding often tips the balance. There was barely a hair's breadth between the two sides over three days of gripping cricket, but the decisive factors proved to be expensive dropped catches by Gloucestershire and wonderfully athletic fielding from Middlesex.

The all-round excellence of Frank Tarrant must be acknowledged, but in his 152 he was dropped by Mills in the slips when he had scored ten, and at 71 Jack Board missed an easy stumping. On the second evening, with every run vital, Page was twice dropped, at cover point when he had made five, and at third man with his score on eleven. He only made twenty, but when Page came in Middlesex were 75 for 5 and in grave danger. In the end only Pelham Warner made a higher score, and the margin of victory could hardly have been closer. Warner's sympathetic captaincy was excellent on that tense final day, and his insistence on good fielding bore handsome fruit. This was his first season as Middlesex captain – even though he had led England to both Australia and South Africa – and he made it clear that he wanted to groom young players. In turn that meant the fielding would improve, and that season Middlesex were the best in the country in that respect. Tarrant was a reliable slip, Trott could gather anything with those huge buckets he called hands, Page was an excellent outfield (as befitted a soccer international), Colbeck and Moon had Cambridge blues for hockey and soccer respectively and their speed around a cricket field was spectacular. Gloucestershire just could not match such all-round athleticism.

At the start of the game, Middlesex lay in fourth position in the

GLOUCESTERSHIRE *v* MIDDLESEX

At Bristol, 30 July – 1 August 1908

MIDDLESEX

*Mr. P. F. Warner c Brownlee b Ford	22	– c Roberts b Dennett	37
F. A. Tarrant c Parker b Dennett	152	– b Parker	11
†Mr. L. J. Moon c Board b Dennett	35	– lbw, b Parker	2
A. E. Trott c Board b Parker	3	– c Jessop b Dennett	12
Mr. E. S. Litteljohn b Ford	14	– c Mills b Dennett	0
Mr. W. P. Harrison, junr. b Dennett	23	– b Parker	19
Mr. C. C. Page b Parker	0	– c Brownlee b Dennett	20
Mr. L. G. Colbeck b Dennett	8	– not out	7
Mr. J. T. Dixon c Board b Dennett	7	– c Board b Dennett	0
E. H. Hendren c Board b Dennett	4	– c Roberts b Dennett	0
E. Mignon not out	1	– c and b Dennett	6
B 8, 1-b 1	9	B 1, 1-b 2, n-b 2	5
	278		119

1/ 2/111 3/120 4/175 5/252 6/ 7/ 8/ 9/   1/7 2/60 3/60 4/60 5/75 6/ 7/ 8/ 9/104

Bowling: *First Innings* – Parker 35–12–84–2; Dennett 39.1–18–59–6; Ford 17–5–39–2; Brownlee 1–0–8–0; Mills 4–0–38–0; Roberts 8–0–28–0; Dipper 3–1–13–0. *Second Innings* – Parker 23–8–41–3; Dennett 31.3–14–61–7; Brownlee 6–4–6–0; Mills 2–0–6–0.

GLOUCESTERSHIRE

†J. H. Board c Harrison b Tarrant	9	– b Trott	29
T. Langdon c Moon b Tarrant	95	– c Colbeck b Trott	15
A. E. Dipper b Tarrant	0	– b Tarrant	0
A. E. Winstone b Tarrant	31	– b Tarrant	12
Mr. L. D. Brownlee c Dixon b Trott	10	– c and b Trott	0
*Mr. G. L. Jessop run out	72	– c Tarrant b Trott	34
Mr. F. B. Roberts c Dixon b Trott	6	– c Trott b Tarrant	1
Mr. P. H. Ford b Tarrant	21	– b Trott	3
E. G. Dennett c and b Tarrant	14	– c Warner b Tarrant	22
P. T. Mills c Harrison b Tarrant	0	– b Tarrant	0
C. W. L. Parker not out	8	– not out	1
B 9, l-b 3	12		
	278		117

1/14 2/14 3/63 4/98 5/220 6/229 7/ 8/ 9/   1/20 2/20 3/53 4/54 5/90 6/90 7/ 8/ 9/

Bowling: *First Innings* – Tarrant 35.1–8–93–7; Mignon 6–1–19–0; Trott 35–11–89–2; Dixon 5–0–22–0; Hendren 6–0–20–0; Harrison Jr 3–0–23–0. *Second Innings* – Tarrant 27–8–56–5; Trott 26–7–61–5.

Umpires: R. G. Barlow and A. Millward.

Middlesex won by two runs.

table, pressing hard on Kent, Surrey and Yorkshire. The county championship was full of interest that year, although cricket was having to compete with other sporting attractions. London was staging the Olympic Games and the prestige of the Goodwood race meeting was reflected in the attendance of the King and Queen on all four days. Sport was proving to be truly the opium of the masses at the start of August 1908, as the barometer rose every day. There were no Test matches that summer and county cricket enjoyed a monopoly among the game's devotees.

The first day at Bristol belonged to Frank Tarrant. He took three hours to reach his hundred, but after that his next fifty came in three quarters of an hour. As usual, he was acquisitive on the leg-side, and after Board's missed stumping, he celebrated by driving nine fours in successive scoring strokes. Tarrant's value to his side was clear after he was at last dismissed; George Dennett cleaned up the tail and the last five wickets went for 26 runs. Tarrant was not done with for the day, however. He opened the bowling with his slow left-arm spin and took the first two wickets for 14. Langdon and Winstone played out time to reach 59 for 2.

When Eddie Mignon reported a leg strain on the second morning, Middlesex had to reconcile themselves to being without one of the best fast bowlers of that summer. Mignon was a curious character; capable of devastating bursts, he was the Chris Old of his day, never sure he was fit enough to bowl long spells. Warner would often remonstrate with his reluctant spearhead, telling him, 'You should be prepared to bleed for Middlesex.' Mignon did not really see the point of all that and he was finished with county cricket by the time he was twenty-eight. His luck did not improve after that: he died of pneumonia, aggravated by malaria, when he was twenty-nine.

Mignon's reluctance to bowl in the Gloucestershire match threw an even heavier burden on Tarrant and, as usual, he did not fail his side. At this time he was the best all-rounder in England, and for eight seasons he performed the 'double'. He was an Australian, and when he qualified to play county cricket in 1905 some Middlesex members felt it was wrong to import a foreigner at the expense of an Englishman. They soon got over that when Tarrant started winning matches with his sensible batting and slow medium bowling. Tarrant always seemed one jump ahead of the herd: after a glittering career in England, he returned home and built up a considerable fortune buying and selling racehorses in India and

Australia. He numbered many Indian princes among his friends and never seemed to put a foot wrong in his life – in stark contrast to his fellow Australian and team-mate, Albert Trott.

It was Tarrant and Trott who bore the brunt of the bowling on that second day at Bristol, and they clawed their side back in the game, after Gloucestershire had arrived at 200 for 4. Then Jessop was out after a comparatively restrained eighty minutes. The rest of the batting collapsed in the same manner as their opponents a day earlier, and the scores were exactly level after two innings. Soon Middlesex were in trouble in their second innings: Moon left at seven, and only thirty runs came in the first hour. Three wickets fell at sixty (Warner batted an hour and a half for 37), and when Trott played a rash shot, Middlesex were 75 for 5. Then, for some unaccountable reason, the Gloucestershire fielding fell apart, and although they reduced Middlesex to 105 for 9 at the close, they ought to have taken the various chances offered. The wicket was beginning to show signs of wear and tear, much to the enjoyment of Dennett, and Gloucestershire would not wish to be delayed by the last-wicket pair the following morning.

Mignon managed to hobble to the wicket next day, and he added an invaluable fifteen with Colbeck. Mignon retired to a comfortable seat to rest his aches and pains as his colleagues took the field. Gloucestershire needed just 120 to win, and one purple patch from Jessop would do the trick; conversely Tarrant was equally capable of matching the efforts of Dennett with the ball. The ball was to turn considerably from Tarrant's end, and Trott managed to show he had not lost his touch completely.

With twenty on the board, Langdon was caught at cover and one run later Alf Dipper, in his first season, picked up a 'pair', dismissed the same way in each innings. Board and Winstone added 32 in half an hour, and then Trott took a magnificent low return catch to get Brownlee. Warner must have purred at the quality of Middlesex's fielding and catching, and they were to surpass themselves. For a time, however, Gloucestershire prospered as the solid, dependable Board kept Jessop company. At 90 for 4, with Jessop making 34 out of the last 36, the game looked a certain victory for the home side; a couple more overs of Jessop's unique batting and it would be over. With just thirty needed, Jessop was splendidly caught high to his right at slip by Tarrant. One run later Trott, who had switched to round the wicket, bowled Board with a beauty that turned a long way. Then Trott caught Roberts at slip and Gloucestershire went into a contemplative lunch at 93 for 7. They must have noticed Warner's shrewd field placings for Jessop; a man placed on the square leg boundary was ideally situated to cut down two pull shots that ended up as singles rather than eight runs.

After lunch Dennett chanced his arm and hit Trott for ten in an over. The score moved to 115, five short of victory and it looked as if Middlesex's splendid out-cricket would be in vain. Then Ford was bowled by Trott's quicker one, and at 116 Tarrant bowled Mills with one that came in with the arm. One wicket left, four runs needed. One good blow would do it, and Charlie Parker aimed one off his first ball. He spooned the ball just over Tarrant's head for one run as the bowler desperately covered the stumps at his end in case of overthrows. Tarrant bowled the last ball of his twenty-seventh over. It proved to be the last delivery of the match – Dennett aimed a drive at a good length ball, it turned into him and he skied a dolly catch to Warner at point. Middlesex had won a desperately close match by two runs, with the two Australians bowling unchanged in the second innings. Above all it had been their fielding that turned the game.

It must have been a delight to watch a match of such closeness and tension, a match that saw three left-arm spinners (Parker, Dennett and Tarrant) open the bowling. Any captain that uses such a bowler as the spearhead at the start of an innings has the game's interests at heart. Eddie Mignon did his side a favour by collecting that leg strain.

19
Sussex *v.* Nottinghamshire
1911

Some games are remarkable for a great finish or a spectacular collapse when the match was there for the taking. This one stands out for just forty minutes of play on a cold, miserable afternoon beside the sea. In that time Edwin Boaler Alletson made an indelible imprint on cricket history.

Inevitably a statistical emphasis must be placed on Ted Alletson's remarkable performance, so I would ask the reader to grit the teeth of concentration, read this paragraph slowly and then we can return to the narrative. Yet a considered appraisal of his innings is rewarding. At lunch on the final day, with the last Nottinghamshire pair together, Alletson was 47 not out after fifty minutes batting. Forty minutes after the resumption, he was out for 189, made out of 227. He made 115 out of 120 in seven overs after lunch, with the last 89 coming in fifteen minutes. One over cost Tim Killick 34 runs, the greatest amount at that time, only surpassed fifty-seven years later by Garfield Sobers. Alletson lost five balls during all the mayhem, so his ratio of runs to minutes would have even more astonishing if around ten minutes had not been wasted looking for spares. In all, 152 runs were scored in forty minutes after the interval – and Alletson made 142 of them. Seventy deliveries were bowled and Alletson's partner, Bill Riley, faced just nineteen of them.

It was the most devasting spell of hitting in history and, despite thrilling assaults in recent years by the likes of Botham and Sobers, it still boggles the mind. Yet Alletson almost missed the game through an injured wrist, and he had the bracing seawaters at Brighton to thank for an improvement in the injury. Early on his great day, he had gone to bathe in the sea in the hope that his wrist would loosen up a little. He knew that he had only been

SUSSEX *v* NOTTINGHAMSHIRE
At Hove, 18–20 May 1911

NOTTINGHAMSHIRE

*Mr. A. O. Jones b Cox	57	– b Leach	0
J. Iremonger c and b A. E. Relf	0	– c Tudor b Killick	83
G. Gunn st Butt b Cox	90	– st Butt b R. Relf	66
J. Hardstaff b Cox	8	– c Butt b A. E. Relf	7
J. R. Gunn c R. Relf b Killick	33	– b R. Relf	19
W. R. D. Payton c Heygate b Killick	20	– lbw b A. E. Relf	0
W. W. Whysall b Killick	1	– c Butt b A. E. Relf	3
G. M. Lee c and b Killick	10	– c Cox b Leach	26
E. B. Alletson c Killick b A. E. Relf	7	– c Smith b Cox	189
†T. Oates not out	3	– b Leach	1
W. Riley c Smith b Killick	3	– not out	10
B 5, n-b 1	6	B 3, l-b 2, w 2, n-b 1	8
	238		412

1/2 2/91 3/117 4/190 5/198 6/201
7/222 8/225 9/235 10/238

1/5 2/127 3/139 4/181 5/182 6/184
7/185 8/258 9/260 10/412

Bowling: *First Innings* – A. E. Relf 19–5–40–2; Leach 11–2–53–0; Vincett
4–0–31–0; R. Relf 11–0–36–0; Cox 25–4–58–3; Killick 10.2–4–14–5.
Second Innings – A. E. Relf 33–13–92–3; Leach 19–2–91–3; Vincett 3–1–25–0;
R. Relf 19–6–39–2; Cox 9.4–2–27–1; Killick 20–3–130–1.

SUSSEX

R. R. Relf b Jones	42	– c Oates b Jones	71
J. Vine b Jones	77	– c Payton b Riley	54
Mr R. B. Heygate c Lee b Iremonger	32	– b J. Gunn	13
G. R. Cox c Alletson b Riley	37	– st Oates b Riley	5
A. E. Relf c and b Jones	4	– c Oates b Riley	0
Mr C. L. Tudor c Oates b Riley	23	– b J. Gunn	4
E. H. Killick c Hardstaff b Lee	81	– c Lee b Riley	21
G. Leach b Lee	52	– b J. Gunn	31
*Mr C. L. A. Smith not out	33	– not out	12
J. H. Vincett c Iremonger b Lee	9	– not out	1
†H. R. Butt b Riley	13	–	
B 4, l-b 3, w 1, n-b 3	11	N-b 1	1
	414	(8 wickets)	213

1/74 2/138 3/176 4/196 5/198
6/272 7/342 8/368 9/386 10/414

1/112 2/139 3/139 4/139 5/144
6/148 7/198 8/212

Bowling: *First Innings* – Iremonger 34–7–97–1; Riley 39.4–5–102–3; J. Gunn
29–2–87–0; Jones 22–2–69–3; Alletson 1–0–3–0; Lee 14–1–45–3. *Second
Innings* – Iremonger 14–2–34–0; Riley 33–9–82–4; J. Gunn 25–7–41–3. Jones
5–1–24–1; Lee 4–0–31–0.

Umpires: A. A. White and H. Wood.

Drawn.

picked in the first place because Tom Wass was injured, and that
he had to make his presence felt at the start of this 1911 season.
He managed that in no uncertain terms.

Ted Alletson had threatened something of this nature for several
seasons. He first played for Nottinghamshire in 1906, yet he did
not make his first half-century for them until 1909. At the start of
the 1911 season his top score was only 81; he was now twenty-
seven and well aware that his rugged approach to batting would
soon have to pay dividends or else he would have to return to his
job as a wheelwright on the Duke of Portland's estate. The Duke
at least had faith in Alletson. He promised him a hundred pounds
when he made his first century for the county. Yet as a batsman
in the lower order, Alletson had little chance to stay long enough
to get a hundred, even if his concentration lasted more than half
an hour. He was ideally equipped for the role of big hitter: over
six feet tall, weighing fifteen and a half stone, he was massively
built across the chest and shoulders. His arms were so long that
the span measured six feet six inches between both sets of finger-
tips, and his hands were huge, powerful enough to grip the extra
thick rubber he liked to wrap around his two pound three ounce
bat. Alletson had one other great asset as a hitter: he played
straight. Once he lined up the bowling, he could hit safely and
long.

The Duke of Portland was not the only man who had confidence
in Ted Alletson. Gilbert Jessop, who knew rather more about such
matters, wrote in *London Opinion:* 'Of all the English big hitters at
the present moment, for pure distance Alletson of Nottinghamshire
deserves to be placed first. It is not necessary for him to make his
best hit to clear the majority of our grounds. When he has had a
little more experience it will be no surprise to me to read of big
scores as well as big hits from his bat.' This was written in 1910,
a year before Alletson's memorable afternoon. Of all cricketers,
Jessop was the best qualified to assess the combination of nerve,
technique and aptitude that makes a consistent hitter; not for the
first time, Jessop showed that a genius can also be a shrewd judge
of another cricketer.

By May 1911 Alletson knew that he had to start turning promise
into hard facts. In the previous game he had batted at number nine
and made six as Leicestershire were beaten by an innings. He did
not get a bowl, and noticed with some disquiet that he was now
placed three rungs down the batting order, after going in at six

the previous summer. The warning signs were clear, and when he began to feel pain in his wrist he kept it quiet in case it would be used as an excuse to drop him. On the first day of the Sussex match he made just seven before Tim Killick caught him; Killick would pay for that transgression two days later. Sussex replied attractively, making 117 for 1 in an hour and a half before the close. On the second day Alletson was allowed one over of innocuous medium pace as Sussex built up a big lead. Nottinghamshire finished on 152 for 3, still 24 behind, with the Gunn brothers unbeaten and surely their only hope of saving the game.

On a cold, bleak morning, in front of a handful of shivering spectators, Ted Alletson walked out to make history. The circumstances were not propitious – Nottinghamshire were 185 for 7, just seven runs on and he had to face two very good bowlers, the brothers Relf. Robert Relf was a cunning, teasing slow bowler (just the type to lure a big hitter to self-destruction) while Albert was an immaculate medium-pacer with the knack of extracting deceptive pace off the pitch. Yet the wicket was the traditional pre-War Hove surface, fast and true. A decade earlier, Fry and Ranji always seemed to be not out 150 at Hove around teatime, with the tail-enders bathing in the sea, girding their loins for a long bowl next day. The wicket had not changed all that much in character since then; it took a great bowler in Maurice Tate to extract advantage from the pre-lunch sea fret in the 1920s.

So at least Alletson could play the bowling on its merits and not concern himself with any uneven bounce or deviation. He started well, reaching double figures in five minutes. With twenty-five minutes to go before lunch, Sussex tried a double bowling change. George Leach, fast right-arm, and Tim Killick, slow/medium left-arm came on for the Relf brothers. Alletson had an escape in Killick's first over when he edged one to slip. It flew to the left hand of George Cox, who could not keep control of it. Alletson was 42 at the time. Cox made amends soon after when he caught Garnet Lee – the stand was worth 73 in forty minutes and at least they had given the meagre crowd some entertainment. When Leach bowled Oates in his next over to make it 260 for 9, lunch was taken. No doubt Sussex would have liked the whole afternoon free, but they should not be delayed very long. This big lad Alletson had played well, though: 47 not out with some good blows. Pity old George Cox had spilled that one. Never mind – his luck can't last. . . .

It lasted for another forty minutes after lunch, long enough to make Ted Alletson famous. Before he went out again, he asked his captain A.O. Jones if it really mattered what he did, with the side only eighty-four runs ahead and the last pair together. The captain replied that it did not. 'Then I'm not half going to give Tim Killick some stick,' replied Alletson. No doubt he remembered that Killick had him caught at slip the previous year at Hove, while he would have gone the same way that morning if George Cox had been a little more alert. Someone had to yield – and Alletson was determined it would be Killick.

Bill Riley, the new batsman, safely negotiated the four balls left on Leach's over on the resumption, and then Alletson prepared to take Killick. Now Killick was a fine bowler – coached by Alfred Shaw, that disciple of line and length, he had figures of 4 for 2, 7 for 10 and 5 for 2 in championship cricket. He was accurate, guileful, with a clever change of pace – a good test for a bold hitter. In Killick's first over after lunch, Alletson got to his fifty with a four off the second ball, then took another, then a single. Riley was left with two balls to face, but took a single off the second to steal the strike. After Alletson pointed out that the number eleven's function was to give his partner the strike and run when he was told, they settled down to a brilliant partnership. Riley did his duty and took a single off the first ball of Leach's over and Alletson proceeded to hit him for two, four, two, two, and then a single off the last ball. Time for another dart at Killick.

The first ball was straight driven for six and he took two fours, a two and another straight six to make it 22 in the over. The only drawback was that he had forgotten to steal the strike in the heady excitement of driving a soaring straight six. Riley did not fail him, however; he scampered three off the second ball of Leach's over and Alletson then hit him for thirteen off the last four balls. A snick for three off the final delivery brought him his hundred and also the strike. Alletson's hundred had come just sixteen minutes after his score had stood at 47.

In the next two overs, Alletson hit eleven off Killick and seventeen off Leach. Each time, Riley was left to block the last ball, leaving Alletson time to catch his breath. Then Tim Killick began the seventh over after lunch. With the bespectacled bowler just 5 feet 6 inches tall, and weighing no more than ten stone, it looked the kind of physical contest that used to adorn those Charles Atlas body-building advertisements – and Alletson proceeded to kick cricketing sand in poor Killick's face. He took 34 off this seventh over as Killick committed the unpardonable sin for a slow bowler of sending down two 'no balls'. To be fair to him, he was so concerned to avoid the fearsome straight drives that he jumped out of the way as soon as he delivered the ball and did not know where he was in relation to the bowling crease. Alletson scored from seven of the eight deliveries (46604446), with a mixture of skimming straight drives, one back foot slash that broke the pavilion window and damaged the bar, and another which smashed the pavilion clock.

The score was now 380 for 9. In five consecutive overs, Alletson had made 97 out of a hundred, and Riley had only had to play five deliveries. Not surprisingly, Killick was taken off and George Cox tried his slow left-arm spin. Albert Relf came on for Leach at the other end. The next two overs produced just eight runs as Alletson tried to sort out the new line and Riley struggled to get him the strike against fielding that had suddenly tightened up. After that short reconnaissance, Alletson had one final glorious burst, taking fifteen off Relf, including a single off the last ball. He then hit Cox for two leg-side boundaries, ignored the chance of a single, then lofted the fourth ball high and straight. He hit it rather too high and it was beautifully taken by the Sussex captain, C.L.A. Smith, on the boundary edge. The crowd, by now intoxicated with such fabulous hitting, claimed that Smith's back foot was breaking the boundary line as he took the catch, and that the catch was therefore not valid, a point later confirmed by the Nottinghamshire players. That did not trouble Alletson – he accepted the word of a gentleman and walked away. Perhaps he knew that he had run out of luck. Perhaps he thought that a lead of 237 was more than enough and that it was now time to try to bowl out a demoralized Sussex side.

Sussex nearly lost. They had three and a quarter hours to bat and Bill Riley followed up his sensible batting with some good bowling. Happily, Leach and Killick, those shell-shocked bowlers, had the last laugh as they stayed together for an hour to save the game. They deserved something tangible from the day. Ironically Alletson's great innings did not get any extra points for his county; Sussex got three to Nottinghamshire's one because they led on first innings.

Just one cricket reporter watched that amazing final day. The Sussex scorer lunched rather well, so he was less than vigilant in his duties thereafter. As a result, the bowling analysis for Sussex is missing, while in the Nottinghamshire scorebook, it is inked over the pencil version and is rather ambiguous. However we do know for certain that Alletson hit eight sixes, twenty-three fours, four threes, ten twos and seventeen singles. Most of his boundaries came from booming straight drives, the sixes mainly going over long-on. Years later, George Gunn recalled, 'The two Relfs and Joe Vine were in the long field and the ball fizzed through them as if they were ghosts.' Bob Relf said he simply hit firm-footed: 'He made no attempt to get to the pitch of the ball, but unless it was right up to him, hit under it, straight off the middle of the bat. I was out at long-off and some of his drives were carrying as far as the hotel or over the stand to the skating rink.' At one stage there were five balls on the roof of that skating rink. If Alletson had played this innings before 1910, some of the sixes would have been fours, because the ball had to go clean out of the ground, but the difference would have only been a handful of runs. It was a truly astonishing innings, whatever the regulations.

Of the three main protagonists in the historic post-lunch session, Tim Killick was the one to prosper. He retired in 1913 and became the Sussex scorer for many years before dying at the age of seventy-three. Poor Bill Riley was killed by a shell splinter in Belgium in 1917, aged thirty-one. As for Ted Alletson, he lived till he was seventy-nine, but he never again scaled the heights of that cold afternoon at Hove. He sometimes threatened to do so – in his next match, he hit sixty against Gloucestershire in half an hour and he once hit Wilfred Rhodes for three successive sixes. He was given a Test trial in 1911, but he looked out of his class and managed only fifteen and eight. *Wisden* had some harsh things to say about his overall performance in the summer of 1911, when he could only average twenty-four, and he was dropped for a time in the next season. His most successful season was 1913 – a modest 634 runs at 21.13 – and after two more games in 1914, he dropped out of first-class cricket. His career average stood at 18.47, with fourteen fifties and one solitary century. What a century it was, though.

Ted Alletson remains the classic example of a cricketer who dazzled just once. It was a shame that he had to be judged by the standard he had achieved in forty minutes of a life that lasted seventy-nine years. It was a pity that he sought to improve his defence instead of concentrating on his natural asset – the ability to hit a cricket ball out of sight. Even in those uncomplicated days, over-theorizing and meddling from coaches could dilute a cricketer's effectiveness. That has to be the main reason for Ted Alletson's sudden eclipse. Any man who could bat the way he did on 20 May 1911 should have been able to stage many repeat performances.

20

Derbyshire *v.* Yorkshire
1914

Ten years earlier, the lovely Chesterfield ground had seen one of the most spectacular batting extravaganzas (see chapter 12). Now it was the turn of the bowlers. In the space of twenty-one deliveries, Derbyshire lost eight wickets for four runs, the greatest collapse in the game's history. No doubt the bowling of Wilfred Rhodes and Alonzo Drake was devastating: they had, after all, the blissful chance to bowl on a wet wicket with sunshine drying it out. Yet somehow Arthur Morton managed to score fifty out of Derbyshire's total of sixty-eight – or to be precise, fifty out of sixty runs that came from the bat.

We know enough about Wilfred Rhodes, but Alonzo Drake was a tragic figure. He had genuine all-round talent, but two factors prevented him from achieving greatness. The Great War came at the end of the 1914 season in which he had bowled magnificently; four seasons were to be lost before first-class cricket could be resumed. By then Alonzo Drake was dead. Heart failure had claimed him at the age of thirty-four. In the last two games of the 1914 season, Drake took nineteen wickets, including 10 for 35 in one innings against Somerset, but he never played for Yorkshire again. Perhaps it was a portent when he was bowled for nought in his last innings at Brighton, as the warmongers mobilized.

When Yorkshire came to Chesterfield in mid-July, Drake had taken seventy-three wickets with his slow-medium left-arm bowling. Over the next month he was to strike an irresistible vein of form, taking another eighty-five wickets. It was a glorious way to end a career. The same applied to his bowling partner, Major Booth – so named after the Salvation Army leader. Booth was also a fine all-rounder (he did the 'double' twice) and with his swerve, speed off the pitch and cunning off-spin, he was the natural

DERBYSHIRE v YORKSHIRE
At Chesterfield, 16–18 July 1914

DERBYSHIRE

Mr. L. Oliver lbw b Rhodes	43	– c Rhodes b Booth	1
A. Morton b Booth	35	– c Dolphin b Rhodes	50
J. Bowden c and b Rhodes	9	– c Dolphin b Rhodes	2
A. G. Slater lbw, b Booth	14	– b Drake	5
Mr. G. Curgenven b Rhodes	4	– b Drake	0
S. W. A. Cadman b Drake	25	– lbw, b Rhodes	2
Mr. C. N. B. Hurt b Booth	1	– b Drake	0
*Capt. R. R. Baggallay st Dolphin b Rhodes	42	– c Holmes b Drake	0
Mr. T. Forester c Kilner b Booth	3	– st Dolphin b Drake	0
†J. Humphries run out	0	– not out	0
J. Horsley not out	0	– lbw, b Rhodes	0
B 1, l-b 3, n-b 1	5	B 4, l-b 3, n-b 1	8
	181		**68**

1/66 2/89 3/90 4/96 5/122 6/124
7/149 8/179 9/179

1/27 2/31 3/64 4/67 5/68 6/68 7/68
8/68 9/68

Bowling: *First Innings* – Booth 25–7–61–4; Hirst 11–2–30–0; Rhodes 23.2–8–54–4; Drake 9–1–31–1. *Second Innings* – Booth 7–1–25–1; Hirst 3–1–17–0; Rhodes 7.4–2–12–4; Drake 3–0–6–5.

YORKSHIRE

W. Rhodes c and b Horsley	39
B. B. Wilson b Horsley	27
D. Denton c Humphries b Cadman	77
R. Kilner st Humphries b Morton	38
G. H. Hirst lbw, b Cadman	21
A. Drake c Oliver b Horsley	18
M. W. Booth c Humphries b Horsley	3
E. Oldroyd not out	28
P. Holmes c Humphries b Horsley	32
*Sir A. W. White c Baggallay b Morton	5
†A. Dolphin b Horsley	1
B 4, l-b 4	8
	297

1/68 2/73 3/175 4/187 5/220 6/225
7/228 8/290 9/295

Bowling: *First Innings* – Forester 20–8–44–0; Morton 36–9–74–2; Slater 16–4–49–0; Cadman 21–7–45–2; Horsley 20–3–77–6.

Umpires: F. G. Roberts and W. Richards.

Yorkshire won by an innings and 48 runs.

successor to Schofield Haigh. In 1914 he took 155 wickets, and he and Drake were a tremendous combination. The future for Yorkshire cricket looked very bright with these two young bowlers backing up Rhodes and Hirst, to give them four genuine all-rounders. Yet both Drake and Booth were dead when first-class cricket resumed in 1919: Drake through a weak heart, while Booth fell on the Somme in 1916. He was just thirty, one of many fine cricketers to suffer the ultimate fate.

In mid-July of 1914 cricket seemed a pleasant distraction from the affairs of state. The Irish question dogged the politicians, Mrs Pankhurst was re-arrested after violent scenes at a Suffragette meeting in London and the King inspected the Fleet at Spithead. The jingoistic headlines in *The Times* ('Forty Miles of Fighting Ships', 'An Imposing Array of Aircraft') suggested that a short, sharp fight with Germany would be enough to re-assert our position in the world and humiliate the insufferable Bismarck. While the politicians postured, and the fighting men flexed their muscles, the flower of English manhood enjoyed the last weeks of a glorious summer – for many of them the last English summer they would ever see.

It was rare to have a rain-affected game in the summer of 1914 and, on the first day at Chesterfield, Derbyshire made 113 for 4 before the weather closed in after lunch. On the second day the home side lost their last six wickets for 68 and Yorkshire made good progress. David Denton was typically audacious, making 77 in two hours, and at the close Yorkshire led by 43 with five wickets left. They still had much to do if they were to get a win out of this game.

It rained in the night and Yorkshire made quick runs in the morning while the pitch was at its easiest. They left Derbyshire needing 116 to avoid an innings defeat, or five hours to bat out time. More pertinently the sun was now shining strongly and the wicket would undoubtedly be difficult as it dried out.

At lunch Derbyshire had made 28 in twenty minutes for the loss of Oliver. Already Arthur Morton was showing that he could score at speed, and with safety if support came at the other end. Morton was a tough, nuggety all-rounder, who had first played for the county eleven years earlier at the age of twenty. He twice took a hundred wickets in a season, and in a weak batting side he tended to sell his wicket dearly. In this 1914 season he was in good form with the bat, ending up with a thousand runs to set alongside his fifty wickets. Morton loved the challenge that Yorkshire cricket presented. It brought out the best of him as a cricketer and later as an umpire. He was once standing in a Yorkshire game when Emmott Robinson came out to field as substitute and had the greatest pleasure in seeing off the excitable Robinson when he appealed for lbw from square leg. Morton turned to him and shouted, 'Tha's not playin' in this match Emmott, so shoot thi' mouth.' Such a man would not be unduly perturbed by a clutch of Yorkshiremen gathered round him on a wet wicket at Chesterfield.

If Morton was undisturbed, his partners were less assured. Bowden was caught behind at 37 and Slater hung on for a time as Morton picked off the runs. With the score at 59 for 2, Drake became the fourth bowler to be used as Yorkshire began to get a little concerned that wickets were not tumbling on what was now a genuine 'sticky'. With his eighth ball, Drake bowled Slater: 64 for 3. Next over Cadman fell to Rhodes to make it 67 for 4. Off the third ball of his third over, Drake had Baggallay taken by slip from a ball that bounced sharply: 68 for 5. The next delivery took Curgenven's middle stump, then the fifth ball pitched leg-stump and took Hurt's off bail. Off the final ball, Dolphin stretched to a wide one and stumped Forester brilliantly. Drake had taken four wickets in four balls, the first Yorkshire player to do so. Would he make it six in six from his next over?

Wilfred Rhodes soon blocked such fanciful notions. In four balls he had Morton caught behind and trapped Horsley lbw to wrap up the match. Morton had hit eight boundaries in a truly gallant innings, but he was overshadowed. Drake had taken five wickets in his last ten deliveries and Derbyshire's last six wickets had fallen at 68. Here is the sequence for the twenty-one balls that decimated Derbyshire – 0W0010 (Drake), 110W00 (Rhodes), 01WWWW (Drake), 0W0W (Rhodes). Morton completed his remarkable fifty with a single the ball before Drake started his sequence of four in four. He then had to watch the collapse from the safety of Drake's end, but he only lasted two more balls. No one can say he had not earned his bonus for a fifty. The innings lasted just over an hour; considering the state of the pitch and the fall of ten wickets, that was an impressive scoring rate by Derbyshire. Correction – by Arthur Morton.

It was not the first time that Drake had performed the hat-trick – two years earlier Essex had provided him with one. It was the twelfth time that a bowler had taken four in four, the last occasion

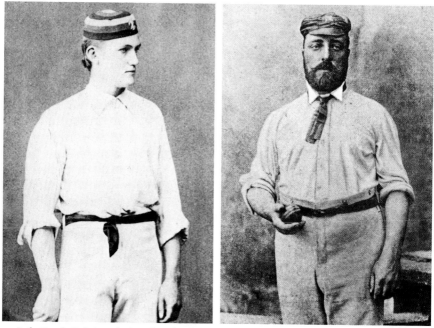

Left: Frank Cobden, the bowler who transformed the Varsity match of 1870 (chapter 1).
Right: Alfred Shaw, one of the most accurate bowlers of all time and a useful batsman.
His all-round talents tipped the scales in the gripping Gents *v.* Players match of 1881
(chapter 4)

The Australian touring party of 1882 that beat England at the Oval, leading to the famous
newspaper announcement that initiated the battle for the Ashes (chapter 5). Standing,
from left to right: S.P. Jones, A.C. Bannerman, G.J. Bonnor, F.R. Spofforth, J.McC.
Blackham, G.E. Palmer, G. Giffen, T.W. Garrett, H.H. Massie, P.S. McDonnell.
Seated: W.L. Murdoch, H.F. Boyle, T.P. Horan

Below: Frederick Spofforth, known as 'The Demon' – the great Australian bowler who shattered English complacency in two historic matches (chapters 3 and 5)

Above: Gilbert Jessop, the most legendary hitter of a cricket ball in history. Just one Test hundred, but its lustre remains undimmed (chapter 11)

George Hirst (*left*) and Wilfred Rhodes, two great all-rounders for Yorkshire and England. Matchless temperaments (chapter 11) and wonderfully consistent (chapter 13)

Left: S.M.J. ('Sammy') Woods, Australian-born but devoted to Somerset. Inspiring captain, spectacular all-rounder, he ordered champagne after Somerset had astounded the cricket world by beating the mighty Yorkshire in 1901 (chapter 9)

Far left: Percy Perrin, one of cricket's unluckiest players: 343 not out and still finishing on the losing side (chapter 12)!

Left: Arthur Mailey, expansive human being, expensive leg-spinner, with a highly developed sense of humour that relished his analysis of 4 for 362 against Victoria in 1926 (chapter 22)

Hedley Verity: 10 for 10 in seventy minutes as the Headingley pitch dried out after a thunderstorm (chapter 25)

Left: Albert Trott, an all-rounder with a touch of genius but with a cricketing and personal deathwish (chapter 14)

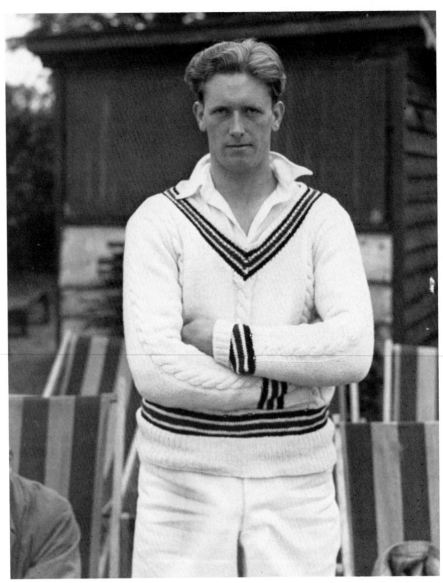

Maurice Tremlett, pictured in May 1947 – the month when he burst onto the first-class scene with such flair and rich promise (chapter 29)

Opposite
Left: Clarrie Grimmett – keen golfer, wonderfully tight bowler whose serene temperament failed him one day in 1929 (chapter 24)

Right: Cliff Gladwin batting in 1949, just a few months after he guided England to a famous victory in Durban (chapter 31). Better known as an excellent fast-medium bowler, nevertheless a leg-bye off one of Gladwin's thighs achieved immortality for the brawny boilersmith from Doe Lea Pit near Chesterfield

Above: Bill Woodfull and Bill Ponsford – pitiless, prolific openers for Victoria and Australia between the wars on pluperfect wickets. At their most merciless in the match against New South Wales in 1926 (chapter 22)

Jim Laker – a wry smile was never far from his lips, especially after he ruined a Test Trial in 1950 in his home town of Bradford (chapter 33)

being 1907 when both Albert Trott and Frank Tarrant achieved the feat. Ironically Drake and his Yorkshire team-mates suffered Derbyshire's fate in their next match at Leeds, when Nottinghamshire bowled them out for 75 as the sun baked a wet wicket. They were rescued in the second innings by eighty from Drake and won the match. Alonzo Drake seemed to have a decisive influence in every game he played during that final summer of the Golden Age: it was as if the gods knew what they had in store for him. In retrospect no one could begrudge him a transient place in the sun.

21

Warwickshire v. Hampshire

1922

In any anthology of extraordinary cricket matches, this one just clamours for inclusion. One needs a keen sense of the ridiculous to get somewhere near an understanding of how a team bowled out for fifteen could win handsomely by 4.20 on the final afternoon.

More than half a century later I was privileged to collaborate in the autobiography of E.J. 'Tiger' Smith, Warwickshire's wicket-keeper in the Hampshire match. A man of utter conviction and clear-eyed recollection, 'Tiger' was still embarrassed by this game until the day he died, fifty-seven years later. While many have tried to probe the cricketing reasons for the astonishing reversal of fortunes, 'Tiger' firmly stuck to his guns: it was all the fault of the Warwickshire committee, in particular the autocratic club secretary, R.V. Ryder. Just before lunch on the second day, with Hampshire still thirty behind with only four wickets left, the committee sent out a message to the Warwickshire captain on the field of play. Freddie Calthorpe opened the envelope and read that the committee wanted to see some cricket before going into an afternoon meeting; he should delay taking the new ball which would undoubtedly polish off the Hampshire innings. Calthorpe, a gentle, popular soul, did as he was told and Hampshire's astonishing recovery was launched as Billy Quaife bowled forty-nine overs of legspin at the age of fifty. To the end of his days, the eyes of 'Tiger' Smith would blaze whenever this game was mentioned: fortunately one cannot defame the dead, no matter how hard the old man cursed the name of R.V. Ryder.

On the first day it was the Hampshire captain who should have been embarrassed, but Lionel Tennyson never acknowledged such

WARWICKSHIRE v HAMPSHIRE

At Birmingham, 14–16 June 1922

WARWICKSHIRE

L. T. A. Bates c Shirley b Newman	3	– c Mead b Kennedy	1
†E. J. Smith c Mead b Newman	24	– c Shirley b Kennedy	41
Mr. F. R. Santall c McIntyre b Boyes	84	– b Newman	0
W. G. Quaife b Newman	1	– not out	40
*Hon. F. S. G. Calthorpe c Boyes b Kennedy	70	– b Newman	30
Rev. E. F. Waddy c Mead b Boyes	0	– b Newman	0
Mr. B. W. Quaife b Boyes	0	– c and b Kennedy	7
J. Fox b Kennedy	4	– b Kennedy	0
J. A. Smart b Newman	20	– b Newman	3
C. C. Smart c Mead b Boyes	14	– c and b Boyes	15
H. Howell not out	1	– c Kennedy b Newman	11
L-b 2	2	B 6, l-b 4	10
	223		158

1/3 2/26 3/44 4/166 5/177 6/184
7/184 8/200 9/219

1/2 2/77 3/85 4/85 5/85 6/89 7/113
8/143 9/147

Bowling: *First Innings* – Kennedy 24–7–74–2; Newman 12.3–0–70–4; Boyes
16–5–56–4; Shirley 3–0–21–0. *Second Innings* – Kennedy 26–12–47–4;
Newman 26.3–12–53–5; Boyles 11–4–34–1; Brown 5–0–14–0.

HAMPSHIRE

H. A. W. Bowell b Howell	0	– c Howell b W. G. Quaife	45
A. S. Kennedy c Smith b Calthorpe	0	– b Calthorpe	7
Mr. H. L. V. Day b Calthorpe	0	– c Bates b W. G. Quaife	15
C. P. Mead not out	6	– b Howell	24
*Hon. L. H. Tennyson c Calthorpe b Howell	4	– c C. Smart b Calthorpe	45
G. Brown b Howell	0	– b C. Smart	172
J. A. Newman c C. Smart b Howell	0	– c and b W. G. Quaife	12
Mr. W. R. Shirley c J. Smart b Calthorpe	1	– lbw, b Fox	30
Mr. A. S. McIntyre lbw, b Calthorpe	0	– lbw, b Howell	5
†W. H. Livsey b Howell	0	– not out	110
G. S. Boyes lbw, b Howell	0	– b Howell	29
B 4	4	B 14, l-b 11, w 1, n-b 1	27
	15		521

1/0 2/0 3/0 4/5 5/5 6/9 7/10 8/10 9/15

1/15 2/63 3/81 4/127 5/152 6/177
7/262 8/274 9/451

Bowling: *First Innings* – Howell 4.5–2–7–6; Calthorpe 4–3–4–4. *Second Innings*
– Howell 63–10–156–3; Calthorpe 33–7–97–2; W. G. Quaife 49–8–154–3;
Fox 7–0–30–1; J. Smart 13–2–37–0; Santall 5–0–15–0; C. Smart 1–0–5–1.

Umpires: A. J. Atfield and B. Brown.

Hampshire won by 155 runs.

an emotion. The colourful Tennyson was incapable of sheepishness, unless it was over something important like being blackballed from his club because his drinks bill had not been paid for a year. The grandson of the former Poet Laureate, Lionel Tennyson would have been a boon companion to hell-raisers like Bill Edrich and Keith Miller of later vintage. He squeezed the grape of social opportunity until the pips begged for mercy; every day had to be lived as if on a twenty-four hour pass from the horrors of the Somme. Such a positive attitude made Tennyson into a very good captain. He would speculate to accumulate on the field (and do the same off it with gusto), and no game could be pronounced dead if he was in charge. In his time he was also a fine, aggressive bat. By 1922 he was at his peak, having played some brave innings against Gregory and McDonald the year before as the Australians blitzed the English batting.

When Tennyson won the toss on the first day at Edgbaston, he took one look at the soft wicket and asked Warwickshire to bat. They were bowled out cheaply enough and, if it had not been for a stand of 122 by Calthorpe and Santall, Tennyson would have been entirely justified. By the time Hampshire started batting at four o'clock the wicket had dried out, and it was now true and easy-paced. Hampshire were a very good batting side: Mead, Brown and Tennyson had played for England the previous summer, while Bowell had great promise and Kennedy and Newman were consistent all-rounders. Hard then to understand how they could be bowled out for fifteen in forty minutes.

It was the third lowest total in first-class cricket and it could so easily have been less. One ball from Harry Howell evaded 'Tiger' Smith down the legside and went for four byes, while Tennyson snicked a four through the slips that could have been taken. Mead hit the only authentic boundary, a hook off Calthorpe. He remained six not out at the end and ever after he protested, 'Nobody bowled me anything that I couldn't play in the middle of the bat.' That was confirmed to me by 'Tiger' Smith. He said too many batsmen played back, rather than forward. In his opinion, Howell bowled the fastest of his career that day, while Calthorpe made the ball swing late and sharply. Everything went Warwickshire's way for forty minutes with every chance that went to hand being taken and a wicket falling whenever a batsman made an error. They never recovered from being 0 for 3, and the dismissal of Day – bowled off stump by one that started outside leg – seemed to inhibit the others.

It was all very bizarre, and to his eternal credit Lionel Tennyson realized that. As they prepared to follow on, the captain bluffly announced, 'Never mind, we'll make 500 now.' The Hampshire team was used to Tennyson's endearing little ways and no one took much notice of his laudable effort to whistle up their spirits. With Kennedy, Day and Bowell all gone before the close, it was hardly a stirring comeback. Hampshire ended on 98 for 3, with Mead looking imperturbable and the captain exasperated by the leg-breaks of Billy Quaife. Tennyson was still fuming back in the dressing-room when Freddie Calthorpe popped his head round the door and asked if the amateurs would care to join him in a round of golf when the match was over next day. It was too much for Tennyson: he delivered a volley peppered with Anglo-Saxon profanities and declared that Hampshire would still be batting at lunch on the final day and that they would also win the match. For good measure he wagered Calthorpe ten pounds that Warwickshire would lose, and as word spread, he struck several more bets with his customary bravado.

One assumes the correspondent of The Times was unaware of Tennyson's bold façade, because his match report the following morning contained this splendid piece of pomposity: 'Major Tennyson will probably never forget his experiment of putting Warwickshire in to bat first.' Experiment! The captain was simply following sound cricketing logic, a decision supported by the old sweats in the Hampshire team. It was not his fault that they had batted so badly when Warwickshire were dismissed. Tennyson's mood was hardly improved when he dealt with a stack of mail on that second morning – especially the droll suggestion that Hampshire should give up the game and take up painting spots on rocking horses. He showed that letter to his side. They were not amused. Something had to be done.

Within an hour Hampshire had slid further into trouble. Mead, after looking totally at ease, was bowled middle stump by an inswinging yorker. Then Tennyson was caught in the slips off his rival captain, who tried very hard to catch his eye as he walked back to the pavilion. It was 152 for 5, still fifty needed to make Warwickshire bat again. George Brown, that tough, grizzled left-hander started to bat with commendable restraint, but when he lost Jack Newman at 177 there seemed no hope. The Old Etonian

Shirley hung around long enough to see Brown reach his fifty after two hours of self-denial, and the pair had added 85 before he was lbw. When McIntyre was beaten for pace, Hampshire were 274 for 8, just 69 ahead with more than a day still outstanding. That golf match seemed a certainty for lunchtime tomorrow.

Then the game threw up the unlikeliest hero. Walter Livsey came in with strict instructions from his captain, He was to stay there, supporting Brown, and he was expected to change the habit of a lifetime and get behind the ball, instead of backing away to square leg. Now Livsey was also Tennyson's valet, and we may safely assume he knew when the bibulous Bacchanalian meant business. It was irrelevant that Livsey had only reached double figures three times so far that season, that Howell would test his nerve with some fast deliveries – he had to stay there. Brown kept Howell away from Livsey as much as possible, and the little wicket-keeper began to relax. Billy Quaife was given some terrible punishment at the other end as Warwickshire realized that Brown's intensely competitive spirit was wresting the game away from them. The committee had long retired into their deliberations and the change bowlers had been banished, but the balance had swung. The ninth-wicket pair added 177 in 140 minutes until Brown was out just before the close for a heroic innings that lasted four and three quarter hours. Then Livsey assumed control, growing visibly in stature. He knew he was now the senior partner and shepherded the twenty-three-year-old Stuart Boyes. At the close Livsey was 81 not out and Hampshire led by 267. One assumes Livsey was not made to pack Tennyson's kit that evening after he had laid aside his own bat.

Hampshire added another 46 on the third morning, and Livsey completed the first hundred of his career. Boyes was equally comfortable and it took a ball that kept low to dismiss him. So Warwickshire needed 314 in about five hours. All the psychological initiative had passed to Hampshire, and although the score was 77 for 1 just after lunch the bowlers were not to be denied. Alec Kennedy – who took 205 wickets that summer – and Jack Newman were too experienced, too resourceful to let Warwickshire off the hook. They took five wickets in an hour, as Tennyson turned the screw with prehensile fielders perched around the bat. It was too much for a demoralized, angry, tired opposition. The side bowled out for fifteen triumphed by 155 runs two days later. The man from *The Times* was right in one sense: Tennyson would never forget asking Warwickshire to bat first. After the game, he was seen attempting a rather elephantine highland fling in the showers, before trawling the Warwickshire dressing-room for his winnings.

Mercifully for Hampshire they did not have another fixture for four days. Time enough to savour the atmosphere and to make a sizeable dent in Tennyson's windfall. While the Warwickshire committee upbraided Calthorpe for losing the match, his opposite number poured out the laughing liquid like a sailor on shore leave. No wonder his professionals loved him; this match had been typical Tennyson. Ever since he had been wounded three times in the Great War, Tennyson had approached life with gratitude that he had survived the worst experience any generation could suffer. Thus a cricket match would always be approached by Tennyson with panache; it would remain a fascinating hors d'oeuvre to the main course of evening entertainment, a game to be savoured but only a game. Strange how men with such an attitude often make excellent captains.

22
Victoria *v.* New South Wales
1926

The statisticians enjoyed themselves around Christmastime, 1926. The New South Wales bowlers were less enthusiastic, as Victoria piled up a new record innings total for first-class cricket. They had become rather used to dipping their bread: four years earlier Victoria had made 1059 against Tasmania and won by an innings and 666 runs. They just failed to improve on that fantastic winning margin, but that was the only cloud on their horizon.

For those who like to see a worthy balance between bat and ball, games like this are an obscenity. After the Great War, the wickets in England and Australia became particularly easy-paced. If it rained the pendulum swung towards the bowler, but at least the batsman could still retain some self-respect by displaying an impeccable defensive technique or a bold, attacking policy. When the wickets were pluperfect, all the poor bowler could do was wheel away, hoping for a mistake. Thus the 1920s saw the rise and rise of acquisitive accumulators; the contrast between dashers like Trumper, Jessop and MacLaren was painfully acute.

No one enjoyed this imbalance more than Don Bradman. From his first-class debut in 1927, he slaughtered bowlers on wickets that gave them little hope. A century on every third visit to the wicket over a twenty-year period is a tribute to Bradman's voracity, but also the quality of pitches that invariably played like smooth billiard tables. If Bradman had not existed, Bill Ponsford would have been an acknowledged marvel. He was eight years older than Bradman and by the mid-1920s he had perfected the art of accumulation. In the Tasmania game in 1922 he made 429, to topple MacLaren's 424 made in 1895. He scored 1146 in five

VICTORIA *v* NEW SOUTH WALES

At Melbourne, 24–29 December 1926

NEW SOUTH WALES

N. E. Phillips c Blackie b Liddicut.......	52	– lbw, b Kartkopf.........................	36
J. G. Morgan c Love b Liddicut..........	13	– c King b Liddicut......................	26
*T. J. E. Andrews st Ellis b Hartkopf .	42	– b Liddicut.................................	0
A. F. Kippax b Liddicut......................	36	– b Hartkopf	26
†A. T. Ratcliffe c Ryder b Liddicut.....	2	– c Morton b Hartkopf	44
A. A. Jackson c Ellis b Blackie	4	– not out.......................................	59
J. E. P. Hogg not out...........................	40	– c Hendry b Liddicut	13
A. A. Mailey b Ryder	20	– c Morton b Hartkopf	3
J. N. Campbell lbw, b Blackie.............	0	– c Ryder b Hartkopf...................	8
R. L. A. McNamee b Ryder	8	– b Liddicut.................................	7
H. V. McGuirk b Ryder	0	– b Hartkopf	0
B 4...	4	B 8..................................	8
	221		**230**

1/25 2/95 3/122 4/133 5/152 6/152
7/207 8/208 9/217

1/67 2/67 3/77 4/112 5/164 6/184
7/189 8/206 9/229

Bowling: *First Innings* – Morton 15–4–43–0; Liddicut 21–7–50–4; Ryder
9–1–32–3; Blackie 16–3–34–2; Hendry 3–2–1–0; Hartkopf 17–1–57–1.
Second Innings – Morton 11–0–42–0; Liddicut 19–2–66–4; Blackie 3–1–16–0;
Hartkopf 16.3–0–98–6.

VICTORIA

W. M. Woodfull c Ratcliffe b Andrews	133
W. H. Ponsford b Morgan	352
H. S. T. L. Hendry c Morgan b Malley	100
*J. Ryder c Kippax b Andrews.............	295
F. L. Morton run out............................	0
H. S. B. Love st Ratcliffe b Malley......	6
S. P. King st Ratcliffe b Malley	7
A. E. V. Hartkopf c McGuirk b Malley	61
A. E. Liddicut b McGuirk	36
†J. L. Ellis run out...............................	63
D. D. J. Blackie not out........................	27
B 27...	27
	1107

1/375 2/594 3/614 4/631 5/657 6/834 7/915 8/1043 9/1046

Bowling: *First Innings* – McNamee 24–2–124–0; McGuirk 26–1–130–1; Mailey
64–0–362–4; Campbell 11–0–89–0; Phillips 11.7–0–64–0; Morgan
26–0–137–1; Andrews 21–2–148–2; Kippax 7–0–26–0.

Victoria won by an innings and 656 runs.

innings in the month of December 1927, including 437 against Queensland. Bradman topped that two years later with 452 not out, but it was Ponsford who had set the standard of gargantuan scores. He made thirteen scores of two hundred and more, averaged 84.57 in the Sheffield Shield and 65 in his career. Yet he was distinctly unmemorable in style. Squarely built, he seemed ponderous although his footwork invariably took him into the right position. He was very strong around the leg stump and was a past master at pushing the ball around for ones and twos, drawing in the field, then hitting the ball a little harder to reach the boundary. Ponsford's pads always seemed wider than anyone else's; he seemed unbowlable. Yet a class fast bowler could sort him out, as Larwood proved on his two tours to Australia. A great player of spin, Ponsford was very much at home on the slower English wickets, where he could manipulate the ball with his powerful top left hand. It was all very unglamorous, compared with the Australian charmers of yesteryear, but in more pragmatic times, men like Ponsford at least ensured immunity against defeat.

His opening partner was just as big an aesthetic disaster. Bill Woodfull had a short back lift and a strange chopping way of making his shots that resembled a guillotine. He seemed to have no momentum to his arms or wrists, yet somehow Woodfull scored all round the wicket. He was known as 'the wormkiller' for the way he could dig out a low delivery, and it was almost impossible to hit his stumps on true, blameless Australian wickets. He and Ponsford became Australia's regular opening pair, and they emasculated many a fine bowler over a decade. Yet no one ever skipped along the road in joyous anticipation of seeing these two walk out to bat. The metronome had replaced the sorcerer.

Woodfull and Ponsford were both abstemious men, so they were unlikely to have supped too well over the Christmas break during the New South Wales game in 1926. On Christmas Eve, New South Wales had been bowled out for just 221. They were without Herbie Collins, Warren Bardsley, Charlie Macartney, Johnny Taylor, Jack Gregory, Bert Oldfield and Charlie Kelleway for various reasons, but at least their other batsmen were on form, particularly their graceful, prolific captain Alan Kippax. Yet they contrived to discover bizarre ways of getting out against a Victorian side immeasureably weaker in bowling than batting.

On 27 December, suitably refreshed, Victoria passed the opposition score without losing a wicket. Woodfull and Ponsford were to add a further 154 before they were parted. Ponsford outscored Woodfull comfortably, his century coming in 125 minutes, his double hundred in 203 minutes and his triple century in 285 minutes. Their opening stand of 375 came up in just 223 minutes, with Woodfull stirring himself to hit five boundaries. At least the new batsman put the bowling in perspective once Woodfull's careworn innings had ended. H.L. Hendry (known as 'Stork' because of his extreme height and thinness) came in and crashed the ball around as though playing in a charity match. It looked as if he was trying to get caught on the boundary, but the fielders were too shattered to offer anything but a vague flap at the disappearing ball. At close of play, Victoria had made 573 for 1, with Ponsford 334 not out and Hendry 86 not out in the final ninety-seven minutes. Victoria had batted for 322 minutes, and only four maiden overs were bowled.

None of those four maidens was bowled by Arthur Mailey: he would have been outraged at such containment. To Mailey, every ball had to take a wicket, otherwise there was no point in bowling. He was forty at the time and too steeped in his ways even to consider tucking up the batsmen. Mailey was an ideal leg-spinner: he had very strong hands that gave him prodigious powers of spin, and a teasing flight. He simply loved to make the ball buzz and fizz, and it is impossible to imagine Arthur Mailey attempting off-spin or seam bowling. He was always happy to buy his wickets, and he brought that refreshing attitude into the grim arena of Test cricket. When he bowled Jack Hobbs with a full toss in the crucial Oval Test of 1926, he burst out laughing; in the same game he was met by his captain in the morning as he walked into the hotel after an all-night session of carousing. He disarmingly promised Herbie Collins he would get five wickets that day – and he did. At various stages a labourer, cartoonist, journalist and painter in oils, Arthur Mailey was at all times a philosopher, *bon viveur* and advocate of cricket's finer feelings. The gluttony of Victoria's batsmen would never strike a responsive chord in his idealistic breast.

As Mailey wheeled away at one end, indulging his flights of fancy, Ponsford continued the carnage the following morning. At 352 his luck ran out and he played a ball into his stumps. Hendry had already gone at 594 after 117 minutes of slaughter, and Ponsford's dismissal made it 614 for 3 – almost a crisis. Ponsford had batted for six hours, hit thirty-six fours and given one chance

– a possible stumping when he had made 265. If the bowlers thought a reprieve was in store, they were soon disillusioned. The Victorian captain Jack Ryder proceeded to drive with enormous power with a full swing of the bat. He did not need to worry about the ball deviating – the wicket was too benign for that – so Ryder just hit through the line. The loss of Love and King was irrelevant. At 657 for 5 he found an excellent partner in Albert Hartkopf, another prodigious hitter. Hartkopf bowled leg-spin, but he was a good enough bat to make eighty in his only Test, against England in 1924. Now he watched Ryder decimate an attack that had caved in a long while ago, apart from the whimsical Mailey, who was still going through his bag of tricks. They added 177 in 94 minutes before Mailey picked up his fourth wicket. It was now 834 for 6 and Ryder still had an appetite for the ludicrous fray. Liddicut, who eventually made three hundreds for Victoria, indulged himself for a time, then the Sheffield Shield record of 918 was passed. After just 574 minutes, Victoria reached a thousand. It fell to Jack Ellis, the wicket-keeper, to make the historic stroke and he ran down the other end, waving his bat wildly, shouting, 'Long live Victoria!' Ellis's hysterical reaction seemed almost as ridiculous as his captain's refusal to declare.

By this time, Arthur Mailey had reached his own personal triple century. Ryder hit him for another six and finally gave a catch to mid-on. His 295 had come in 245 minutes, with six sixes and thirty-three fours, and even though he had made some thrilling shots, it was now an irrelevance. That is unless you believed that it was important to pass Victoria's score of 1059 made four years ago. Clearly it was: sixteen runs later, after Morton had been run out, Jack Ellis cut a ball past point and again vouchsafed his love of Victoria.

Yet Ryder still carried on. Bow-legged, forty-four-year-old Don Blackie carved away for a time until Ellis was run out. The innings had lasted for 633 minutes, an astonishing scoring rate if the contest had been even. It was not: the bowlers never had a chance. Yet the fielding had stood up uncommonly well, with Tommy Andrews outstanding in the covers. Amid the devastation, Arthur Mailey retained his sense of humour, remarking that it was a pity Ellis had been run out as he was just finding his length. He felt his figures would have been better if a chap in the stand had caught Ryder early in his innings.

It would have been a miracle if New South Wales had avoided

defeat after starting their second innings 886 behind. Yet Ratcliffe made a bright 44 and Archie Jackson gave a glimpse of his precocious genius at the age of seventeen. What a pity that greedy pragmatists like Woodfull and Ponsford dominated that period of Australian cricket, rather than the sickly Jackson or the stylish, charming Kippax!

At least there is one satisfying sting in the tail from this farcical game. Five weeks later, in the return match, Victoria were caught on a rain-affected pitch and bundled out for 35. At one stage they were 19 for 8 and only one batsman reached double figures. They were dismissed for 181 after following on, and lost by an innings and 253 runs on the third day. Victoria may have been without Woodfull, Ponsford, Ryder, Love and Hartkopf (who had compiled 847 of that 1107), but nevertheless it was good to see gluttony reap its eventual whirlwind. It certainly kept Arthur Mailey amused over the years. . . .

23
Surrey *v*. Kent
1928

'Kent, with six wickets in hand and a lead of 29 runs, can only be afraid of one thing – rain.' That magisterial forecast by *The Times* came after the first day of this splendid match. It was yet another example of how cricket writers love to shoot themselves in the foot – the compulsive yen to make sweeping forecasts seems to rebound on the writer so often. They consistently ignore the human element like inspiring captaincy or an attack of funk by talented batsmen. These were the two main ingredients in this game, as Surrey took the last ten Kent wickets for 52 after they appeared dead and buried.

With a man like Percy Fender as captain, it was always unwise to write off Surrey. What he achieved with a limited bowling attack on the placid Oval wickets almost qualified him for membership of the Magic Circle. In his time as captain Surrey always had the batting, but the bowling was threadbare; yet somehow Fender would conjure up victories by a mixture of cheek, cunning, tactical sagacity and luck. The season of 1928 was a typical one for Surrey, with nine batsmen making over a thousand runs, but only Fender taking a hundred wickets with his leg-breaks. The bowling support he had was mundane – the honest, untiring pace of Alan Peach, the occasional slow bowling of Monty Garland-Wells, the medium pace of Tom Shepherd and in his first season, the erratic, expensive Alf Gover. Yet Surrey finished sixth in the table because Fender did the 'double' while ardently pursuing the half chance out in the field. The Kent match was a classic example of how Fender could turn impending defeat into breathless victory.

Kent came to the Oval at the top of the table. Lancashire, lying second, had just beaten them by eight wickets, but the neutrals wanted Kent to lift the title. Lancashire had enjoyed many

SURREY v KENT
At the Oval, 28–31 July 1928

SURREY

J. B. Hobbs c Legge b Freeman	6	– c Beslee b Freeman 109
A. Sandham c Freeman b Marriott	29	– lbw, b Freeman.............. 17
A. M. Ducat c Woolley b Freeman	22	– c Marriott b Freeman 33
T. F. Shepherd c Marriott b Woolley	6	– lbw, b Marriott.............. 17
T. H. Barling b Freeman	19	– lbw, b Freeman.............. 17
Mr. H. M. G-Wells c Freeman b Marriott	5	– lbw, b Marriott.............. 2
*Mr. P. G. H. Fender c Beslee b Freeman	22	– c Legge b Beslee.............. 42
R. J. Gregory lbw, b Marriott	3	– b Freeman....................... 0
H. A. Peach not out	6	– c Ashdown b Marriott.... 25
†E. W. J. Brooks st Ames b Marriott	2	– not out........................... 1
A. R. Gover c Ames b Marriott	0	– c Ames b Beslee.............. 0
B 6, l-b 3, n-b 2	11	B 11, l-b 7, n-b1 19
	131	**282**

1/9 2/53 3/61 4/69 5/77 6/103 7/123 8/123
9/131 10/131

1/44 2/111 3/173 4/191 5/
193 6/215 7/215 8/254 9/
282 10/282

Bowling: *First Innings* – Beslee 4–1–7–0; Ashdown 4–4–0–0; Marriott
24.5–12–41–5; Freeman 28–8–58–4; Woolley 5–1–14–1. *Second Innings* –
Beslee 9–3–26–2; Ashdown 11–2–35–0; Marriott 29–3–81–3; Freeman
31–4–101–5; Longfield 3–0–9–0; Hardinge 2–0–11–0.

KENT

W. H. Ashdown c Gregory b Gover	9	– b Fender........................... 44
H. T. W. Hardinge c Fender b G-Wells	38	– c Gregory b Fender......... 25
F. E. Woolley c G-Wells b Shepherd	51	– c Shepherd b Fender....... 14
†L. E. G. Ames run out	96	– c Barling b Peach............ 8
Mr. J. A. Deed b Fender	10	– c Brooks b Peach............ 5
*Mr. G. B. Legge c Fender b G-Wells	52	– c Brooks b Fender............ 6
Mr. T. C. Longfield c Fender b G-Wells	2	– not out........................... 6
Mr. B. H. Valentine b Fender	2	– run out........................... 1
G. P. Beslee b Garland-Wells	0	– c Fender b Peach............ 6
A. P. Freeman not out	4	– c Gover b Peach.............. 0
Mr. C. S. Marriott c Hobbs b Fender	8	– c Garland-Wells b Fender 0
B 8, l-b 1, n-b 2	11	N-b 1....................... 1
	283	**116**

1/13 2/86 3/111 4/142 5/253
6/260 7/262 8/263 9/264

1/64 2/80 3/89 4/92 5/103
6/103 7/105 8/116 9/116

Bowling: *First Innings* – Gover 24–4–76–1; Peach 9–0–34–0; Garland-Wells
18–7–35–4; Fender 26.4–9–78–3; Gregory 6–1–19–0; Shepherd 17–2–30–1.
Second Innings – Peach 23–6–36–4; Garland-Wells 7–1–25–0; Fender
23–8–53–5; Shepherd 2–1–1–0.

Umpires: J. Moss and W. A. Buswell.

Surrey won by 14 runs.

successful seasons – they had won the championship for the last two summers – and they lacked the charm and panache of Kent, a side that believed in attractive batting and slow bowling. Kent had acquired a deserved reputation as the most dazzling team in the land; they were the opponents every shrewd beneficiary chose for his benefit match because they always brought in the crowds. Ever since the start of the century Kent had never slipped below eighth place in the championship, and one of their strongest assets was their genuine commitment to going all out for victory, to make things happen by positive means. They were to lose this Surrey match when they temporarily mislaid that commitment.

The first day went according to plan for the championship leaders. Fender won the toss and he would have fielded had he the bowlers to capitalize on a wicket that favoured spin. He rightly reasoned that it was up to his batsmen to get a good enough score to enable him to attack Kent in the last innings when presumably the ball would be turning even more. After all 'Tich' Freeman was in his customary deadly form (he had just completed two hundred wickets for the season) and he would have been an awkward proposition on the final afternoon. Within a quarter of an hour, Freeman was on at the Pavilion End, with C.S. Marriott plying his leg-breaks and googlies at the Vauxhall End. Hobbs and Ducat were both out to catches at slip from sharply turning leg-breaks and at lunch Surrey were in trouble at 81 for 5. Fender, as usual, opted for a positive response and tried to hit the spinners out of the attack, but he soon cut a long-hop to deep point and retired, cursing himself. Marriott wrapped up the innings with three wickets in nine balls and already it seemed as if Kent were impregnable. Gover and Peach opened for Surrey and bowled poorly. Frank Woolley, another Kent man in matchless form, hit Fender for two sixes and a four in the over before tea and although he was soon out afterwards from a mishit, it did not seem to matter. Les Ames and his captain, Geoffrey Legge, settled down to a productive stand, and at the close Kent's lead was already 29 with six wickets in hand.

On the second day Fender tried all he knew to stem the flow of runs, but the wicket was now playing easier and the stand between Ames and Legge prospered. Ames off-drove superbly, Legge's cutting was deft, and it came as a surprise when the captain was out to a slip catch after they had added 111. Fender took the catch off a hard snick. In the opinion of *The Times*, it 'would have hit many another on the shins'. Fender was that kind of fieldsman. After that, Kent rather lost their way. Ames was unluckily run out, then Tom Longfield seemed to forget his handsome strokeplay that had impressed so much that season for Cambridge. Like his son-in-law Ted Dexter, he occasionally disappeared into a shell of technical self-absorption when the bowling was there for the taking. With Fender and Garland-Wells sticking gallantly to the task, Kent were winkled out and had to settle for a lead of 152 after they must have fancied at least three hundred.

When Hobbs and Sandham started off like a train Kent had their spinners on within half an hour. Hobbs engaged in a fascinating duel, playing well forward to smother the spin and rocking back whenever their length strayed. He made a beautiful hundred and, characteristically, gave away his wicket after he had passed three figures. Perhaps Hobbs was satisfied simply with the landmark; he had been upset a few days earlier when he had been passed over for the Gents v. Players game at Lord's. Hobbs had been out of action for several weeks with a torn thigh muscle and he had not been asked if he was fit for the big game. This glittering hundred showed what the Players' side would be missing when the game started across London in two days' time.

No one else in the Surrey side matched Hobbs' mastery that day. Sandham was trapped lbw, playing back to Freeman's straight one, then he had Ducat playing too soon and deep mid-off took the catch. When Gregory went first ball, Surrey were 215 for 7, a lead of just 63, with Fender and Peach the last remaining hopes. These two had enjoyed many a rollicking partnership over the years (including 171 in forty-two minutes against Northamptonshire in 1920), and they now garnered some valuable runs. Fender played the watchful role, while Peach hit well with an engagingly crooked bat. They managed at least to set Kent a target which was far from derisory, although 131 on a blameless pitch with such powerful batting was comfortably within their compass.

It had been a fascinating day. Great batting from Hobbs and over after over of fascinating slow bowling. Woolley could still nip in with valuable wickets with his left-arm spin, while Freeman was prodigious. Marriott was a fine bowler, with cunning flight and the patience to bowl well on wickets that favoured the batsmen. He played just one Test for England and hardly failed: 11 for 96 at the Oval against the West Indies in 1933. He was never picked again, one of the game's many enduring oddities. For thirteen years he shared his summer duties – enhancing Kentish glamour as well as coaching cricket at Dulwich College. He was a happy man, ideally suited for the temperamental trials of leg-spin. Marriott, Woolley and Freeman took eighteen of Surrey's twenty wickets in this match: such faith in slow bowling would baffle a modern captain.

Kent began the final day needing 131 to win. After heavy overnight rain, there was no play till 12.30. Fender, ever alert to the psychological nuances, brought all the Surrey side out to look at the wicket and indulged in agonized thumb-pressing. The Kent players watched from their dressing-room window, wondering if Fender was indulging in kidology. The hour before lunch must have reassured them. The roller was wet when it had finished with the pitch, but the dampness seemed to anaesthetize the surface and the ball did not misbehave at any stage. Fender opened with himself and Peach, wisely believing that he could not afford early waywardness from the young Gover. The Kent openers, Wally Hardinge and Bill Ashdown, seemed unperturbed. Hardinge, secure and reliable, was enjoying the best season of his career yet he hardly played a shot in the hour before lunch. He made thirteen while Ashdown scored 44 with a succession of beautiful offside strokes. In retrospect Kent should have crammed on at full speed in this first hour when the pitch was dead, but their openers were so experienced that they surely knew what they were doing. . . .

As the players filed out after lunch, Fender could be seen on his haunches, prodding away at the pitch. Was he trying to unnerve the batsmen or did he really see possibilities in it for the bowlers? At 58 for 0, Kent could afford to smirk at Fender's little foibles; even if the openers were to be parted, a dart or two from Frank Woolley would soon settle it. At 64, Fender got Ashdown and the real contest was on. Woolley had already passed 2000 runs for the season and he was to add another thousand more before its end – yet that was still not enough to gain him a place on the England tour to Australia that winter! He had learned of his omission the day before – strange that the England selectors in those days made up their minds with more than a month of the season still to go – and one can assume he was in the mood to work off his frustration with a few good blows in the dying overs of this game. He got to fourteen at his usual speed, then he was caught at slip off his gloves. A shame for the crowd, but there were still a few batsmen of class left who could be relied on to finish off the proceedings with a flourish. Hardinge was not one of them and his dismissal to a good catch at mid-on was a merciful relief for everyone.

Now the self-belief began to flood through Surrey's ranks. Peach bowled an immaculate length on the off-stump, bringing one back now and then and getting some lift. Fender went through his bewildering variations in spin and the fielding was keenness itself. Ames, Legge and Deed all went cheaply – and the way the two Old Malvernians sat on the splice while adding eleven singles was hardly in the great Kentish tradition. It was now 103 for 6, but surely the gifted young Valentine and the elegant Longfield had the strokes to clinch it? They had the shots but not the composure. At 105, Valentine ignored one of cricket's oldest maxims when he claimed a second run to a misfield by Sandham at mid-on. He was easily run out. Three wickets left, 26 needed. Longfield tried to hit his way out of the mess, but he lost Beslee at 116. At the same total, Gover caught Freeman from a skier at mid-off. In came Marriott, a batsman in the great traditions of hopelessness; in his career he was to make more wickets (724) than score runs (555). Such a man was not cut out for heroics against a side with the scent of victory in its nostrils, driven on by the best current captain. Without another run being added, Marriott was caught at mid-off and Kent had thrown it away.

They could not blame the wicket. Admittedly it was more difficult after lunch, but the sun never came out to turn a rain-affected pitch into a 'sticky wicket'. The warm atmosphere dried it out, but conditions were hardly hazardous. A good, solid professional would have grafted away perfectly comfortably on it. That is what Hardinge tried to do, but he neglected the opportunity to score off several loose deliveries before lunch, when the pitch was easy. The young amateurs brought up on perfect public-school wickets watched an experienced player struggling and probably came to the conclusion that the Oval pitch had become a demon. Deed, Legge, Longfield and Valentine were not up to this stern test of their temperaments while Ames, Ashdown and Woolley all got out at the wrong time.

Kent contrived to lose the game, with their last six wickets falling for thirteen runs, but it was Fender who first made them conceive of defeat. With subtle gamesmanship, the occasional histrionic gesture and some shrewd field placing, he let Kent think a target of 131 was difficult. It was not – but Fender was a great one for grabbing the opposition by the windpipe and asphyxiating them.

No one made more out of his meagre resources as captain than Percy Fender, yet he was never asked to captain England.

It proved to be a bad week for Kent. They lost the next match to Nottinghamshire by nine wickets, while Lancashire overtook them at the top of the table. That is how the championship ended and Kent were left to regret their uncharacteristic passivity in the Surrey match.

24
Queensland *v.* South Australia
1929

Few bowlers have done more than Clarrie Grimmett to win a game from a hopeless position, then throw it away in a moment of carelessness. Grimmett had taken a hat-trick when his side desperately needed it but then he gave away the match with two aberrations in a couple of seconds. With the last pair together and the scores level, Grimmett dropped a simple catch at cover point: to compound the felony, he shied the ball wildly in the direction of the bowler and it sped away for an overthrow. Queensland had won by one wicket and the villain of the piece was a man who invariably could be relied upon to do the sensible thing. Memories of Gerry Hazlitt came flooding back (chapter 16), but at least Hazlitt had the excuse of extreme, excitable youth. At the age of thirty-seven, Clarrie Grimmett only ever got excited when anyone suggested he ought to buy a drink.

By common consent, Grimmett was the shrewdest, most calculating Australian bowler of this century. Unlike Arthur Mailey, he did not believe in buying wickets with his leg-spin; accuracy and relentless pressure were his tools of the trade, plus a memory for weaknesses and a small degree of spin that was just enough to find the bat's edge. Grimmett did not believe in beating a man all ends up with an outrageous delivery, if that batsman was still at the crease after the cries of 'oh, hard luck, Clarrie' had died down. Bill O'Reilly, his friend and team-mate for many years, swears he never saw Grimmett bowl a long-hop – Arthur Mailey would average one an over. On each of his three trips to England, Grimmett took over a hundred wickets and he never showed any mercy on an opponent. He had taken years to break into regular first-

QUEENSLAND *v* SOUTH AUSTRALIA
At Brisbane, 22–26 February 1929

SOUTH AUSTRALIA

*V. Y. Richardson c O'Connor b Thurlow....	15	– b Hornibrook	25
G. W. Harris b Rowe.....................................	61	– lbw, b Oxenham.............	10
†A. T. Hack lbw, b Thurlow	1	– lbq, b Oxenham.............	0
H. E. P. Whitfield b Nothling.....................	5	– lbw, b Oxenham.............	65
W. C. Alexander b Oxenham.........................	66	– c O'Connor b Hornibrook	0
D. G. McKay run out......................................	4	– c Levy b Hornibrook......	40
M. D. Hutton b Oxenham	4	– c O'Connor b Nothling ..	7
C. V. Grimmett b Hornibrook	1	– b Oxenham.....................	4
T. W. Wall c Nothling b Hornibrook	3	– c Rowe b Hornibrook ...	13
J. D. Scott c Gough b Oxenham	4	– st O'Connor b Hornibrook ..	
		....	2
T. A. Carlton not out....................................	7	– not out...........................	10
B 12, l-b 1, n-b 1	14	B 2, l-b 4, n-b 1.......	7
	185		183

1/20 2/23 3/36 4/130 5/148
6/166 7/167 8/169 9/177

1/29 2/29 3/41 4/41 5/130
6/154 7/158 8/158 9/160

Bowling: *First Innings* – Hornibrook 18–3–48–2; Thurlow 12–1–40–2;
Nothling 7–1–21–1; Oxenham 19.1–5–30–3; Bensted 5–0–26–0; Rowe
4–0–6–1. *Second Innings* – Hornibrook 27.3–7–60–5; Thurlow 10–0–40–0;
Nothing 8–1–12–1; Oxenham 21–5–43–4; Bensted 3–1–5–0; Rowe
4–0–10–0; Thompson 3–1–6–0.

QUEENSLAND

*†L. P. D. O'Connor b Wall...............	2	– b Wall............................	19
C. A. McCoombe c Richardson b Wall..........	1	– c Whitfield b Wall	17
R. K. Oxenham c Hack b Wall.....................	2	– b Grimmett.....................	17
R. M. Levy c Harris b Wall	4	– not out............................	85
F. C. Thompson run out	37	– b Wall.............................	5
W. D. Rowe c McKay b Whitfield.................	2	– lbw, b Grimmett..............	0
Dr. O. E. Nothling c Wall b Grimmett..........	50	– lbw, b Grimmett..............	1
F. J. Gough c Hack b Grimmett.....................	21	– st Hack b Grimmett........	0
E. C. Bensted c Wall b Whitfield....................	40	– c Carlton b Grimmett.....	20
P. M. Hornibrook b Whitfield.......................	14	– b Carlton	8
H. M. Thurlow not out.................................	0	– not out............................	0
B 8, l-b 5, w l, n-b 1	15	B 2, l-b 6, n-b 1.......	9
	188		181

1/8 2/9 3/13 4/15 5/21 6/95
7/116 8/148 9/179

1/33 2/42 3/48 4/55 5/96
6/160 7/160 8/160 9/178

Bowling: *First Innings* – Wall 17–0–57–4; Whitfield 10.1–3–31–3; Scott
9–2–22–0; Carlton 8–2–14–0; Grimmett 15–3–49–2. *Second Innings* – Wall
13.4–2–57–3; Whitfield 6–0–33–0; Scott 6–0–25–0; Carlton 10–4–8–1;
Grimmett 17–4–49–5.

Umpires: J. P. Orr and J. Bartlett.

Queensland won by one wicket.

class cricket (he was thirty-three when he first played for Australia), and his burning desire to prove himself never left him. He may have looked inoffensive enough – small, wiry, always wearing a cap – but he was a fierce competitor. And a safe field anywhere, with a good pair of hands. If any player could be relied upon to keep his head during a tense finish, it would be Clarrie Grimmett.

When the two sides gathered on a rainy Friday in February 1929, they were playing simply for self-respect. New South Wales had already won the Sheffield Shield, but South Australia would finish second if they beat Queensland; if not, Victoria would steal in. When Vic Richardson won the toss he decided to bat, even though a lot of rain had fallen recently in the area. The wicket was slow, but reliable for batting and South Australia did not impress. The outfield was slow, but positive strokes were few and far between. Harris batted almost three hours, with just two boundaries. Alexander only hit one and batted 147 minutes. On a grey day, in poor light, it was hardly a promising harbinger for an exciting game.

It was considerably brighter the following day, when Queensland managed a lead of three runs on first innings, after being 21 for 5. The day closed with South Australia losing Harris and Hack for 29. Early on Wall bowled fast and with hostility as the batsmen misjudged the pace of the pitch. The partisan crowd cheered Hornibrook to the echo when he cover drove Wall for three to give them the lead; the noise suggested that Australia had just beaten England in a Test. Grimmett was hampered by the slow pitch and by bad catching, with three catches dropped off him in successive overs. Overall, it had been an interesting day with promise of more to come. The hysteria of the Brisbane crowd seemed disproportionate to the structure of the match, but one supposes that Sheffield Shield cricket had assumed a higher status that season, with Percy Chapman's England side thrashing the Australians by 4/1. In such circumstances, the Australian cricket fan seeks consolation elsewhere, rather than enjoy the efforts of the Poms.

Bowlers still reigned supreme on the third day. Queensland ended it on 80 for 4, needing another 101 to win. The day ended with honours still even, the result poised on the proverbial knife-edge. South Australia were disappointed to slump to 183 all out from 154 for 5, but Queensland stood at 48 for 3, then 55 for 4 when they batted late in the day. They were indebted to Roy Levy, a pugnacious little left-hander, for righting the ship and playing out time steadily in the company of Benstead. It took South Australia 287 minutes to make their 183, but the play was always absorbing and there seemed every prospect of a close finish.

Queensland got to 96 on the fourth morning before their fifth wicket fell, with Benstead turning Grimmett into the hands of short leg. Levy got to his fifty in 103 minutes, with his off-driving an impressive feature: at the age of twenty-two, he looked a fine prospect in his second game for the State. He and Oxenham looked well set as the score crept towards 150. Within the space of fifteen runs, Grimmett was rested, then brought back: he was the main hope of testing the batsmen's nerves with his testing accuracy and guile. At 160, with only 21 needed, he bowled Oxenham off his pads; he had played a valuable support innings, lasting eighty minutes. It was a pity he could not be there at the finish, but no doubt Levy would see them home. One ball later, the doubts began to flow as Rowe was lbw first ball. There were four balls left of Grimmett's over, but the umpires ruled that lunch had to be taken and the players trooped off with Grimmett on a hat-trick.

Thirty-five years later, Fred Trueman would lunch on a similar possibility, with the possible third wicket proving to be his three hundredth in Tests. The hat-trick did not materialize that day at the Oval, but at Brisbane in 1929 Grimmett made it. He had Gough stumped and had dragged South Australia back into the match when all had seemed lost. Eight for 160 and there was no better bowler around who could be relied upon to finish off the tail to snatch a victory. There would be no loose deliveries, just a relentless pressure on the batsmen from a master bowler.

Hornibrook had other ideas though. He had played nervelessly in the first innings and he relished the battle now. He blocked the last three balls of Grimmett's over, and did not worry when Levy took a single off the first ball of the next, and exposed him to the pace of Wall. He never saw the first three balls, but a run off a no-ball gave Levy the strike again and he responded by driving Wall for a splendid three. Hornibrook blocked the last ball and left Levy to face Grimmett; a single off the first ball left the number ten batsman to fend for himself again. The first six balls to Hornibrook were successfully negotiated, then Hornibrook on-drove Grimmett impressively to the boundary. Just ten runs needed and the crowd had sensed victory, despite Grimmett's parsimonious and threatening bowling.

Wall's next over saw six men posted in the slip area – yet

somehow Levy steered a single through the field. Next ball was played away through the leg-side cordon by Hornibrook for a single. Then Levy played uppishly through the slips for another single: on another day he would have been safely caught. Then an astonishing decision by Vic Richardson, the South Australian captain: he took off Grimmett and brought on the slow left arm of Carlton. It was the third time over a period of forty runs and an hour's play that Grimmett had been taken off, yet one would have thought he had done enough to stay on. He was surely the only bowler who could be relied upon to bowl properly in a tight situation; perhaps his costly aberration in the field later on stemmed from rumination over Vic Richardson's decision to take him out of the attack at a decisive stage. Perhaps the captain believed that a slow left-arm spinner had more of a chance against a left-hand bat (Levy), yet Grimmett could bowl the 'googly' at will. Better left-handers than Levy had been undone by it.

Levy played out a maiden from Carlton, then Hornibrook steered Wall away for a single. Levy then clipped Wall away for three, as two fielders desperately raced after the ball to stop it going to the boundary. Hornibrook deflected the next ball for one more and at the end of a costly over from Wall, two runs were needed to tie and three to win, with two wickets standing. Carlton bowled the next over and it was clear that Hornibrook wanted to finish the game in one stroke: he lunged at several deliveries and it was no surprise when he was bowled, smearing across the line at the sixth ball. Nine wickets down for 178 and Hugh Thurlow, a man with little batting pretensions, came in to partner Levy. If Queensland lost this one, Hornibrook would be to blame for not supporting the little left-hander. Thurlow did the necessary by blocking the last two balls of Carlton's over, and Levy then took up the cudgels. Wall bowled three balls in a row outside the off-stump and Levy ignored them as the crowd roared, 'Bowl on the wicket!' The fourth ball was in the appropriate area, but Levy played it calmly down through the slips for one run. Thurlow negotiated the rest of the over and Levy had to face Carlton. Off the second ball, he sneaked a single to mid-on and Thurlow played out the remaining six balls.

So the scores were level when Wall bowled to Levy. The field was well in by now; it was a case of a wicket or defeat. Levy left the first three deliveries as they passed by on the off-side, with the crowd baying for a wide. Off the fourth ball, Levy decided to chance his arm: he launched himself at an off-side delivery and hit it straight to Grimmett at cover point. Levy turned away in disgust, convinced that he had lost the game. To everyone's astonishment, Grimmett dropped the ball. The batsmen started to run, Grimmett threw the ball in a temper and it missed both bowler and stumps by several yards. Wall was not behind the stumps in the textbook fashion, but there was still no excuse for such a wild throw from such an experienced cricketer.

It seemed ironic that a twenty-two year-old with so little experience should play such a splendid, match-winning innings while a man of Grimmett's pragmatic nature should panic at the last gasp. Levy (199 minutes, seven boundaries) was carried from the pitch by the esctatic supporters, while Thurlow modestly accepted the plaudits for his supporting role. Irony has never been far from a perception of cricket's foibles, and Clarrie Grimmett never forgot the moment when his temperament let him down. He was still foxing first-class cricketers at the age of forty-eight, as the Second World War loomed and when he retired, he was garlanded with praise. Yet one moment in a frenetic finish in February 1929 underlined that even the coolest of cricketers can be subject to human frailties.

25
Yorkshire *v.* Nottinghamshire
1932

A glance at Hedley Verity's analysis in the second innings would suggest that the batsmen had been afflicted by a form of creeping palsy. How else to justify the fall of ten wickets after lunch for 29 runs in seventy minutes? In his last three overs Verity took 7 for 3, including the hat-trick, and twice he took two wickets in two balls. The wicket, of course, helped Verity: it was drying out after an overnight thunderstorm. Yet why did he get the full hand, while Bill Bowes and George Macaulay went unrewarded at the other end? Those two were hardly shrinking violets when it came to picking up cheap wickets, and no Yorkshire side would ever have conspired to ensure one man took all ten wickets. It would also be wrong to lambast the batting. At that time Nottinghamshire had one of the best batting line-ups in county cricket: their last five in the order eventually made twenty-five hundreds in first-class cricket and there was not a rabbit to be seen. At this stage of the 1932 season, Nottinghamshire were lying in third place behind Yorkshire and Kent. They were a stern test. Until the first hour after lunch on the final day, they more than held their own.

Yet Hedley Verity was in a class of his own when it came to wrapping up an innings when conditions favoured him. This was only his second full season, yet at the age of twenty-seven, he was already the finished product as a left-arm spinner. Verity had learned much from Wilfred Rhodes in the pivotal season of 1930 when Rhodes eased himself out to allow Verity to get valuable experience. He clearly kept his ears open when the old taskmaster spoke: Verity varied his pace according to the condition of the wicket, tossing it up and going for extra spin when it was wet or

YORKSHIRE v NOTTINGHAMSHIRE
At Leeds, 9–12 July 1932

NOTTINGHAMSHIRE

W. W. Keeton b Rhodes	9	– c Macaulay b Verity	21
F. W. Shipston b Macaulay	8	– c Wood b Verity	21
W. Walker c Barber b Bowes	36	– c Macaulay b Verity	11
*Mr. A. W. Carr c Barber b Verity	0	– c Barber b Verity	0
A. Staples b Macaulay	3	– c Macaulay b Verity	7
C. B. Harris lbw, b Leyland	35	– c Holmes b Verity	0
G. V. Gunn b Verity	31	– lbw, b Verity	0
†B. Lilley not out	46	– not out	3
H. Larwood b Leyland	48	– c Sutcliffe b Verity	0
W. Voce b Leyland	0	– c Holmes b Verity	0
S. J. Staples b Leyland	0	– st Wood b Verity	0
B 8, l-b 6, w 2, n-b 2	18	B 3, n-b 1	4
	234		**67**

1/15 2/15 3/40 4/46 5/67 6/120 7/159 8/233
9/233

1/44 2/47 3/51 4/63 5/13
6/63 7/64 8/64 9/67

Bowling: *First Innings* – Bowles 31–9–55–1; Rhodes 28–8–49–1; Verity 41–13–64–2; Macaulay 24–10–34–2; Leyland 8.2–3–14–4. *Second Innings* – Bowes 5–0–19–0; Verity 19.4–16–10–10; Macaulay 23–9–34–0.

YORKSHIRE

P. Holmes b Larwood	65	– not out	77
H. Sutcliffe c Voce b Larwood	0	– not out	54
A. Mitchell run out	24		
M. Leyland b Voce	5		
W. Barber c and b Larwood	34		
*Mr. A. B. Sellers b A. Staples	0		
†A. Wood b Larwood	1		
A. C. Rhodes c A. Staples b Voce	3		
H. Verity b Larwood	12		
G. G. Macaulay not out	8		
W. E. Bowes not out	1		
B 5, l-b 5	10	B 4, 1-b 4	8
(9 wickets) *	163	(0 wickets)	139

*Innings declared closed.

1/1 2/37 3/122 5/125 6/128 7/135 8/152
9/154

Bowling: *First Innings* – Larwood 22–4–73–5; Voce 22–2–52–2; S. J. Staples 7–2–8–0; A. Staples 11–3–20–1. *Second Innings* – Larwood 3–0–14–0; Voce 10–0–43–0; S. J. Staples 18.4–5–37–0; A. Staples 6–1–25–0; Harris 3–0–12–0.

Umpires: H. G. Baldwin and W. Reeves.

Yorkshire won by ten wickets.

breaking up, or bowling slow/medium on fast pitches. He had an inswinging yorker that was reminiscent of George Hirst, and he went about his job in a quiet undemonstrative way. Hedley Verity was the only English bowler who consistently tested Don Bradman to the full on all wickets, because, as Bradman acknowledged, 'There was no breaking point with him.' The only modern equivalent in pace and controlled mastery is Derek Underwood, yet even in his pomp on uncovered wickets, Underwood could not match Verity's record. In each of his nine full seasons, he took 150 wickets and he averaged 185. On a statistical basis Verity is the bowler of the century, with 1956 wickets at the incredibly low average of 14.87 in a decade of batting largesse on generally placid wickets. Seven times he took nine wickets in an innings as well as all ten twice.

The weather played right into Verity's hands for the Nottinghamshire match. Over the weekend it was the hottest since August 1930 and clearly thunderstorms were in the air. Nottinghamshire realized that, so they occupied the crease for 132 overs on the opening day and crawled to 234. The wicket was dry and easy-paced, and Verity showed his value as a stock bowler by taking 2 for 64 in 41 overs. He was simply tireless, nagging and cunning when the batsmen held the aces; when he had the whiphand he was as deadly as any bowler in history. It took some bright hitting by Harold Larwood to brighten up the Nottinghamshire innings. He came in at 150 for 7 and added 74 in eight-five minutes with Ben Lilley. Larwood's huge six and four other boundaries again confirmed he was a handy bat; on Monday he would show his more publicized ability.

Off the third ball of the second morning Larwood had Herbert Sutcliffe caught at third slip. Sutcliffe had made his hundredth hundred in the previous game and his was still the prized Yorkshire wicket. Larwood had his tail up and Arthur Mitchell had to retire hurt after he had struck him on the back of the right hand. Wilf Barber and Percy Holmes rallied with a stand of 85, but Holmes was bowled leg-stump and Larwood swept through the batting. By the time a cloudburst washed out play at 3.55, Larwood had taken 5 for 73 (including 3 for 3 after lunch) and Yorkshire were struggling at 163 for 9, still 71 behind. It was hard to see how they could manufacture a win against some tough opposition, led by that granite man, Arthur Carr. Some sides at that time were beaten psychologically by Yorkshire before they ever walked on the pitch, but not Nottinghamshire. Between 1925–31, they had never fnished out of the top five in the table, and Arthur Carr captained the side with a blend of unyielding toughness and finesse that even Yorkshiremen admired.

However Carr could do nothing about the storms that lashed the North of England for the next twelve hours. In just five hours, 4.92 inches flooded Cranwell in Lincolnshire, as much rain as usually fell throughout the whole of July and August. The Leeds area took the full brunt – hardly surprising given the intense, clammy heat of recent days – and that surely meant there would be no more play in the Nottinghamshire game. Astonishingly, a warm drying wind and wonderful work by the groundstaff permitted play to start only an hour late at 12.30. The Nottingham-shire players could hardly believe it. For their part Yorkshire knew they had the match won, as long as Hedley Verity did himself justice.

Yorkshire promptly declared and put the onus on their opponents. They could opt simply to bat out the rest of the day, taking five points for the first innings lead, or get some quick runs for a declaration and hope to bowl out Yorkshire as the wicket deteriorated. The top three (Kent, Yorkshire and Nottinghamshire) were separated by just twenty-eight points, though Nottingham-shire had two games in hand. It seemed logical that Arthur Carr would want to deny Yorkshire a chance of victory, so he would try for a draw by occupying the crease. Whatever the permutations, defeat seemed out of the question for Carr and his men, barring a miracle. Time was not on Yorkshire's side and Carr would not make things easy for them.

The hour's play before lunch confirmed that Nottinghamshire were looking for a quiet time at the crease, a chance to boost their batting averages and a sedate draw. Although Keeton hooked Bowes for three and then four in his first over, they did not take any risks. At lunch they were 38 for 0, with Keeton and Shipston both on 18 and in no real trouble. Verity had needed close atten-tion, as seven successive maiden overs suggested, but he had not as yet turned the ball disconcertingly on the soft, sluggish wicket.

Something freakish happened over lunchtime to freshen up the pitch. Perhaps it was the gradual drying process that meant the ball would now turn and lift. Perhaps it was the quality of Verity's bowling. He settled in to a mesmerizing groove, making class batsmen play at deliveries they should have either left alone or played differently. Verity just dripped away at the stone like a Chinese water torturer and he would not let go. His flight was a teasing masterpiece and when the ball pitched, his powerful finger spin made it fizz away from the right-hander – always the delivery that gets a good player.

Immediately after lunch, it was clear that Verity expected the ball to turn a good deal more. He doubled the slip cordon and Macaulay caught Keeton there at 44. At the other end Macaulay started to bowl around the wicket to two slips and two short legs, turning his off-break sharply into the right-hander. It would not be long before he started to harvest a few victims: these were the kind of conditions he exploited so skilfully. Judging by the hurried, late adjustments indulged in by Willis Walker, the pitch was now very difficult for batting, but Walker would not give away his wicket. He watched Shipston caught at the wicket, then his captain collected a 'pair'. Carr was out in almost the same way as the first innings, beautifully caught in front of the sightscreen by Barber. It was typical boldness by Carr; a man who had hit forty-eight sixes in 1925 had enough confidence to try to hit his way out of trouble and break Verity's stranglehold. No one could blame him for the attempt.

At 63 for 3, Walker played a perfectly sound defensive stroke, but the ball turned at the very last instant, took the edge and flew low to Macaulay's right hand at first slip. Next ball, Charlie Harris went the same way, caught at second slip. George Gunn's son, George Vernon, came in and was lbw to a ball of good length that shot through low. A hat-trick to Verity and soon he almost did it again. At 64 for 6 he got Arthur Staples, then Larwood was superbly caught by Sutcliffe, running back from extra cover after Larwood had followed Arthur Carr's bold policy. Verity's hat-trick ball was the first of his nineteenth over and Ben Lilley snicked it over the slips for three fortuitous runs. The reprieve was short-lived, as Verity polished off Bill Voce and Sam Staples in successive deliveries. He could not go for another hat-trick because he had dismissed everyone. The analysis of 10 for 10 remains a world record to this day for a bowler taking all ten wickets, surpassing George Geary's 10 for 18 in 1929. Since lunch Verity's figures read: 12.4 – 9 – 10 – 10. He took seven wickets in his final three overs, and the only scoring stroke was that snick for three by Ben Lilley. In contrast Macaulay bowled twenty-three overs and went empty-handed on a pitch ideally suited to him.

The game had been won and lost in three overs by Verity. The stuffing was knocked out of Nottinghamshire and Voce and Larwood held no terrors for Holmes and Sutcliffe as they embarked on the target of 139. They cruised home in ninety-five minutes, and Yorkshire went to the top of the table. They stayed there for the rest of the summer.

It seems strange now to read the hosannahs of praise that rained down on Yorkshire for declaring on the final morning. Neville Cardus, writing in the *Manchester Guardian*, declared, 'It is good to hear a trumpet call to decisive action sounding from out of the North. The victory will do more good to cricket than anything else that has happened to it for years. Here was the pre-war gesture, here was cricket of the spirit which once on a time made the game a theme for poets.' One gets used to Cardus going elegantly over the top, but in the same edition, a *Guardian* editorial praised the boldness of Yorkshire. Hardly a mention of Verity's wondrous exploits, it was all about the bold declaration. Well modern cricket has its justified detractors, but I cannot think of any county captain who would not have done the same today in similar circumstances. It was the only way to win the game, with time running out and the championship race hotting up. So why all the fuss about declaring behind? Could it be that first-class cricket in 1932 was hidebound by conservatism and safety-first policies? Perish the thought! We are always being told that the players of yesteryear were more dynamic, glamorous and talented. Must be true. . . .

Hedley Verity was certainly not glamorous nor dynamic, simply equipped with a great talent for being able to bowl at the right speed for the appropriate pitch. He was the fourth member of that great slow left-arm tradition associated with Yorkshire – from Edmund Peate in 1879, through to Bobby Peel, Wilfred Rhodes, ending in 1939 with Verity. His last day on a county ground saw him take 7 for 9 against Sussex. That was 1 September, 1939; exactly four years later, his death was announced. Captain Hedley Verity of the Green Howards was shot by a sniper in Sicily while guiding his men towards a ridge. His last words were: 'Keep going, keep going.' Every batsman who had been tormented by this great bowler knew that Hedley Verity always kept going.

26
Leicestershire *v.*
Warwickshire
1936

A great cricket match should encapsulate many varied emotions preferably ending in a thrilling, nerve-tingling finish. This match satisfied all the basic requirements, as Leicestershire's last pair added eleven runs on a bowler's wicket to win by a solitary wicket. For George Geary it was a game of contrasting emotions. His side won at the last gasp, he took 12 for 12 in a single day, as well as top scoring in Leicestershire's first innings. Unfortunately for Geary's pocket, this was also his benefit game, and his all-round efforts were so outstanding that only a smattering of spectators bothered to turn up on the final day. With the weather cold and rainy throughout, it was hardly ideal for cricket watchers. As a result George Geary picked up precisely £10 from his benefit match.

That was hard on a great player and vastly popular man. At the age of forty-two, Geary needed some security. Not even a man of his inexhaustible stamina could expect to last much longer in first-class cricket, and county clubs had a deserved reputation for casting great servants aside when their powers seemed on the wane. At that time, the beneficiary had to bear the whole expenses of his chosen match. He had to pay players, umpires, scorers, policemen, gatemen and the travelling expenses for the opposition – as well as fork out for his own team's expenses when they played the return fixture that season. The beneficiary did not always have a free hand with the fixture list, because some county clubs preferred to pocket the money from profitable games. During the Depression days in the 1930s, it was common for a county club to suggest a ten per cent reduction in wages among the professionals, and other clubs were circularized to find out what they were paying. The

LEICESTERSHIRE *v* WARWICKSHIRE
At Hinckley, 23–26 May 1936

WARWICKSHIRE

N. Kilner c Smith b Geary	14	– b Smith	15
A. J. W. Croom not out	69	– c Smith b Shipman	1
W. A. Hill lbw (N), b Smith	0	– c Marlow b Geary	7
*Mr. R. E. S. Wyatt b Smith	1	– b Geary	19
F. R. Santall b Smith	4	– c Geary b Smith	19
H. E. Dollery b Prentice	17	– lbw, b Geary	0
G. A. E. Paine b Geary	1	– c and b Geary	7
†J. A. Smart b Geary	0	– c Marlow b Geary	2
J. H. Mayer lbw, b Geary	5	– lbw, b Geary	1
W. E. Hollies b Geary	4	– b Geary	0
W. E. Fantham b Geary	1	– not out	4
B 9, l-b 7, w 1	17	B 2, l-b 1	3
	133		**78**

1/21 2/26 3/28 4/32 5/60 6/63 7/63
8/91 9/117 10/133

1/2 2/22 3/28 4/58 5/62 6/62
7/70 8/73 9/73 10/78

Bowling: *First Innings* – Smith 21–5–57–3; Geary 25.5–12–36–6; Astill 1–1–0–0; Prentice 6–1–23–1. *Second Innings* – Smith 16–2–48–2; Geary 13.3–8–7–7; Shipman 2–0–10–1; Marlow 2–0–10–0.

LEICESTERSHIRE

A. W. Shipman b Mayer	14	– b Wyatt	5
L. G. Berry lbw (N), b Mayer	6	– lbw, b Hollies	18
N. F. Armstrong lbw, b Wyatt	0	– c Smart b Mayer	15
F. T. Prentice b Hollies	23	– c Wyatt b Mayer	0
G. S. Watson c Wyatt b Mayer	0	– c Paine b Hollies	6
*Mr. C. S. Dempster b Hollies	11	– not out	32
G. Geary c Wyatt b Hollies	25	– lbw, b Hollies	0
W. E. Astill b Hollies	9	– lbw, b Hollies	1
H. A. Smith b Mayer	5	– c Santall b Hollies	14
W. H. Marlow c Croom b Mayer	13	– b Hollies	6
†P. Corrall not out	0	– not out	0
L-b 2	2	B 4, l-b 3	7
	108	(9 wkts.)	**104**

1/13 2/14 3/22 4/22 5/41 6/60 7/88
8/93 9/103 10/108

1/15 2/37 3/38 4/38 5/49
6/69 7/69 8/87 9/93

Bowling: *First Innings* – Mayer 10.4–3–19–5; Wyatt 9–2–16–1; Paine 6–0–34–0; Hollies 10–4–19–4; Fantham 2–0–18–0. *Second Innings* – Mayer 19–4–35–2; Wyatt 5–0–23–1; Hollies 20.1–10–39–6.

Umpires: G. Beet and G. M. Lee.

Leicestershire won by one wicket.

hard-pressed professional had to hope he could hang on for a benefit, then get lucky with the weather and the opposition. It would not be in his best interests if a rain-affected wicket led to a batting lottery and a two-day defeat for either side: the club would not be terribly sympathetic just because the bowlers had done their job properly.

So George Geary wanted to fare well but not so well that the game would be over early. That was a difficult circle to square for such a gifted, whole-hearted cricketer. He and Ewart Astill had shouldered the burden of match-winning bowlers and reliable batsmen for more than twenty years; without these two, Leicestershire would have dropped out of county cricket. If Astill was the better bat, Geary was the better bowler. Tall and powerful, he had a fast-medium style with a beautiful action. Off a short run, his stock ball would move in off the seam, but he also bowled the leg-cutter and the occasional straight one. Geary could use the shine of the new ball profitably and bowl all day when the batsmen were on top: in the Melbourne Test of the 1928/9 series, he took 5 for 105 in eighty-one overs in exhausting heat. Such a man was the very best type of cricket professional – cheerful, talented and a wonderful support to a young amateur captain. R. E. S. Wyatt, who played in this match, likened Geary's bowling style to that of Alec Bedser: 'George was not quite so quick, but they both had a beautiful action and great variety. Both had short run-ups and used their full height at delivery. I always felt the experts were wrong to compare Alec Bedser to Maurice Tate: for me, Alec's model was George Geary.'

Even George's genial nature took a knock when he arrived at the Hinckley ground for the start of his benefit match. It was bitterly cold, with rain in the air and just about two hundred turned up, when at least five thousand would have been there given fine weather. Only eighty minutes' play was possible, in which Warwickshire struggled to 60 for 5. Geary began with an uncharacteristic wide, but he soon settled into his customary groove. At the other end Haydon Smith, tall, right-arm fast, was a handful as he made the ball rear up from a good length. The spasmodic showers kept the wicket fresh, and Warwickshire could not have been sorry to see a heavy drizzle wipe out play just after tea.

It was still cold and gloomy on the Monday, but at least the rain kept away. The two thousand souls who braved the elements saw a remarkable day's cricket, in which twenty-nine wickets fell

for three hundred runs. It ended with Leicestershire on 41 for 4,
needing another 63 to win. The day belonged to Geary in more
ways than one – 12 for 12 in the day, 13 for 43 in the match and
the top score when he alone realized the bowlers had to be
attacked. He hit the first three balls after lunch to the boundary,
then belted two sixes off Fantham, as every run proved precious.
Warwickshire would have been lost without Croom's unbeaten 69,
the fourth time he had carried out his bat. Yet Leicestershire fared
little better against the pace of Danny Meyer and the accurate leg-
spin of Eric Hollies. They lost all ten wickets in ninety-five minutes,
and a lead of 25 looked as if it might prove crucial.

Geary had already found a spot at the Pavilion End in the first
innings, and now he proceeded to work his way through the second
innings. He came on at 16 and was soon hitting that troublesome
spot. For a quarter of an hour before the tea interval, it looked as
if Wyatt and Santall had worked him out, but that was illusory:
the last five wickets went down for fifteen. The innings only lasted
a hundred minutes and Geary had once more shown his mastery.
Yet his brilliance had scuppered his chance of a bumper crowd
on the third day. The last fifty minutes of the second day saw
Leicestershire lose four wickets and judged by the regularity of
dismissals so far, the game would be all over by lunch the following
day. The canny folk around this mining town would not be
throwing good brass away on an hour or so of cricket.

It took eighty minutes to finish it – and a grand game of cricket
it turned out to be. Unfortunately for George Geary, the takings
at the gate were minimal and he could barely cover his expenses.
He was also out first ball at a particularly tense stage – whatever
happened to the 'one off the mark' for the beneficiary? That went
by the wayside when there was a match to be won. Geary's
dismissal left Leicestershire 35 adrift, with seven men gone. Eric
Hollies was bowling his nagging leg-spin from the end where Geary
wrought havoc, while Meyer kept the batsmen quiet at his end by
an immaculate length. Leicestershire had just one trump card left:
Stewart Dempster was still in, and as long as he was there, the
game could be won. Dempster had never been coached, but he still
remains one of New Zealand's greatest batsmen. He captained
Leicestershire for three seasons, each time heading the batting averages, and he left behind memories of an attractive, attacking style.
At the start of this game he was heading the national averages, yet
he was struggling to come to terms with the vagaries of the wicket.

In the first six overs of the final day he faced twenty-four balls and managed just three singles – not Dempster's usual rate of progress.

When Geary was out, the captain continued to play cautiously and left the hitting to his fast bowler, Haydon Smith. He buffeted fourteen of the next eighteen with some unorthodox blows until Hollies had him caught by fine leg, running towards square leg. Marlow pulled the first ball he received from Hollies to the boundary, then added a couple of singles. Marlow, a left-hand bat, was a useful performer – three years earlier he had added 157 for the last wicket with Ewart Astill against Gloucestershire, and he was an ideal man to support Dempster in the tense final stages. The tension was now afflicting both sets of players: at 93, Marlow popped up an easy return catch to Hollies, but to everyone's astonishment, Hollies stumbled, his hand bumped into his knee and he spilled the easiest of chances. Yet Marlow did not learn from this escape. He swung wildly at the very next delivery and his stumps were shattered.

So Leicestershire needed eleven more, with only Paddy Corrall, the wicket-keeper, left to help Dempster. Somehow Corrall survived the rest of Hollies' over and the perilous way he negotiated it seemed to have convinced the captain that he had to win the match before Hollies got to Corrall again. Off the first ball of Meyer's over, he straight drove a magnificent six, a considerable feat against a bowler of Meyer's pace and control. Possibly Dempster had made up his mind to play the shot if it landed in the right slot, but it worked. He then cut Meyer for two, stole a quick single and got up the other end to face Hollies. Warwickshire now realized that they had to dismiss Dempster to win the match and they crowded him. The first ball of Hollies' over was on-driven for two and a thrilling game was over. Dempster had batted more than an hour and a half for 32 not out, and he had guided his team from the ruins of 69 for 7 on a pitch that heavily favoured the bowlers. It had never recovered from its weekend soaking and Hollies was a particular handful on the final day. He never bowled a loose ball, a great performance from a leg-spinner, especially one so young.

Half a century later, R. E. S. Wyatt looked back on this game and told me, 'It serves to illustrate the fact that the game is much more interesting when the wickets aren't covered. Low-scoring matches are often absorbing.' Amen to that; a judicious display of batting from a fine player proved decisive in a game where only two men scored more than thirty. Croom's performance was admirable; 1936 was also his benefit year and, like George Geary, his match against Sussex was badly disrupted by rain. The beneficiary did not even manage to get a bat and the takings were derisory. Luckily for Croom, Warwickshire were rather more supportive of their beneficiaries than other counties and a few fund-raising activities brought him the sum of £679. Geary was less fortunate, but he was not the kind of man who bemoans his luck.

For George Geary, the chance to play the game he loved all round the world was enough of a blessing. He carried this cheerful resilience into retirement and became a superb coach at Charterhouse School. His pride and joy there was Peter May, who always paid generous tribute to the inspirational qualities of a much-loved man. Anyone who knew George Geary will testify that he did not need a lucrative benefit to possess life's riches.

27
Somerset *v*. Gloucestershire
1938

When you are the sole hope of the side during a last-wicket stand, it helps if you have nerves of steel and the ability to inspire your partner. If you have been told by the medical experts that batting is totally unsuitable for your health, then you have every good reason for approaching the task with all the enthusiasm of a turkey in December. Yet Wally Luckes managed consistently to steer Somerset to unlikely victories from his bunker in the late order. In this match, he did it by hitting two boundaries off the third and fourth balls of the final over. It was a magnificent climax to a great game and no more than Somerset had come to expect from a man who ought not to have been playing cricket for a living.

Wally Luckes was always a neat, unobtrusive wicket-keeper, with a penchant for natty leg-side stumpings that stamped his class on the proceedings. In a more glamorous side than Somerset's, he might have played for England, but he was content to render twenty-five years' service of a consistently high standard. Yet he ought to have been lost to the county game in his early years on the staff: doctors warned him that the stresses of batting would only aggravate an already delicate constitution. He missed many games in the early 1930s and re-appeared on the understanding that he would concentrate solely on his wicket-keeping and that batting would not occupy his attention. All very well, but Wally Luckes had a streak of cussedness that never allowed him to accept such a subdued role. He made himself into one of the best lower order batsmen in English cricket in the thirties. Once or twice he managed to inveigle a place higher than ten or eleven and he then showed his true colours – for example, his 121 not out against

SOMERSET v GLOUCESTERSHIRE
At Taunton, 4–7 June 1938

GLOUCESTERSHIRE

Mr. B. O. Allen c Lyon b Hazell	52	– run out	28
C. J. Barnett lbw b Wellard	41	– c and b Wellard	0
G. M. Emmett b Wellard	18	– lbw b Wellard	6
*Mr. W. R. Hammond c Luckes b Hazell	6	– not out	140
J. F. Crapp b Buse	33	– b Wellard	29
W. L. Neale c Luckes b Hazell	13	– c Luckes b Wellard	6
Mr. B. H. Lyon c Gimblett b Hazell	0	– c Longrigg b Hazell	88
R. A. Sinfield b Wellard	0	– not out	0
†A. E. Wilson b Andrews	38	– c Andrews b Kinnersley	32
C. J. Scott lbw b Andrews	9		
L. M. Cranfield not out	5		
B 1, l-b 3, w 1, n-b 1	6	B 4, l-b 3, n-b 2	9
	221	(7 wkts. dec.)	338

1/68 2/108 3/116 4/120 5/150 6/150 7/150
8/195 9/204

1/9 2/25 3/54 4/96 5/119
6/280 7/338

Bowling: *First Innings* – Wellard 30–6–77–3; Andrews 15.1–0–48–2; Buse 17–4–48–1; Hazell 16–2–42–4. *Second Innings*: Wellard 32–7–85–4; Andrews 13–1–76–0; Buse 27–6–86–0; Hazell 27–6–72–1; Kinnersley 5–2–10–1.

SOMERSET

H. Gimblett c Wilson b Emmett	67	– c Allen b Sinfield	7
F. S. Lee lbw b Sinfield	56	– c Allen b Barnett	18
Mr. M. D. Lyon b Hammond	48	– lbw b Barnett	19
H. T. F. Buse c Wilson b Scott	27	– c Emmett b Hammond	79
*Mr. E. F. Longrigg c Hammond b Sinfield	7	– b Sinfield	24
Mr. J. W. Seamer c Allen b Scott	23	– run out	34
W. H. R. Andrews c Wilson b Barnett	6	– c Barnett b Emmett	2
Mr. K. C. Kinnersley c Allen b Scott	12	– c and b Emmett	7
A. W. Wellard b Hammond	21	– c Barnett b Scott	68
†W. T. Luckes lbw b Scott	2	– not out	18
H. L. Hazell not out	0	– not out	0
B 1, l-b 4, w 1, n-b 1	7	B 7, l-b 1	8
	276	(9 wkts.)	284

1/98 2/174 3/174 4/186 5/220 6/231 7/245
8/262 9/268

1/22 2/32 3/50 4/181 5/154
6/157 7/172 8/253 9/276

Bowling: *First Innings* – Hammond 33.2–8–64–2; Scott 19–2–42–4; Sinfield 39–20–57–2; Barnett 10–1–21–1; Cranfield 6–0–33–0; Emmett 9–1–52–1. *Second Innings* – Hammond 17–3–57–1; Scott 15–3–51–1; Sinfield 29.4–10–68–2; Barnett 17–5–50–2; Cranfield 2–0–5–0; Emmett 6–0–36–2; Neale 2–0–9–0.

Umpires: A. Dolphin and E. Robinson.

Somerset won by one wicket.

Kent in 1937 from the lofty position of number five. Later in this 1938 season, he made 90 not out at number ten against Leicestershire in the Bath Festival. At the age of thirty-seven, there was no man more likely to sell his wicket dearly from such a low position in the order.

This local derby over Whitsuntide 1938 represented the very best of county cricket. A continual ebb and flow of fortunes, some spectacular batting, gallant bowling and a great finish. All this in perfect weather: a prolonged drought over Europe followed by recent rains had led to the breaking up of some county pitches, with the result that a batsman could never really believe he was in for a long time. There was always the chance that a bowler would turn the game upside down in the space of a few overs and, as a result, interest never flagged. Add the spice of two rivals from the same part of the country and the ingredients were there for a gripping struggle. On the first day, Charlie Barnett showed the kind of form he was soon to display against Australia in the Trent Bridge Test, when he just missed a hundred before lunch. Barnett made 41 out of 68 for the first wicket, but the medium-pace of Wellard and the pinpoint accuracy of Hazell's left-arm spin picked up five wickets for 34 in fifty minutes after lunch. Hammond, with a thousand runs under his belt already, was cheered all the way to the wicket in recognition of his ascent to the England captaincy, but he was soon picked up by the reliable Luckes, and Neale and Lyon went in the same over. Bev Lyon's brother fared rather better when Somerset batted. 'Dar' Lyon, as he was known, was home on leave from Gambia, where he was a magistrate, and he gave a tantalizing glimpse of the batting grandeur he had shown a decade earlier when he was one of the best uncapped players in the country. Lyon had missed out on county cricket for the previous three seasons as he built up his legal career and, although he was now thirty-seven, his power in the drive remained undimmed. He finished on 43 not out from half an hour's batting, as Somerset ended up 167 for 1, with the prospect of a handy lead. Harold Gimblet had hammered 67 out of 98 in ninety minutes, including three superb straight sixes, and the tempo did not slacken when he was out.

Yet Somerset fell away on the second day. Lyon did not last very long, and Frank Lee laboured for two hours and twenty-five minutes. Somerset went into the lead with just three wickets down, but a spell of 3 for 8 by the young fast bowler Colin Scott brought

Gloucestershire back into the game after lunch. The lead was a disappointing 55, but when half the Gloucestershire side were out for 119 that Somerset collapse was put in perspective. Unfortunately for them, one of the not-out batsmen was W. R. Hammond. He was determined to make up for his first innings failure, and the presence of an eight thousand crowd on Bank Holiday and the need to maintain his marvellous form with the Australian series imminent both combined to bring out the best from a prince among batsmen. He gave one very difficult chance to Wellard at point when he had made 31 but that was all. At the close, Hammond was 83 not out, Lyon 24 and Gloucestershire 183 for 5, a lead of 128. The Somerset fielding had been excellent, the cricket gripping, but the genius of one man could make all the difference.

On the third morning, Hammond cruised to his sixth hundred of the season, a summer that saw him make thirteen in all, plus 3000 runs. He seemed to have reached the full ripening of his maturity, and there appeared no earthly reason why he would not make a century every time he glided majestically to the crease. That summer he made seven hundreds in eight successive innings, and the grandeur of his batting was a genuine palliative to the worrying news coming out of Europe every day. During this game David Lloyd George had addressed an open-air meeting at Stafford in which he railed at the Government for appeasing the dictators of Europe and undermining the integrity and power of the League of Nations. The word 'appeasement' was to recur time after time during the uneasy summer of 1938 – almost as much as a Hammond century.

Hammond declared at lunchtime, asking Somerset to get 283. Gimblett and Lee went before they had passed 32, and when Lyon was out lbw the score was 50 for 3. Yet those runs had come in fifty minutes, and if only someone could stay there long enough to anchor the innings there was still hope for Somerset. Bertie Buse was that man. He was never a stylish player – all crouching, ungainly discomfort – but Bertie Buse never gave his wicket away unwittingly. When Arthur Wellard came out to join him at 172 for 7, the target was 112 with a possible sixty-five minutes left. The pairing was ideal, as Buse manipulated the bowling for ones and twos, while Wellard simply smashed it out of sight. Wellard was to take 172 wickets in 1938, as well as hit fifty sixes. He played for England against Australia at Lord's, which was no more than his due for a typically wholehearted season. One quarter of his runs in his career came in sixes and in this innings, we saw six of them, plus five other boundaries. Two of them came in succession off Emmett, another off Sinfield went into the car park, one into the scorers' box and – revenge for yesterday's dropped catch – one off Hammond disappeared out of the ground. When Wellard was caught in the deep (and what a characteristic way to go) he had hit 68 out of 81 in forty minutes. Buse had rocketed from 58 to 66 during that time. Now he had to break out of his three-hour vigil and steer the side home. The target was thirty in twenty-five minutes. When Buse left at 276, five minutes remained and eight runs were needed. There was time for just one more over and the frail Wally Luckes and the roly-poly Horace Hazell knew they would not get them in singles.

Hazell had that engaging, comfortable air of a Somerset farmer who had just wandered onto the ground from a cattle auction and fancied a bit of a game with his mates out there in the middle. Appearances were deceptive: he may have enjoyed a couple of bottles of Bass at lunchtime, but that never lead to prodigality when he bowled. He was a grudging spinner who saw no pleasure in the ball disappearing back over his head into the River Tone. Equally he saw no reason why he should not hang around at the crease when he batted. At that time he was the best number eleven in county cricket, having persuaded Luckes he could go up one rung in the order. Hazell had an impeccable forward defensive stroke, an excellent cover drive and the placid temperament that would always see his partner to his hundred or the side to a narrow win. Truly Somerset had the ideal men out there as the final over started.

The bowler was to be Reg Sinfield, a talented off-spinner about to make his England debut at Trent Bridge and dismiss Don Bradman into the bargain. For the past decade Sinfield had prospered in similar circumstances, and he would not bowl badly over the next few minutes. Would the batsmen risk losing a local derby, or would they consider a bowler of Sinfield's class too problematical? The first two deliveries yielded no clue as Luckes blocked them. The third was driven straight back past the bowler, a lovely low skimmer that cracked against the pickets. Three balls to go, four to win. Would Sinfield fire it in? To his eternal credit, he went for the dismissal, tossing it up and inviting Luckes to go for glory or defeat. Luckes went for the shot and away it soared towards the long-on boundary. He had not connected cleanly, but it was dropping towards the rope, fading rapidly. Jack Crapp, right on the boundary edge, raced towards the dipping ball, fully aware that he had to make a catch or the game was lost. He just ran out of time, the ball dropped at his toes and bounced past him to the boundary. The game was Somerset's and Crapp was left to rue a matter of inches as the faithful of Taunton rushed onto the field to cheer their two heroes. Hazell displayed a turn of speed that would have astonished local publicans but Luckes was less fortunate; he was grabbed and carried shoulder high to the pavilion. Once inside, he permitted himself the rare luxury of a brandy – for medicinal purposes. He was badly shaken by a crowd reception that was hardly common in those days.

It had been the perfect finish to the perfect game and credit was shared in equal measure between the two sides. Hammond's declaration was eminently fair – considering the danger posed by the likes of Wellard, Lyon and Gimblett – and unsung heroes like Buse and Luckes deserved their ovations. The crowd had seen a great batsman make another glittering hundred and a spin bowler trust his own skill and rely on flight and courage when the game was there for the taking. It was not the fault of Reg Sinfield that Wally Luckes was the man for the occasion.

Three weeks later, Luckes and Hazell showed it had been no fluke when Somerset went to Trent Bridge. They won with two minutes to spare, courtesy of the usual last-wicket pair. This time Hazell was the hero: he cut Voce to the boundary, then calmly turned him to leg for a couple. No one could accuse Luckes and Hazell of inconsistency.

28
Gloucestershire *v*. Derbyshire
1939

You can never really tell what will happen in a cricket match. Even the greatest players sometimes fail to remember that. Take Walter Hammond: in this match he was so convinced that a two-day victory was in sight that he claimed the extra half-hour to finish the job. At that stage, Gloucestershire needed just 39 with five wickets left. The ensuing overs brought Derbyshire back in the game and the following morning they squeezed home by one run.

Hammond was never one to spurn the chance of social activity away from cricket. He was a solitary, brooding man on many a cricket day, but he assiduously cultivated profitable contacts of either sex when his cricket gear was packed away. Hammond was not the life and soul of the party in his own dressing-room; he only gave of himself out there in the middle, where he proved himself one of the greatest of all cricketers. By 1939 his social contacts had brought him a lucrative post with a tyre company; he could thus afford to turn amateur and claim the England captaincy that was barred to him if he remained a professional. He had captained England at home against Australia, then in South Africa and, in this climactic summer, against the West Indies. On this second day of the Derbyshire match, the captain's thoughts were no doubt straying to Kennington Oval, where he and Tom Goddard were due to play for England two days later. The prospect of a free day in London must have seemed irresistible to Hammond as he watched his team cruise to expected victory on the Thursday night. Why not finish the job now and motor down to London that evening? With Hammond's predilection for female company common knowledge on the county circuit, his team-mates were in

GLOUCESTERSHIRE v DERBYSHIRE
At Cheltenham, 16–18 August 1939

DERBYSHIRE

D. Smith lbw b Barnett	30	– b Lambert	8
A. F. Townsend c Crapp b Lambert	1	– c Wilson b Lambert	5
A. E. Alderman lbw b Scott	3	– b Scott	2
T. S. Worthington c Hammond b Lambert	31	– lbw b Lambert	13
G. H. Pope b Scott	29	– b Scott	57
A. E. G. Rhodes c Barnett b Lambert	45	– b Scott	0
A. V. Pope c Goddard b Lambert	7	– c Wilson b Lambert	9
*Mr. T. D. Hounsfield c Wilson b Scott	36	– c Crapp b Scott	4
†H. Elliott not out	10	– not out	9
T. B. Mitchell lbw b Scott	0	– c Barnett b Lambert	11
W. H. Copson run out	0	– c Crapp b Lambert	23
L-b 1	1	B 2, l-b 5	7
	193		148

1/10 2/15 3/55 4/86 5/96
6/117 7/152 8/192 9/192

1/12 2/15 3/17 4/39 5/44
6/48 7/65 8/81 9/123

Bowling: *First Innings* – Scott 16–3–68–4; Lambert 16.3–1–79–4; Barnett 5–1–8–1; Goddard 8–0–32–0; Sinfield 2–0–5–0. *Second Innings* – Scott 17–2–52–4; Lambert 14.2–1–69–6; Barnett 1–1–0–0; Goddard 5–1–20–0.

GLOUCESTERSHIRE

C. J. Barnett c Alderman b Copson	24	– c G. H. Pope b A. V. Pope	16
G. M. Emmett c Hounsfield b Copson	13	– b Mitchell	58
W. L. Neale b A. V. Pope	0	– c Smith b Mitchell	27
*Mr. W. R. Hammond lbw b A. V. Pope	10	– c Hounsfield b Rhodes	87
J. F. Crapp b Copson	6	– c Alderman b G. H. Pope	40
Mr. A. H. Brodhurst b Copson	0	– b Rhodes	0
R. A. Sinfield not out	19	– b Mitchell	5
†A. E. Wilson b Copson	1	– c and b Mitchell	1
C. J. Scott b A. V. Pope	0	– c and b Mitchell	4
T. W. J. Goddard c Hounsfield b A. V. Pope	3	– c Townsend b Copson	4
G. E. E. Lambert b A. V. Pope	2	– not out	1
L-b 3	3	B 12, l-b 4	16
	81		259

1/23 2/24 3/48 4/52 5/52
6/63 7/65 8/66 9/76

1/26 2/44 3/125 4/199 5/199
6/246 7/247 8/253 9/259

Bowling: *First Innings* – Copson 13–1–45–5; A. V. Pope 13.3–4–25–5; G. H. Pope 1–0–8–0. *Second Innings* – Copson 17–1–74–1; A. V. Pope 13–1–25–1; G. H. Pope 12–1–38–1; Mitchell 20.5–2–75–5; Rhodes 10–1–31–2.

Umpires: H. Elliott and E. J. Smith.

Derbyshire won by one run.

no doubt that the captain's motives were not solely geared to letting his men have a day off. Altruism was never Walter Hammond's strongest quality. Had it been so, he would probably not have been such a great player.

Perhaps Hammond felt he and everyone else were in the last throes of a normal life before the flames of war licked at them. There were enough warnings around: the papers were full of advertisements for service uniforms and overcoats. On 11 August, half of England had been plunged into a blackout lasting four hours. Homes and factories were in darkness over twenty-eight counties, a grim foretaste of the deprivations to come. On the first day of this Derbyshire match, Germany told Poland she would not negotiate over Danzig. German troops massed on the Slovak-Polish border in readiness for the final provocative invasion that would spark off war in just over a fortnight. Yet the British Government still viewed the gathering war clouds with its customary *sangfroid:* the Foreign Secretary, Lord Halifax returned to his holiday retreat in Yorkshire after three strenuous days at the Foreign Office. He let it be known that he might have to return urgently to London. The Prime Minister, Neville Chamberlain, was equally unflappable; he was not due back in London until 21 August from his holiday. The atmosphere was simply unreal. Cricket must have seemed incidental, yet to many it probably provided a slice of sanity.

The weather helped to foster a balmy, relaxed mood. It was now the warmest spell in England since early June and the Cotswolds looked breathtakingly pretty as Gloucestershire prepared for the second match of the Cheltenham Festival. They were third in the table, nurturing hopes of a championship title for the first time this century; nearly forty years on, those hopes are still springing eternal in optimistic breasts. On the first day, twenty-three wickets fell for 203 runs as the fast bowlers revelled on a fast, hard pitch containing one or two treacherous areas. Scott and Lambert, Gloucestershire's two young fast bowlers, were much more threatening than the off-spin of Goddard, who had already taken more than 180 wickets that season. Gloucestershire fared even less impressively against pace bowling, losing eight wickets after tea for just 33. They then grabbed three Derbyshire wickets for 29 before the close, and there seemed every prospect of a two-day win for someone.

At 48 for 6 in their second innings, Derbyshire were deep in trouble. Then George Pope, that underrated all-rounder, pulled them round, with valuable aid from Bill Copson. Lambert went for 19 in one over including two huge straight sixes from Copson. So Gloucestershire now needed 261 to win, the highest score of the match on an unreliable wicket. Almost everything would depend on a batsman of genius who had a great incentive to finish the job that day. Barnett and Sinfield were out for 44 when Hammond revived the innings. He added 81 with George Emmett and his mastery against the dangerous leg-spin of Tommy Mitchell was thrilling. Emmett hardly faced a ball from Mitchell and, as long as Hammond stayed in, the game was Gloucestershire's. It came as a surprise when he was out after three hours, caught at cover point – but he had brought his side to the brink of victory. At the scheduled close at 6.30, Gloucestershire stood 39 away from victory with half their wickets left. The stumps were pulled up by umpires Elliott and Smith, but Hammond strode out onto the pitch to claim the extra half-hour. It did not work – two more wickets fell for 25, and at seven o'clock they were still fourteen short. Billy Neale was 24 not out and almost everything would depend on him.

The Times reflected the usual sycophantic attitude to the current England captain, whoever he was, by praising Hammond's shrewdness. The writer reasoned that Hammond had claimed the extra half-hour because he knew that the dew would help the bowlers the following morning. Furthermore, 'This tactical move may well keep his side in the running for the championship.' Ho, hum – not a word about Hammond's own dismissal when he was winning the match easily. With games starting at 11.30 in the morning, it is hard to see how the last lingering traces of dew could affect a wicket that was being continually baked by a hot sun – but in those conformist days, the England captain must always be supported. It did not matter that Hammond was generally acknowledged to be an awful captain, devoid of flexibility, imagination or man management: he was the England captain and so his writ ran large.

Tommy Mitchell had the final word on the third morning. He caught and bowled Scott after the tall fast bowler had hit him to the boundary. Goddard hit two successive twos off Copson, who then had him caught at mid-off. George Lambert came in with four needed and one wicket to fall. Now Lambert was to become a very useful late-order batsman, but at the age of twenty he was just embarking on his first-class career, and he could not be expected to ward off England bowlers of the calibre of Mitchell

The bread of heaven is scattered over Swansea's waters as Tony Lewis leads the crowd in song after Glamorgan's last ball victory over Essex in 1969 (chapter 40)

Right: Bob Willis's legendary concentration and determination saved his career and won an historic Test for England at Leeds in 1981 (chapter 44)

Far right: Derek Underwood – when the conditions favour his unique bowling talents, he is unplayable. The 1986 Warwickshire side would agree (chapter 49)

Right: Ray Bright is yorked middle stump by Bob Willis at Leeds in 1981 to end one of the most astonishing of all Tests (chapter 44)

Left: Ian Botham's relaxed, fatalistic attitude to England's crisis at Headingley transformed the match and the series (chapter 44)

Chris Tavaré's whole life flashes before him as he turns to see Geoff Miller spare his blushes. Thomson caught Miller bowled Botham (with an assist from Tavaré), and England have snatched the Melbourne Test of 1982 by just three runs after all had seemed lost. In the background the England captain Bob Willis can barely trust the evidence of his own eyes (chapter 46)

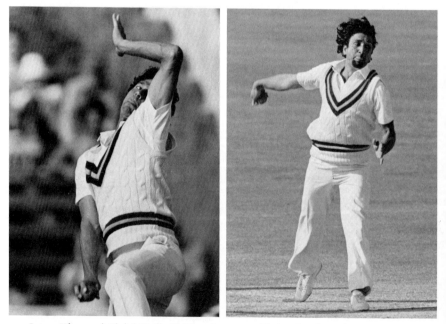

Imran Khan and Abdul Qadir, Pakistan's two world-class bowlers who sensationally destroyed the cream of the West Indies batting at Faisalabad in 1986 (chapter 50)

and Copson. It all depended on Billy Neale, the sturdy farmer who happened to be one of the best players of spin bowling in the county game. A couple of singles were scraped, then Mitchell had Neale caught in the slips. It had all backfired for Gloucestershire and Neale, one of the few close friends Hammond had in the game, had failed at the last. The match had been thrown away in the inordinate keenness to get it finished the previous evening.

It must have been a sombre drive down to London for Hammond, especially when he learned that Yorkshire had won for the fifth time in a row, and Middlesex had beaten Essex by five runs. A fortnight later, the championship race ended with Yorkshire on top, followed by Middlesex with Gloucestershire frustrated in third position. Soon weighty matters like claiming the extra half-hour were to be overshadowed by more important considerations – like the struggle for a civilized world.

29
Middlesex *v.* Somerset
1947

Most cricketers would settle for Lord's as the place to make their first-class debut – and few have made the immediate impact of Maurice Tremlett in the glorious summer of 1947. Against that season's county champions, he took 3 for 47 and 5 for 39, then won the match for Somerset with a cameo of an innings that was chock-full of commonsense and maturity. Somerset won by one wicket and the press hailed a new star. It could not last – nor, sadly, did it.

Tremlett was twenty-four that summer and he looked every inch the golden boy. Tall, fair-haired, with a loose-limbed athleticism, he had built an impressive reputation in club cricket around the Taunton area and his performances for the Army had satisfied the exacting standards of G. O. Allen. His bowling seemed to be Tremlett's major asset: he was a natural fast-medium, who bent his back. He could bring the ball in at a fair speed and he made the batsmen play almost all of the time. With England desperately short of pace bowlers after the War, Maurice Tremlett seemed a godsend. He was young, fit, and seemed to want to bowl all day. He would never compare with the great Miller and Lindwall, but at least he would make the best players hurry their shots. Later Tremlett's career would lapse into anti-climax, but for three days in 1947 it must have seemed a very easy game to him.

On the first morning of his county career, he was badly afflicted by nerves. Eric Hill, a friend from Taunton days, was also making his debut for the first team that day and he recalls, 'He couldn't speak after his first over, he was so nervous about playing at Lord's in front of all those great players. He said to me, "Eric, can't these blokes bat?" and he was pretty overawed by it all. But he bowled it pretty straight after his first over and just got better and better

MIDDLESEX v SOMERSET
At Lord's, 10–13 May 1947

MIDDLESEX

J. D. B. Robertson b Tremlett	39	– b Buse	30
S. M. Brown lbw b Wellard	7	– b Wellard	0
W. J. Edrich c Luckes b Buse	102	– c Lawrence b Wellard	3
D. C. S. Compton c Woodhouse b Buse	6	– b Tremlett	25
J. T. Eaglestone b Buse	0	– c Lawrence b Tremlett	4
*F. G. Mann b Buse	27	– b Tremlett	0
A. W. Thompson c Wellard b Tremlett	5	– b Tremlett	0
†L. H. Compton b Tremlett	11	– b Tremlett	0
J. M. Sims c and b Buse	3	– not out	6
J. A. Young not out	6	– c Luckes b Wellard	1
L. H. Gray c Hazell b Buse	5	– run out	4
B 19, l-b 1	20	B 1, l-b 4	5
	231		78

1/20 2/76 3/99 4/100 5/156 6/184
7/207 8/213 9/221

1/14 2/18 3/56 4/63 5/63
6/63 7/65 8/68 9/69

Bowling: *First Innings* – Buse 33–8–52–6; Wellard 22–4–49–1; Tremlett 24–5–47–3; Hazell 4–0–13–0; Lawrence 12–2–40–0; Meyer 4–1–10–0. *Second Innings* – Buse 4–2–14–1; Wellard 16.3–7–20–3; Tremlett 14–3–39–5.

SOMERSET

F. S. Lee c D. Compton b Young	28	– c Robertson b Young	38
H. Gimblett b Edrich	25	– b Edrich	13
H. T. F. Buse lbw b Gray	1	– c L. Compton b Gray	3
G. E. S. Woodhouse b Edrich	7	– b Edrich	21
*R. J. O. Meyer c Robertson b Sims	1	– b Gray	4
J. Lawrence c Mann b Sims	30	– b Young	19
E. Hill b Edrich	0	– c Edrich b Young	17
†W. T. Luckes c Edrich b Gray	9	– c L. Compton b Gray	26
A. W. Wellard b Edrich	17	– b Edrich	5
M. F. Tremlett c Gray b Sims	5	– not out	19
H. L. Hazell not out	0	– not out	8
B 1, l-b 9, w 1	11	B 4, l-b 1	5
	134	(9 wkts.)	178

1/56 2/59 3/67 4/68 5/68 6/68 7/100
8/117 9/133

1/17 2/47 3/92 4/100 5/101
6/108 7/113 8/151 9/151

Bowling: *First Innings* – Gray 24–10–25–2; Edrich 16–3–46–4; Young 11–6–12–1; Sims 15.4–4–40–3. *Second Innings* – Gray 29.2–7–51–3; Edrich 22–8–47–3; Young 34–14–48–3; Sims 7–0–27–0.

Umpires: A. R. Coleman and J. J. Hills.

Somerset won by one wicket.

as the day wore on.' Tremlett bowled twenty-four overs in all, took three wickets and picked up some favourable press notices. It was a fine opening to the county season at Lord's, with Bill Edrich making a superb hundred in just over three hours before he was wonderfully caught, wide down the leg-side by Wally Luckes. Somerset finished on 59 for 2, with the dangerous Harold Gimblett still there with 24 not out.

On the Monday, twenty-three wickets fell and Maurice Tremlett became an overnight sensation. First Bill Edrich showed him how to use the new ball, as Somerset lost four wickets for nine. Middlesex led by 97 when they batted again and, for a time, they had few worries. Tremlett did not bowl well in his first spell from the Pavilion End: he strayed down the leg-side and the elegant Jack Robertson picked him off his legs profitably. At 60 for 3, Tremlett returned from the Nursery End and the transformation was immediate. He straightened up his break-back and made the batsmen play at every ball. In five overs, he took 5 for 8, four of them clean-bowled. Denis Compton was beaten for pace, playing a perfectly sound defensive stroke, while at the other end Robertson essayed a crude hook shot with his head in the air. Johnny Lawrence took two great catches at leg-slip, and Middlesex lost their last seven wickets for just eighteen. Tremlett's deceptive pace had disconcerted everyone; Leslie Compton had to go to hospital to get some blood released after being nailed inside the thigh area by one of Tremlett's vicious break-backs. It was rare to see a young bowler rely on old-fashioned line and length, rather than pace and swerve. Fleet Street was impressed – the *Daily Telegraph* headline was 'Young Bowler's Amazing Spell at Lord's' – and within the space of five overs he had arrived.

Tremlett still had one more decisive contribution to make, but for the moment he watched Somerset's early batting falter in their chase for 176. At 17, Gimblett was bowled off-stump without playing a stroke and Lawrence went lbw in the same disappointing fashion. When Frank Lee was caught in the slips fending off a short rising ball, Arthur Wellard came in with the score 92 for 3. It made sense to promote the big hitter because Middlesex's bowling was so tight; a few rugged blows might loosen the stranglehold. Unfortunately the weather helped Middlesex. In the gathering gloom, Edrich bowled fast and straight and he made Woodhouse play on and then bowled Wellard. At 101 for 5 at the close,

Somerset still needed another 75 and much depended on the obdu-rate Bertie Buse.

On a beautiful May morning, the temperature rose to 82 degrees, the warmest May day for two years – and the cricket remained gripping. Admission was free and the public thronged through the gates, perhaps aware that momentous deeds lay ahead. At 113 for 7 – with Meyer and Buse both cut down by Gray's pace – only one team seemed certain of victory. Then Wally Luckes showed his serene temperament for the umpteenth time. He found a partner of similar bravery in Eric Hill. It was an unnerving experience for Hill: he had made nought in his debut innings and now, with a 'pair' looming, he was surrounded by close fielders and accurate bowling by Gray and Edrich, then Young. They defied the new ball, and added 38 in sixty-five minutes, dealing almost exclusively in singles. It looked as if they might win it on their own until they were both out at 151 – Luckes was caught behind, then Hill brilliantly taken wide on the right side at slip by Edrich. It was now 151 for 9. The time was just after one o'clock, and with 25 needed the tall, striking figure of Maurice Tremlett came out to join Horace Hazell, a man who looked the exact opposite.

As we have already seen, Hazell was an excellent tail-ender (chapter 27), but it was expecting a lot to shield young Tremlett while trying to gather another twenty-five runs against such tight bowling. Somerset could not expect any more heroics from the young man – he had done more than enough in his first game. Hazell was nearly out twice when the stand was in its infancy, as he edged one perilously near to second slip, then his leg-stump was shaved by a ball from Jack Young. Somehow they survived till lunch, when they still needed fifteen. Apart from one injudicious heave, Tremlett had batted responsibly, leaving anything not pitched on the stumps, while Hazell was simply Hazell.

After lunch Hazell stroked a splendid four through the covers. With Young bowling his left-arm spin so naggingly, there was nothing else to hit until Tremlett took his courage in both hands. Young tossed one up to tempt him, and he majestically struck him over long-off for a long, soaring six. He then played Young past mid-on for three more. Two to win. Another sweet on-drive brought the winning runs and the batsmen ran another single for good measure, just in case there were any discrepancies later on. It had been a triumph of character and determination over high-class opposition and the Middlesex players recognized that by standing back and applauding Tremlett off the field. It was a typically sporting gesture from one of the most chivalrous county teams of all time, and it was hard to demur with the verdict of *The Times*: 'As noble a game of cricket as any man could ever hope to play in or any spectator be privileged to watch.' It had been tense and skilful throughout – but above all friendly. Both sets of players seemed to relish the chance of uncomplicated sporting combat after the years of tragedy, and this match set the tone for a sun-kissed season which still turns middle-aged cricket fans into dewy-eyed romantics whenever the year 1947 is mentioned.

For Maurice Tremlett, it was the greatest match of a career that lasted fourteen more years and included three England caps. That may seem a harsh judgement on such a talented all-rounder, but he was put under the microscope right at the start of his county career and he never managed to do himself justice. That soaring straight six – the turning point in the Middlesex game – remained his trademark, to the delight of every cricket purist. He was a lovely clean hitter, and on his good days there were few better stylists. Yet it was his bowling that fell away spectacularly. No one expected him to emulate his deeds at Lord's every week, but his natural talent was soon confused by a succession of well-meaning coaches. They tried to mould a natural bowler into the genuine fast-bowling article – chiding him about the position of his head, his feet and hips at the moment of delivery. Soon Tremlett hardly knew where to pitch the ball as he fretted about his technical defects. He had never claimed to be anything other than an uncomplicated fast-medium bowler who liked to give the ball a healthy crack as well, but the public burden of expectation dragged him down. He was billed as the young man who would meet Australian fire with Anglo-Saxon reliability, but he knew better than anyone that he had flaws. During the Middlesex match, E. W. Swanton encapsulated the yearning of the English cricketing world for a genuine fast bowler when he wrote, 'We must restrain ourselves from rushing into superlatives about a young cricketer on the strength of one notable performance, but Tremlett's possibilities stand out for all to see. He may become a truly fine bowler.' He did not: within three years he was bowling far too many wides and he had little idea where the ball was going after it had left his hand. After that, he became little other than a change bowler, who would occasionally be wheeled on to try to break up a partnership.

Too much was expected of Tremlett the bowler. In another era, when the fast bowling cupboard was fairly well-stocked, he might have been given time to ease himself naturally into the game, away from the spotlight. It seems significant in retrospect that in his second first-class match he made a 'pair' and did not take a wicket; within a few days, the Lord's glow was being tarnished. Eric Hill feels that Tremlett was rather relieved when he eventually took the hard decision to let his bowling go: 'I think he realized it was easier scoring runs than busting a gut with the ball when it's all going wrong. Tremmie was a pretty shrewd guy.' He settled for batting elegantly and excitingly, and for a period of four seasons he was one of the best county captains. For a man of his great natural talent, a record of sixteen hundreds and a batting average of 25 is sadly disappointing: perhaps the men with the coaching manuals were mainly responsible, perhaps the fault lay in Maurice Tremlett's unassuming nature. Whatever the area of responsibility men of inferior abilities have played a good deal more for England than the one who loved to hit bowlers straight back over their heads.

30

Surrey *v*. Middlesex
1948

Don Bradman's juggernaut of an Australian side were not the only crowd-pullers in the 1948 season. A thrilling race for the county championship delighted the millions of cricket-lovers who saw the attractions of the county game as another example of a slow return to normality after the ravages of war. It was a time for unaffected enjoyment, whatever austerity packages Sir Stafford Cripps was unveiling. How appropriate then that the game which decided the county championship of 1948 should be decided by a tall, whimsical man who perennially saw the funny side of life, whatever the exigencies.

Jim Sims was a genuine cricket character. For a quarter of a century he adorned the Middlesex side with his all-round skills, but more importantly with his great good humour. Somehow Jim could always defuse the tensest situation with a dry quip out of the side of his mouth; he followed Patsy Hendren as the clown of the Middlesex side, and on the county scene of the 1940s, Jim Sims was the most popular player around. He was that rarity – a man who could still give of his best while relishing his sense of the ridiculous. It seems natural that he should be a leg-spin and googly bowler – traditionally a breed of cricketer who needs to be a philosopher. He could also bat. In his early days with Middlesex he often opened the innings and he made four hundreds in his career. Yet it was an innings of just 36 not out that underlined his sterner side and in the process robbed Surrey of the 1948 championship.

Early in August, Surrey were vying at the top of the table with the current champions, Middlesex. Of course Glamorgan were mounting a concerted challenge, but no one outside the Principality gave them a chance. The London sports fan has never been short

SURREY v MIDDLESEX
At the Oval, 7–10 August 1948

SURREY

L. B. Fishlock b Young	82	– b Young	11
E. A. Bedser c Robins b Young	2	– absent ill	0
H. S. Squires c Gray b Young	10	– c D. Compton b Young	12
M. R. Barton c L. Compton b Young	5	– c Sims b Young	6
J. F. Parker c Edrich b Young	11	– lbw b D. Compton	30
E. R. T. Holmes hit wkt b D. Compton	5	– c Robins b Young	0
J. C. Laker c Robertson b Young	0	– c Dewes b D. Compton	17
A. V. Bedser c Mann b Young	11	– c L. Compton b Young	1
G. S. Mobey c and b D. Compton	0	– b Young	0
W. S. Surridge not out	16	– c Brown b Young	19
J. W. McMahon lbw b D. Compton	7	– not out	0
B 4, 1-b 3	7	B 6, l–b 1	7
	156		**103**

1/17 2/42 3/54 4/86 5/92 6/98 7/131
8/132 9/134

1/17 2/17 3/23 4/37 5/63 6/66
7/100 8/103 9/103

Bowling: *First Innings* – Edrich 6–1–8–0; Gray 16–4–27–0; Young
39–15–50–7; D. Compton 28–8–64–3. *Second Innings* – Edrich 2–0–9–0;
Gray 4–0–13–0; Young 21.1–8–47–7; D. Compton 19–7–27–2.

MIDDLESEX

J. D. Robertson c Mobey b McMahon	16	– c Laker b A. Bedser	17
F. G. Mann c Surridge b A. Bedser	2	– c Surridge b McMahon	29
W. J. Edrich c E. Bedser b Laker	19	– c Fishlock b Surridge	4
D. C. S. Compton b McMahon	14	– c Parker b A. Bedser	4
R. W. V. Robins lbw b McMahon	21	– c Mobey b McMahon	38
J. G. Dewes c Surridge b A. Bedser	14	– c Parker b Laker	4
S. M. Brown c Barton b Laker	5	– lbw b A. Bedser	4
L. H. Compton c Parker b Laker	5	– b Laker	2
J. Sims b Laker	15	– not out	36
J. A. Young c McMahon b A. Bedser	4	– c McMahon b Laker	0
L. Gray not out	1	– not out	0
B 1, l-b 1	2	L-b 4	4
	118		**142**

1/2 2/30 3/45 4/66 5/77
6/90 7/98 8/98 9/104

1/8 2/13 3/21 4/33 5/35
6/97 7/101 8/109 9/110

Bowling: *First Innings* – A. V. Bedser 14–5–25–3; Surridge 6–0–20–0;
McMahon 11–3–20–3; Laker 13.1–0–51–4. *Second Innings* – A. V. Bedser
14.1–5–25–3; Surridge 8–1–23–1; McMahon 7–1–25–2; Laker 14–0–65–3.

Umpires: P. T. Mills and H. Cruice.

Middlesex won by one wicket.

of confidence in his own favourite team, and the general feeling was that the winner of this local derby at the Oval would lift the title. Stan Squires, that elegant Surrey batsman, could not have chosen a better game for his benefit; despite poor weather over the first two days, the turnstile rattled merrily throughout.

On the first day, play was delayed for three and a half hours and then George Mann put Surrey in on a pitch no doubt affected by the rain. From the Vauxhall End, Jack Young took the first four wickets with his accurate left-arm spin and only Laurie Fishlock played him with any confidence. Surrey finished on 120 for 6, with five wickets to Young and Fishlock 74 not out. On the Monday, Fishlock was bowled 'through the gate' for an invaluable 82, but the others could make little headway against the spin of Young and Compton. The catching was excellent, especially Compton's return effort from a full pitch that was hammered straight back by George Mobey. When Middlesex batted, George Mann – on the day it was announced he was to lead England in South Africa – was picked up at short leg in the first over. When Jack McMahon came on to bowl left-arm spin from around the wicket, he had Jack Robertson caught behind at once. Bill Edrich was then taken at long-on, and when McMahon bowled Compton with a 'chinaman' and trapped Walter Robins lbw, Middlesex were 77 for 5. The pitch was now awkward, with sunshine drying it out, and McMahon bowled over the wicket to three short legs, making the odd ball stand up. The day ended with Middlesex 90 for 5, with every prospect of some gripping play on the final day. It would be too much to expect a positive result – too much time had been lost – but neither side would just play for the draw. Neither captain was a passive leader, and in any event the stakes were too high not to gamble.

The last day was dramatic, pulsating and a marvellous advertisement for the county game. *The Times* said, 'This was county cricket for which one has so longed in these days of drawn-out Test Matches.' It was certainly a pleasant contrast to the inexorable march towards supremacy from the Australians; at least this game offered a prospect of victory to both sides, rather than humiliation for England. No less than 23 wickets fell for 273 runs on this final day, most of them to the spinners. Early on, the last five Middlesex wickets went for just 28, leaving them 38 runs behind. Again Young and Compton bowled beautifully. They took every Surrey wicket in the match, and only a stand between Jack Parker and

Stuart Surridge offered any respectability. Some of the catches were brilliant – Sid Brown took a wonderful effort at deep extra cover to get Surridge, while Jim Sims belied his 45 years to run round from mid-on to mid-off to catch Michael Barton.

So the game was wide open. Surrey's collapse had reduced the game's destiny to a simple equation: Middlesex needed 142 in 145 minutes. With their strokeplayers, Middlesex would not be worried about the time factor, but could they surmount the spin of McMahon and Laker and the cutters of Alec Bedser? Within an hour, it seemed not. They were soon 21 for 3, with Brown lbw, Edrich rashly caught at mid-on and Compton taken in the slips. When Robertson was caught at bat/pad and Dewes picked up at slip, they were 35 for 5. Then a thrillling counter-attack from two amateurs who knew no other way. Walter Robins ran like a hare between the wickets, George Mann drove superbly, and they had added 62 in half an hour when Mann fell in the gallant manner, caught in the deep. Four runs later, Leslie Compton was bowled middle stump. Middlesex needed 41 with just three wickets left. Then Robins was caught behind and surely that was the end of Middlesex.

Jack Young came out to join Jim Sims, who had seen all this kind of stuff before and was unlikely to let it all perturb him. On the other hand, Young was hardly the most reliable of tail-enders, in complete contrast to his unstinting accuracy and patience as a bowler. Sims cajoled him, telling him to play straight, to leave the heroics to his senior partner, and for a time it worked. Then with 22 needed, Young could not resist temptation any longer. Jim Laker tossed one up, Young swung lustily and McMahon took a good, swirling catch at mid-wicket. That catch must surely have sealed it, despite the presence of Sims.

Yet Laurie Gray, the last man, was a different proposition from Jack Young. Although he averaged around seven with the bat throughout his career, he was capable of long periods of passive resistance, while a better player prospered at the other end. In 1939 he had added 83 in forty-five minutes for the last wicket with Denis Compton against Essex – and Gray's contribution was 1 not out. His highest score was only 35 not out, but he was not the worst number eleven in the business. All he had to do was keep out the straight deliveries and run when he was told by Jim Sims. For his part, Sims batted gloriously: he now started to hit some magnificent on-side shots and ran like someone half his age. His ability to count to six served his side nobly in the last tense overs. He edged a single off the last ball of one Laker over, then off-drove Bedser for a couple and nicked another single to keep the strike for Laker's next over. He then pulled one to the mid-wicket boundary, and edged the final ball past slip's right hand for a precious one. By now, there were ten minutes left, one run to win and the last pair together. Bedser bowled to Sims and he shovelled an inswinger in the direction of square leg. It was not an elegant shot, it stayed rather long in the air, but they all count. Middlesex had won by one wicket and Jim Sims had made 36 of the last 41 runs.

He had his luck, of course. He was dropped twice in the slips during the frantic last minutes, and a couple of deliveries from Laker just went over his leg-stump. Jim Laker must have been disappointed with his figures – an England spinner should not have conceded four and half runs per over in favourable conditions. Yet Laker was still learning his trade and he had been sorted out unceremoniously by the Australians that summer. Within a season or so, he was the best spinner in the world and running through sides in conditions similar to the Middlesex match.

Not even the Surrey players could have begrudged Jim Sims his final glory day. He was such a popular man. Few professionals of that time were lucky enough to get two benefits in five years, but that was Jim Sim's reward after his first game had been washed out in 1946. That committee decision was a measure of his popularity, and he never lost the priceless ability to make people laugh with him rather than at him. For many years he was the Middlesex scorer, and no old pro was less prone to drone on about the old days to the new order. He died amongst cricketers, in a Canterbury hotel the night before he was due to open up the Middlesex score-book for the 1973 season with a match against Kent. Jim Sims would have wanted to go amid the relaxed ambience that generations of genial county cricketers have created.

Poor Stan Squires was less lucky. His benefit match was very successful, but he only lived another fifteen months to appreciate the hard-earned cash. He died of leukaemia, after the best season of his stylish career. It was decent sportsmen like Stan Squires who helped consolidate the admirable reputation of the English professional cricketer after the war years. Jim Sims did not exactly harm that reputation either . . .

An ironic postscript on this great game: Middlesex could only finish third, despite their crucial Oval win. Surrey finished second, just four points behind the surprise winners, Glamorgan. All things being equal, Surrey would have won the championship had Jim Sims not chosen the time to remind us that he was more than just a handy man with a quip.

31
South Africa *v.* England
DURBAN, 1948

The definition of an exciting finish to a Test might be when all the players forget to snatch some souvenir stumps as they race off the field in excitement or dismay. On that basis, the Durban Test of England's 1948/9 tour ranks high as one of the greatest finishes in Test history. England clinched victory off the last ball of the game, and as the players raced away from the steady drizzle and crepuscular gloom the two sets of stumps remained unchallenged.

The main focus of attention had switched to Cliff Gladwin's thigh. As human limbs go, it ranked fairly low in the aesthetic league, but it had brought England their precious victory. The brawny, bluff fast bowler from Chesterfield's mining community had taken the last ball on the thigh and hared up the other end as if his very life depended on it. His partner, Alec Bedser, managed to get in at the danger end, while Gladwin waved his bat exultantly. In the pandemonium of the dressing-room Gladwin posed for photographs of the most famous thigh in cricket and expressed the fond hope that the eventual bruise would never fade.

At the start of that final over, one of four results was possible. England needed eight to win, South Africa wanted two more wickets, and a tie or a draw was perfectly possible. The light was fearful and the nearby hills were totally hidden by the heavy rain. We were down to human elements like courage, nerve and luck, with technical skill almost irrelevant. Lindsay Tuckett, the bowler, could not grip the ball properly in such damp conditions, and neither the fielders nor the batsmen could sight the ball satisfactorily. If 'Dickie' Bird had been umpiring, they would have been off the field two hours ago, but mercifully both sets of players wanted victory above all. It was that kind of match throughout.

Unusually for South Africa, poor weather dogged all four days

SOUTH AFRICA *v* ENGLAND
(First Test)
At Kingsmead, Durban, 16–20 December 1948

SOUTH AFRICA

E. A. B. Rowan c Evans b Jenkins	7	– c Compton b Jenkins	16
O. E. Wynne c Compton b Bedser	5	– c Watkins b Wright	4
B. Mitchell c Evans b Bedser	27	– b Wright	19
*A. D. Nourse c Watkins b Wright	37	– c and b Bedser	32
†W. W. Wade run out	8	– b Jenkins	63
D. W. Begbie c Compton b Bedser	37	– c Mann b Bedser	48
O. C. Dawson b Gladwin	24	– c Compton b Wright	3
A. M. B. Rowan not out	5	– b Wright	15
L. Tuckett lbw b Gladwin	1	– not out	3
N. B. F. Mann c Evans b Gladwin	4	– c Mann b Compton	10
C. N. McCarthy b Bedser	0	– b Jenkins	0
B 3, l-b 2, n-b 1	6	B 1, l-b 5	6
	161		**219**

1/9 2/18 3/69 4/80 5/99 6/148
7/150 8/152 9/160 10/161

1/22 2/22 3/67 4/89 5/174
6/179 7/208 8/208 9/219
10/219

Bowling: *First Innings* – Bedser 13.5–2–39–4; Gladwin 12–3–21–3; Jenkins 14–3–50–1; Wright 9–3–29–1; Compton 2–0–5–0; Watkins 3–0–11–0. *Second Innings* – Bedser 18–5–51–2; Gladwin 7–3–15–0; Jenkins 22.3–6–64–3; Wright 26–3–72–4; Compton 16–11–11–1.

ENGLAND

L. Hutton c McCarthy b A. M. B. Rowan	83	– c Dawson b Tuckett	5
C. Washbrook c Wade b Mann	35	– lbw b Mann	25
R. T. Simpson c Begbie b Mann	5	– (6) c E. A. B. Rowan b McCarthy	0
D. C. S. Compton c Wade b Mann	72	– b McCarthy	28
A. J. Watkins c Nourse b A. M. B. Rowan	9	– b McCarthy	4
*F. G. Mann c E. A. B. Rowan b A. M. B. Rowan	19	– (3) c Mitchell b McCarthy	13
†T. G. Evans c Wynne b A. M. B. Rowan	0	– b McCarthy	4
R. O. Jenkins c Mitchell b Mann	5	– c Wade b McCarthy	22
A. V. Bedser c Tuckett b Mann	11	– not out	1
C. Gladwin not out	0	– not out	7
D. V. P. Wright c Tuckett b Mann	0	–	
B 2, l-b 12	14	B 9, l-b 10	19
	253	**(8 wickets)**	**128**

1/84 2/104 3/146 4/172 5/212 6/212 7/221
8/247 9/253 10/253

1/25 2/49 3/52 4/64 5/64
6/70 7/115 8/116

Bowling: *First Innings* – McCarthy 9–2–20–0; Dawson 3–0–16–0; Tuckett 6–0–36–0; A. M. B. Rowan 44–8–108–4; Mann 37.4–14–59–6. *Second Innings* – McCarthy 12–2–43–6; Tuckett 10–0–38–1; A. M. B. Rowan 4–0–15–0; Mann 2–0–13–1.

Umpires: R. G. A. Ashman and G. L. Sickler.

England won by two wickets.

of the Test. Yet the resultant erratic nature of the pitch and the encouragement it gave to the bowlers kept the game open – in stark contrast to England's last visit to Durban, the infamous Timeless Test of the 1938/9 tour. This time runs had to be earned, and the three half-centuries made were worth at least a hundred in less hazardous circumstances.

George Mann, leading England in his first Test, lost the toss, but fine bowling by Gladwin and Bedser in a humid atmosphere, backed up by brilliant fielding, restricted South Africa to a disappointing score. There was time for just seven balls and one run to England before bad light and rain ended play for the day. Next day only three hours' play was possible, and England reached 144 for 2, with Hutton 81 not out and Compton on 17. The off-spin of Rowan and the slow left arm of 'Tufty' Mann restricted the batsmen, and they were beginning to turn the ball when a thunderstorm ended proceedings. With just two days left, it was hard to see how either side could win, especially with the weather so uncertain.

At dawn on the third morning, George Mann went to the ground and took a decision which altered the course of the match. The groundsman told him that the longer he delayed rolling the pitch, the more difficult it would be for batting. Seven minutes of rolling were allowed and the groundsman said it would crack and crumble on the baked surface if he waited. Mann agreed and so conditions became even more difficult for batting. On the third day, twelve wickets fell for 199 and there now seemed every prospect of a definite result. Compton's 72 on a broken wicket was a classic, a signpost to his genius. His footwork against the spinners was bewitching and, if he had got out cheaply, England would have lost the game. Instead he guided them to a lead of 92, and at the close South Africa had lost four men for 90. The initiative lay with England, provided the weather held.

One of the greatest days in Test history started favourably for the home side. Billy Wade and Denis Begbie added 85 in eighty two minutes, and Begbie even hit Bedser for six, a genuine collector's item. Mann switched his bowlers around in desperation and finally he caught Begbie off Bedser and Jenkins bowled Wade round his legs. Rowan and Tuckett lingered for a time, but soon after half past three, South Africa were all out for 219. That left England a possible 135 minutes in which to get 128.

England's intentions were clear off the first ball, which was cut fiercely by Hutton to gully, where Dudley Nourse took it on the knee and went down like a sack of potatoes. He needed five minutes of medical attention, which did nothing at all for the scoring rate. Then Washbrook swung at his first ball and was dropped on the long leg boundary by Wynne. Rain fell shortly afterwards, lopping off another ten minutes, and when Hutton was taken at silly mid-on, it seemed as if England would never manage to accelerate in deteriorating conditions. The captain ran out to the wicket at 25 for 1, and he and Washbrook added a swift 24 before Washbrook was lbw. Mann was hitting out at everything by now and he was dropped twice in the gathering gloom. Finally his luck ran out and Mitchell took a brilliant slip catch: 52 for 3.

The drizzle was now persistent and both bowlers and batsmen were hampered. Cuan McCarthy, a strapping nineteen-year-old was a fearsome proposition in the murky light and he fired out Watkins, Simpson and Evans to reduce England to 70 for 6. One hour to go, 56 needed and four wickets in hand. 'Roley' Jenkins ambled out to join Compton, surely England's last hope. Compton asked 'Roley' if he was worried about fast bowling and he answered in his usual cheerful way, 'Don't worry about me, mate – I'll prop and cop for you.' He was as good as his word and they stole singles here and there as the tension rose. The England players had locked themselves in their dressing-room, and those who could not bear to watch paced up and down. With half an hour left, England needed another 33. At 115 for 7, with just thirteen needed, Compton was bowled after again demonstrating his character and nerve. One run later, Jenkins was given out caught at the wicket, after aiming a swat at a short ball after it had passed him – a decision that still annoys the genial 'Roley' almost forty years later. So with ten minutes left, England had come a long way – but they still needed another twelve.

Alec Bedser – brave, sensible and no mug with the bat – was already out there and he was joined by a grinning giant called Cliff Gladwin. In retrospect, Gladwin was the ideal man for the situation. When you hail from a mining community, where tragedy can stalk hand-in-hand with poverty, you tend to be able to put sporting matters in perspective. Gladwin looked as if he was actually enjoying all the tension as he came to the crease. He passed Dudley Nourse, the opposition captain, who inquired testily, 'What have you got to smile about?' and back came the classic reply, 'Coometh the hour, coometh the man!' How right he was. . . .

Gladwin nearly botched it up, though. He lifted one ball to Tuckett at mid-on, but he missed it in the gloom and they ran two. Then Bedser was almost run out as they stole a hair-raising single. The senior partner was left to face the last over with eight needed. It was to be bowled by Lindsay Tuckett, a fastish, reliable bowler with the reputation of bowling straight. In the misty drizzle that could be enough to win the game. Bedser heaved at the first ball, missed and they ran a leg-bye. Seven needed in seven balls. Gladwin took the next one on the rise and planted it in the direction of deep midwicket – a genuine tailender's slog. Eric Rowan was out there for the catch, but he had come in too far and the ball sailed over his clutching fingers, bounced once and rolled over the boundary. A four: three needed in six. They got another leg-bye down to long leg off the third ball. Five balls in which to get two runs – surely it was England's game? Tuckett dried the ball on a towel while Bedser bent down to touch his toes, for something to do amid the tension. Off the fourth ball, Bedser drove hard to mid-off where Nourse made a great stop and dared the batsmen to run. They did not. Bedser swung at the fifth ball and it hit him in the stomach; the crowd roared a frantic appeal, even though the ball was passing a foot over the stumps. Three balls to go, two to win. Bedser stabbed the next delivery to cover for a single to bring the scores level. Now it was all up to Gladwin.

Before the seventh ball, Bedser called up to the wicket to tell his partner that Billy Wade, the wicket-keeper, was standing well back in case of byes or an awkward bounce. Bedser said, 'If you miss it, run like mad, because I'll already be on my way.' Gladwin missed it, but forgot to run. Bedser did not and he was sent back with an anguished scream by Gladwin. The giant Bedser managed to cram on the brakes and get back. He then noticed that Wade was in such a nervous state that he had not picked up the ball cleanly and that they could have got the vital single. They would have to go for it next time, wherever the ball was to land.

Tuckett bowled the last ball of the match, with a draw or England win imminent. It was a perfectly good delivery, around leg-stump and short of a length. It smacked against Gladwin's thigh as Bedser charged forward, bellowing, 'Run! Run!' The ball came out to 'Tufty' Mann at short leg and while he fumbled for it, Bedser dived forward to safety. He came up under a pile of bodies and looked up to see Gladwin waving his bat around at the other end. Only then did Bedser know England had won, courtesy of a solid lump of Derbyshire thigh.

The South Africans sat stunned for five minutes in their dressing-room, letting the impact of the struggle sink in. There would be time enough for post-mortems, and within five minutes they were offering their generous congratulations to England. It was hard on Cuan McCarthy, who had bowled at full speed for an hour and half in daunting circumstances, while still finishing on the losing side after taking six cheap wickets. Yet England had played the more positive cricket throughout, and the way they approached the run chase spoke volumes for the attitude of the players and their positive captain. Without the injury to Nourse and the stoppage for rain, England would have had another fifteen minutes in hand. If Compton had got out early during his crucial partnership with Jenkins, South Africa would have won. If Eric Rowan had obeyed the old maxim of standing with his heels on the boundary rope he would have caught Gladwin's desperate smear. If anybody but 'Tufty' Mann had been placed at short leg in the final over, there would have been a run-out: Mann's spectacles were covered by the driving rain and he could not sight the ball instantly when Gladwin produced the final leg-bye. By the time Mann had gathered the ball, Bedser had lumbered past him. It is fair to say that George Mann's captaincy was more subtle and inspiring than that of Dudley Nourse and Mann's dawn visit to the ground on the third day was highly influential.

The abiding memory from a pulsating match must be the cheerful resilience of Cliff Gladwin. He never thought South Africa would win, not even at the start of the last over. He called down the pitch to Bedser, 'Don't worry, my little champion – we're going to get them' and he actually believed that. As he proudly displayed a bruise on his left thigh, his team-mate Jack Young was trying to wheedle £25 out of press photographers for an exclusive picture, but he soon gave up. It was not a time for financial opportunism, it was a moment for genuine good fellowship in the glow of a great victory. The last word must go to Cliff Gladwin and his matter-of-fact reaction as he ran that historic leg-bye: 'Strangely enough, I thought of what the Derbyshire team would think, and the boys at the pit where I worked.' It was no more than you would expect from Doe Lea Pit's most famous boilersmith and storekeeper.

32
Bombay *v*. Maharashtra
1949

This is one of those games that really gets the statisticians salivating. It set a new world record aggregate of 2376 runs, beating the total of 2078 from the Bombay *v*. Holkar game four years earlier. Nine hundreds were scored and three batsmen made a hundred in each innings. The game lasted seven days, with no rest day. Bombay became the first side to score more than six hundred in each innings – and Maharashtra lost, even though they scored over a thousand runs in the match. I almost feel the need to have a calculating machine alongside me as I write the account of a bizarre game of cricket.

It was billed as a semi-final for the Ranji trophy, the cricket championship of all-India; in truth; it was a graphic example of man's inhumanity to man. Anyone not besotted with this dotty game called cricket would be entitled to ask the point and purpose of a match that lasted so long and inflicted so much pain on the bowlers. Yet cricket in India has always seemed essentially timeless – that is until the recent interest in one-day cricket, fostered by the 1983 World Cup triumph. In the 1940s in particular, gargantuan scores were the norm for Indian cricket: nine of the current record partnerships for the ten Indian wickets were set up in the 1940s. Double and triple centuries were as common as gastric upsets. It was all so very pointless, if the object was the greater good of Indian cricket. The national team remained chopping blocks for the established opposition throughout the period. When their batsmen encountered anything other than a perfect wicket they capitulated, while their bowlers operated under a collective inferiority complex.

This match revealed a marked disparity between the two sides, even if the vanquished salvaged some points near the end. Bombay were the best side in India, with so many fine players choosing to

MAHARASHTRA v BOMBAY

At Poona, 5–11 March 1949

BOMBAY

*K. C. Ibrahim b Dhanawade	32	– c Bhandarkar b Dhanawade.	59
†M. K. Mantri c Nana Joshi b Choudhari	200	– b Nimbalkar	2
P. J. Dickinson b Dhanawade	5	– lbw b Rege	40
U. M. Merchant c Nana Joshi b Gokhale	143	– st Bhandarkar b Choudhari	156
P. R. Umrigar b Dhanawade	57	–	
K. M. Rangnekar st Nana Joshi b Gokhale	0	– st Bhandarkar b Choudhari	94
D. G. Phadkar b Gokhale	131	– c Rege b Gokhale	160
M. M. Dalvi lbw b Choudhari	28	– b Choudhari	43
G. S. Ramchand b Choudhari	11	– not out	49
M. N. Raiji lbw b Gokhale	27	– st Bhandarkar b Choudhari	75
K. K. Tarapore not out	0		
Extras	17	Extras	36
	651	(8 wickets, declared)	714

1/101 2/107 3/357 4/433 5/433 6/462 7/521
8/553 9/648

1/4 2/165 3/181 4/483 5/518
6/571 7/627 8/714

Bowling: *First Innings* – Nimbalkar 25–4–86–0; Deodhar 20–3–65–0; Rege
49–22–86–0; Gokhale 11.4–2–35–4; Dhanawade 47–7–195–3; Choudhari
41–1–149–3; Joshi 1–0–10–0; Datar 2–0–8–0. *Second Innings* – Nimbalkar
17–1–107–1; Deodhar 15–4–42–0; Rege 28–4–71–1; Gokhale 29–6–86–1;
Dhanawade 27–1–126–1; Choudhari 47.5–0–210–4; Joshi 3–0–12–0; Datar
4–0–24–0.

MAHARASHTRA

K. V. Bhandarkar c Mantri b Tarapore	15	– c Rangnekar b Ramchand	47
S. G. Palsule b Phadkar	18	– c Rangnekar b Phadkar	97
P. G. (Sham) Joshi c Phadkar b Ramchand	1	– b Tarapore	57
M. C. Datar c Raiji b Tarapore	143	– b Tarapore	86
M. R. Rege b Tarapore	133	– c Mantri b Phadkar	100
B. B. Nimbalar st Mantri b Tarapore	25	– b Ramchand	21
S. D. Deodhar c Rangnekar b Tarapore	28	– b Phadkar	146
*Y. N. Gokhale b Phadkar	4	– run out	23
†P. G. (Nana) Joshi c Merchant b Tarapore	13	– absent – hurt	
S. D. Dhanawade c Merchant b Phadkar	12	– not out	0
D. G. Choudhari not out	9	– st Mantri b Tarapore	2
Extras	6	– Extras	25
	407		604

1/32 2/33 3/36 4/294 5/324 6/361 7/366
8/380 9/387

1/84 2/235 3/260 4/285
5/447 6/484 7/593 8/603
9/604

Bowling: *First Innings* – Phadkar 50.2–9–142–3; Umrigar 4–1–14–0; Tarapore
64–21–119–6; Ramchand 23–5–53–1; Raiji 18–1–54–0; Dickinson
2–0–16–0; Dalvi 1–0–3–0. *Second Innings* – Phadkar 48.3–16–178–3;
Tarapore 56–9–180–3; Ramchand 33–4–121–2; Raiji 31–5–84–0; Dalvi
8–4–13–0; Rangnekar 1–0–3–0.

Bombay won by 354 runs.

work – and therefore play cricket – in the country's industrial centre. Among them was one Patrick Dickinson, an unusual name to be found jostling among the Umrigars and the Merchants. Dickinson had made a thrilling hundred for Cambridge in the 1939 Varsity match; he did not return to the cloistered calm after the War, preferring to stay in India. He of all the players in this remarkable game must have appreciated its unreality. In contrast to the experienced, efficient Bombay side, Maharashtra were a collection of callow youths from the colleges around Poona – the cricketing equivalent of naive subalterns leading their troops over the top at Ypres and the Somme. At least these college boys escaped with nothing worse than a lesson in the facts of life.

On the first day, Bombay scored 366 for 3. To his chagrin, Patrick Dickinson missed out on the run feast after coming in at 101 for 1. He lasted just a few minutes and had to watch Mantri make a disdainful double hundred. Perhaps Dickinson lacked the killer instinct: at King's College School, Wimbledon, he would have been indoctrinated with concepts like compassion. There was little enough of that on show on the second day, when Bombay batted on for nine hours in all. Maharashtra were 34 for 2 at the close, but at least they had the satisfaction of restricting the batsmen to just another 285, while losing seven wickets. All credit to the captain, Raja Gokhale, whose analysis for some intelligent swing bowling on a plumb wicket should qualify for some sort of heroism award. The captain must have despaired of his players ever taking a catch: Umrigar was dropped off an easy chance in the slips when he had made fourteen, while Phadkar ought to have been caught and bowled by Choudhary when he had made 45. The batsman gratefully eased to his second fifty in just 34 minutes and played with his customary elegance. He might have been troubled by that fine spinner, Sayaji Dhanwade, but he had been put out of action after spraining his right shoulder in the morning.

In its review of the second day, *The Times of India* described Bombay's position as 'comfortable, though none-too-safe'. One would hate to imagine what constituted that august journal's version of a crisis. When Maharashtra lost their third wicket for 36 on the third morning, they were the side who were 'none-too-safe', but a splendid stand of 258 between Datar and Rege revived them. The weather at least favoured Bombay – it was a good deal cooler with a refreshing breeze – but the wicket was still blameless. The only bowler to do more than just turn his arm over hopefully was the left-arm spinner Tarapore – 2 for 75 off 42 overs. At the close, with the score 308 for 4, the game was beginning to meander along gently in the time-honoured Indian way.

Progress was comparatively frenetic on the fourth day. The college boys collapsed feebly to Tarapore's spin and were all out just before lunch. Three batsmen pushed simple catches to short-leg, Gokhale did not play a captain's innings, perishing to a slog that took his off-stump and once more it seemed like men against boys. In twenty-two overs that morning, Tarapore had taken 4 for 44, with six maidens. Bombay decided not to enforce the follow-on (presumably leave of absence from work was open-ended) and they made 255 for 3 by the close, a lead of 499. Merchant and Phadkar had added an unbroken 74 in the last three quarters of the day, and they at least were looking forward to the fifth morning.

Their partnership was eventually worth 302 in 195 minutes, and they both made their second hundreds of the match. Phadkar's was the more attractive innings, while Merchant plodded on, eschewing any off-side strokes and getting most of his runs with the sweep. Then Dickinson waded in with 40 in thirty-eight minutes and at close of play Bombay were 672 for 7, a lead of 916. Six catches had been dropped in the day and, if the fielders had bothered to stir themselves, they would have got somewhere near another half-dozen. It had been oppressively hot and the bowlers simply went through the motions. The pitch was totally devoid of pace, so that when the spinners induced an error, the batsmen still had time to adjust. In the space of five hours, Bombay had scored 417 for the loss of five wickets, and the cautious *Times of India* risked the following observation: 'Bombay are now virtually certain of their victory.'

Yet Bombay were not yet satisfied. On the sixth morning they flogged another 42 runs in a quarter of an hour before declaring. Maharashtra needed just 959 for victory. Not surprisingly, Bombay seemed over-confident in the field, and they dropped Palsule three times in the slips. They bowled listlessly, and a more positive attitude by the batsmen disrupted Tarapore's leg-trap. Phadkar, troubled by his batting exertions, could only bowl medium-pace due to a shoulder strain. Rege thrashed around for a fortuitous century and Palsule ended up 94 not out from a total of 273 for 3. For those who cared, they still needed another 686. The *Times of India* preferred to babble on about the prospect of new batting records. Indian cricket was like that in those days.

After the seventh and final day, the press dusted down the adjectives marked 'gallant', 'heroic' and 'courageous', then garlanded them round the necks of the young Maharashtra batsmen. They made another 331 in 270 minutes before they lost the last of their six wickets. At 593 for 6, they were entertaining grandiose dreams, but the end came swiftly, just twenty five minutes before the close. Perhaps the prospect of an eighth day was too awful for either side to contemplate. The most pleasing aspect of the day was the stylish, progressive attitude of Datar, Deodhar and Joshi. They soon realized that the Bombay bowlers were clueless and listless and they cashed in elegantly. Deodhar was last man out after four and a half hours and, at the end, no Bombay bowler was keen to inquire about his figures.

If the seventh day was the most attractive one, the match remains a ridiculous exercise in Parkinson's Law. The scoring rate was good throughout – 274 was the lowest total in a day – but how can so much time be spent on a game of cricket? The selfish attitudes of most of the batsmen made Don Bradman look a cavalier philanthropist. Games like this should act as a warning to those who maintain that four-day cricket on covered wickets would solve England's ills. When the bat is so much in charge, the players are powerless and the result is a meaningless fiesta for Frindalls. Thankfully, bold cricketers like Kapil Dev, Srikkanth and Engineer have guided Indian cricket away from the dark recesses of statistical freaks. It is no coincidence that their international stock has risen in the process.

33
England *v.* The Rest
1950

'Are these your best bowling figures, Mr Laker?' The question from the local newspaper reporter signified he would have been more at home covering crown court cases or the deliberations of the finance and general purposes committee. Instead he had to put several questions to this tall, laconic Surrey player; even more baffling, the cricketer had a Bradford accent, so why was he playing in the South? Jim Laker smiled that sardonic grin and confirmed to the hapless newshound that 8 for 2 was a career-best. Anyone who had ever played the game could only dream about such an analysis.

By 1950 Jim Laker had already suffered enough at the hands of the England selectors to feel unabashed at the thought of wrecking a Test Trial. His later experiences left him even more amused at their discomfiture. What could they possibly glean from a match supposedly featuring the cream of English cricket, when the whole thing was over just before lunch on the second day? The press fulminated over the frailties of the Rest's batsmen, with the *Manchester Guardian* saying the game was 'a ruthless indictment of their weaknesses', while *The Times* moaned: 'It is impossible to believe that the miserable total of 27 could not have been improved by what is assumed to be the second best eleven available in this country.' Yes, yes, yes – but what about Laker's bowling? Does a man get no credit for a faultless bowling performance? Surely the batting was only as good as the bowling would allow? If, in these days of covered wickets and fast bowling intimidation, a spinner took 8 for 2 we would laud him to the skies rather than berate the batting. In 1950 Jim Laker still had to convince many sceptics of his worth.

Despite his obvious class, Laker's introduction to Test cricket

ENGLAND *v* THE REST
At Bradford, 31 May–1 June, 1950

THE REST

D. J. Kenyon c Evans b Laker	7	– lbw b Hollies	9
D. S. Sheppard lbw b Bailey	4	– b Laker	3
G. H. G. Doggart c Bailey b Laker	2	– st Evans b Hollies	2
P. B. H. May c Hutton b Laker	0	– b Laker	2
D. B. Carr c Bailey b Laker	0	– st Evans b Hollies	2
E. A. Bedser lbw b Laker	3	– c Evans b Hollies	30
R. T. Spooner b Laker	0	– c Yardley b Bedser	22
R. O. Jenkins not out	0	– c Bedser b Hollies	3
R. Berry b Laker	0	– c Yardley b Bedser	16
F. S. Trueman st Evans b Bedser	1	– not out	0
L. Jackson c and b Laker	5	– st Evans b Hollies	1
B 3, l-b 1, w 1	5	B 4, l-b 6, n-b 3	13
	27		113

1/7 2/10 3/10 4/10 5/18 6/19 7/20
8/20 9/21

1/12 2/27 3/32 4/32 5/42 6/84 7/91
8/110 9/112

Bowling: *First Innings* – Bailey 6–4–3–1; Bedser 9–3–12–1; Laker 14–12–2–8;
Hollies 7–5–5–0. *Second Innings* – Bailey 5–2–6–0; Bedser 9–2–22–2; Laker
18–4–44–2; Hollies 22.4–13–28–6.

ENGLAND

L. Hutton b Trueman	85
R. T. Simpson st Spooner b Berry	26
W. J. Edrich lbw b Jenkins	46
J. D. Robertson c Sheppard b Berry	0
J. G. Dewes c Doggart b Berry	34
N. W. D. Yardley c Trueman b Jenkins	13
T. E. Bailey c Spooner b Berry	7
T. G. Evans run out	1
J. C. Laker not out	6
A. V. Bedser c Jackson b Jenkins	5
W. E. Hollies st Spooner b Berry	4
L-b 1, n-b 1	2
	229

1/59 2/155 3/156 4/162 5/187 6/212
7/214 8/214 9/214

Bowling: *First Innings* – Jackson 12–3–38–0; Bedser 13–0–60–0; Jenkins
10–0–38–3; Berry 32–10–73–5; Trueman 9–3–18–1.

Umpires: W. H. Ashdown and H. Elliott.

England won by an innings and 89 runs.

had been fraught in the two previous years. He was dropped twice in the 1948 series against the Australians, was not taken on the South Africa tour, and played only once in the four-Test series against New Zealand in 1949. By the time he came to his home town of Bradford for the 1950 Test Trial, Laker was twenty-eight and well aware he had one or two things to prove. Modern cricketers would call it 'a pressure situation', but Laker was the kind of man who viewed both triumph and failure with the same admirable equanimity. He would simply do his best.

Norman Yardley won the toss for England on a bright, sunny morning and had no hesitation in taking the field. There had been a lot of rain in the area recently and Yardley was well aware that Bradford was a paradise for spinners when the pitch had been dampened. It was perfectly natural to bring on Laker early, even though Trevor Bailey and Alec Bedser had made the ball get up in their opening spells. David Sheppard was first out, lbw without playing a stroke to Bailey, and then Laker came on with the score 10 for 1. The fun was only just beginning. . . .

Laker operated from the Football Ground End and he took advantage of a slight dip in the wicket to turn the ball immediately. Off his second ball, Hubert Doggart was caught by the most forward of the three short-legs and Peter May pushed the fifth delivery into the finer of the short-legs, playing forward. Then Donald Carr tried to hook a ball that was not short enough for the shot and he skied it to midwicket. Laker, operating from round the wicket, had found his line and length at once and the score was now 10 for 4, with the legside field looking very expectant. With the score on 18, Don Kenyon was caught at the wicket off one that went with the arm; Kenyon was the only batsman to shape up with any conviction. Laker relaxed his tormenting accuracy for just one ball, sending down a full toss to his county colleague, Eric Bedser, to allow him 'one off the mark'. Eric played it studiously to mid-on, where his twin brother Alec had positioned himself a few yards back to give him a comfortable single. After that lull in the hostilities, Laker returned to the attack: Eric Hollies had been brought on at the other end and he saw no reason why he should share any of these cheap wickets with a man who, however talented, might keep him out of the England team. At 19, Bedser was lbw to a quicker one, and in Laker's next over he bowled Dick Spooner and Bob Berry with two beauties 'through the gate'. Laker had now taken 7 for 1, but Fred Trueman spoiled the analysis with an inside edge for a single. A combination of a brilliant leg-side stumping by Evans and the bowling of Bedser accounted for Trueman, but Laker was not to be denied the last man. When Les Jackson smashed one straight back at him, Laker hung on to the missile and it was all over on the stroke of lunch. In just 110 minutes, the Rest had been dismissed for 27, the lowest score in a match of such importance. Laker had conceded two singles (one a gift, the other fortuitous) and he had beaten the previous lowest analysis for an eight-wicket haul – Edmund Peate's 8 for 5 for Yorkshire against Surrey in 1883.

None of Laker's friends from his bank clerk days in Bradford were there to see him – after all it was a working day – and with his parents dead, his only local living relative was an elderly aunt. Although the local boy had made good, he had never returned to Yorkshire after joining the Army when he was eighteen. He was now an adopted southerner, despite the flat vowels, and one can only imagine the full-throated approval that would have greeted such a feat by a Yorkshire county player. That bothered Laker not a jot; he had taken a look at the wicket before play started and he knew what had to be done. Most of the batsmen played right into his hands by pushing out firm-footed, and the four amateurs from Oxbridge had looked all at sea. They had piled up handsome runs in the Parks and at Fenner's, where the ball did not misbehave, but Laker on a wet wicket at Bradford was a different matter. 'Roley' Jenkins, who was undefeated by Laker, sniffs dismissively: 'Those public schoolboys were taught to play off the front foot and they left the gate open, and didn't use their feet. They didn't seem to know about leaving the bat beside the pad.' Fred Trueman, unsurprisingly, endorses that comment and says that it was poor technique as much as great bowling that led to the humiliation. 'The ball didn't turn square, it just did enough to beat the bat. The University players had never seen anything like it.'

After lunch, the experienced players showed them how to play the turning ball. Eric Bedser bowled off-spin from Laker's end right from the start, but he was mastered by Len Hutton and Reg Simpson. They posted fifty in even time, getting to the pitch of the ball masterfully. The wicket had not eased that dramatically since lunch, but Hutton's innings was that of a master craftsman. Bill Edrich was almost as impressive when he came in and only Bob Berry looked at all threatening with his left-arm spin. Meanwhile Fred Trueman was fretting away, wondering why he was not bowling. Finally Len Hutton said to the Rest's captain, Hubert Doggart, 'I suppose you know Fred's in the side for his bowling, not his batting,' and he was brought on at four o'clock. Hutton's reward was to be bowled by Trueman with a beautiful inswinger which hit the top of the off-stump at a fair old pace. As Fred was keen to point out, 'it were with the old ball, too'.

England led by 202 on first innings, and before the first day had finished they had reduced the Rest to 27 for 2. Laker had taken another wicket, bowling Sheppard for 3. He must have looked forward to reading the morning's papers.

On the second morning, the wicket had dried out a little. Hollies found a helpful spot at his end and exploited the conditions better than Laker. Eric Bedser even had the temerity to drive Laker to the sightscreen, while lovers of cricket curios could enjoy the sight of one twin brother bowling to the other – Alec to Eric Bedser. The Rest's innings fizzled away quietly a quarter of an hour before lunch, leaving the selectors wondering if they should ignore everything they had seen. Next day, they picked three spinners – Laker, Berry and Hollies – for the first Test at Old Trafford. Laker injured his hand while batting and took 1 for 86, while Berry and Hollies bowled West Indies to defeat on a dustbowl. So Laker was again dropped and he also missed that winter's tour to Australia. Not until 1956 could Jim Laker be certain of his place in the England team – and we all know what he did to the Australians that year. No wonder he adopted a rather cynical view of life while a player.

It is also a mystery why Bradford was chosen for a Test Trial. Certainly it was a good batting wicket in those days, but rain would always turn it into a paradise for spinners. Around 1950, Bob Appleyard and Johnny Wardle used to get stacks of wickets there for Yorkshire, so there was every chance that the match would become a farce. It was; but it is hard to blame Jim Laker's excellence for that.

34
Surrey *v.* Warwickshire
1953

The least a modern county side would expect after losing in less than a day would be a dose of 'naughty boy nets', or a vote of confidence in the captain from the chairman of the cricket committee. At worst, the skipper would be given a metaphorical loaded revolver and told to demote himself. The media would be babbling on about 'Loamshire's Day of Shame' and a petition would be circulating the county ground. In 1953 things were rather more civilized: Warwickshire stayed on in the capital for a couple of extra days and dined in the House of Commons with, among others, the Foreign Secretary. This welcome lack of hysteria stemmed from the quality of Warwickshire's opponents and their ill-fortune in being trapped on a wicket that favoured a great bowling side.

Although Warwickshire's batting only lasted two hours and twenty-five minutes, there was no shame in that. They were caught on a pig of a wicket, with the sun drying a wet ground and the Surrey bowlers desperate to get at them. Across London there was no play at Lord's, where thousands had flocked to watch the Australians play the MCC, but the new Oval drainage worked wonders and the game started at midday. At that time Alec Bedser was the greatest medium-pacer in the world, about to enjoy a memorable year as England's spearhead in the Ashes battle – and he would not be passing up the chance to prove his early season form in such favourable conditions. Although the wet turf might have hampered many bowlers of Bedser's size, he kept his feet and bowled magnificently, using the strong crosswind cleverly and, in effect, bowling fast leg-breaks, The catching in the close positions had to be seen to be believed. In less than twenty minutes, Warwickshire were 8 for 3, all of them to Bedser. Tom Dollery

SURREY v WARWICKSHIRE
At the Oval, 16 May 1953

WARWICKSHIRE

F. C. Gardner c Laker b A. Bedser	7	– c Laker b A. Bedser	7
T. W. Cartwright lbw b A. Bedser	0	– lbw b Laker	9
D. D. Taylor c Fletcher b A. Bedser	0	– lbw b A. Bedser	20
†R. T. Spooner c Whittaker b A. Bedser	16	– c and b Laker	0
*H. E. Dollery c Lock b A. Bedser	8	– c Surridge b Laker	0
R. E. Hitchcock c Whittaker b Lock	3	– c A. Bedser b Laker	0
A. Townsend c McIntyre b Lock	7	– run out	0
R. T. Weeks not out	0	– c Surridge b A. Bedser	0
C. W. Grove c Fletcher b A. Bedser	3	– c Constable b Laker	10
K. R. Dollery c Brazier b A. Bedser	0	– not out	0
W. E. Hollies c Laker b A. Bedser	0	– c sub b A. Bedser	0
L-b 1	1	– B 2, l-b 3, n-b 1	6
	45		**52**

1/3 2/3 3/8 4/27 5/30 6/36 7/42
8/45 9/45

1/20 2/22 3/26 4/26 5/26
6/32 7/32 8/49 9/52

Bowling: *First Innings* – A. Bedser 13.5–4–18–8; Surridge 6–1–17–0; Lock 7–2–9–2. *Second Innings* – A. Bedser 13.4–7–17–4; Laker 13–6–29–5.

SURREY

E. A. Bedser b K. Dollery	5
D. G. W. Fletcher c Townsend b Weeks	13
B. Constable c Grove b K. Dollery	37
T. H. Clark c K. Dollery b Hollies	2
A. F. Brazier c Townsend b Hollies	6
G. J. Whittaker b K. Dollery	0
†A. J. W. McIntyre c and b K. Dollery	9
J. C. Laker c H. Dollery b Hollies	18
*W. S. Surridge b Grove	19
A. V. Bedser not out	5
G. A. R. Lock retired hurt	27
L-b 4, n-b 1	5
	146

1/5 2/27 3/50 4/61 5/65 6/77 7/81
8/108 9/119

Bowling: Grove 10.1–3–29–1; K. Dollery 11–4–40–4; Weeks 8–1–24–1; Hollies 10–4–48–3.

Umpires: L. H. Gray and E. Cooke.

Surrey won by an innings and 49 runs.

and Dick Spooner added nineteen, the best stand of the innings, with Spooner in particular playing well until he mistimed a drive to mid-off. Tony Lock brought off one of his specialities in the leg-trap to get Dollery, and Bedser wrapped it up with the last three wickets in one over. In just seventy-five minutes, Warwickshire were all out.

Surrey would be expected to struggle against class bowling on such a wicket – after all, their bowling was always their strongest weapon – but unfortunately Warwickshire lacked the firepower. Eric Hollies was his usual consistent self, but Charlie Grove and Keith Dollery were no Bedsers, even though admirable county bowlers. So Surrey pressed ahead, determined to get quick runs in order to get the opposition in again before the wicket eased. They passed Warwickshire's score with just two men out, but a mid-innings slump left the tail with much to do. Bernie Constable played well, Stuart Surridge hit Hollies for three sixes in four balls and Laker drove one from Grove out of the ground. The last half-hour of the innings saw the addition of sixty-five runs, and the only jarring note for Surrey was the injury to Lock. He was hit over the eye by a ball from Grove and taken to hospital. He was not seriously injured and, to his chagrin, missed the fun as Warwickshire batted again on a pitch now taking a great deal of spin.

With Surrey leading by 101, Jim Laker opened the bowling with Alec Bedser at 5.30. By 6.40 the game was over after Surridge had claimed the extra half-hour at 49 for 7. Warwickshire started reasonably well, getting to twenty without loss – then five wickets went down for six runs. Laker took the second hat-trick of his career and they were three good players – Dick Spooner, Tom Dollery and Ray Hitchcock. When the left-hander Hitchcock walked in for the hat-trick ball, he was disconcerted to see the Surrey players already congratulating Laker on getting three in three! They felt that a left-hander had no chance against a class off-spinner who would be bowling one that would take the edge of the bat at speed – and to Hitchcock's annoyance, they were absolutely right. It must have galled a good player to see the opposition write you off first ball, but their confidence serves to confirm the quality of the bowling and the wicket.

While Laker was taking his hat-trick, Alan Townsend was just about to step into a hot bath. This fine all-rounder was due to bat at number seven and reasoned that the earlier batsmen would at least prolong the game for another half-hour to the close. He was just testing the water when an anguished cry from the dressing-room told him he was next man in. They threw his whites and pads on him, propelled him out of the door with a bat in his hand, and one wag shouted, 'Leave the water in the bath – he won't be long!' They were right: with his senses disorientated, he was soon run out.

Meanwhile, Eric Hollies was contemplating the realistic possibility of yet another 'pair'. Eric was a magnificent county leg-spinner, but not even his wife would have claimed any batting expertise for this genial son of the Black Country – indeed he is one of the rare cricketers who took more wickets than he scored runs. A career batting average of 4.94 indicates that Eric was often a godsend to bowlers anxious to finish off a game and this Surrey match was no exception. Eric had his pride, however; one nought in a game was enough, he would rather not get a 'pair'. He expressed this opinion to Alec Bedser as he walked past him with the score 52 for 9 and Alec – who was very fond of Eric – promised he would let him have one to get him 'off the mark'. The big fellow ambled up, sent down an absolute lollipop and Eric tried to smash it out of sight. He only succeeded in hammering it straight to short-leg who took an absolute blinder. Poor Eric was disconsolate, the Surrey players tried desperately not to laugh and, for the fortieth time, a first-class match was over in a day.

That great catch to get Hollies summed up Surrey's fielding that day, even without the prehensile Lock in the second innings. Alec Bedser recalls, 'Our close catching could not have been improved by any side at any stage. They were a wonderful boost to the bowlers.' Bedser feels that it was simply his day; he bowled leg-cutters that pitched middle and leg, and the ball did what he wanted it to do. He made the point that the batsmen were out of form, with a damp start to the season, and that Warwickshire were very unlucky to come up against such an attack on such a wicket. Tom Dollery, Warwickshire's captain, agreed: 'It was an absolute pig of a wicket. The top had gone off it by the end of the day and Alec Bedser was hitting you in the face with unplayable deliveries. If we'd had their attack, the roles would have been reversed.' Alan Townsend points out that like all great sides, Surrey at that time would never let up on the opposition: 'They snapped up half-chances all the time, they expected to get wickets with every ball. Honestly, we didn't play all that badly that day.' The total of sixteen Surrey catches out of twenty wickets gives some hint of their fielding brilliance.

So Warwickshire were now faced with a social dilemma at seven o'clock on a Saturday night in London. By all the cricketing canons, it was a case of back up to Birmingham straight away, tail between the legs. Yet the players had been invited to dine at the House of Commons on the Monday night by their local Member of Parliament; should they risk offending that worthy dignitary or stay down amid the fleshpots, delaying the retreat to Birmingham? Tom Dollery rang the club secretary, Leslie Deakins, and the message came back that it would be rude to spurn such a munificent gesture. They would dine at the Commons. So the players spent an extremely pleasant couple of days at the club's expense in London: no wonder Warwickshire have enjoyed a reputation for treating its players well! They took in some of the cricket at Lord's on the Monday, and in the evening enjoyed the historical, political and gastronomic delights of the Mother of Parliaments. Alan Townsend recalls the droll sight of watching Sir Anthony Eden chase his peas around his plate while sitting opposite Sir Walter Monckton, a recent president of Surrey County Cricket Club, but also the Duke of Windsor's confidant at the time of the Abdication. Seldom can a group of vanquished cricketers have been so far away from the proverbial sackcloth and ashes.

35
Somerset *v*. Lancashire
1953

Exactly three weeks after Warwickshire's debacle at the Oval, Somerset followed suit at Bath, much to the chagrin of one of that city's favourite sporting sons. Bertie Buse went to the City of Bath School, worked in a local solicitor's office, played rugby for Bath then joined the Somerset staff to play cricket. Since 1929 he had given valuable, underrated all-round service to the county; he was popular, reliable, the very best type of professional cricketer. You could be sure that he would be handsomely rewarded when his time for a benefit was due. Bertie had to wait twenty-four years for that day, and when it came, what could be more natural than to stage it in his home city?

How was Bertie to know that his benefit match would be over in a day, leaving him actually contemplating a loss on the event? He had to pay for all the expenses of staging the game, plus Lancashire's hotel and travelling bills — so he was left with little to show for a match in front of a good crowd in beautiful weather. To a certain extent Bertie contributed to the nightmare in the same way as Albert Trott back in 1907 (chapter 14). If Bertie had not bowled so well in Lancashire's innings, the game would have gone into a second day, and the crowd receipts would have helped compensate for a truncated match — but Bertie Buse always tried his best and would never have throttled back in the Somerset cause. It was just his bad luck that the Queen had been crowned a few days earlier. . . .

The groundsman at the Bath ground only had three full working days on the wicket after the Coronation. Due to the appropriate festivities he had not been able to tend the pitch because too many people were tramping all over the ground, toasting Her Majesty's health and enjoying the funfair and stalls. By the time all that

SOMERSET v LANCASHIRE

At Bath, 13–15 June 1953

SOMERSET

H. Gimblett run out	0	– c Wharton b Tattersall ...	5
J. Lawrence c Ikin b Tattersall	8	– c Wharton b Statham	0
R. Smith c Place b Tattersall	9	– b Statham	0
M. F. Tremlett c Statham b Tattersall	4	– b Statham	1
H. T. F. Buse c Grieves b Tattersall	5	– c Grieves b Tattersall	3
†H. W. Stephenson c Marner b Tattersall	8	– b Tattersall	14
*B. G. Brocklehurst c Marner b Hilton	2	– c Hilton b Tattersall	2
D. P. T. Deshon c Edrich b Tattersall	0	– c Wharton b Statham	9
S. S. Rogers st Parr b Hilton	7	– c Grieves b Tattersall	0
J. Redman c Place b Tattersall	1	– not out	27
B. A. Langford not out	7	– b Tattersall	8
B 2, l-b 2	4	B 1, l-b 9	10
	55		**79**

1/12 2/13 3/17 4/22 5/34 6/40 7/40
8/47 9/47

1/3 2/3 3/5 4/7 5/26 6/27
7/36 8/37 9/44

Bowling: *First Innings* – Statham 8–4–14–0; Tattersall 12.4–4–25–7; Hilton 5–1–12–2. *Second Innings* – Statham 10–4–13–4; Tattersall 11.3–2–44–6; Hilton 2–0–12–0.

LANCASHIRE

*C. Washbrook lbw b Buse	20
J. T. Ikin c Tremlett b Buse	8
W. Place lbw b Buse	11
G. A. Edrich c Brocklehurst b Buse	2
K. J. Grieves c Tremlett b Lawrence	2
A. Wharton b Redman	21
P. T. Marner b Redman	44
M. J. Hilton b Buse	19
†F. D. Parr not out	15
J. B. Statham c Tremlett b Langford	6
R. Tattersall c Stephenson b Buse	2
B 4, l-b 4	8
	158

1/22 2/33 3/41 4/44 5/46 6/116 7/117
8/140 9/155

Bowling: Buse 12.4–3–41–6; Redman 6–1–32–2; Smith 1–0–8–0; Langford 3–0–18–1; Lawrence 8–2–31–1; Tremlett 2–0–20–0.

Umpires: A. E. Boulton-Carter and J. S. Buller.

Lancashire won by an innings and 24 runs.

debris had been cleared, there were just a few days to go before an important cricket match that should last the full three days. When the pitch was mowed on the Wednesday (three days before the game), hardly any grass came off and, on the Saturday morning, the texture of the wicket owed more to dried moss than grass. The Somerset captain Ben Brocklehurst recalls, 'There were pebbles and acorns in it and it was quite the most dangerous pitch that any of us had played on.' Roy Tattersall, Lancashire's match-winning off-spinner, remembers looking at the wicket before the game started and being able to move the surface! Now the cock-up theory rears its indiscriminate head again: local rumour had it that the council workmen in charge of the Bath ground sent the appropriate turf for relaying to a village and the cricket pitch ended up with the turf for the village green. The likes of Brian Statham and Roy Tattersall were a big enough handful on good wickets, but no one would think to bat against them on a village green! Whatever happened to the turf we shall never know, but clearly the process of knitting together had not worked during the winter, so that Bertie Buse lost the most important payday of his county career. It was not as if the ground authorities were caught unawares; the previous year, the wicket turned an angry reddish colour and Middlesex could only get 52 in the fourth innings of the match, with thirteen of those coming in extras.

Lancashire's captain, Cyril Washbrook, showed what he thought of the pitch by opening with Tattersall's off-spin alongside Statham. At that time, Statham was genuinely fast and this, combined with his legendary accuracy, meant he was unplayable. He was too much of a gentleman to intimidate the batsmen deliberately, but the ball did the most amazing things and he was a frightening proposition. Brian Langford, later a fine off-spinner, was making his Somerset debut at the age of seventeen, and he recalls missing every ball in one Statham over. 'Then Cyril Washbrook took him off, thank God – he must have seen how frightened I was! The big problem was the uneven bounce – one would go past your nose and the next would hit you on the ankle. And, don't forget, no helmets in those days!' Roy Tattersall modestly attributes his success in the game to Statham's relentless pressure at the other end: 'I was the lesser of the two evils and they either holed out to me, trying to get some runs, or they played forward defensively and I had them picked up in the leg-trap, as the ball did funny things. They just couldn't get a run against Brian, so they had to try it against me.'

Somerset lasted ninety minutes first time round, and when Washbrook was asked what sort of roller he would like, he asked for the harrows! When Lancashire went in, they were under orders to get quick runs and avoid serious injury. They struggled to 46 for 5, then Peter Marner and Alan Wharton produced the most controlled batting of a remarkable day. They added seventy in twenty-five minutes, hitting Johnny Lawrence for fifteen in one over, smashing the poor beneficiary for eighteen in the next over, and later Jim Redman also went for eighteen. Marner, showing the type of clean hitting that underlined his class, kept his head over the ball and hit through the line like a Botham. Admittedly the bowling was not as taxing as Lancashire's, but in the context of the game Marner's innings was outstanding, especially at the age of seventeen.

Somerset went out to bat again at 4.10, and the wicket was now even worse. Every time the ball pitched, it took large chunks out of the pitch, and soon Somerset were 7 for 4, three of them to Statham. Buse and Harold Stephenson added a precious nineteen, with the wicket-keeper hitting Tattersall for ten in two balls, but Somerset never had a chance. At 5.15 they were 44 for 9, and it was left to Redman and Langford to add 35 with some bold hitting. The end came mercifully at 5.35, with twenty-two players relieved that they had escaped serious injury. The bowler only had to pitch the ball in a certain area and the batsman was helpless and physically threatened.

Bertie Buse was deluged with sympathy as the crowds filed out of the ground. With the weather set fair, and most people still in festive mood after the Coronation, he could have expected a generous windfall from three full days. Yet Bertie took the reverse with his customary stoicism. Roy Tattersall remembers him with affection: 'Bertie wasn't the sort of chap to get upset, even at something like this. Whenever he was bowling he'd just smile if he beat the bat. No fuss, just a genuine enjoyment from playing the game.' Brian Langford agrees: 'Bertie was a gentleman, he would not moan about his bad luck. He just got on with the job.' Such admirable unflappability had its reward eventually. The plight of Bertie Buse touched so many hearts that he received countless donations for the rest of that summer. Even on the one and only day of his benefit match, he was touched by the generosity of the travelling Lancashire supporters and, in succeeding weeks, he would often open a letter from a well-wisher and a cheque would fall out. In the end Bertie made as much from his benefit year as if the Lancashire game had drawn packed houses for three days. His personal reputation helped – genuine cricket fans can easily spot a loyal, uncomplaining player – and many admired his decision to have his benefit game in his home town, rather than Taunton. Modest, amiable, phlegmatic, Bertie Buse at last got what he deserved. A sum of £2814 for his benefit was about par for the course in those days, and a good deal more than Bertie Buse initially expected.

There was also a happy sequel in the next match of the Bath Festival. After an emergency meeting of Somerset's executive committee the groundsman was sent to the local market to find something that would bind the pitch together. He came back with bull's blood and it worked, although the bowlers were careful not to lick their fingers as they walked back to the mark. A mixture of marl, water and bull's blood compacted the surface and it was not so dangerous in the next two games. Brian Langford took twenty-five wickets in those two matches – it must have seemed an easy career to him at the age of seventeen – but the most popular individual performance came from Bertie Buse. In the match immediately after the Lancashire fiasco, he made 102. Perhaps you do get your just desserts in the end. The fact that there has only been one first-class game to finish in a day since Bertie Buse's match suggests that groundsmen have become rather more efficient. Modern players who bemoan the deadening quality of current wickets might pause to consider if they would like to play on pitches like the one at Bath in Coronation Year.

36

England *v*. Australia
OLD TRAFFORD, 1956

Laker's Match. Enough said. Australia lost the Old Trafford Test by an innings and 170 runs to J. C. Laker, Esq. If ever a record could claim to be imperishable, it is Laker's feat of taking 19 for 90 in a first-class match. No one else has taken more than seventeen wickets in a first-class match, and it would take either a highly developed imagination or a fantastic sequence of events to create another nineteen-wicket scenario for one man. Just for a change, the use of hyperbole is justified: it was a fabulous achievement.

One of the more remarkable sub-plots of Old Trafford 1956 is that Laker had already taken all ten wickets that summer against the Australians, this time for Surrey. He had been up all night with two sick children and hoped that Surrey would bat first thing. Yet Laker had to bowl forty-six overs on a very good batting wicket and Stuart Surridge, his captain, cajoled him to take 10 for 88. There was little turn for him at the Oval compared to Old Trafford and most of his wickets were catches at slip or behind the wicket. When sceptics point out that Laker was indebted to the wicket's vagaries at Old Trafford, they might remember a classic piece of spin bowling on a good wicket earlier in the season.

They might also consider the case of Tony Lock. Laker's Surrey team-mate could only take one wicket at Old Trafford, despite his customary commitment. Lock was one of the game's great triers and would be expected to pick up a shoal of wickets in such conditions. Yet he tried too hard and ended up with 1 for 106 in the match. Godfrey Evans, the England wicket-keeper that day, says: 'Locky kept pulling the ball down and I was taking it chest-high. When it turned for him, it just went too far. Jim had the right idea – pitch the ball up and let it turn a little off the pitch.' Peter May, England's captain, feels the crucial difference lay in the

ENGLAND *v* AUSTRALIA
(Fourth Test)
At Old Trafford, Manchester, 26–31 July 1956

ENGLAND

P. E. Richardson c Maddocks b Benaud	104
M. C. Cowdrey c Maddocks b Lindwall	80
Rev. D. S. Sheppard b Archer	113
*P. B. H. May c Archer b Benaud	43
T. E. Bailey b Johnson	20
C. Washbrook lbw b Johnson	6
A. S. M. Oakman c Archer b Johnson	10
†T. G. Evans st Maddocks b Johnson	47
J. C. Laker run out	3
G. A. R. Lock not out	25
J. B. Statham c Maddocks b Lindwall	0
B 2, l-b 5, w 1	8
	459

1/174 2/195 3/288 4/321 5/327 6/339 7/401 8/417 9/458 10/459

Bowling: Lindwall 21.3–6–63–2; Miller 21–6–41–0; Archer 22–6–73–1; Johnson 47–10–151–4; Benaud 47–17–123–2.

AUSTRALIA

C. C. McDonald c Lock b Laker	32	– c Oakman b Laker	89
J. W. Burke c Cowdrey b Lock	22	– c Lock b Laker	33
R. N. Harvey b Laker	0	– c Cowdrey b Laker	0
I. D. Craig lbw b Laker	8	– lbw b Laker	38
K. R. Miller c Oakman b Laker	6	– (6) b Laker	0
K. D. Mackay c Oakman b Laker	0	– (5) c Oakman b Laker	0
R. G. Archer st Evans b Laker	6	– c Oakman b Laker	0
R. Benaud c Statham b Laker	0	– b Laker	18
R. R. Lindwall not out	6	– c Lock b Laker	8
†L. V. Maddocks b Laker	4	– (11) lbw b Laker	2
*I. W. Johnson b Laker	0	– (10) not out	1
Extras	0	– B 12, l-b 4	16
	84		205

1/48 2/48 3/62 4/62 5/62 6/73 7/73
8/78 9/84 10/84

1/28 2/55 3/114 4/124 5/130 6/130
7/181 8/198 9/203 10/205

Bowling: *First Innings* – Statham 6–3–6–0; Bailey 4–3–4–0; Laker 16.4–4–37–9; Lock 14–3–37–1. *Second Innings* – Statham 16–10–15–0; Bailey 20–8–31–0; Laker 51.2–23–53–10; Lock 55–30–69–0; Oakman 8–3–21–0.

Umpires: D. E. Davies and F. S. Lee.

England won by an innings and 170 runs.

fact that Lock's stock delivery was going away from the right-hander and so they could leave a few that were spinning viciously. 'Jim just dripped away at their nerves, realizing that they had got a little obsessional about him and the wickets that year. To be honest, the wicket was not that difficult.' Whatever the reasons, only one England player was less than chuffed in the after-match celebrations, as everyone else toasted Jim Laker.

Before the game, Cyril Washbrook, England selector and alleged expert on Old Trafford, prophesied that it would be the greatest batting wicket of all time. The chairman of selectors, G. O. Allen, disagreed and voted against playing an extra seamer. For the first day and a half, Washbrook looked to have got it right, as England piled up a score that at least put them beyond defeat. The off-spinner Ian Johnson and the leg-spinner Richie Benaud did not look very penetrative, and it seemed to augur a lot of work for Laker and Lock. At tea on the second day, Australia were 62 for 2. Thirty-five minutes later, they were all out for 84. Why? The light was fine and the pitch dry with a small degree of turn. The only ball that did anything untoward was the one that pitched on Neil Harvey's leg-stump and hit the off. Laker took seven wickets in the space of twenty-two deliveries and the batsmen were simply mesmerized by his reputation and control. Peter May was right: they had got themselves into a state about the turning wickets in a damp summer and the likes of Mackay, Miller and Archer looked as if they had never held a bat in their lives.

Laker's 9 for 37 had only been bettered in Test history by George Lohmann's 9 for 28 for England against South Africa in 1895/6, but little did we know that a new record would be established within a few days. Laker finished off the second day with another wicket when Australia followed on, but it was not one to brag about – Neil Harvey hit a full toss straight to mid-wicket to complete a 'pair'. Yet Australia ended the day in a comfortable manner which suggested that they would, as usual, battle to save the game. Now the weather came to their aid. Just forty-five minutes' play on Saturday saw Jim Burke caught in the leg-trap for 33 and, in another fifty minutes on Monday, Ian Craig and Colin McDonald added another 27 runs and Australia ended on 84 for 2. The wicket was very damp indeed and all Laker could seemingly offer was accuracy. England began to resign themselves to a moral victory.

On Tuesday it rained hard until dawn. The captains disagreed about the condition of the pitch and play started ten minutes late. Until lunch the batsmen were not troubled; the pitch was sluggish and it was taking too long to dry out for England's peace of mind. Craig and McDonald looked immovable. Over lunchtime the clouds dispersed and a strong wind joined forces with a bright sun and began to work its influence on the pitch. At 2.25 Craig was beaten through the air and off the pitch and trapped lbw, after four hours and twenty minutes of watchful, mature batting. The roof started to cave in around the Australians as Laker bowled with six fielders around the bat. Archer turned an off-break into the leg-trap with the air of a man giving catching practice, Miller used his pads instead of his bat and was yorked, while Mackay's torment ended when he offered a supine catch to slip. They had gone from 114 for 3 to 130 for 6 with the time now 2.55. At last McDonald found a doughty partner in Richie Benaud. They stayed together for eighty minutes – McDonald picking up runs on the leg-side off a frustrated Lock, and Benaud wasting time by asking for a guard each over and gardening the pitch after every ball. This served only to increase the frustration of the volatile Lock, whereas Laker viewed the proceedings with his usual calm, detached manner at the other end. It was a time for cool heads and there was no better man in such a situation than Jim Laker.

The pair were still together at tea, and May had even rested his two spinners in favour of Oakman and Bailey. That had not worked, so the Surrey spinners were reunited with four wickets needed in two hours. The second ball after tea turned sharply and McDonald turned it into the hands of Oakman at short-leg. He had batted magnificently for 337 minutes, and given the bulk of his team-mates an embarrassing lesson in skilled defensive play. At five o'clock, Benaud played back to Laker and the ball hurried through to bowl him. Laker had now equalled the first-class record of seventeen wickets in a match and everyone on England's side (apart from Lock) was willing him to take the last two wickets. At 5.15 Lock secured the record by catching Lindwall. Lock bowled the next over with all his usual demonic fervour, but he could not break through. At 5.20 Laker bowled the second ball of his fifty-second over to Len Maddocks, the Australian wicket-keeper; Maddocks went back instead of forward, the ball hit his pads and he was out lbw. Maddocks went forward to shake Laker's hand, and a few England players walked up and patted the bowler on the back. Laker strolled off the pitch with that detached air, softly whistling to himself while his colleagues followed a respectful pace or two behind, contenting themselves with measured applause. Judging by Laker's demeanour, you would have thought he had taken nought for plenty.

A quarter of a century later, Jim Laker and I talked about that astonishing day. He was simply philosophical about the chain of events that made history: 'If that game was played again a million times over, you'd never get the same situation. I wasn't particularly excited inside – nobody kissed me, that's for sure. I was doing my job and I tried to detach myself from everything. I gave a thought to every ball I bowled.' Colin Cowdrey stood at slip for most of the game and he cannot forget Laker's calmness: 'The batsmen played and missed so often, yet you couldn't tell from his expression. He was in perfect rhythm. Jim made the batsmen play at every ball, with a little drift in the air and just enough turn.'

How much was it a case of great bowling or mesmerized batting? Certainly Laker had the 'hex' on the Australians throughout that year. In the previous Test at Leeds, he and Lock had taken eighteen of the twenty wickets and, whenever he went into their dressing-room at Old Trafford, the Australians stopped playing cards, looked at him, then at his fingers as if he were a magician. Yet McDonald, Burke and Craig showed the wicket was not hopeless for batting; perhaps it was yet another case of a great bowler exerting psychological pressure on vulnerable players who were out of form.

So many amusing vignettes came out of this historic match. There was the sight of Tony Lock cursing and throwing the ball away whenever he took a catch off Laker. The hero of the day toasted the crowd in Lucozade and, when he stepped back into the dressing-room, Lock had changed and gone to his car. Alan Oakman has dined out on his five catches ever since, so much so that the youngsters in Warwickshire's second eleven groan whenever their coach is asked his memories of the game. 'Twenty years later, I sat next to Jim at a dinner and when I was billed as the man who took all those catches in Laker's Match, Jim leaned over and whispered, "Christ, you're not still living on that are you?" But you've got to make the most of it, haven't you?'

That is the one thing Jim Laker did not do. He was too great a bowler to rely on one performance for a place in the Pantheon and he was too self-mocking and whimsical a man to talk about it unless pressed. He never forced his past deeds into conversations, never commented on the amazing reasons why the England selectors did not trust his marvellous ability. To Jim Laker, it was all rather amusing: picking a couple of long-odds winners out of the *Sporting Life* was a considerably more taxing exercise. It was typical of Laker's wry sense of humour that one incident stands out from that remarkable day. On the way home from Old Trafford he stopped for a pie and a pint in a pub at Lichfield. He stood in a corner of the bar, munching away contemplatively, listening to the chatter of the regulars about this chap Laker. He watched about eight of his wickets on the television in the bar, drained his pint and walked out. Nobody recognized him. Jim thought that was very funny.

37
Border *v.* Natal
1959

For fifty-one years, Northamptonshire had jealously guarded its proud record of the worst combined innings total in a first-class match (see chapter 17). Then at the Jan Smuts Ground in East London, their colours were lowered, with a total of thirty-six far too good for one of forty-two. Furthermore, Northants had batted a man short during their heroic spell of incompetence: Border had no such excuse, all eleven men were fully fit and found wanting.

It would be safe to say that the wicket favoured the bowlers at the Jan Smuts Ground just before Christmas 1959. Certainly twenty-three wickets fell on the first day, a day when play did not start until two o'clock because of heavy rain. Yet it was the imbalance between the two sides that was most graphic. Cricket had been strongly rooted in Natal since the military presence there during the Boer War had established an Anglophile passion for the game and instilled the necessary disciplines needed to flourish at the highest level. Only Transvaal consistently compared with Natal as South Africa's premier side and, at the start of the sixties, Natal were about to carry all before them. They were to win the Currie Cup in this 1959/60 season, and another six times in a row, sharing it with Transvaal in 1965/6. They enjoyed the same supremacy as Surrey in English county cricket during the 1950s, with a production line of fine players. In contrast, Border were the country cousins, out of their depth. They first entered the Currie Cup in 1897/8, but the district of Cape Province around East London that comprises its cricket catchment area has never been able to hang on to promising young talent. Too often the talented schoolboys have gone to pastures new while furthering their academic studies at university. Border have never won the Currie Cup, and their

BORDER v NATAL

At Jan Smuts Ground, East London, 19–22 December 1959

NATAL

*D. J. McGlew c Hagemann b Knott..	0	– c During b Schreiber	22
T. L. Goddard lbw b Knott	4	– lbw b Knott	0
M. K. Elgie b Hagemann	11	– not out	162
R. A. McLean b Knott	0	– c Hagemann b During	23
C. Wesley c and b Hagemann	11	– b Schreiber	36
L. Morby-Smith c Muzzell b Hagemann	0	– c Griffith b Schreiber	43
G. M. Griffin c Hagemann b Knott	22	– st Kirsten b Schreiber	5
A. F. Tillim c Schreiber b Hagemann ..	0	– did not bat.	
†M. S. Smith c Griffith b Hagemann ..	33	– lbw b Schreiber	2
P. M. Dodds b Knott	8	– c Knott b Schreiber	0
J. M. Cole not out	0	– did not bat.	
N-b 1	1	L-b 1	1
	90	(For 8 wkts. dec.)	**294**

1/0 2/15 3/15 4/18 5/21 6/47 7/47
8/50 9/90

1/0 2/13 3/13 4/46 5/80 6/145
7/267 8/294

Bowling: *First Innings* – Knott 13.3–2–40–5; Hagemann 13–2–49–5. *Second Innings* – Knott 15–5–24–1; Hagemann 10–3–37–0; Schreiber 39–5–126–6; Tainton 3–0–13–0; Commins 4–1–16–0; Griffith 1–0–5–0; Muzzell 3–0–23–0; During 15–4–49–1.

BORDER

A. F. Hagemann b Cole	2	– c Smith b Griffin	3
P. J. Muzzell lbw b Goddard	0	– b Griffin	0
P. Fenix b Goddard	0	– c Smith b Cole	1
K. N. Kirton c Elgie b Cole	4	– c Smith b Griffin	3
N. During b Goddard	9	– c Smith b Cole	1
*K. T. Commins c Tillim b Goddard ..	0	– c Smith b Griffin	0
W. M. Tainton c Elgie b Cole	0	– not out	7
M. H. Griffith lbw b Goddard	1	– b Griffin	0
S. Knott c Cole b Goddard	0	– c Smith b Griffin	0
E. F. Schreiber c McLean b Cole	0	– c Smith b Cole	1
†N. Kirsten not out	0	– c McLean b Griffin	2
Extras	0	B 1, l-b 1	2
	16		**20**

1/2 2/2 3/2 4/8 5/11 6/11 7/12 8/16
9/16

1/1 2/4 3/5 4/5 5/10 6/10 7/11 8/12
9/15

Bowling: *First Innings* – Griffin 1–1–0–0; Goddard 11–9–3–6; Cole 11–4–13–4. *Second Innings* – Griffin 13–6–11–7; Goddard 4–3–1–0; Cole 9–7–4–3.

Umpires: T. M. Gunton and A. L. Haiden.

Natal won by 350 runs.

only claim to fame is that Tony Greig began his first-class career with them.

When the two sides met at East London, it was Border's first match in the 'A' section of the Currie Cup. It was to be a harsh introduction to life among the big boys. They started well enough: Cummins won the toss, put Natal in and they made their lowest score against Border. Four of the first five Natal batsmen were Test players, but they only managed fifteen between them. Had it not been for some gallant batting by Geoff Griffin and Malcolm Smith it would have been even more embarrassing. A series of dropped catches did not do Border any favours either.

A score of ninety by mighty Natal was enough to set the press-box phones buzzing, but they soon had more sensational tidings to impart. Trevor Goddard, fresh from a double hundred against Rhodesia, now showed the other side of his all-round talents. His nagging left-arm medium pace brought him 6 for 3, including the hat-trick (Griffith, Knott and During). At the other end, Cole was a trifle short of a length at the start of his spell, but he soon learned where to put the ball after watching Goddard. There was still forty-five minutes' play left after Border were skittled out and in that time, Natal lost 3 for 39 to lead by 113. Judging by Border's efforts with the bat, they could declare overnight and still win comfortably. The *Natal Mercury* pithily summed up the day's efforts thus: 'It was a bad wicket and even worse batting.'

On Monday morning it began to resemble a proper cricket match. Kim Elgie, a sensible, unfussy batsman, hit his second first-class century, with a six and twenty-two fours in 260 minutes and he added 122 in seventy minutes with Lynton Morby-Smith. Colin Wesley also joined Elgie in a partnership worth 65 in seventy minutes. The pitch appeared as docile as it had looked lethal on Saturday, and Edwin Schreiber had to work hard with his patient off-spin.

The blameless nature of the pitch on Monday only served to highlight Border's shocking inadequacy. There was some excuse for capitulating to the canny seam bowling of Goddard on a wet wicket, but not when it had rolled out easy-paced after sunshine. All Geoff Griffin had to do was bowl somewhere near the off-stump and the batsmen did the rest. Natal's wicket-keeper Malcolm Smith helped himself to seven catches, John Cole also enjoyed himself at the other end and it was all over in ninety-seven minutes. With Border 11 for 7 at one stage there was a real chance that the lowest-ever total of twelve might be toppled, but Peter Tainton soon put a stop to such statistical flights of fancy. Tainton batted for fifty-seven minutes and never looked in the slightest trouble. He showed there was nothing wrong with the wicket, it was simply a case of young players being overawed in the company of their superiors.

Geoff Griffin must have thought that cricket was a lovely pastime at this stage. The tall, blond fast bowler was just twenty and beginning to look a natural successor to Neil Adcock as the spearhead of the South Africa side. In this 1959/60 season, Griffin took thirty-five wickets (average 12.23), and he was an automatic selection for the tour to England. He was not to know it, but his days as a front-bowler were numbered. There had been one or two grumbles about his action during this first successful season in the Currie Cup; it had stemmed from a school accident that gave him a discernible crook in his right arm. He could not straighten his right arm naturally and at the moment of delivery, Griffin looked distinctly suspicious. A widespread disquiet among the game's rulers about throwing had sparked off a genuine desire to stamp out the problem and Griffin was to suffer the consequences. He was called for throwing three times in the early part of the England tour, then his fate was sealed at the Lord's Test. Griffin was no-balled eleven times by Frank Lee and then in an exhibition game after the serious stuff had ended, Sid Buller no-balled him persistently. Griffin had to finish his last over underhand and that was the last we saw of him as a Test bowler. Ironically, Griffin had taken a hat-trick earlier in that Lord's Test, the first by any Test bowler at headquarters.

It seemed a pity that such a pleasant, dignified young man had been allowed to come this far without official reprimands back home. He bore the ordeal with immense self-control and saw out the tour as a batsman. When he returned home, he played several seasons for Rhodesia as a batsman. Yet Griffin's name will always be remembered for his bowling, or at least his attempts at legitimate bowling. Perhaps we have all been too harsh on Border's batsmen for their abject display in the second innings: it cannot have been a pleasure for young players to try to keep out someone impersonating a javelin thrower.

38

Yorkshire *v.* Hampshire
1962

On the afternoon of 29 June, 1962 Brian Sellers was not a happy man. The autocratic chairman of Yorkshire was never all that pleased when his side was about to lose, but this time it was even more galling than usual. Hampshire, the team that had interrupted Yorkshire's run of championship successes the year before, were about to inflict a significant defeat on Sellers' side. They needed just seven runs to win, with five wickets left and both sides seemingly going through the motions. It was too much for Sellers, the man who had grown accustomed to Yorkshire titles, both as captain and chairman. He stormed off the ground in one of his legendary furies and nobody dared suggest he stayed around. Half an hour later, he received a phone call at home from the club secretary, J. H. Nash: he thought the chairman might like to know that Yorkshire had taken the last five wickets for one run and had romped home by five runs.

That decisive period of play represented Yorkshire cricket at its best – dynamic bowling by Fred Trueman and Ray Illingworth, wonderful close catching and an irresistible will to win that would not be denied. It was a triumph of will as much as anything, as Fred Trueman recalls: 'That was the greatness of Yorkshire cricket at its best; we never knew when we were beaten. We had men who could catch anything anywhere in the field and for the bowlers that was always a fantastic boost.' It was particularly satisfying to beat Hampshire: the Yorkshire players were convinced that they had won the title in 1961 through generous declarations, with the brilliant Roy Marshall often leading the successful run chase. Ray Illingworth says: 'They chased declarations that we were never given. Out of ten games against Hampshire we would expect to win eight of them, because we were the better side. As a result

YORKSHIRE v HAMPSHIRE
At Bradford, 27-29 June 1962

YORKSHIRE

J. B. Bolus lbw b Heath	31	– c Harrison b White	0
K. Taylor c Gray b Shackleton	1	– lbw b Heath	7
P. J. Sharpe c Horton b White	5	– c and b Shackleton	13
D. E. V. Padgett c Livingstone b Shackleton	10	– lbw b Shackleton	5
W. B. Stott c Harrison b Shackleton	15	– b White	21
R. Illingworth c Sainsbury b Heath	7	– c Harrison b White	13
*J. V. Wilson c Livingstone b Shackleton	51	– c Barnard b Shackleton	45
F. S. Trueman c White b Shackleton	8	– c Wassell b Shackleton	41
D. Wilson c Harrison b Shackleton	19	– lbw b Shackleton	4
†J. G. Binks c Wassell b Shackleton	3	– c Wassell b White	12
M. J. Cowan not out	1	– not out	0
Extras	0	B 4, l-b 9, n-b 2	15
	151		**176**

1/7 2/18 3/41 4/49 5/63 6/75 7/85
8/139 9/148

1/1 2/22 3/26 4/31 5/55 6/70 7/137
8/145 9/176

Bowling: *First Innings* – Shackleton 31–7–78–7; White 20–4–52–1; Heath 10–3–21–2. *Second Innings*—Shackleton 34–16–67–5; White 19–5–55–4; Heath 14–3–39–1.

HAMPSHIRE

J. R. Gray b Trueman	9	– c Binks b Trueman	78
H. Horton c Sharpe b Trueman	67	– c Binks b Cowan	12
H. M. Barnard c Sharpe b Trueman	23	– b D. Wilson	6
M. Heath c and b D. Wilson	18	– c Trueman b Illingworth	0
D. A. Livingstone c Sharpe b D. Wilson	12	– lbw b Taylor	26
P. J. Sainsbury c D. Wilson b Taylor	9	– lbw b Illingworth	15
*A. C. D. Ingleby-Mackenzie c Cowan b Taylor	10	– c Cowan b Illingworth	8
†L. Harrison c Binks b Cowan	1	– c J. Wilson b Illingworth	1
A. Wassell lbw b Trueman	0	– not out	0
D. Shackleton c Sharpe b Trueman	2	– b Trueman	0
D. W. White not out	6	– c Trueman b Illingworth	1
B 4, l-b 4	8	B 10	10
	165		**157**

1/10 2/102 3/103 4/126 5/145 6/155
7/156 8/157 9/159

1/28 2/41 3/97 4/127 5/135 6/156
7/156 8/156 9/157

Bowling: *First Innings* – Trueman 23.2–9–34–5; Cowan 24–6–50–1; Taylor 10–5–16–2; Illingworth 6–1–14–0; D. Wilson 8–0–37–2; Bolus 2–1–6–0. *Second Innings* – Trueman 24–9–49–2; Cowan 17–6–30–1; D. Wilson 13–7–25–1; Illingworth 22–12–33–5; Taylor 5–4–10–1.

Umpires: W. E. Phillipson and W. H. Copson.

Yorkshire won by 5 runs.

there was always a bit of edge when we played Hampshire around that period.'

Unfortunately for the impartial observer, Roy Marshall could not play in this Yorkshire game. He had been sent home with German measles, and his brilliant strokeplay would be missed. Yet the other great Hampshire match-winner was in attendance, and Derek Shackleton proceeded to dominate the Yorkshire batsmen with his maddening accuracy and skilful use of seam and swing. He bowled unchanged for three hours and forty minutes, and only Brian Bolus (attractively) and Vic Wilson (obdurately) looked the part. Yorkshire had slumped to 85 for 7 before Wilson rallied the side, with the last four wickets responsible for more than half the total. In contrast Hampshire went for their shots, and although Trueman pegged them back with two wickets in the final half-hour, a close of play score of 103 for 3 augured well for a useful lead.

Hampshire must have been disappointed to make do with a lead of only 14, especially after Danny Livingstone (55 minutes for 12) and nightwatchman Malcolm Heath (90 minutes for 18) had built solid foundations. The cricket was keen and tense (Yorkshire's rate of scoring 2.47 an over, Hampshire's 2.26) and Trueman showed his competitive steel when he hit Livingstone on his cap with a beamer, then appealed for lbw after the batsman had recovered! By teatime Yorkshire faced the prospect of a two-day defeat. They were 61 for 5, a lead of only 41: Bolus had been brilliantly caught behind, Taylor and Padgett leg before, Sharpe gave an easy catch to the bowler and Stott was yorked after a few defiant shots. There was a suspicion of a ridge at Shackleton's end, but there had been too many loose strokes. The captain, Wilson, and Trueman put it all in perspective with a stand of 67 in seventy-five minutes. Trueman was at his most belligerent, smearing 'Butch' White back over his head for six, and picking up five, courtesy of a wild throw from Livingstone. By 5.30 Yorkshire led by a hundred and Shackleton was tiring after yet another marvellous display of seam bowling. Wilson hit him for three boundaries in an over, during which he was also missed at slip by Barnard. When Trueman was caught in the gully, Jimmy Binks came in to give sensible support to his captain. They closed on 175 for 8 (Wilson 45 not out, Binks on 12), and with a lead of 161, there was nothing in it after two engrossing days.

Round one went to Hampshire on the final morning, with the

last two wickets going down for one run. So Hampshire needed 163 to win with the rest of the day stretching ahead of them. Trueman looked hostile in his opening spell (rapping Jimmy Gray on his right glove) and the batsman almost played on to Mike Cowan, but the openers weathered the early assaults. They got to 28 after fifty minutes when Henry Horton was out, and twenty minutes later Mike Barnard was yorked by Don Wilson. Livingstone swept Illingworth for six and at lunch, with Gray looking indomitable, Hampshire were 60 for 2 and slightly the favourites. After lunch Livingstone still continued to play with ominous freedom until Ken Taylor was brought on as partnership breaker and at once had Livingstone lbw. Gray advanced to his fifty with measured tread and got there after two and a half hours. Peter Sainsbury was lbw at 127 for 4, but still you had to fancy Hampshire, especially if their captain, Colin Ingleby-Mackenzie, connected with a few of his ambitious blows. Luckily for Yorkshire, he was out to a brilliant running catch by Cowan for the second time in the match – this time at wide long-on. That made it 135 for 5, with the experienced Leo Harrison next man in. He turned his first ball from Trueman into the huge right hand of Vic Wilson at short leg – and he dropped it. The despairing groan from the crowd was no help to Wilson, a man who regularly held blinding catches in that position, but what a time for a rare aberration! It did not improve the black mood of Brian Sellers.

Gray and Harrison lasted till tea, with Gray 66 not out, playing the sheet anchor role to perfection. They needed just 23 to win with half the side still to bat. During Illingworth's first over after tea, a ball stood up off a length and it went for four byes: could the wicket possibly have deteriorated in the space of half an hour? Judging by the way the Hampshire batsmen looked solicitously at the pitch, they thought so – and Yorkshire sensed they still had an outside chance. With the total on 156, Vic Wilson made amends for his earlier lapse by catching Harrison in the leg-trap. Then Gray flicked at a rising ball from Trueman and was caught behind. The next ball yorked Shackleton and suddenly Hampshire were 156 for 8. White steered the hat-trick ball through the vacant third slip area for a single. That summed up Yorkshire's dilemma: they wanted the wickets but they could not afford to allow a snick to go through a crowded slip area to the boundary. If they could have spared a third slip, Trueman would probably have had a hat-trick, but he had his revenge in the next over when he caught White at backward short leg. It was now 157 for 9 and Malcolm Heath and Alan Wassell needed to find six runs from somewhere against a Yorkshire side that smelt blood. Wassell survived a testing over from Trueman, but then Illingworth had Heath jubilantly caught inches off the ground by Trueman in the leg-trap. The last pair had never looked like withstanding the inexorable pressure from the close fielders and resourceful bowlers.

The transformation after tea had been remarkable. Trueman had looked subdued, out of luck, while Illingworth looked in vain for some sharp turn. Yet he took 3 for 4 in five overs after tea. Perhaps the secret lay in the eventual use of an attacking field, with two short legs breathing down on the batsmen. Whatever the reasons, Yorkshire at last looked themselves, after appearing mystifyingly passive for most of the match. It was that air of defeatism which had annoyed Brian Sellers so much. Ray Illingworth says the pitch had helped the bowlers throughout: 'Bradford at that time was one of the few places where you would get a green turner. There was bounce, which helped the spinner and the fast bowler, but also the strokemaker. So we had a good cricket wicket and when we at last sniffed victory, we were experienced enough to go for it. In the end, they lacked a bit of character, because we should never have come back from that position.' Fred Trueman pays tribute to Jimmy Gray's sportsmanship which possibly turned the match: 'He got a very thin edge to me and walked immediately. I don't think the umpire would have been able to give him out because the edge was so faint, but Jimmy didn't hang around. If he had been there at the end, they would have won.'

It is pleasant to think that Jimmy Gray's sense of honour helped Brian Sellers recover his good humour. One hopes that he would have expected nothing less from his young charges at Yorkshire. Within two months the chairman was celebrating yet another championship, with the remarkable win over Hampshire assuming crucial significance.

39
Ireland v. West Indies
1969

Sion Mills is hardly the place to find a West Indian cricketer: as likely a sight as Ian Paisley orating on the Savannah. Perhaps that's why Sion Mills is as warm a memory for the Caribbean cricketer as Culloden might be for the Scottish fighting man. It was here, fifteen miles from Londonderry, that the West Indies suffered the most ignominious defeat in its history on a bright, breezy day. The town of one street and sixteen hundred souls could hardly believe it, either; perhaps the little people really did have an influence on matters Hibernian.

A cursory look at the scorecard suggests that Ireland either played twenty-two men or the West Indians were made to bat the wrong way round. Not a bit of it. West Indies won the toss and decided to bat, so they cannot complain if they misread the conditions. It is true that they must have been tired after being kept in the field at Lord's the previous evening as the Test ended in an exciting draw – but then only six of that side played the following day. Their captain, Gary Sobers, stayed behind for treatment on his injured knee and the manager, Clyde Walcott, had to come out of retirement to play, but they still had enough quality in their ranks to beat Ireland, even if it was the weakest West Indies tour party since the War. The likes of Basil Butcher, Clive Lloyd, John Shepherd and Joey Carew should not have been troubled by amateurs who only played forty overs games at the weekend.

During my research I was lucky enough to watch a video recording of the West Indies innings, and it was not an impressive sight. Certainly the wicket was very green after heavy rain, no doubt the ball 'stopped' when they tried to play forcing shots, but their efforts to combat the unfamiliar conditions were feeble.

IRELAND *v* WEST INDIES

At Sion Mills, Londonderry, 2 July 1969

WEST INDIES

G. S. Camacho c Dineen b Goodwin ..	1	– c Dineen b Goodwin	1
M. C. Carew c Hughes b O'Riordan ..	0	– c Pigot b Duffy	25
M. L. C. Foster run out......................	2	– c Pigot b Goodwin	0
*B. F. Butcher c Duffy b O'Riordan ...	2	– c Waters b Duffy	50
C. H. Lloyd c Waters b Goodwin	1	– not out..	0
C. L. Walcott c Anderson b O'Riordan	6	– not out..	0
J. N. Shepherd c Duffy b Goodwin	0		
†T. M. Findlay c Waters b Goodwin ..	0		
G. C. Shillingford not out	9		
P. Roberts c Colhoun b O'Riordan	0		
P. D. Blair b Goodwin........................	3		
B 1..	1	L-b 2..	2
	25	(4 wkts.)	78

1/1 2/1 3/3 4/6 5/6 6/8 7/12 8/12 9/12   1/1 2/2 3/73 4/78

Bowling: *First Innings* – O'Riordan 13–8–18–4; Goodwin 12.3–8–6–5. *Second Innings* – O'Riordan 6–1–21–0; Goodwin 2–1–1–2; Hughes 7–4–10–0; Duffy 12–8–2–2; Anderson 7–1–32–0.

IRELAND

R. H. C. Waters c Findlay b Blair........	2
D. M. Pigot c Camacho b Shillingford	37
M. S. Reith lbw b Shepherd	10
J. Harrison lbw b Shepherd.................	0
I. J. Anderson c Shepherd b Roberts...	7
P. J. Dineen b Shepherd.......................	0
A. J. O'Riordan c and b Carew...........	35
G. A. A. Duffy not out........................	15
L. P. Hughes c sub b Carew................	13
L-b 2, n-b 4.................................	6
(8 wkts., dec.)	125

1/19 2/30 3/34 4/51 5/55 6/69 7/103 8/125

*D. E. Goodwin and †O. D. Colhoun did not bat.

Bowling: Blair 8–4–14–1; Shillingford 7–2–19–1; Shepherd 13–4–20–3; Roberts 16–3–43–1; Carew 3.2–0–23–2.

Umpires: M. Stott and A. Trickett.

Ireland won by 9 wickets.

Whenever they tried to hit out, they got out. Afterwards, Clyde Walcott said: 'These are not conditions we are used to, but Ireland bowled extremely well and also took their catches.' True enough, but one would have thought Test players had it in them to adapt; more than one of them had played English county cricket and so the pitch at Sion Mills was not remarkably different from a slow, damp wicket in April. The two Irish bowlers who decimated the innings were experienced cricketers who knew how to exploit the conditions. The captain, Doug Goodwin, bowled leg-cutters from a good, high action while Alec O'Riordan operated from over the wicket with his left-arm seamers. Today, O'Riordan remembers above all the poor batting: 'They played bad shots early on, there was a stupid run out and we fielded well. The common fault was playing too early on the damp, slow pitch. I was barely medium pace that day because the run-ups were so wet, so I just concentrated on putting it on the spot.' It was some consolation to O'Riordan for missing his brother's wedding, although his family had long become accustomed to cricket taking priority in the life of the only man to score 2000 runs and take 200 wickets for Ireland.

While watching the West Indies debacle it struck me that both the crowd and the Irish players were very low-key about the whole affair. At the fall of every wicket, there was a ripple of applause, isolated pats on the shoulder of the bowler from assorted team-mates, but little of the self-indulgent melodramatics that have since become the norm in first-class cricket. Perhaps everyone on the ground was too bemused to take it all in, but the only man who seemed in danger of going over the top was the television commentator, busy dusting off his 'Boys' Own Stuff' hyperboles. The Irish team simply went out there and relied on the West Indians to shoot themselves in the foot. Everything went according to plan and Doug Goodwin can never have had an easier time as captain. There were no tactical niceties to consider, the ball was not disappearing into the crowd every over; all he had to do was persevere with himself and O'Riordan. Over the years the rumour has gained currency that the West Indies had over-indulged in local hospitality the night before. It is hard to see where they would have found the time to do so, considering that they would not have arrived until late in the evening from London. From what I could glean from the video recording, their batsmen tried to knuckle down after the loss of early wickets, but they were just not up to the job of grafting away and punishing the loose ball. A total of sixteen maidens in 25.3 overs hardly indicates that the visitors were the victims of Caribbean indiscipline.

At the start, Camacho and Carew were both out mishooking to mid-wicket and Foster was run out by a smart piece of fielding at mid-off. With the score 3 for 3, Lloyd and Butcher needed to work hard. Their timing was awry throughout, and Butcher was caught at gully, playing forward loosely: 6 for 4 in the eleventh over. After labouring for twenty-five minutes, Lloyd was caught at mid-on, trying to dig out a yorker: 6 for 5 after forty-five minutes. Clyde Walcott was already at the wicket, his bat sounding as if it were broken every time it made contact with the ball, and the crowd sat stunned. When John Shepherd walked out to join his manager, the television commentator announced 'Ireland are now through to the West Indies tail,' an interesting way of dismissing Shepherd's three hundreds and thousand runs for Kent in the previous season! Yet Shepherd did not play like an all-rounder, and when he slashed one hard off the back foot, Gerry Duffy caught it nonchalantly, pocketed the ball and grinned at his team-mates. In the sixteenth over, it was 8 for 6, with Walcott surveying the ruins, and wondering what he could say at the post-match reception. He had got off the mark with a desperate slog for two over mid-on, but his footwork was predictably immobile and no amount of vigorous patting of the pitch could obscure the technical defects that creep into the game of any forty-three-year-old heavy man who no longer practises. At least he hung around for a time, playing one good shot off the back foot through the covers for a single, smearing one from Goodwin just over mid-on's head for two, then picking up a comfortable single with a controlled shot past point. After an hour, the score was 10 for 6, with fourteen maidens out of the nineteen overs. Walcott had made exactly half the runs when he was caught at cover by Ivan Anderson, playing an airy shot with his head in the air. Goodwin had 4 for 6 off eleven overs when Findlay was taken at the third attempt by Robin Waters at mid-off and the score stood at 12 for 8.

When Roberts hit O'Riordan straight up in the air, the improbable loomed — a hat-trick to end the innings. Events had been sufficiently bizarre that there was no telling where fantasy would end and reality re-emerge. For just one over, reality took over: Blair hit the hat-trick ball down to long leg for the first boundary of the innings, the third ball was smacked over mid-off for three, another went the same place for two and a couple of singles were also taken. Thirteen runs came off that O'Riordan over and the West Indies had reached the dizzy heights of 25 for 9. Goodwin put a stop to all the nonsense by clipping Shillingford's off-stump as he tried to hit him towards Londonderry. All out for 25 in eighty-five minutes and, amid polite applause, the Irish team walked off in calm contentment, with Goodwin shyly leading them in. The press men squabbled for use of the phone, the sports desks of Fleet Street asked to have the score repeated to check any typographical errors and the West Indies made a mental note to avoid the town of linen mills for the rest of their lives.

Perhaps the calm reaction to the astonishing morning's play stemmed from a fear that the West Indies would be an even more fearsome proposition on this wicket, that Ireland would not muster double figures. They need not have bothered. Ireland passed the total of twenty-five for the loss of just one wicket and under the laws relating to one-day cricket, they were permitted to bat on. Joy of joys, they even had the luxury of a declaration, then dismissed Camacho and Foster for just two runs. Carew and Butcher made 72 in thirty-four overs and West Indies ended a momentous day at 78 for 4. The record books however state that Ireland beat the West Indies by nine wickets and no one in Sion Mills will ever forget the time that weekend cricketers became kings for a day.

The *Daily Telegraph* called it 'a stew of truly Irish ingredients'. Heaven knows what they made of it in the cane fields of Barbados and in the Jamaican rum shops. One thing they ought to know, almost twenty years after the event: the proud successors to Headley and Constantine let themselves down by bad technique, not by a carefree attitude. They did not try to hit the cover off every ball, they were simply not up to the job, even though they tried hard. In the history of West Indies cricket, it was a fluke, a one-off, but try telling that to the gentlefolk of Sion Mills.

40

Glamorgan *v.* Essex

1969

This was a tremendous game of cricket, won off the last ball in circumstances that defied description for all those who had seen a certain Glamorgan cricketer field over the years. For Ossie Wheatley was no Clive Lloyd in the field: he was closer to Harold Lloyd when the ball came anywhere near him. For a decade, he was an outstanding opening bowler with Oxford University, Warwickshire and Glamorgan. With a superb action and an excellent late outswinger, Wheatley was a match for the best batsmen. Yet it was one uncharacteristically swift piece of fielding that secured his place in the affections of the Glamorgan faithful.

Wheatley had been brought out of virtual retirement for the closing stages in the race for the 1969 championship. The previous season, he had taken eighty-two wickets as Glamorgan finished second; now his experience and class would be vital in the run-in. Glamorgan were leading Gloucestershire by twelve points by the end of August 1969, but if they were to land the title for the first time since 1948 they had to beat either Essex or Worcestershire in the next two matches. Glamorgan lacked really penetrative bowling, but their fielding was brilliant – apart from a rather senior seam bowler – and their batting was attractive and positive, with Majid Khan its star turn. Under the quixotic captaincy of Tony Lewis, they had a happy approach to the game that deserved to succeed. The good folk of Swansea who thronged in to see the Essex game could only agree. For many it was the perfect way to spend a Bank Holiday weekend, and both sides deserve equal credit for making it such a memorable game.

By 1969 Essex were beginning to emerge as a team for the future. Under Brian Taylor's benevolent despotism, men like Keith Fletcher, John Lever, Ray East and Stuart Turner were coming

GLAMORGAN *v* ESSEX

At Swansea, 30 August – 2 September 1969

GLAMORGAN

A. Jones c Boyce b Turner	75	– c Taylor b Lever	69
R. C. Davis lbw b Boyce	2	– b Lever	2
Majid Jahangir c Turner b East	23	– b Turner	28
*A. R. Lewis c Taylor b Turner	1	– c Irvine b Lever	21
B. A. Davis c Ward b East	78	– c Irvine b Hobbs	5
M. A. Nash c Edmeades b Lever	14	– not out	36
P. M. Walker c Barker b Hobbs	14	– c Ward b Boyce	50
†E. W. Jones c Fletcher b East	0	– st Taylor b Hobbs	28
A. E. Cordle c Taylor b Boyce	20	– b Hobbs	30
D. J. Shepherd not out	2	– not out	2
O. S. Wheatley c and b Hobbs	0		
B 4, l-b 3, n-b 5	12	B 8, l-b 2, n-b 3	13
	241	**(8 wickets)**	**284**

1/5 2/58 3/65 4/156 5/196 6/210
7/210 8/230 9/239

1/8 2/50 3/90 4/109 5/144 6/181
7/227 8/272

Bowling: *First Innings* – Boyce 18–3–52–2; Lever 15–5–38–1: East 19–3–63–3; Turner 20–8–44–2; Hobbs 11.1–2–32–2. *Second Innings* – Boyce 25–5–79–1; Lever 22–4–64–3; East 9–3–19–0; Turner 11–1–31–1; Hobbs 36–16–78–3; Fletcher 1–1–0–0.

ESSEX

B. Ward c R. C. Davis b Wheatley	31	– c R. C. Davis b Wheatley	21
B. E. Edmeades lbw b Nash	4	– c Lewis b Wheatley	10
G. Barker lbw b Wheatley	17	– st E. W. Jones b. R. C. Davis	28
K. W. R. Fletcher lbw b Wheatley	49	– c B. A. Davis b R. C. Davis	44
B. L. Irvine b R. C. Davis	109	– b Shepherd	29
K. D. Boyce c B. A. Davis b Shepherd	16	– c Lewis b R. C. Davis	11
*†B. Taylor c Cordie b R. C. Davis	70	– c Lewis b Wheatley	5
S. Turner not out	23	– c R. C. Davis b Shepherd	2
R. N. S. Hobbs not out	8	– c E. W. Jones b Shepherd	17
R. E. East (did not bat)		not out	14
J. K. Lever (did not bat)		run out	2
B 1, l-b 7, n-b 1	9	B 4, l-b 1	5
	(7 wkts., dec.) 336		**188**

1/5 2/48 3/63 4/139 5/165 6/294
7/304

1/29 2/36 3/43 4/109 5/123 6/125
7/131 8/163 9/185

Bowling: *First Innings* – Nash 24–5–84–1; Wheatley 26–3–77–3; Cordle 8–2–32–0; Shepherd 28–10–78–1; Walker 3–0–20–0; R. C. Davis 10–1–36–2. *Second Innings* – Nash 3–0–16–0; Wheatley 10–0–40–3; Cordle 4–0–33–0; Shepherd 11–0–56–3; R. C. Davis 9–0–38–3.

Umpires: D. J. Constant and G. H. Pope.

Glamorgan won by one run.

through to supplement seasoned players such as Gordon Barker and Brian Edmeades, with Lee Irvine proving a sound overseas purchase. Essex were shaping up well in the championship table, but they had their eyes on talent money in the John Player League which had just been launched that year. They hoped to finish third and a win over Glamorgan on Bank Holiday Sunday would do very nicely. Tony Lewis admits that he talked about the aims of the respective sides that weekend to Brian Taylor and Keith Fletcher, and all three expressed the hope that Essex and Glamorgan would get what they deserved. As it turned out, Essex won by one run on Sunday while Glamorgan triumphed in the county game by one run – each time off the last ball. Cynics might tap the side of their noses and look knowingly, but Tony Lewis insists there was no collusion. 'I simply asked Brian Taylor to approach the three-day game as if it were May – in other words go for the runs if I declared. He was as good as his word, and they tried to win right to the last ball. But there was no deal done.' The key to the chivalrous atmosphere in the three-day match lies in John Lever's observation: 'It was always a pleasure to play Glamorgan around that time because they had so many nice guys. Both sides always went out to win, there was never any aggro.' David Constant, one of the umpires, confirms that point: 'If every game was played in the spirit I saw in that particular match, there would never be any worries at all. It was a classic – great individual performances, wonderful atmosphere, excellent sportmanship. I have lovely memories of that game.'

In front of a crowd of six thousand, Glamorgan started the match in confident style. Alan Jones and Roger Davis added 91 in just under two hours in the face of superb bowling and wonderful fielding. Glamorgan declined from 196 for 4 to 210 for 7, and they finished up nine runs short of their fourth bonus point. Essex made 63 for 3 by the close and the big surprise was that no batsman had really got in for a big score on an excellent wicket and a lightning fast outfield.

Lee Irvine was the first man to cash in on the favourable batting conditions on Bank Holiday Monday. Twelve thousand packed the ground and they saw rich entertainment: Essex made another 268 in seventy-two overs, then Glamorgan made 123 for 4 in the remaining two hours fifty minutes, chasing quick runs for a possible declaration on the final day. Irvine and Taylor added 129 in ninety minutes and everyone else batted positively: Fletcher made a cultured 49, the dangerous Keith Boyce made 16 in twenty minutes, including one enormous six, and Irvine punished everyone except the enduringly canny Don Shepherd. Essex, true to their word, declared at four o'clock, 95 ahead, and invited Glamorgan to throw down the gauntlet. They did their best, getting to fifty in the first nine overs, but then Davis was bowled behind his legs. Majid played a delightful cameo innings for half an hour, but then he was disturbed by a needless public address announcement and he was bowled swinging across the line. Lewis also played freely before he was caught low down at slip, and Brian Davis was beautifully taken at deep mid-off before the deficit was wiped out. Glamorgan were now in trouble; there was plenty of time left in the match and they needed a period of retrenchment before hoping to launch another assault around lunchtime. In that context the valuable forty-five minutes occupied by Peter Walker and Alan Jones at the end of the second day was to prove highly significant.

No one could argue that Glamorgan's best crowd since the War had seen a magnificent day's cricket. Essex had looked the better side while Glamorgan's nerve ends seemed to be fraying. No matter: almost four hundred runs had been scored in the day by high-class batting, not Sunday League slogging. That was some consolation to the worried Glamorgan supporters, although John Woodcock in *The Times* could hardly be blamed for writing: 'I doubt now whether Glamorgan can pull the match back.' With a lead of just twenty-eight, and not a great deal of batting to come, one could see his point.

On the final morning, Peter Walker played a vital role for three and three quarter hours, as Glamorgan inched towards some sort of respectability. The crowd slow-handclapped him for a time, but they seemed to be unaware that Glamorgan needed to be there till at least lunchtime, otherwise Essex would have far too much time in which to get the runs. Essex needed to have a twitch or two of anxiety in their run chase if Glamorgan were to have any chance, because the wicket was still excellent. Cordle's innings of an hour should also not be forgotten and, by lunch, Glamorgan had done well to scrape together a lead of 141 with three wickets left. After that they had an enjoyable swish against the new ball, with Malcolm Nash clubbing five boundaries in two overs from Boyce and Lever. Essex were left with a target of 190 in fifty-five minutes plus twenty overs. Would they go for them? The rate was five an over, but the short boundaries, fast outfield and good wicket were all highly relevant. . . .

Essex kept their word and Brian Ward in particular set off like an express train. Then Ossie Wheatley did exactly what he had been brought into the side to do – with the ball still new, he fired out Edmeades, Ward and Taylor in three consecutive overs and Essex were now 43 for 3. Yet they kept going and Irvine and Fletcher added 66 in ten overs. At the start of the final twenty overs, they were 89 for 3, but then Fletcher was out at 109 to a wonderful diving catch at short mid-wicket by Bryan Davis. At 123, Irvine was bowled behind his legs and two runs later Boyce launched himself into a spiralling shot that was beautifully taken by Lewis, running back from mid-on. Other sides would have shut up shop at that dismissal, but not Essex. Gordon Barker, that highly competent, experienced Yorkshireman, had seen these kind of situations before; he paused for a few overs to right the ship then, in the company of Robin Hobbs, resumed the offensive. When Hobbs was out, Ray East came in with the clear intent to keep going for victory.

The last over was entrusted to the offspin of Roger Davis. Essex needed seven runs and Glamorgan two wickets. Essex also knew that if the scores were level at the end, they would get an extra five points as the side batting second. At that stage of the season, they were lying seventh in the table and the extra few points might just help them to squeeze into the talent money at the season's end. So the incentives for both sides over the next six deliveries were attractive enough. Off the first two balls, easy singles were taken to the deep-set field. Essex now needed a boundary and Barker was stumped off the third ball, giving the charge to Davis in search of it. Three balls left, five to win and the last man, John Lever, out there with Ray East. Over the next few years, these two would establish reputations as genuine comedians and much-loved characters in an era that became increasingly serious – but in 1969, they were just a couple of young lads anxious to make the grade in the professional game. Their captain had told them to go for the runs until the very death, so they had no second thoughts about that. They picked up a single each off the next two balls, which left them needing three off the last delivery of the match.

John Lever had the strike, and to an inexperienced player the atmosphere must have been daunting. The Swansea ground is a marvellous amphitheatre when full, with vast banks of spectators all around the bowl of the field. The partisan crowd were not only roaring on Glamorgan that day, they were supporting Wales. Just a few weeks earlier, they had seen the Prince of Wales enthroned at Caernarvon Castle and what better way to celebrate belatedly than to win the county championship? To all intents and purposes, this tall, blond young man from Essex was all that stood in their way of a famous win. Tony Lewis shuffled his fielders around, checking that they could all hear him above the din and he remembered just in time to bring Ossie Wheatley in from the third man boundary. As Lewis recalls, 'Ossie was a magnificent bowler who ought to have played for England, but as an athlete he was not terribly well put together. To be frank, he was the biggest carthorse in the county game at that time. So I had to be sure he would not be exposed if the batsmen played it slowly down to him at the boundary edge. So I brought him up to a position that was halfway between backward point and third man. You see, he had a fine throw and from that position they couldn't possibly run three to him.'

Wheatley was about fifty yards away from the bat when Davis bowled the last ball. Lever glided it through the region of third slip and set off for runs. Lewis thought, 'Oh God, it's going down to Ossie's corner and he'll have to turn and chase it, he'll never get there!' Lever recalls, 'Ossie was the slowest mover in county cricket, and I was pretty confident of getting at least two runs, which would have tied the scores and got us the bonus points. I hadn't reckoned on what was about to happen. . . .' What happened was that Wheatley moved to his left, gathered up the ball comparatively smoothly in one hand and fired in a lovely, flat strong throw to the wicket-keeper. Lever had not even bothered to look as he turned at the bowler's end and continued charging back for the second run. He was out by a good four yards as Wheatley's throw dipped, hit the gloves of Eifon Jones halfway up the stumps and the bails were taken off exultantly. Glamorgan had triumphed by one run and the hero was a specialist bowler with no claims to fielding or batting prowess. When he really had to do it, Ossie Wheatley came up with a throw from the Colin Bland manual.

Grown men wept unshamedly as the Welsh crowd burst into spontaneous song. As the warmth of the choristers washed all over the ground, Tony Lewis took a delighted bow from the players' balcony. Inside, Ossie Wheatley was reminding those who cared to listen that he had always had a good, flat throw, that it was simply a case of getting to the ball in enough time. Don Shepherd, the grizzled senior pro, kept insisting 'We haven't won the title yet, you know,' but few heeded his words of caution. It was a time of emotion, for 'Bread of Heaven', 'Sospan Fach' and many full-throated choruses. It would be some time before the celebrants would get round to appreciating the gallant efforts of Essex.

It was a match that embodied all the best qualities of the English – and the Welsh – county scene. Romantics were delighted that a marvellous finish was orchestrated from the unlikeliest source – the athleticism of Ossie Wheatley. Perhaps Don Shepherd's scepticism was well founded: he had seen one miracle that day to last him a lifetime, and it would be wrong to expect anything else. Within three days, even Shepherd permitted himself the luxury of a glass of champagne when the title came back to Wales after Worcestershire were defeated at Cardiff.

41
Sussex *v.* Surrey
1972

This was one of those games where most of the excitement was crammed into the last quarter of an hour when the batsmen were reduced to gibbering wrecks and somehow the bowlers got out of jail after the key had seemed firmly lodged in the jailer's pocket. Correction, not bowlers – bowler. For Pat Pocock chose this match to turn in one of the most remarkable spells of bowling. He took seven wickets in eleven balls as Sussex blew the simple task of getting eighteen off the last three overs with nine wickets in hand. Thanks to Pocock, Sussex lost eight wickets in eighteen balls while making fourteen runs – the most dramatic collapse since Alonzo Drake and Wilfred Rhodes wrought such havoc at Chesterfield in 1914 (chapter 20). Never has the dull term 'draw' been so misleading.

Until six o'clock on Tuesday, 15 August, the match had followed a fairly routine pattern, even if some good cricket had been played. Both sides had made up for the loss of almost all the first day's play with some positive batting on Monday. Surrey advanced from 38 for 0 to 300 for 4 declared, while Sussex closed on 110 for 3. After putting on 130 for Surrey's first wicket, Mike Edwards and Roy Lewis both got out, mistiming their shots in the quest for bonus points. In the last hour of the day, the spin and guile of Pocock and Intikhab troubled Sussex and they were indebted to a fine unbeaten half-century from Roger Prideaux. Given a couple of sensible declarations on the final day, there was every prospect of a good finish.

Prideaux got his hundred, then after Sussex declared behind, Surrey took up the challenge and made some quick runs before Mickey Stewart declared for the second time. It was a typical Eastbourne wicket – helping the seamers early on with the new

SUSSEX v SURREY
At Eastbourne, 12–15 August 1972

SURREY

*M. J. Stewart not out	34	– not out... 1
R. M. Lewis c Greenidge b M. A. Buss	72	– st Parks b Spencer 28
D. R. Owen-Thomas c Parks b Spencer	31	– c Griffith b M. A. Buss.............. 32
Younis Ahmed c Parks b Phillipson	26	– c A. Buss b Joshi 26
G. R. J. Roope not out......................	43	– not out... 21
M. J. Edwards c Joshi b M. A. Buss ...	81	– c Phillipson b Spencer................ 6
Intikhab Alam (did not bat)................		– c Spencer b Joshi 6
B 6, l-b 7....................................	13	B 4, l-b 6............................ 10

(4 wkts., dec.) 300   (5 wkts., dec.)............................ 130

1/130 2/167 3/212 4/232   1/8 2/61 3/95 4/101 5/117

A. R. Butcher, †A. Long, P. I. Pocock and R. D. Jackman did not bat.

Bowling: *First Innings*—Spencer 22.5–4–56–1; A. Buss 17–3–74–0; Phillipson 13–1–37–1; M. A. Buss 15–3–58–2; Joshi 15–5–62–0. *Second Innings*—Spencer 11–0–29–2; A. Buss 12–1–35–0; M. A. Buss 5–1–29–1; Joshi 6–0–27–2.

SUSSEX

G. A. Greenidge c Long b Butcher	6	– b Pocock.................................... 68
P. J. Graves b Pocock.........................	35	– c Roope b Jackman 14
R. M. Prideaux not out......................	106	– c Jackman b Pocock 97
M. A. Buss c Long b Pocock...............	8	– b Pocock.................................... 0
†J. M. Parks c Roope b Intikhab	29	– c and b Pocock 2
*M. G. Griffith not out......................	29	– c Lewis b Pocock....................... 6
J. Spencer lbw b Intikhab...................	0	– not out... 1
J. D. Morley (did not bat)...................		– st Long b Pocock........................ 0
A. Buss (did not bat)...........................		– b Pocock..................................... 0
U. C. Joshi (did not bat).....................		– run out 1
B 6, l-b 7.....................................	13	B 4, l-b 8, w 1.................... 13

(5 wkts., dec.) 226   (9 wkts) 202

1/12 2/80 3/104 4/117 5/190   1/27 2/187 3/187 4/189 5/200
                               6/200 7/200 8/201 9/202

C. P. Phillipson did not bat.

Bowling: *First Innings*—Jackman 7–1–29–0; Butcher 15–4–33–1; Pocock 24–8–69–2; Intikhab 26.1–6–82–2. *Second Innings*—Jackman 13–1–62–1; Butcher 3–0–13–0; Pocock 16–1–67–7; Intikhab 12–2–47–0.

Umpires: D. J. Constant and A. G. T. Whitehead.

Drawn.

ball, but rolling out flat and easy-paced thereafter. It needed declarations to keep the interest flowing and both captains were aware of this. Sussex were asked to get 205 in seventy minutes plus twenty overs and this was fair enough, given that Surrey would have their spinners on a fair amount.

Peter Graves and Geoff Greenidge came out at 3.30 and climbed into Robin Jackman and Alan Butcher from the start. Graves was out after twenty-five minutes with the score 27, but already Intikhab had come on at the other end. Prideaux joined Greenidge and the former England batsman looked in ominously good form. On his day, few contemporaries drove the ball so powerfully and safely off the front foot and the hundred came up in ninety-five minutes with few alarms. Pocock was proving very expensive and the wicket was giving no assistance to either his off-spin or Intikhab's leg-breaks. By six o'clock it was all over bar the final rituals. Prideaux and Greenidge had added 160 in eighty minutes and at 187 for 1, Sussex needed only eighteen with three overs to go. With nine wickets in hand all they had to do was to push the ball around for ones and twos with just one boundary needed.

Pat Pocock began the eighteenth of the last twenty overs with the simple aim of bowling accurately, hoping to make the batsmen work for the measly runs that were still outstanding. He had no inkling at all that he was about to enter the record books: 'The ball wasn't turning at all, and Prideaux and Greenidge were plonking us about all over the place. It looked a nine-wicket win.' Off the first ball of the eighteenth over, Pocock bowled Greenidge and Mike Buss suffered the same fate third ball. Jim Parks got two runs off the fourth ball, failed to score off the fifth and was caught and bowled from the sixth. 'He played a little bit early to me, looking to off-drive, and I had to nip in front of Prideaux to sprawl and catch it. I skinned all my arms diving for it, but the lads just thought I'd made hard work of taking a simple looper!' Whatever the leg-pulling, Pocock had done exceptionally well to take three wickets in one over at a cost of two runs. At least Sussex would now have to work for the last sixteen in two overs.

Robin Jackman was to bowl the penultimate over: a good choice, given his accuracy and combative temperament. He, of all bowlers, would strive to make it difficult for the batsmen. Jackman chose the worst moment to deliver a bad over – he went for eleven, including a six over long-on by Mike Griffith. Says Jackman, 'I felt terrible. In those days a seamer rarely got hit back over his head for six, although it's commonplace nowadays with all these big bats and confident young players. But Pat had done so well at the other end that I thought we still had a chance of a draw when I started my over. Now I'd blown it. . . .'

Pat Pocock was always an optimist in his genial, talented career. He expected to take wickets, even when the conditions were against him, as they were at Eastbourne in 1972. Just because Sussex needed another five runs with six wickets in hand did not stop him from trying his hardest. For his part, Prideaux must have fancied a hundred in each innings and one good blow would also finish the match. Off Pocock's first ball, Prideaux went for it, but he top-edged a sweep and Jackman caught him near the boundary, backward of square. The batsmen crossed while the ball was in the air and Griffith holed out in 'cowshot corner', going for the clinching blow. Jerry Morley came in and it slowly dawned on the fielders that Pocock was on a hat-trick. It had occurred to the bowler a good deal quicker, and he was ready for Morley when the batsman charged down the pitch at him. Pocock bowled a quicker one, Morley played over the top of it and Arnold Long was left to complete a routine stumping. Morley walked off, convinced the stumping was a formality, even though the ball had hit Long's pads and rebounded half a yard away. For an instant, the action was frozen in a time warp until Pocock shouted at Long 'Well bloody stump him then!' and finally the keeper grabbed the ball and took off the bails. It was hardly a classic slow bowler's stumping, but Pocock had his hat-trick, the second of his career, and things were getting rather interesting in this final over. It was now 200 for 7 with three balls left and five runs needed.

John Spencer got a single off the fourth ball, so just one slog would do it. Tony Buss went for it but he was bowled, heaving across the line. Pocock had taken four wickets in five balls. Sussex still needed four to win with one ball to go. Joshi aimed a desperate heave at it, but could only get one as he was run out going for an impossible second. The last over had yielded five wickets, two runs and a hat-trick. Sussex had finished three runs adrift and Surrey needed just one more wicket. As the players walked off, Mickey Stewart turned to a knot of spectators and said, 'I told you so, this is how we stage-manage these things at Surrey!' At the start of the final over, he had amazed those spectators by turning to them and saying, 'We are going to win this, you know, it's in the bag.' He admits he was only pulling their leg, but treasures the look on their faces.

It had taken ten minutes to bowl that final over, with all the comings and goings of the batsmen. Pocock had taken 7 for 4 in his last two overs and here is the full sequence of those last three overs – WOW2OW (Pocock)/410060 (Jackman)/WWW1WW. Sussex should have walked it by calm acceptance of the many singles that were there for the taking. With eleven coming off the penultimate over, it was even more remarkable that Surrey did not lose. Fifteen years later, with county batsmen more used to pacing a run chase, it would be more difficult to botch up a similar opportunity. In 1972 the John Player League was still in its infancy and the Benson and Hedges Cup had only started that season – so perhaps the county player was unaccustomed to a sensible reaction to the frenetic finishes that are now part-and-parcel of modern cricket.

One telephone call serves to exemplify the crazy events of that last over. It came through to the Surrey dressing-room from the club coach, Arthur McIntyre, and it was answered as Pocock was setting his field for the last six balls of the match. The coach was given the bare outline of the day's events and he concurred with the verdict, 'We're going to lose, coach.' The ensuing conversation gives something of the flavour of those last few minutes: 'Hang on coach, Percy's just got Prideaux'; 'We've just caught Griffith'; 'I'll hang on, then'; 'Coach! Percy's done the hat-trick!'; 'I'll hang on, then;' 'Percy's done it again, coach! Four in five!'; 'I'll hang on, then'. When Joshi ran himself out off the next ball, Arthur McIntyre was still hanging on: soon he would get the whole story from the mouth of 'Percy' Pocock. Knowing the famous Pocock loquacity, I imagine it was a fairly expensive phone call.

42
Derbyshire *v.* Lancashire
1975

On away trips, the first question a county cricketer usually asks after waking up is 'What's the weather doing?' That was certainly Jack Simmons's initial query to the waiter who brought in his early morning cuppa to his hotel room in Buxton one June morning in 1975. Now this particular waiter's command of the English language was on a par with dear old Manuel in 'Fawlty Towers' – so when he told Simmons 'it is snowing', the worthy Lancastrian thought something had surely got lost in the translation. So Jack tried to wake up his room-mate David Hughes and staggered to the window to check on the weather. He drew the curtains, looked up at a clear blue sky, chuckled at the waiter's pidgin English and then looked down on the street below. There was snow on the ground. It was Monday, 2 June. This would be no ordinary day in county cricket.

The Lancashire players made their bemused way to the ground at Buxton and waited for the sun to dry out the wicket. Jack Simmons ate his usual hearty lunch and joined the players in the dressing-room who were watching the steam rise from the pitch as the sun got to work. Then it got very dark. It started to snow again and for twenty minutes a blizzard enveloped the highest county cricket ground in England. No one could see the other side of the playing arena, nor the surrounding houses. Then the clouds lifted to reveal a Christmas scene straight out of a card manufacturer's catalogue. Clive Lloyd dashed around trying to find a photographer to capture the moment when the West Indian picked up a snowball for the first time in his life. Players of vast experience who thought they had seen everything stood gaping at the scene. When the warm atmosphere reacted on the snow-covered ground

DERBYSHIRE *v* LANCASHIRE
At Buxton, 31 May – 3 June 1975

LANCASHIRE

B. Wood b Russell	26
*D. Lloyd c Swarbrook b Russell	69
F. C. Hayes c Page b Harvey-Walker	104
C. H. Lloyd not out	167
A. Kennedy c sub b Miller	5
†F. M. Engineer c Morris b Russell	18
J. Simmons not out	55
B 10, l-b 22, n-b 1	33
(5 wkts.)	477

1/45 2/175 3/240 4/261 5/306

D. P. Hughes, K. Shuttleworth, P. Lever and P. G. Lee did not bat.

Bowling: Stevenson 14–3–50–0; Glenn 12–3–36–0; Russell 34–10–119–3; Swarbrook 17–1–111–0; Miller 14–0–94–1; Harvey-Walker 9–2–34–1.

DERBYSHIRE

A. Hill c Engineer b Lever	0	– c D. Lloyd b Lee	2
J. B. Bolus c Engineer b Wood	11	– c Shuttleworth b Hughes	14
M. H. Page c Simmons b Lee	13	– c Engineer b Lee	15
A. Morris run out	4	– c Simmons b Lever	26
A. J. Harvey-Walker c D. Lloyd b Lee	7	– c Kennedy b Lever	26
F. W. Swarbrook not out	1	– c Engineer b Lever	0
G. Miller c D. Lloyd b Hughes	2	– b Lever	0
*†R. W. Taylor c C. H. Lloyd b Hughes	0	– c D. Lloyd b Lever	4
P. E. Russell c Kennedy b Lee	1	– c Hayes b Hughes	0
K. Stevenson c Engineer b Lee	0	– not out	0
M. J. Glenn absent ill	0	– absent ill	0
B 2, n-b 1	3		
	42		87

1/2 2/20 3/25 4/35 5/38 6/41 7/41 8/42 9/42

1/7 2/25 3/39 4/72 5/72 6/72 7/85 8/85 9/87

Bowling: *First Innings*—Lever 8–1–18–1; Lee 13.2–11–10–4; Wood 2–2–0–1; Hughes 9–5–11–2. *Second Innings*—Lever 5.2–2–16–5; Lee 17–9–26–2; Hughes 12–5–26–2; Shuttleworth 6–1–16–0; Simmons 4–1–3–0.

Umpires: H. D. Bird and A. E. G. Rhodes.

Lancashire won by an innings and 348 runs.

to create the effect of a giant cauldron, everyone started to look for a camera.

The Meteorological Office at Bracknell dipped into its box of platitudes and pulled out a plum. 'It was just one of those oddities that we have from time to time,' a spokesman pronounced. From time to time? Not since 11 July 1886 had there been such widespread snow in England after May. As well as Buxton, Bradford's play was snowed off and the start at Colchester was delayed. While the Lancashire players enjoyed the novelty of Clive Lloyd frisking around in the snow, it slowly dawned on them that they had lost their chance of winning this match. Clearly there would be no play that day, and there could be little prospect on Tuesday. The snow had cascaded down and it was now a groundsman's nightmare.

There had been no forecast of such freakish weather and Lancashire had been looking forward to another profitable day. On Saturday, they had piled up 477 for 5, the biggest score yet for a hundred overs innings and Derbyshire had replied with 25 for 2 in fifteen careworn overs. Derbyshire had lost two young seam bowlers before lunch with heat exhaustion; it was bad enough to be missing the injured Mike Hendrick and Alan Ward, but when Michael Glenn and Keith Stevenson staggered off, their side were left with sixty-odd overs to bowl and just Geoff Miller, Fred Swarbrook and Phil Russell to see them through. Every innings was suspended after a hundred overs in those days, and Lancashire slaughtered the decimated attack in stifling heat. Clive Lloyd hit eight sixes, with his last 67 runs coming in thirty-seven minutes, and poor Swarbrook received a savaging from which he never really recovered.

With Derbyshire languishing at the bottom of the championship table, second-placed Lancashire strongly fancied their chances of another comfortable victory. The snow seemed to have put a stop to that, and on the final morning, they arrived at the ground without their cricket bags. David Lloyd recalls: 'Buxton is traditionally a wet area and after all that snow, we didn't think there was a chance of play. We couldn't believe it when we started on time.' Harold 'Dickie' Bird had been at the ground for hours by then, fussing and clucking like a mother hen, wondering if he dare pronounce the pitch playable. 'We had difficulty getting the pitch cut on the morning, because it had been left open to the elements. But the surrounds were okay and when Derbyshire used the heavy roller, it didn't fetch up too much water. It was very warm and the conditions dried out remarkably. We had to play, even though I was worried what the snow had done to the wicket.'

With good reason, Dickie. It turned out to be an old-fashioned 'sticky' wicket, where the ball did the most remarkable things. Dickie Bird wondered how Les Jackson would have bowled on it, while David Lloyd felt Derek Underwood would have been unplayable. Lancashire used their seamers because they could stand up satisfactorily in their run-ups and as a result they bowled unplayable, dangerous deliveries at speed. Geoff Miller shudders at the memory: 'The worst I've ever played on. Good length balls went straight up in our faces.' Bob Taylor remembers: 'It was lethal. If you were lucky, you'd get a glove to the rearing ball and deflect it to a close catcher.' At one stage Peter Lever asked to be taken off: it was only a few months since he had hit Ewan Chatfield in the face with a bouncer in New Zealand, and Chatfield had nearly died. Lever was badly shaken by that incident and here he was, bowling on a horrible pitch with batsmen genuinely frightened. The aptest comment on the conditions came from Ashley Harvey-Walker when he came in to bat. The first delivery roared past his head from a good length as he played forward. That was enough for him: he walked towards Dickie Bird at square leg and handed over his false teeth! The umpire stood there, like Hamlet contemplating the skull of Yorick, while David Lloyd at short leg also took his false teeth out in self-preservation. The ordeal was soon over for Harvey-Walker as he fended one off his face for a gentle catch; he turned away and asked David Lloyd if he had caught the ball, and when that was confirmed, the batsman said with feeling: 'Thank God for that.' Several other batsmen shouted 'Please catch it' as they hit the ball up in the air. Jack Simmons remembers being very worried about the safety of some batsmen: 'We were glad to come away without seriously injuring anybody. Both sides knew that whoever was batting on that day would lose the match and for the first time I can recall, I wanted the game to be over as soon as possible with everyone in one piece.'

Derbyshire lost sixteen wickets for 104 on that frightening Tuesday – Glenn was absent ill in each innings – and they suffered one of the heaviest defeats in county cricket's history. Apart from Harvey-Walker's false teeth, there was one amusing incident. It came in the second innings as Brian Bolus came out to bat. As he made his splay-footed way out to the wicket, with his large pads flopping around as usual, he said to the Lancashire fielders: 'Ah reckon this is goin' to be another desperate nought!' The Lancashire lads appreciated such black humour in these desperate circumstances and they felt genuinely sorry for Bolus and the others.

Dickie Bird cannot remember standing in a game where the conditions altered so drastically – from batsmen's paradise to a terror track. With pardonable Yorkshire emphasis, Dickie told me that he would have loved to watch great technicians like Leonard Hutton and Geoffrey Boycott at work on that final day. I imagine both worthy gentlemen would have pleaded a prior appointment or at least a high temperature.

43
Surrey *v.* Leicestershire
1975

In a two-horse race, odds of 5 to 1 against victory are always worth contemplating. One can only hope that a few lucky punters had a piece of that on a baking hot July afternoon at the Oval in 1975, because they would have cleaned up an hour later. Surrey stood at 29 for 5, while chasing – or rather limping – after a victory target of 93 when the odds of 5 to 1 were offered in the Oval bookies' tent. When they had slumped to 51 for 8, then 65 for 9, the odds must have been even more tempting – and at five o'clock, when Surrey had scraped home by one wicket, many a betting slip was being torn up in anger.

This match followed a remarkable series of symmetrical events, with innings of 259, 68, 283 and 93 for 9 in that order. The wicket favoured bowlers throughout, and Ray Illingworth took the first hat-trick of his career without realizing it. Apart from dashing batting, the game had all of the ingredients that lead to deep enjoyment – brave recoveries, long spells of spin bowling and two unlikely heroes conjuring up a one-wicket win when everything seemed against them. It was doubly satisfying that the two match-winners were men who gave immense pleasure to the connoisseur over a twenty-year period – Intikhab Alam and Pat Pocock. The portly, gentle Pakistani was one of the most popular overseas signings, a resourceful, accurate leg-spinner and hard-driving batsman, while Pocock never lost that fresh, coltish approach to the game despite the whimsies of England selectors, fallibilities of umpires and unimaginative captains who preferred a diet of seam to the joys of spin bowling. Apart from his high-class offbreaks, Pocock was also one of the best number eleven batsmen in the business, as he was to demonstrate in this match.

Both sides lay handily placed in the championship table at the

SURREY v LEICESTERSHIRE
At the Oval, 5–8 July 1975

SURREY

*J. H. Edrich c Balderstone b McKenzie	1	– b McVicker	14
A. R. Butcher b McVicker	33	– c Illingworth b McKenzie	0
G. P. Howarth c Steele b McVicker	37	– c Tolchard b McKenzie	0
Younis Ahmed b McKenzie	4	– c Birkenshaw b McKenzie	9
G. R. J. Roope c and b Booth	13	– lbw b Higgs	1
D. R. Owen-Thomas lbw b Higgs	33	– b Illingworth	14
†L. E. Skinner c Tolchard b McVicker	24	– b Illingworth	6
Intikhab Alam b Higgs	54	– not out	20
R. D. Jackman not out	42	– c Davison b Illingworth	0
G. G. Arnold b McVicker	11	– b Illingworth	8
P. I. Pocock c Davison b McVicker	0	– not out	10
L-b 1, n-b 6	7	L-b 9, n-b 2	11
	259	**(9 wkts.)**	**93**

1/14 2/67 3/74 4/88 5/102 6/145
7/167 8/233 9/259

1/0 2/0 3/13 4/27 5/29 6/48 7/51
8/51 9/65

Bowling: *First Innings*—McKenzie 19–6–34–2; Higgs 24–6–67–2; Booth
20–3–76–1; McVicker 28.5–9–56–5; Steel 8–3–19–0. *Second Innings*—
McKenzie 8–4–16–3; Higgs 17–6–29–1; McVicker 6–1–16–1; Illingworth
93–3–20–4; Balderstone 2–1–1–0.

LEICESTERSHIRE

B. Dudleston c Skinner b Arnold	22	– c Skinner b Intikhab	44
J. F. Steele lbw b Arnold	2	– c Roope b Pocock	71
J. C. Balderstone b Arnold	0	– st Skinner b Intikhab	49
B. F. Davison b Pocock	30	– c Roope b Butcher	20
*R. Illingworth b Arnold	0	– not out	41
†R. W. Tolchard b Arnold	0	– c Jackman b Arnold	12
J. Birkenshaw b Pocock	2	– c Skinner b Jackman	11
P. Booth c Edrich b Jackman	0	– b Jackman	0
N. M. McVicker c Skinner b Intikhab	3	– c Skinner b Jackman	5
G. D. McKenzie c Jackman b Pocock	0	– b Intikhab	18
K. Higgs not out	2	– c Edrich b Pocock	2
L-b 7	7	B 3, l-b 7	10
	68		**283**

1/2 2/11 3/40 4/40 5/40 6/45 7/50
8/66 9/66

1/85 2/140 3/173 4/208 5/226
6/245 7/245 8/253 9/276

Bowling: *First Innings*—Arnold 13–6–17–5; Jackman 11–2–32–1; Intikhab
Alam 4.4–2–3–1; Pocock 12–7–9–3. *Second Innings*—Arnold 22–3–63–1;
Jackman 15–5–28–3; Intikhab Alam 29–9–76–3. Pocock 38.5–15–59–2:
Butcher 21–9–36–1; Roope 2–0–11–0.

Umpires: W. L. Budd and A. E. G. Rhodes.

Surrey won by one wicket.

start of the game. Leicestershire had just chalked up their third win on the trot and they were on course for the title that was duly won in September. Their trump card was a varied, experienced bowling line-up: the great Australian seamer, Graham McKenzie was supported by England's Ken Higgs and the uncomplaining, underrated Norman McVicker, while the spin bowling comprised Ray Illingworth, Jack Birkenshaw, Chris Balderstone and John Steele. They appeared well-equipped for every eventuality, especially on an Oval wicket that was now dusty and cracking up after a prolonged hot, dry spell. On the opening day, Surrey could never really break free from tight bowling. They recovered from 102 for 5, due to a jolly stand of 66 between Intikhab and Robin Jackman, and Intikhab's ninety-minute innings contained the most attractive batting of the day. The fact that Leicestershire took seven overs to score just three runs by the close confirmed that the wicket was far from reliable.

The events of Monday morning confirmed the dubious nature of the pitch. Leicestershire went from 40 for 2 to 40 for 5, with Geoff Arnold getting a great deal of lift from the dry surface. Then Pocock got some crucial turn and mopped up the tail. It looked as if a two-day game was on the cards, but then the wicket eased dramatically after Leicestershire followed on 191 behind. Steele and Duddleston settled in and looked as if they could stay there all week as conditions became more and more benign. The crowd slow-handclapped the batsmen as they took 44 overs to make 85, but they were doing a good job for their side. When Duddleston was caught behind at 85, Steele carried on the anchor role till he was caught at leg-slip with the score on 140. The dangerous Davison was taken in the gully before Leicestershire closed at 185 for 3, still six behind – but they had a fair amount of batting still to come. One of their strengths lay in the amount of good bowlers who could also bat and Tolchard's batting was a vital adjunct to his wicket-keeping. That night Ray Illingworth told his rival captain John Edrich that Leicestershire would win if they could set Surrey a target of around 120; he thought the ball would turn a lot on the final day. Edrich did not believe his former England captain and looked forward to a comfortable win.

On the third morning Illingworth batted sensibly, but Jackman ripped out three men with the new ball. McKenzie and Higgs defended stoutly until they lost patience, and Leicestershire were disappointed to set a target of only 93. With a man such as

Illingworth in charge of the side, Surrey would not be handed the game on a plate and after the first over, they knew they would struggle. Butcher was taken round the corner off the second ball of the innings and, when Howarth was caught behind in the same over, the fight was on. At 13, Younis Ahmed was caught in the slips, Roope was lbw at 27 and Edrich yorked at 29. Then Illingworth finally brought himself on and proceeded to take the first hat-trick of his twenty-four-year career. Skinner was bowled off the last ball of his third over, and Owen-Thomas and Jackman went at the start of his fourth over: 51 for 8. Arnold slogged a couple of boundaries, but then Illingworth ensnared him – 65 for 9 and Illingworth had taken 4 for 6. Surely Leicestershire would not be long delayed.

They reckoned without the skill of Intikhab and the obduracy of Pat Pocock. Now and then Pocock would surprise people, with a gritty, gutsy batting effort that seemed totally at variance with his genial, chatty person. He never appeared to be the man you would choose to bat for your life, but when he wanted to he would take a lot of shifting. This time he did not think that Leicestershire deserved to win, and believed that the earlier Surrey batsmen had told themselves there was something radically wrong with the wicket. He would try to shame them by playing forward with bat and pad close together, whacking the occasional loose delivery and above all supporting Intikhab, a man who could win the game with a few well-judged blows.

The pair inched slowly towards the target by a sensible, low-key approach. Illingworth even tried the slow left-arm of Balderstone for a couple of overs, then he brought himself back from round the wicket. All of a sudden, Pocock danced out to Illingworth and hit him for a skimming, flat six. It passed just over the head of Chris Balderstone at long-off and landed in the pavilion. At the moment of contact with the ball, Pocock shouted 'Run!' and Intikhab shouted back 'How many?' to receive the triumphant reply, 'Bloody six!' Intikhab looked at his partner, then at the dark, glowering countenance of Illingworth and burst out laughing.

That was the decisive shot of the partnership. Surrey now believed they could do it, even though the ball was both turning and springing up off a length from the Vauxhall End. The tea interval arrived at 4.45 and the players had to go off, even though just two more runs were needed. Illingworth was glad of the respite, hoping that the tension would get to the batsmen, but after nine more balls, Surrey were home thanks to a leg-bye and a single from Intikhab. The last wicket pair had added 28 in forty-five minutes and it was a popular performance. 'I don't mind losing, but not to you, Percy!' was Barry Duddleston's remark to the proud number eleven, but it was made in good-natured banter. Looking back, Pocock says, 'I loved every minute of it, I honestly thought we could do it. At one stage, Inty grinned at me and said, "We're going to stroll it, Percy," and I must say it was a great thrill to be there at the end with one of the favourite cricketers of my career. I loved the way Inty would tell me exactly what he was about to do – then do exactly the opposite. But he was a lovely man who brought great joy to the game.'

Ray Illingworth was not quite so effusive about the result. 'We were very disappointed, because we had got back in the game after being out of it for long periods. It would have been great to win it after following on. The quickies were tired after a long bowl, so I had to persevere with the spinners. It was just one of those things – but don't forget Percy's not the worst number eleven.' Well, Pocock is grateful for the tribute but feels Illingworth erred in bringing back McKenzie instead of Higgs. 'From the Vauxhall End there was a worn patch, and if you hit that it stood up and throated you. Higgs was hitting it five balls an over, but McKenzie only managed it once an over. The patch was as big as a doormat, but McKenzie lacked the accuracy to find it. Although he was faster than Higgs, he was almost light relief. If Higgs had stayed on, I think eventually one of us would have copped the unplayable ball.'

Well, even former England captains and current commentary box pundits can make tactical errors. Those of us who enjoyed Pocock and Intikhab over the years as bowlers remain grateful that Homer nodded for once to let them bat their way to an improbable victory.

44
England *v.* Australia
HEADINGLEY 1981

Now we really are deep into script rejection time. Anybody who sat down and penned a scenario on the lines of this game would be laughed out of every publisher's office. It was sensational enough when England became only the second side in Test history to win after having to follow on, but the sequence of events that led to the transformation is even more remarkable.

Headingley 1981 will always be remembered as the game won by Ian Botham and Bob Willis when all seemed lost: phoenix from the ashes and all that. Yet either player could easily have been missing as England tried to fight back in the series after losing the first Test and drawing the second. Botham had lost the England captaincy in sad circumstances at Lord's, and many good judges felt he ought to be rested in the hope that his all-round brilliance would soon be restored. Mike Brearley, the man chosen to lead England at Leeds, was unsure; he sounded out Botham in the nets on the eve of the Test and was prepared to see him stand down if the player felt it was in the best interests of the side. Bravely and typically Botham would not hear of it – whatever his private torments, he persisted in his public stance that the wheel of fortune would soon spin his way again. Bob Willis was equally vulnerable before the Leeds Test. After struggling with a chest infection at Lord's he had been originally left out for the following Test. He was under several clouds at that time: at the age of thirty-two the fast bowling machinery was beginning to clank, and a serious knee operation in the spring made him realize he was running out of time, even though it had proved a success. It was also his benefit year and, allied to his frustrations as Warwickshire captain, he was not in the best frame of mind for the stern struggles of an Ashes series. Willis desperately wanted to play at Leeds, but his current

ENGLAND *v* AUSTRALIA
(Third Test)
At Headingley, Leeds, 16–21 July 1981

AUSTRALIA

J. Dyson b Dilley	102	– c Taylor b Willis	34
G. M. Wood lbw b Botham	34	– c Taylor b Botham	10
T. M. Chappell c Taylor b Willey	27	– c Taylor b Willis	8
*K. J. Hughes c and b Botham	89	– c Botham b Willis	0
R. J. Bright b Dilley	7	– (8) b Willis	19
G. N. Yallop c Taylor b Botham	58	– (5) c Gatting b Willis	0
A. R. Border lbw b Botham	8	– (6) b Old	0
†R. W. Marsh b Botham	28	– (7) c Dilley b Willis	4
G. F. Lawson c Taylor b Botham	13	– c Taylor b Willis	1
D. K. Lillee not out	3	– c Gatting b Willis	17
T. M. Alderman not out	0	– not out	0
B 4, l-b 13, w 3, n-b 12	32	– L-b 3, w 1, n-b 14	18
(9 wickets declared)	401		111

1/55 2/149 3/196 4/220 5/332
6/354 7/357 8/396 9/401

1/13 2/56 3/58 4/58 5/65 6/68 7/74
8/75 9/110 10/111

Bowling: *First Innings* – Willis 30–8–72–0; Old 43–14–91–0; Dilley
27–4–78–2; Botham 39.2–11–95–6; Willey 13–2–31–1; Boycott 3–2–2–0.
Second Innings – Willis 15.1–3–43–8; Old 9–1–21–1; Dilley 2–0–11–0; Botham
7–3–14–1; Willey 3–1–4–0.

ENGLAND

G. A. Gooch lbw b Alderman	2	– c Alderman b Lillee	0
G. Boycott b Lawson	12	– lbw b Alderman	46
*J. M. Brearley c March b Alderman	10	– c Alderman b Lillee	14
D. I. Gower c Marsh b Lawson	24	– c Border b Alderman	9
M. W. Gatting lbw b Lillee	15	– lbw b Alderman	1
P. Willey b Lawson	8	– c Dyson b Lillee	33
I. T. Botham c Marsh b Lillee	50	– not out	149
†R. W. Taylor c Marsh b Lillee	5	– c Bright b Alderman	1
G. R. Dilley c and b Lillee	13	– b Alderman	56
C. M. Old c Border b Alderman	0	– b Lawson	29
R. G. D. Willis not out	1	– c Border b Alderman	2
B 6, l-b 11, w 6, n-b 11	34	– B 5, l-b 3, w 3, n-b 5	16
	174		356

1/12 2/40 3/42 4/84 5/87 6/112
7/148 8/166 9/167 10/174

1/0 2/18 3/37 4/41 5/105 6/133
7/135 8/252 9/319 10/356

Bowling: *First Innings* – Lillee 18.5–7–49–4; Alderman 19–4–59–3; Lawson
13–3–32–3. *Second Innings* – Lillee 25–6–94–3; Alderman 35.3–6–135–6;
Lawson 23–4–96–1; Bright 4–0–15–0.

Umpires: D. G. L. Evans and B. J. Meyer.

England won by 18 runs.

mental state was always highly relevant to his form as a fast bowler. Unlike Botham, Willis was never a confident cricketer and he worried about whether a decline in pace and accuracy was temporary or terminal. During this particular period, he and I had many soul-searching conversations and I cannot imagine an England strike bowler ever having a lower morale. When he heard he had been left out for Leeds, he was even more depressed. He had to swallow his pride and assure the selectors that if he could get through a second eleven match earlier in the week, then he would be fit for Leeds if wanted. The selectors did want a fit, dedicated Willis – but they and the bowler in question took a big risk in reinstating him to the squad.

Willis made it into the eleven, but on the first day nothing happened to improve his morale. He bowled well enough, beating the bat many times. The cloud cover made the ball swing and the dry pitch was uneven in bounce, so Australia must have been happy to close on 203 for 3, with John Dyson making a valuable, if pedestrian, hundred. Botham, the other legend on trial, swung the ball around and took a wicket, but he cannot have been happy with that meagre return in such favourable bowling conditions. On the following day, Botham worked his way through the order, while Willis continued to bowl unluckily, especially against Kim Hughes. The Australians must have been delighted to get to 400 and England's wayward line and poor catching helped them. The feeling persisted that if Lillee, Lawson and Alderman had been operating over these two days, then England would not have reached 200. Approaching the halfway point in the Test, Australia still looked the better side, as they had done for most of the series so far.

It was equally one-sided on the third day. The Australian seamers bowled intelligently and England's technique was found wanting on a wicket that never allowed a batsman to think he was now entrenched. Only Botham took the fight to the enemy, his fifty coming off the same number of balls. He was providing the solitary crumb of comfort so far, with wickets and a dashing innings. Perhaps the wheel of fortune was swinging his way after all. It had missed out Graham Gooch in this match: he was dismissed twice on the Saturday as England followed on. They closed at 6 for 1, still 221 behind. Short of a historic rearguard action from Geoffrey Boycott or prolonged rain, it looked like another Australian victory.

Over the weekend, that air of fatalism which sometimes affects the most bullish of professional cricketers settled on the England team. They knew that they could not hold out for two days on such an unreliable wicket against such a strong three-man pace attack. Kim Hughes, the Australian captain, could afford to ration the overs to a deplorably slow rate in the knowledge that he was keeping one of his three seamers fresh, that eventually an unplayable delivery would come along. The England players gathered at Botham's home on Saturday night for a barbecue, and the consensus was that the pitch would be the decisive factor. They made the ritual remarks about the press sharpening their claws and changed the subject.

On the Monday morning, the England players checked out of their hotel in Leeds. They did not expect to be back for a final day. On the Monday night, they were delighted to sign the register again and Ian Botham, with 145 not out, signed with a flourish. It had been a remarkable day's cricket. At lunch England were 78 for 4, with Willey and Boycott battling to retrieve a score of 41 for 4. The weather would not be aiding England that day – it was bright and breezy – and there seemed little prospect of holding out for another four hours. Just before tea, England stood at 135 for 7, still 92 runs behind. Around this time, the bookmakers offered their own chilling verdict on England's chances. The giant electronic scoreboard flashed up the odds for the match result – England were 500 to 1, Australia 4 to 1 on, and the draw was 5 to 2. It would later emerge that Dennis Lillee and Rod Marsh cleaned up on those odds, unable to resist betting against their own team, while Bob Taylor could not get out of the England dressing-room to place his bet because of the hordes of autograph-hunters.

When Graham Dilley came in to join Botham at 135 for 7, the senior partner summed up the situation with his customary finesse. Botham asked Dilley if he fancied hanging around for a day and a half on such a wicket, and when Dilley demurred Botham offered this famous clarion call: 'Come on, let's give it some humpty.' They certainly did that: in the next eighteen overs, they added 117. Dilley, a clean, hard hitter, actually outscored Botham in that partnership, and at last the bowlers began to look tired and ragged. The pitch remained dubious, but now the snicks were not going to hand the ball was flying over the slips to the boundary and the ball was being struck with murderous ferocity. Alderman went for sixteen in an over as the target of an innings defeat was at last removed. Gradually the crowd stirred from passive resignation to warm support. At least England were going down with a flourish and when Dilley reached his fifty with a glorious crashing off-drive, he was cheered as if he came from Skipton. Soon afterwards, he was bowled, aiming to hit Alderman out of the ground and England had to take stock: 252 for 8, a lead of just 25 and despite the recent heroics, the game could still be over that night.

Chris Old was next man in – a talented striker of the ball, but against a pace attack on a dodgy wicket, he would never win the Brian Close Fortitude Award. Old was pushed down the steps by his team-mates, with imprecations and threats ringing in his ears. He was to get in line, to stay there and support Botham or the match would be over. For his part, Botham carried on wafting at almost everything; he stepped down the pitch and drove Alderman back over his head for a stirring six, then mistimed a booming drive that went over the slips to the boundary to bring up his hundred. He had gone from 39 to 103 with a six, fourteen fours and two singles. The last fifty had taken just forty minutes, and his hundred came up in only eighty-seven balls. In the context of the match, the bowling and the wicket, it was an astounding performance, even if some of the boundary hits were not quite in the intended place.

Old managed to hang around long enough to help add a precious 67, which stretched the lead to 92. Willis strode out to hold up an end while Botham continued to blaze away. By now the crowd were delirious, reminding each other that Botham's wife is a Yorkshire lass and that with a home on Humberside he was really one of them. At the close England stood at 351 for 9, a lead of 124, with Botham unbeaten on 145. In two hours since tea, he had made 106 out of 175. The Australian dressing-room was rather quiet for the next hour. Yet they must have realized they were still in the driving seat. If they could get the last wicket quickly with the new ball on the final morning, they would have the rest of the day to make around 130.

That is exactly what happened. Willis edged Alderman to slip and Botham finished undefeated on 149. He did not think a target of 130 was enough to trouble Australia, and when they swiftly moved to thirteen the result seemed clear-cut. Then the ubiquitous Botham had Wood caught behind. For the next hour it went Australia's way with Dyson and Chappell playing resiliently and

Willis no-balling persistently. Then Brearley made a crucial decision: in response to Willis's plea, he switched him to the Kirkstall Lane End. It was the last throw of the dice for Bob Willis's Test career; if he had not broken through immediately he would have been banished to the outfield for the rest of the match and he would have surely faded into international obscurity. Just when he needed to fire on all cylinders, he rediscovered the inspiration that had been lacking for a year in Test matches. He took 3 for 0 in eleven balls – Chappell was done by an unplayable lifter, Hughes was superbly caught at third slip and Yallop jabbed a bouncer to short leg. At lunch Australia were 58 for 4 – still needing 72 – and the realists were beginning to wonder. Afterwards, Old bowled the admirable Border with a beauty and finally the valued wicket of Dyson fell, caught hooking. When Dilley caught Marsh at fine leg off a hook shot, Australia were 74 for 7; one run later Lawson was caught behind. This was ridiculous; what had Willis been taking between overs? What was wrong with the batting? Had Willis found a ridge?

Just as the crowd geared themselves to roar in a famous victory, Australia at last showed their mettle. From the next four overs, Lillee and Bright plundered thirty-five runs with a mixture of brave shots and fortuitous snicks. Time to get worried again: it was 110 for 8, just twenty short. Then Gatting caught Lillee at mid-on, a running tumbling athletic catch that belied the fielder's generous bulk. In the next over England twice thought they had it won, but each time Old dropped Alderman at slip. The Yorkshire crowd groaned in disappointment; good job the errant catcher was a lad from their own county. Keith Fletcher had been pilloried for years at Leeds for less.

The reprieve did not last very long. Willis stormed in and produced the perfect ball to finish off Bright – a yorker that took the middle stump. This time the crowd invasion was understandable and Willis ran off the field, staring ahead of him as if in a nightmare. He flopped in the bath as pandemonium reigned in the dressing-room and, after trying to take in all the dramatic events of the past few days, he changed, then delivered a famous broadside against the press in a live television interview. Willis had been furious at the campaign waged against Botham and dismayed at the trivialization of cricket coverage in the tabloids. That he chose such a moment of euphoria to vent his contempt served to confirm that he was still not mentally stable after his draining performance on the field. Not until he switched on the 'PM' programme on Radio Four to learn that the game was the lead item did the enormity of it all sink in. 'I just couldn't believe that a cricket match would be the lead story. I thought there must be something more important going on in the world. Then I realized what we had done and I felt proud. I envied Ian Botham's ability to savour the moment at that time – I was always too tensed up about my cricket to do that. Satisfaction was always a slow-burning thing with me.'

Willis feels that Ray Bright's spin should have been used more against Botham when he was running amok on Monday afternoon. Botham has always been likely to perish against a spinner, purely because he does not rate them – he calls them 'step and fetch it' bowlers. In Willis's view, the turning point in the Australian innings was the double dismissal of Hughes and Yallop just before lunch. 'That gave them forty minutes to think about the awful possibility of defeat. Once you get defeatist feelings in the mind, you're halfway to defeat.' He maintains he bowled just as well in the first innings without luck, and that he was equally satisfied with his bowling on the same ground in the 1983 Test against New Zealand and in the following year, when Michael Holding hit him for several sixes with embarrassing ease. 'It's true – on another day I would have got Holding with a bit of luck, but I suppose I used it all up at Leeds in 1981. I have bowled just as well and gone without a wicket, but try telling that to anyone who saw me take 8 for 43 against the Aussies.'

Whatever the merits of Willis's bowling, it helped transform the series. Botham proceeded to dominate the remaining games with irresistible all-round performances and the crowds lapped up the spectacular deeds. Mike Brearley was again hailed as the guru who galvanized Botham, surely a simplistic assumption when you consider Botham's staggering talents. When the luck runs his way, Botham could inspire even if Ronald Reagan was the captain. As for Bob Willis, his England career lasted another three years, and it even took in the captaincy. He has the video of Leeds '81 somewhere in his house. He has never even watched it. He says he is saving it for his dotage. I wonder if the rose-coloured spectacles will be donned?

45
Lancashire *v.* Warwickshire
1982

The car travelling from Southport to Accrington contained two very tired cricketers. David Lloyd, the driver, finally broke the silence and said to his passenger, Graeme Fowler, 'I reckon we'll win this one.' Fowler looked at his friend with pity and said, 'You must be joking.' That first day had ended with Warwickshire scoring over 500 and taking Lloyd's wicket before close of play. Lancashire trailed by 483 with nine wickets left, and yet David Lloyd was talking about victory. Perhaps it was the champagne that Warwickshire had generously provided in celebration of a couple of double hundreds, or perhaps it was the sun – either way Fowler worried for his driver's sanity. Two days later, Lloyd sported a blissful 'told you so' expression. Warwickshire not only contrived to lose, but they did it in style – by ten wickets. This after piling up over 500 on the first day.

The Warwickshire sides in the 1980s have often found themselves in bizarre matches, but this one tops the lot. Collectors of trivia had a field day, as source material for quiz questions kept appearing. We had the first substitute who was allowed to bowl. We had an opening bat who scored a hundred in each innings without running a single. For the first time in cricket history, two batsmen scored double centuries in one innings and finished on the losing side, and they also compiled the highest partnership for a team that eventually lost the match. For good measure, we had a bowler pulled out to join the England squad after the first day – and he was back to bowl later in this match.

Alvin Kallicharran and Geoff Humpage were the two batsmen to score double centuries. They came together at 11.46 with

LANCASHIRE v WARWICKSHIRE
At Southport, 28–30 July, 1982

WARWICKSHIRE

*D. L. Amiss c Abrahams b McFarlane	6	– c Scott b McFarlane	24
R. I. H. B. Dyer c Simmons b McFarlane	0	– c Abrahams b McFarlane	0
T. A. Lloyd c Scott b Folley	23	– b McFarlane	0
A. I. Kallicharran not out	230	– (5) c D. Lloyd b O'Shaughnessy	0
†G. W. Humpage b D. Lloyd	254	– (6) c Abrahams b O'Shaughnessy	21
Asif Din (did not bat)		– (4) c Hughes b O'Shaughnessy	21
S. H. Wootton (did not bat)		– b McFarlane	0
C. Lethbridge (did not bat)		– c Hughes b Folley	18
G. C. Small (did not bat)		– lbw b McFarlane	0
P. J. Hartley (did not bat)		– c Scott b McFarlane	16
S. P. Sutcliffe (did not bat)		– not out	7
B 1, l-b 6, w 1, n-b 2	10	B 1, l-b 2, w 1	4
(4 wkts dec.)	523		111

1/5 2/6 3/53 4/523

1/1 2/1 3/47 4/47 5/47 6/47
7/76 8/81 9/99

Bowling: *First Innings* – McFarlane 11–2–90–2; Folley 15–3–64–1; O'Shaugnessy 15–2–62–0; Simmons 20–2–97–0; Hughes 20–2–79–0; Abrahams 15–3–76–0; D. Lloyd 10.1–1–45–1. *Second Innings* – McFarlane 20–3–59–6; Folley 11–5–19–1; O'Shaughnessy 7.1–0–29–3; Simmons 1–1–0–0.

LANCASHIRE

G. Fowler b Asif Din	126	– not out	128
D. Lloyd c Humpage b Small	10	– not out	88
†C. J. Scott lbw b Brown (sub)	9		
I. Cockbain c Amiss b Kallicharran	98		
*C. H. Lloyd c Humpage b Kallicharran	45		
D. P. Hughes c Small b Kallicharran	14		
J. Abrahams not out	51		
S. J. O'Shaughnessy not out	26		
L. L. McFarlane (did not bat)			
J. Simmons (did not bat)			
I. Folley (did not bat)			
L-b 13, w 3, n-b 19	35	L-b 2, n-b 8	10
(6 wkts dec.)	414	(no wkt)	226

1/34 2/109 3/194 4/305 5/327 6/333

Bowling: *First Innings* – Small 15–4–38–1; Hartley 14–0–66–0; Sutcliffe 38–9–103–0; Lethbridge 14–5–58–0; D. J. Brown (sub) 13–3–47–1; Asif Din 6–1–35–1; Kallicharran 13–3–32–3. *Second Innings* – Small 11–2–30–0; Hartley 9–1–38–0; Sutcliffe 19–5–60–0; Lethbridge 9–2–27–0; Asif Din 5–0–25–0; Kallicharran 6–0–35–0; Lloyd 1–0–1–0.

Umpires: H. D. Bird and J. van Geloven.

Lancashire won by 10 wickets.

Warwickshire struggling at 53 for 3, and when they were finally parted at 5.49 they had added 470. It was the highest fourth-wicket partnership by any county, and the 293 minutes they spent together contained some of the most exhilarating strokes seen on an English county ground this decade. Kallicharran was in a rich vein of form at this stage and his third double century of the season was the usual mixture of disdainful hooks and scintillating drives. He took one look at the dry pitch of even bounce and simply cashed in with the merciless approach of a great player. While Kallicharran provided the steely elegance, Humpage produced the fireworks. In a twenty-minute period before lunch he only scored two runs, and for half an hour just after the interval he was equally circumspect – but apart from those two periods he was tremendously entertaining. As a natural and ready strokemaker, he was perfectly happy to face an attacking field and positive bowling at the start of his innings and he stroked the ball away through the covers with consummate ease. He was determined not to throw away the fruits of the revival after lunch, but when the spinners Abrahams and David Lloyd came on, he helped himself. In all he savaged thirteen sixes, a total only exceeded by the New Zealander John Reid. Although Southport is a small ground, the vast proportion of Humpage's sixes would have been sixes on an area as large as the Oval. When the new ball was taken, the pair savaged 62 in 4.1 overs, 54 of them to Humpage off sixteen balls. It was intoxicating stuff, and the Warwickshire players found it all very funny. Andy Lloyd remembers nominating where each ball would go. 'If they managed to bowl a rare dot ball, we would guess the destination of the next ball – some would say the pavilion, others someone's garden, and with one shot, he put the ball onto the railway track. It was a joke eventually – we kept goading Humpage on and his hitting was unbelievably clean.'

Humpage says he had no intention of piling up a big score. Once he had passed his career best of 146, he simply played his shots, as Kallicharran gave him more and more of the strike. 'I started playing a shot a ball and I knew the lads were enjoying it. I was delighted when my double hundred came up and we just kept going in the absence of any instructions. Finally Dennis Amiss made a signal to us with one finger upraised, so we assumed he meant to go on for just one more over. I tried to hit the first ball for twelve, was bowled and came back perfectly pleased with life.

Then the captain tells me he meant us to keep going until we lost another wicket! I could've got three hundred in that mood!'

Just to end a perfect day for Humpage, he caught David Lloyd off Gladstone Small. Then the champagne corks popped amid that semi-masonic camaraderie of the county circuit, with the Lancashire boys offering sincere congratulations for a tremendous piece of batting from two players. By that time Gladstone Small was on his way to Birmingham: he had been called to join the England team after Derek Pringle had ricked his back earlier that day. It did not matter that Small felt unwell; he was bronchial and missed most of the day's great partnership as he lay down to recuperate. David Brown, the manager, did not tell him about the call until after close of play and sent him off with his best wishes. The following morning, Small did not do himself justice in the nets at Edgbaston and he was sent back to re-join the county match. His place was taken for the morning session by his manager. It was the first time a substitute had been given permission to bowl, and David Brown became the first substitute to take a wicket when he had Scott lbw in his second over. It came as no surprise to those who watched Brown in the indoor nets to discover that he was the best bowler that morning. Time after time the Warwickshire players had said, 'Come on, manager, get your whites on and get out there!' and he was delighted that at the age of forty he could still run up and put the ball on the spot at medium pace. 'What I really liked though was having a nice bowl and not having to do any fielding after my spell had ended. By then Gladstone was back and I could put my feet up back in the pavilion. I'd never have retired if I could get away with spells like that all the time!'

Gladstone Small must have wished he had never left Edgbaston because he ran into some powerful Lancashire batting. Graeme Fowler made exactly a hundred before lunch, going from 26 not out overnight to 126 – and even more pleasing, his good mate David Lloyd had to run for him. Fowler had pulled a hamstring within an hour on the first morning and he did not field for the rest of the game, but he saw no reason why he should miss out on the fun. 'It was a flat wicket, a small ground and the bowling wasn't very demanding, so I just played my shots and got away with it. Because I was restricted in my movements, I found myself concentrating a little more and I played my shots with extra care.' Fowler was well supported by the others, and they declared only 109 behind. By the close poor Robin Dyer had completed a 'pair',

and with him and Andy Lloyd going in successive balls to McFarlane, Warwickshire were 14 for 2. Yet with so much class batting
in the side, it was hard to conceive of anything other than another
day of leather-hunting on the Friday.

Southport is rather like Hove. The ball can swing around in the
morning, then when the sea fret disappears conditions ease for the
batsmen after lunch. That is one of the reasons for Warwickshire's
abject performance on the third day. They were all out just before
lunch for 111, with Les McFarlane returning the best figures of his
career. Now McFarlane's own mother would never claim international status for her son; all he had to do was pitch the ball up,
keep a good line and the Warwickshire batsmen did the rest.
Lancashire fielded magnificently – with the outstanding feature the
short-leg catch by David Lloyd that dismissed Kallicharran second
ball. Four wickets fell at the same score of 47, and at lunchtime
we had the supreme irony of Humpage and Kallicharran posing
for a commemorative photograph beside the scoreboard with their
individual totals standing at 254 and 230 not out. They could have
done with some of those runs on the Friday morning.

Lancashire needed 221 to win in 166 minutes plus twenty overs,
and they cantered home with seven overs to spare. Dennis Amiss
twice dropped Fowler in the slips before he had reached ten and
he proceeded to smash his second hundred of the match, again
with a runner. This time it was Ian Folley, and when Fowler played
and missed at a ball when he was on 49 Folley shouted over from
square leg, 'Hang on Foxy, I've never got a first-class fifty!' David
Lloyd did not fancy running any more of Fowler's runs for him,
so he stayed in as well, guiding the ball into the open spaces like
a good old pro while Fowler enjoyed himself. It was Fowler's
eighth first-class hundred and four of them had now come off
Warwickshire's attack. Within a few weeks he was in the England
team. At one stage in the debacle, Gladstone Small shouted in
exasperation to Fowler, 'Bloody hell, Foxy. It's a shot a ball!' It
was and the atmosphere was no longer as conducive to swing as
it had been in the morning. It was now baking hot, and after a
time Warwickshire knew they were finished. Fowler ended the
game by hitting Asif Din for six, and the fielding side trooped off
unsure whether to laugh or cry. As soon as they saw their
manager's face, they knew that hilarity would not be appropriate,
that it would be a long drive home.

Dennis Amiss summed up the game thus: 'We needed our backsides kicking,' and it is hard to disagree with that. How could Lancashire be allowed to get back into it? Agreed that Warwickshire's bowling was weak, that they were cannon fodder for many batsmen that season – but Lancashire's attack on paper was no better, without the injured Croft and Allott. There was also a vast gulf in the respective quality of fielding. David Brown says that the main reason for the humiliation was the 'third innings syndrome', something that has perturbed him as player and manager for years. 'So often a side relaxes subconsciously after getting a big score at the start. You go in again and everyone leaves the responsibility to the others because you think there is no real pressure on you. All of sudden, you've got a collapse on your hands and given the game away on a plate.' Geoff Humpage agrees: 'There was a lack of application on that Friday morning. We took it easy because the pitch was still so good. If we had grafted harder, we would have got through the period when the ball swung so much.'

Perhaps Warwickshire scored too quickly on the first day. If they had batted till lunchtime on the second day, they would at least have been immune from defeat. Instead they gave Lancashire enough time to get themselves back in the match and have one good session in the field. They still had enough time to pop a few champagne corks on the Friday evening – but there was none left from Wednesday night.

46
Australia *v.* England
MELBOURNE 1982

Eighty years after Fred Tate lost a game for England due to a dropped catch (chapter 10), Chris Tavaré almost did the same at 12.24 on a cold Melbourne morning just after Christmas 1982. It would have been rough on Tavaré after a splendid innings earlier in the game, but he would have only been remembered for a fielding aberration at slip if Geoff Miller had not caught the rebound from Tavaré's hands. At that stage Australia needed just four to win with their last pair together. One good blow would win it for Australia and England looked demoralized – but a combination of a bad shot and outrageous luck brought victory by three precious runs.

Only one other Test has ended in a similarly close margin – Fred Tate's match in 1902. There have been several one-wicket victories, but only two Tests which could have been won by a single boundary. It was fitting that this Test should end so dramatically: it had been a desperately tense affair throughout, and by the end the nerves on either side were twanging like piano wires. Due to the prevailing emphasis on commercialism, there was no rest day, a monstrously unfair decision in the light of the constant travelling in an Australian tour and the draining tension of the Melbourne game. The England players I talked to who played in this Test and the one at Leeds in 1981 all made the point that Melbourne was much more emotionally taxing – at Leeds they had a rest day, while the first three days were very one-sided, and when Botham sparked the revival it was simply a case of riding on a high tide of adrenalin and luck. At Melbourne, every day was remarkably tense and closely fought – the first three innings all finished at the end of each day and the fourth would have followed the same pattern if not for rain. Each day several wickets would fall in the morning

AUSTRALIA *v* ENGLAND
(Fourth Test)
At Melbourne Cricket Ground, 26–30 December 1982

ENGLAND

G. Cook c Chappell b Thomson	10	– c Yardley b Thomson	26
G. Fowler c Chappell b Hogg	4	– b Hogg	65
C. J. Tavaré c Yardley b Thomson	89	– b Hogg	0
D. I. Gower c Marsh b Hogg	18	– c Marsh b Lawson	3
A. J. Lamb c Dyson b Yardley	83	– c Marsh b Hogg	26
I. T. Botham c Wessels b Yardley	27	– c Chappell b Thomson	46
G. Miller c Border b Yardley	10	– lbw b Lawson	14
D. R. Pringle c Wessels b Hogg	9	– c Marsh b Lawson	42
†R. W. Taylor c Marsh b Yardley	1	– lbw b Thomson	37
*R. G. D. Willis not out	6	– not out	8
N. G. Cowans c Lawson b Hogg	3	– b Lawson	10
B 3, l-b 6, w 3, n-b 12)	24	– B 2, l-b 9, n-b 6	17
	284		**294**

1/11 2/25 3/56 4/217 5/227 6/259
7/262 8/268 9/278 10/284

1/40 2/41 3/45 4/128 5/129 6/160
7/201 8/262 9/280 10/294

Bowling: *First Innings* – Lawson 17–6–48–0; Hogg 23.3–6–69–4; Yardley
27–0–89–4; Thomson 13–2–49–2; Chappell 1–0–5–0. *Second Innings* –
Lawson 21.4–6–66–4; Hogg 22–5–64–3; Yardley 15–2–67–0; Thomson
21–3–74–3; Chappell 1–0–6–0.

AUSTRALIA

K. C. Wessels b Willis	47	– b Cowans	14
J. Dyson lbw b Cowans	21	– c Tavaré b Botham	31
*G. S. Chappell c Lamb b Cowans	0	– c sub (I. J. Gould) b Cowans	2
K. J. Hughes b Willis	66	– c Taylor b Miller	48
A. R. Border b Botham	2	– (6) not out	62
D. W. Hookes c Taylor b Pringle	53	– (5) c Willis b Cowans	68
†R. W. Marsh b Willis	53	– lbw b Cowans	13
B. Yardley b Miller	9	– b Cowans	0
G. F. Lawson c Fowler b Miller	0	– c Cowans b Pringle	7
R. M. Hogg not out	8	– lbw b Cowans	4
J. R. Thomson b Miller	1	– c Miller b Botham	21
L-b 8, n-b 19	27	B 5, l-b 9, w 1, n-b 3	18
Total	**287**		**288**

1/55 2/55 3/83 4/89 5/180 6/261
7/276 8/276 9/278 10/287

1/37 2/39 3/71 4/171 5/173 6/190
7/190 8/202 9/218 10/288

Bowling: *First Innings* – Willis 15–2–38–3; Botham 18–3–69–1; Cowans
16–0–69–2; Pringle 15–2–40–1; Miller 15–5–44–3. *Second Innings* – Willis
17–0–57–0; Botham 25.1–4–80–2; Cowans 26–6–77–6; Pringle 12–4–26–1;
Miller 16–6–30–1.

Umpires: A. R. Crafter and R. V. Whitehead.

England won by 3 runs.

while the pitch eased to allow runs to be scored in the afternoon, but then there would again be a clatter of wickets in the evening session. As a result the players could never settle, they knew that one mistake or flash of brilliance could prove decisive.

England felt the greater pressure. They were two down in the series after playing spinelessly at Brisbane and Adelaide, so they had to win the remaining two Tests to square the series and retain the Ashes. The captain, Bob Willis, was near to mental and physical collapse by the time the team arrived at Melbourne for Christmas. He had worried himself to a frazzle over the batting inadequacies and he felt badly let down by the batsmen at Adelaide. After being worked over by the Australian fast bowlers at Brisbane, the English players did not fancy taking first strike at Adelaide. When Willis won the toss, he chose to field first and allow his batsmen time to recover – a decision he bitterly regretted almost at once. Australia made 438, won by eight wickets and Willis had to take it on the chin. He blamed himself for not following his own instincts, yet he did not want to castigate his batsmen in public. The rest-day press conference at Adelaide was one of the worst experiences in Willis's long career, and he still had not recovered from the mauling by the time of the next Test at Melbourne on Boxing Day.

At the eve-of-Test dinner, Ian Botham and Allan Lamb had recommended getting after the Australian bowlers, rather than wait to be rolled over again, courtesy of uncertain wickets and weak umpiring that allowed blatant intimidation from the fast bowlers. Willis wanted to go for crease occupation, but the batsmen argued that timid tactics had done them no good so far, that they should now go for their shots. Willis was determined to field first this time because the wicket looked damp on the first morning. He lost the toss, Greg Chappell agreed with the diagnosis of the pitch and England batted first. They certainly played their shots – none more so than Chris Tavaré who was a revelation as he climbed into the off-spin of Bruce Yardley. Allan Lamb was typically pugnacious, but a slide from 217 for 4 to 284 all out was rather anti-climactic.

Australia's reply followed similar lines: 261 for 6 to 287 all out. The dangerous Hookes, Hughes and Marsh all got in, but mercifully they were seen off before they could put the game beyond England's reach. The crucial dismissal was that of Greg Chappell for a duck. Like all great players he resented the presence of a new bowler, who was feeling his way into the big league. In this case it was Norman Cowans, and Chappell was determined to smash him out of the series and damage his confidence for long enough. Cowans had arrived in Australia with a reputation of waywardness, but surprising speed. Chappell knew enough about cricket history to remember how Tyson and the young Willis made big impressions with little practical experience behind them, so he would take care of Cowans before he became too much of a threat. At Melbourne he went to hook his first ball for six; on a smaller ground it would have sailed over Allan Lamb's head at deep square leg, instead of being comfortably caught. Round one to Cowans – and the boost in his confidence was obvious and significant within the context of the match.

On the third day England were rescued by some solid batting from the middle order and tail. Graeme Fowler led the way with a typically gutsy effort after breaking a toe, and Derek Pringle at last did himself justice at the highest level with an intelligent, defiant innings of three hours, aided by that supreme professional Bob Taylor. The innings lasted 80.4 overs, compared to 81.3 overs in the first and Australia's 79 overs. It was a remarkably even game and no one doubted that a target of 292 would take some getting.

By the last hour of the fourth day, England appeared to be home and dry. Six wickets had fallen either side of tea and Australia were 218 for 9. Norman Cowans had taken six wickets through a combination of speed, accuracy and the vagaries of the pitch. The England management had worked hard on Cowans, and his stamina had been greatly improved. Now he was repaying their faith. Again the vital wicket was that of Chappell – the substitute fielder Ian Gould diving to his left at cover to take a marvellous catch. Gould's ebullience in the field was significant as England chipped away at the Australians amid great tension. Hughes and Hookes added 100 in two hours, when they were both out to marvellous catches – one from Willis, running back at mid-on, and another from Taylor that was an acrobatic miracle. Yardley, Marsh and Hogg were all undone by shooters, and it seemed that the variable bounce would be the crucial factor. Australia needed 74 runs from their last pair and they did not exactly inspire confidence. Jeff Thomson was a competent enough player, but he could not be expected to display the reserves of stamina and concentration to last out for such a long time on this unpredictable wicket. His partner Allan Border was acknowledged as one of the best batsmen in the world, but he was horribly out of form. England had bowled very well at him, tucking him up with short-pitched deliveries and he had dropped down from number five to number six to avoid the new ball. In fading light, on a dubious pitch, Border could not be expected to win the match single-handed.

Border received a boost from an unlikely quarter. Ian Botham is a great friend and, typically, he had been sympathetic towards his miserable run of failure. Botham rated Border very highly as a batsman, even though he always tried his very best to knock his head off -- and it was entirely in character that the Englishman should lend the Australian his favourite bat. Botham believed something as simple as a change of bat would revive the little man's fortunes and Border, by that time, was prepared to try anything. It did him no good in the first innings -- he was bowled by his mate -- but he batted magnificently in the final reckoning. Lest anyone misconstrue Botham's part in Border's rehabilitation, there was never a breath of criticism about the altruistic gesture. Not even Botham's harshest detractors have ever accused him of soft-pedalling against the Australians, and it was simply seen as an act of friendship from a man who values loyalty from his own close pals. On the field of play, Botham still tried his very best to dismiss Border, despite their relationship. Yet Botham's bat almost lost the game for England.

Rain curtailed the final session on the fourth day, but not before Border and Thomson had added 37. Thomson managed to hold on as Cowans tired, while Border seemed to grow in assurance through every over. The ball just eluded the hand on one or two occasions and just occasionally the fielding slipped from its high standards, but England did not seem unduly perturbed that play ended with that final wicket still outstanding. Only 36 were needed for victory, however, and Australia still had hopes of a famous win.

On the final morning no less than 18,000 were allowed free into the ground for a session that might have been over after just one ball. They witnessed eighty-five minutes of gut-wrenching anxiety, during which the last pair added 32 before being separated anti-climactically. Thomson continued to carve at balls pitched on the middle stump, while Border looked masterful. The new ball was taken, but Cowans could not recapture his spark of the previous afternoon. Border picked off singles at will, and Thomson did not have to face too many deliveries per over. Many felt Willis was wrong to give Border so many untroubled singles, but the captain felt all along that if Thomson was exposed to the danger end he would eventually run out of luck. Yet the fielders were beginning to panic as Border manipulated the strike superbly. Once again he looked like Australia's best player – solid, imperturbable, ruthless with the poor delivery. For his part, Thomson, that arch baiter of the Poms, was loving the duel.

With just four runs needed, Willis prepared to bowl an over to Border that was bound to be vital. 'As I started to run in, I thought we'd lost it because they only now needed one shot to do it. So I had to bowl tightly at Border to avoid the boundary, then keep him away from the other end off the last couple of deliveries. We just had to get at Thommo in the next over, otherwise we had lost.' The result was a magnificent over as Willis dredged deep into his reserves of willpower. Border knew what was going on and yet he could not break out of the stranglehold imposed by six fast, straight deliveries and superb, alert fielding that stopped any quick singles. At last England had done something right – those years of playing limited overs cricket had helped them concentrate on the essentials. All the England players I talked to about this match paid tribute to that over by Willis.

England breathed again, but Willis still had to decide who was going to bowl at Thomson. The ball was still new, the damp conditions favoured seam bowling but Cowans had shot his bolt amid all the tension. There was only one man, one cricketer who would relish the challenge – old Golden Arm himself. By 1982 the effervescence and variety had gone from Ian Botham's bowling: long hops were now as plentiful as late inswingers and he was now in the 'four an over' category. He was the last man to use when runs were desperately tight, yet he was the best man to try in the heat of battle. Botham positively relished the responsibility; perhaps he realized that he owed something to his great friend Willis after a disappointing tour so far.

By now the ground was a sea of frenzy, the commentators were babbling away, and even the denizens of the press box were beside themselves. John Woodcock, the admirable correspondent of *The Times*, suddenly moved his typewriter and other journalistic impedimenta to another desk, announcing that he hoped a change of location would break the deadlock and bring England luck. You really are in trouble when a cricket correspondent fingers the metaphorical four-leaf clover, yet it worked. Botham lolloped up to bowl the first ball of his over and proceeded to send down a gentle loosener. It was almost a wide, swinging gently away, with

'hit me' written all over it. This was the one ball that he should
not have delivered at that stage of the match, but he got away with
it. Thomson suddenly played at it like a number eleven batsman
and he got a thick edge to a ball he did not need to play. The
subsequent events are described by a key man in the denouement,
Geoff Miller. . . .

'I was fairly deep at first slip – I was always deep when standing
alongside Bob Taylor, because he liked to take the low ones
without distraction from first slip and that gave him space to dive.
If I'd been up in the normal first slip position, the ball would have
gone over my head. The snick came fast and head high to Chris
Tavaré's left at second slip. He didn't snatch at it, but he was done
for pace. It burst through his hands, but he had taken the pace off
it and it lollipopped up in the air where I grabbed it. I was genuinely
looking for the rebound, but I was lucky to be standing where I
was.' Bob Willis recalls, 'That was typical Botham. I went for him
because of his flair and he bowls a rubbish ball that gets a wicket. If
Thommo hadn't played at it, the umpire would have been perfectly
entitled to call a wide, and where would we have been then?'

The England players ran off the field like demented dervishes,
with even reserved types like Tavaré, Willis and Geoff Cook
hopping and skipping. In the dressing-room, Botham grinned
wolfishly and said, 'You knew you could rely on me, lads,' while
Willis told a press conference that he always thought England
would win. Greg Chappell simply smiled wryly. The media felt
Willis had erred tactically by giving Border so many runs without
exerting undue pressure on him. Willis said they felt that Thomson
was bound to get out eventually, that the pressure would get to
him. Certainly it must have had a bearing on that final shot he
played, because such an experienced cricketer must have known
that Border had the game won if he could just stay there with him.

For sustained excitement, it was a Test in a million. Once again
a sub-standard wicket had produced a great game of cricket, with
no one making more than 89 and no side passing 294. The purists
may have bemoaned the poor batting, but they did not have to dig
the ball out off their ankles, then fend the next one off the face.
Once more the human element had triumphed, with Botham's
outrageous luck making Thomson forget that he was a number
eleven batsman. Many superior batsmen have made the same
miscalculation.

47
Essex *v.* Surrey
1983

It takes a lot to make Keith Fletcher sit in the Essex dressing-room, shaking his head and saying: 'Now I've seen everything.' That was his immediate reaction to eighty-seven deliveries in the previous hour. In that time Surrey had been bowled out for just 14 and nobody could really guess why. It was the lowest total since Northamptonshire's twelve in 1907 (see chapter 15), and the fifth lowest of all time. Yet this was the first occasion in sixty-one years that any side had made 15 or under; modern batsmen had become more serious about their job, there were few genuine tail-enders around any more. The demands of limited overs cricket, the deadening nature of many pitches, the financial rewards now available – all these had conspired to raise the standard of lower order batting. A century ago there was always the chance of a first-class team being whipped out for next to nothing on a bad wicket if their star batsmen were soon out. Often backbone was conspicuous by its absence. Not now: for all the criticism of the modern player, there is never any expectation that a county side would be bowled out for 14.

So why did it happen? How could such a powerful batting line-up succumb so speedily? The short answer is that the ball swung, and swung late so that the batsmen were committed to their shots and the snicks gratefully snaffled. There was nothing wrong with the wicket, although it was dampish after a fair amount of rain. The fact that Surrey easily saved the game next day confirms that the wicket was flat. The humid conditions certainly helped the Essex bowlers, but good county batsmen are used to days like that when the ball moves around a great deal. Usually it is simply a matter of watchful technique, but not in this match. Keith Fletcher says there is no need to hunt for justifications for the freak score,

ESSEX v SURREY
At Chelmsford, 28–31 May 1983

ESSEX

G. A. Gooch b Thomas	1
B. R. Hardie b Clarke	16
*K. W. R. Fletcher c Lynch b Monkhouse	110
K. S. McEwan c Lynch b Knight	45
K. R. Pont b Pocock	12
N. Phillip b Pocock	8
S. Turner c and b Knight	20
R. E. East c Lynch b Clarke	19
†D. E. East c Butcher b Pocock	17
N. A. Foster not out	19
D. L. Acfield run out	0
B 4, l-b 10, n-b 6	20
	287

1/1 2/27 3/113 4/156 5/179 6/222
7/238 8/252 9/276

Bowling: Clarke 20–3–58–2; Thomas 20–2–78–1; Monkhouse 13–2–49–1;
Knight 17–6–33–2; Pocock 19.5–6–49–3.

SURREY

A. R. Butcher c D. E. East b Phillip	2	– c Gooch b Foster	5
G. S. Clinton c D. E. East b Foster	6	– not out	61
A. Needham b Foster	0	– lbw b Phillip	4
*R. D. V. Knight lbw b Phillip	0	– not out	101
M. A. Lynch lbw b Phillip	0		
†C. J. Richards c Turner to Phillip	0		
D. J. Thomas lbw b Foster	0		
I. R. Payne b Phillip	0		
G. Monkhouse lbw b Phillip	2		
S. T. Clarke b Foster	4		
P. I. Pocock not out	0	B 1, l-b 8, w 2, n-b 3	14
	14	(2 wkts)	185

1/2 2/5 3/6 4/8 5/8 6/8 7/8 8/8 9/14   1/11 2/18

Bowling: First Innings – Phillip 7.3–4–4–6; Foster 7–3–10–4. Second Innings–
Phillip 13–2–39–1; Foster 13–2–33–1; Turner 7–3–16–0; Gooch 22–6–45–0;
Acfield 17–7–23–0, R. E. East 1–0–5–0; Pont 5–1–10–0.

Umpires: W. E. Alley and J. W. Holder.

Drawn.

it was simply inexplicable. 'You couldn't account for why it happened, other than the ball swinging late. We kept thinking that someone would come in and slog a few, but no one did.' David Acfield agrees: 'It was a remarkable piece of cricket and we all sat around afterwards, saying "How the hell did that happen?" Usually someone plays a decent innings if you're 10 for 5 or something like that, but everything kept going to hand.' Even more inexplicably, Surrey had four left-handers in their first eight, and three in their top four, yet they were undone by two right-arm bowlers delivering outswingers to the right-hander. That is usually the ball that troubles the professional player, not the ball that comes into the bat – yet to Surrey's left-handers, Foster and Philip were bowling inswingers. They should have been able to play some of them off their legs for runs, but they failed to do so. All very curious.

The conditions were no great help to the Essex bowlers. After the first day was lost to rain, Essex had an untroubled time on an easy-paced pitch. Fletcher made the fifty-ninth hundred of his career with elegance and distinction and Roger Knight must have regretted asking Essex to bat first. An hour later he was even more sorrowful. Two runs came off the first three overs, and there seemed little prospect of an early breakthrough. Then Butcher was caught hooking and Needham bowled, pushing forward defensively. One run later, Knight was surprised to be given out lbw as he went half forward. Then five wickets fell with the score stuck on 8 – Lynch out lbw playing defensively, Clinton caught at the wicket trying to glance, Richards caught low at fourth slip trying a back-foot steer, Payne bowled playing half forward and Thomas out lbw in the same way. It was now 8 for 8, and at the fall of each wicket the Essex players gathered round the pitch and wondered from where the demons had suddenly sprung.

Sylvester Clarke was hauled out of the bath, where he had been enjoying a blissful soak after his twenty overs earlier in the day. A dangerous smiter of the ball, Clarke was determined to put the earlier batsmen to shame. Before he could connect, Graham Monkhouse edged a ball through the legs of Ray East at slip and they managed to run two. Then Clarke heaved Foster to the mid-wicket boundary to take Surrey past the ignominy of twelve, the grisly record shared by Oxford University and Northamptonshire. Clarke was bowled in the same over, trying a similar shot, and then

Monkhouse was lbw to a break-back. All out for 14, it was Surrey's lowest score in their history.

The two Essex bowlers, Foster and Philip, are still amazed at the capitulation of a good batting side. Philip said, 'I just pitched the ball up and let it do the work,' while for Foster it was all a bit of a dream. He was only playing because John Lever was suffering from a hairline foot fracture and Foster was also making a come-back after a serious back injury. One would expect him to ease his way gently back into the first team instead of making such a dramatic impact and he found it very unreal: 'I was too young to appreciate it, because everything was new to me. Mind you, I've got the scorecard framed and it's hanging up on a wall at home!' Keith Fletcher says it was one of the easiest tasks a fielding captain has ever had to face: 'I didn't have to change the bowling, because they kept getting themselves out. Runs were there for the taking because we had a close in-field all the time – but they couldn't score any. It was unbelievable.'

The Surrey players felt the same way. Roger Knight offered no excuses and praised the bowlers, but the rest of the team went back to their hotel, sat around having a drink and suddenly burst out laughing. Pat Pocock said: 'Someone suggested buying Sylvester drinks all night because he was the only one to hit a four. You had to see the funny side of it because it was so ridiculous.' Pocock had the right answer to the television reporter who asked his secret, why he had not been dismissed: 'Because I only faced one ball.' It was that kind of bizarre day.

Normality reigned the following day. For a start it rained and play was delayed for ninety minutes. There was little elbow room for a positive result, so Surrey meandered through a lovely after-noon. The pitch was as docile as on the previous afternoon, but this time there were no sensations. Knight and Clinton picked up some useful batting practice and the match eased peacefully to a close. On the face of it, we had watched a typical county match that failed to yield a result after three days of fencing for an opening. One glance at the scorecard proves this was not a typical county match.

48
Warwickshire *v.* Yorkshire
1983

'You're wasting your time, it'll be over shortly.' That was the greeting thrown at me by a pessimistic gateman as I arrived at Edgbaston. It was just after lunch on the final day and the gateman did not need the perspicacity of a Benaud to deliver his apocalyptic forecast. Warwickshire, needing 299 on a broken wicket, were 136 for 6 and past salvation. Three hours later, they were celebrating an extraordinary win, inspired by a remarkable piece of batting.

Geoff Humpage has always been an attractive batsman in county cricket, a dangerous, clean striker of the ball. Erratic and headstrong on occasions, yes, but a gifted player. On this final afternoon he played a truly great innings, one that would have delighted the most illustrious of players. In four and a half hours, he hit seventeen fours and made an unbeaten 141 in a chanceless style that was simply breathtaking. I cannot believe that anyone could have played better in the circumstances. It is true that cricket is, and must always be, a team game – but this match was won by a single individual, and won gloriously.

To assess the quality of Humpage's performance, consider first the wicket. It was an experimental pitch that had been re-laid eighteen months earlier, but had not bound satisfactorily together. It was under-prepared and the ball went through at wildly differing heights on the dry, powdery surface. On the first two days the ball would either shoot along the ground or rear up off a length and endanger the batsman's teeth. Never was a helmet more welcome. On the final day, the wicket was slower but the bounce was still hopelessly uneven. It helped the spinner more than the seamer, but there was always the probability that any delivery pitched in the right spot would prove unplayable. The two rival managers, Ray Illingworth and David Brown, admitted the pitch was unfit for

WARWICKSHIRE *v* YORKSHIRE
At Birmingham, 25–28 June 1983

YORKSHIRE

G. Boycott c Asif Din b Willis	0	– lbw b Willis	28
R. G. Lumb c Kallicharran b Old	5	– lbw b Ferreira	13
C. W. J. Athey c Asif Din b Old	15	– st Tedstone b Gifford	29
S. N. Hartley b Ferreira	69	– c Asif Din b Ferreira	11
J. D. Love c Amiss b Old	58	– lbw b Gifford	45
†D. L. Bairstow c Humpage b Old	45	– lbw b Gifford	11
P. Carrick b Gifford	6	– b Old	16
G. B. Stevenson c Humpage b Gifford	0	– b Old	5
*R. Illingworth lbw b Gifford	8	–	
S. J. Dennis b Ferreira	4	– (9) b Old	0
P. W. Jarvis not out	5	– (10) not out	1
B 7, l-b 7, n-b 10	24	B 3, l-b 19, n-b 3	25
	239	(9 wkts dec.)	184

1/0 2/20 3/35 4/160 5/168 6/184
7/184 8/210 9/219

1/33 2/53 3/87 4/94 5/125
6/165 7/178 8/182 9/184

Bowling: *First Innings* – Willis 16–5–43–1; Old 26.1–7–63–4; Gifford
38–17–52–3; Ferreira 23–5–57–2. *Second Innings* – Willis 14–2–48–1; Old
13–3–26–3; Ferreira 17–4–41–2; Gifford 19.5–8–44–3.

WARWICKSHIRE

T. A. Lloyd b Dennis	11	– c Athey b Carrick	49
K. D. Smith b Dennis	0	– c Bairstow b Stevenson	2
A. I. Kallicharran c Bairstow b Stevenson	9	– b Illingworth	16
D. L. Amiss c Lumb b Stevenson	41	– lbw b Carrick	15
G. W. Humpage c Illingworth b Stevenson	0	– not out	141
Asif Din b Dennis	1	– b Illingworth	2
A. M. Ferreira lbw b Jarvis	36	– lbw b Illingsworth	13
†G. A. Tedstone lbw b Illingworth	4	– lbw b Stevenson	8
C. M. Old c Bairstow b Stevenson	4	– run out	2
N. Gifford b Stevenson	4	– b Jarvis	14
*R. G. D. Willis not out	2	– not out	16
L-b 11, n-b 2	13	B 7, l-b 11, w 1, n-b 5	24
	125	(9 wkts)	302

1/12 2/16 3/24 4/25 5/26 6/91 7/108 8/115
9/116

1/27 2/56 3/80 4/97 5/100
6/136 7/178 8/180 9/238

Bowling: *First Innings* – Dennis 10–5–24–3; Stevenson 13.2–3–35–5; Jarvis
9–3–28–1, Carrick 4–1–10–0; Illingworth 9–2–15–1. *Second Innings* – Dennis
13–4–46–0; Stevenson 20–2–54–2; Illingworth 37.3–13–71–3; Jarvis
13–4–43–1; Carrick 34–12–64–2.

Umpires: R. A. White and A. G. T. Whitehead.

Warwickshire won by one wicket.

first-class cricket, which prompted the thought that the Inspector of Pitches should have been there on the second day, if that worthy figure had not also been the Warwickshire groundsman, Bernard Flack. It does not take much to fuel the paranoia about suspect pitches in the breasts of county batsmen, but this time they were justified in moaning into their post-match beers after this game.

Yorkshire did well to make 239 on the first day, although Warwickshire did not use the conditions as well as they might. The first ball of the second day proved a relevant augury – it came through to Andy Lloyd at ankle height. After fifteen overs, Warwickshire were 26 for 5. Humpage was caught in the gully pushing forward, then fending off the ball as it shot up at his nose, while Asif Din's off-stump was taken out by a shooter. Dennis Amiss's impeccable technique enabled him to survive for two hours, but then he was caught off his bat handle, unable to get out of the way. It was hopeless, and Yorkshire led by 114 on first innings. When Yorkshire batted, Boycott emulated Amiss for a time until he was lbw to a shooter, and the same fate befell Lumb. Hartley deflected a lifter to short leg, and Athey escaped when one from Willis skidded through like an ice-hockey puck and just missed the off-stump. Love chanced his luck and gathered a pugnacious 45, but they were irrelevant runs, we felt. Warwickshire would not get 150 on this pitch, never mind the lead of 299 that Yorkshire enjoyed at close of play. Jack Bannister wrote in the *Birmingham Post* that 'Bob Willis must have known on Saturday that when he lost the toss he lost the match', a comment that would rebound on the *Post*'s cricket correspondent a day later. He was not the only one to be astonished at the events of Tuesday, 28 June.

As the rival players mingled in the tea room before play started on the third morning, the Yorkshire lads were debating how soon after lunch they would be able to get away from Birmingham. No one could fault their reasoning, but Yorkshire over-confidence has always stuck in the gullets of players from other counties. Geoff Humpage listened to the confident chatter and vowed that he would at least try to whack a few. 'The Yorkies always try to rub your nose in it, they give the impression that they play the real game of cricket, not any other county. So any time you can do them, you like to give it a go.' David Brown had the same feeling: 'In the sixties, I was on the end of a few thrashings from the Yorkies when they were a great side, and they never let you forget it. All I wanted from our lads that day was a bit of pride in their performance and to make it difficult for the opposition. Looking at that wicket, I couldn't expect anything more than that – not even a draw. And as for victory, you'd have to be crackers even to think about that.'

Ray Illingworth was so confident that he declared overnight and his bowlers did not let him down initially. Although Andy Lloyd played positively for a while, Warwickshire had no chance. The ball was turning, seaming and coming through at differing heights; all the Yorkshire bowlers had to do was put the ball on the spot. It was advisable to play off the front foot, but survival was not guaranteed. Humpage came in half an hour before lunch and, at the interval, Warwickshire were 97 for 4 with their best batsmen out. Asif Din left at 100 and Ferreira at 136, after several rugged blows. When I popped into the Warwickshire dressing-room for a chat around that time, I found a mood of relaxed fatalism. No recriminations, just acceptance of the fates that shaped such a wicket. At least Humpage was playing a few shots; they were feeding him too much on the leg-side and he was crashing the ball away through midwicket like a white Viv Richards. It could not last, but at least the cocky Yorkshiremen were being kept out in the field for a while. Geoff Tedstone, the reserve wicket-keeper, who was playing in this match because Humpage was having knee trouble, now kept him sensible company, adding 42 runs. Then Chris Old ran himself out, a desperate disappointment to him because Old wanted to do well against the county that sacked him from the captaincy the previous year. That made it 180 for 8, and the home dressing-room prepared to mouth sportsmanlike platitudes to the Yorkies. Norman Gifford made his way out to the wicket to join Humpage and the ensuing conversation was not without significance:

Gifford: 'I can stop in, you know.'
Humpage: 'Shall I give it a go then?'
Gifford: 'You bloody well won't – make the buggers work for it. Don't give 'em anything. We can win this.'

At that stage, Humpage was just past his fifty. It was twenty minutes to tea, and Warwickshire still needed 119. He looked at Gifford to see if he was joking, but the old boy also had a long memory about thrashings by Yorkshire and he was serious. They lasted till tea – 183 for 8, Humpage 60 not out. The welcome in the dressing-room for Humpage was respectful for the way he played, and curious about the state of the wicket. They only had to look at the confident swagger of the opposition in the tea-room to get the answer to that one. Yorkshire were still going to win, but at least they were having to fight for it.

After tea, Gifford continued to play with admirable *sangfroid* – nicking a single now and again, ignoring the occasional delivery that would have tested the greatest of techniques and exhorting Humpage to greater deeds. Yorkshire took the new ball and Humpage hammered it. Suddenly they started to bowl badly. The awful prospect of defeat manifested itself as Humpage missed nothing wayward. Gifford had lasted for thirty-one overs when he missed a full toss by Jarvis and was bowled; to this day he cannot imagine how he contrived to do that. Still, it had been a marvellous effort and he did not forget the team's interests as he passed Humpage. 'Don't give it away, we can still do it!' he told him.

Back in the dressing-room, the Warwickshire players were astonished that a full toss could claim Gifford after such admirable, skilled resistance. They had to blame somebody – so they picked on Anton Ferreira. The genial South African had left his seat to answer a call of nature, and when he was away Gifford had fallen. He was ordered to stay put in his seat until the match was over, and David Brown issued the same instructions to everyone else. No one would be moving until the last decisive moment, proof indeed that at last Warwickshire thought they had a chance.

Surprisingly that view was not shared by the emerging hero out in the middle. Humpage still felt he would be undone by an unplayable delivery. The loping figure of Bob Willis was a comforting sight – he would be guaranteed to sell his wicket dearly – and they gathered for a tactical pow-wow:

Willis: 'What do you think?'
Humpage: 'I'll have a go.'
Willis: 'Okay.'

Men of action do not need to be verbose, and Humpage was as good as his word. He got to his glittering century with 16 in one over from Dennis, then he hit 10 off the next from Jarvis. Suddenly the last-wicket target of 61 seemed just possible, especially if Humpage had a few more overs like those two. At once Illingworth went on the defensive. He placed eight, sometimes nine men on the boundary to thwart the power of Humpage's driving – this

with a new ball less than ten overs old. Somehow he still managed
to pierce the field and the score climbed. With twenty runs to go,
the Yorkshire heads were drooping and Humpage was delighted
to overhear this exchange:

Illingworth: 'Who should I put on to bowl now?'
Boycott: 'Don't ask me, you're the captain.'

Humpage says he knew that they were beaten once he heard that
little burst of frustration, because earlier Boycott had been very
supportive to the bowlers. Now he was distancing himself from
Illingworth, letting him stew in his own juice. Yet there were still
a few alarms in store for Warwickshire. Both batsmen survived
confident appeals for lbw, and Phil Carrick beat Willis outside
the off-stump and watched it go agonizingly close. Even more
dramatically, Willis was dropped behind the stumps by Bairstow
with just a handful of runs needed. At the other end, Humpage
was thunderstruck: 'It was a ridiculous shot to play at that time.
He went for the off-drive against Illingworth, got an inside edge
and it hit the middle of Bairstow's gloves. Somehow he shelled it
out, even after grovelling to try to catch the rebound. It was roughly
reminiscent of one of my bad days behind the stumps!' Back in
the Warwickshire dressing-room, the players were amazed that the
captain would try such an ambitious stroke. When the collective
heads came out of hands, Dennis Amiss spoke for everyone when
he shouted in exasperation: 'What a bloody shot to play!' Yet
Willis was still there, after an uncharacteristic aberration, and one
look at the Yorkshire players confirmed that the crucial and final
phase of the match was over. A few minutes later, Humpage swept
a four to the boundary and the home players sprung out of their
seats in joy.

Warwickshire had won with fifteen balls to spare, and Humpage
had made 110 out of the last 150 from the bat. Amid the immediate
euphoria, Gifford said it was one of the three best centuries he had
seen in his long career – four years later he stands by that. 'The
Yorkies were disgusted that anyone should get so many runs in
such conditions and they started to think what they'd say back
home if they lost. You could see the heads droop – but it was
Humpage's brilliance that caused that.' David Brown agrees: 'The
bowlers can let it slip just as much as the batters when the pressure
is on. They felt they should have got Humpage out cheaply, and
they weren't up to the test of character. They didn't bowl well,

but it was magnificent batting that won it for us.' Ray Illingworth felt that Yorkshire lost the game, rather than Warwickshire winning it: 'I was annoyed at some atrocious bowling with the second new ball. I never thought they'd get them, but Humpage was magnificent.'

Humpage pays tribute to the support of Gifford and Willis, two of the best tail-enders of their time in the game. 'Both played spin so well, going forward and making late adjustments. As experienced Test players, their temperaments were excellent. A younger player might have got excited in such a situation, but apart from Bob's daft shot near the end they were terrific. I never thought we had a hope in hell until we saw them arguing among themselves. Before that they had been going through the motions, expecting the wicket to do the work for them. Their seamers bowled two yards quicker in the first innings.'

The only jarring note to be struck in the euphoric Warwickshire dressing-room came from Anton Ferreira. The tension of the last wicket stand had proved too much for him, and he suffered the fate of every small boy at some stage. The ban on moving and several cups of tea had conspired against even the awesome frame of Ferreira, and as his side inched towards a spectacular victory, he had to answer nature's call right there in his chair. He is still waiting for David Brown to pay that cleaning bill.

49
Kent *v*. Warwickshire
1986

If you glanced at the Warwickshire scorecard in their second innings and ignored the date, you would swear it was an early excerpt from Derek Underwood's great career. It has all the makings of another relentless performance on a wet wicket, the kind of inexorable, ruthless display that earned Underwood the soubriquet of 'Deadly'. Not so – it was achieved on a dry wicket in a season of covered pitches, the kind of conditions many thought would emasculate Underwood's unique talents. A match return of 9 for 59 off 67.5 overs suggests that the old maestro still knew a trick too many for the younger generation.

Since wickets have been covered over the past five years, Derek Underwood's influence has declined. This is not to deny his greatness – his accuracy, stamina, wrist action and command of flight still remain top class – but he rarely bowls out a side for next to nothing any more. Derek knew this would happen, once the game's administrators decided that uncovered wickets constituted a lottery. The feeling was that wickets exposed to the elements made the game one-sided, with bowlers cracking the whip and batsmen unable to develop a proper technique. Many influential people at Lord's believed that high-class cricketers were moulded on good playing surfaces, with batsmen learning their trade slowly and bowlers having to develop subtlety, rather than relying on the elements to do their job for them. This ignored the qualities of men like Dennis Amiss, Geoffrey Boycott, Norman Gifford and Derek Underwood – men who had mastered the basics on uncovered wickets and then adapted when the pitches became flatter and more uniform. One of the saddest aspects of recent county cricket has been the decline of the spinner, and there is no doubt that he would still be an influential figure if wickets were

KENT v WARWICKSHIRE

At Folkestone, 3–5 September 1986

WARWICKSHIRE

A. J. Moles b Baptiste	82	– b Davis	8
P. A. Smith c Marsh b Cowdrey	11	– c C. Cowdrey b Underwood	14
A. L. Kallicharran c Marsh b Baptiste.	2	– c C. Cowdrey b Underwood	2
D. L. Amiss b Davis	73	– c C. Cowdrey b Underwood	5
†G. W. Humpage c Marsh b Baptiste.	19	– c Tavaré b Underwood	23
Asif Din c Davis b Underwood	11	– c C. Cowdrey b Underwood	5
A. M. Ferreira st Marsh b Davis	26	– c C. Cowdrey b Underwood	0
K. J. Kerr c Marsh b Baptiste	1	– c C. Cowdrey b Davis	3
G. C. Small b Davis	28	– c Aslett b Underwood	2
T. A. Munton c Marsh b Underwood.	0	– not out	0
*N. Gifford not out	2	– b Davis	2
B 3, l-b 5, w 2, n-b 2	12	N-b 1	1
	267		65

1/21 2/32 3/146 4/195 5/196 6/219
7/221 8/246 9/247 10/267

1/11 2/18 3/26 4/29 5/56 6/56 7/59
8/62 9/65 10/65

Bowling: *First Innings* – Ellison 12–1–26–0; Baptiste 26–9–53–4; C. Cowdrey 12–1–49–1; Davis 28.5–4–83–3; Underwood 32–18–48–2. *Second Innings* – Baptiste 8–3–12–0; Underwood 35.5–29–11–7; Davis 31–18–38–3; Tavaré 2–1–4–0.

KENT

M. R. Benson c Ferreira b Small	2
N. R. Taylor c Moles b Small	10
C. J. Tavaré c Humpage b Gifford	43
D. G. Aslett b Gifford	63
G. R. Cowdrey c Humpage b Gifford.	7
*C. S. Cowdrey lbw Small	100
E. A. Baptiste lbw Gifford	22
†S. A. Marsh b Gifford	70
R. M. Ellison b Kerr	8
D. L. Underwood b Kerr	1
R. F. Davis not out	0
B12, l-b 21, n-b 3	36
	362

1/2 2/23 3/114 4/131 5/150 6/224
7/328

Bowling: *First Innings* – Small 21–4–64–3; Smith 2–0–13–0; Ferreira 9–2–32–0; Gifford 49.5–15–96–5; Kerr 46–2–120–2; Munton 2–0–4–0.

Umpires: K. J. Lyons and A. G. T. Whitehead.

Kent won by an innings and 30 runs.

uncovered. Cricket history is full of gallant performances against a top-class spinner operating on a rain-affected wicket, but the alteration in conditions of play has eradicated that. As a result a great bowler like Derek Underwood has been in retreat in recent years. Just once in 1986 he managed to remind us of his awesome control and pitiless dominance.

By the time Warwickshire came to Folkestone, Underwood was a tired man. It was his benefit season, always a draining year, and he was also unhappy with his form. 'You have to set yourself standards and I was annoyed that I was going to finish up with so few wickets for the season. I hadn't had one wicket conducive to me all season and, when I heard that John Childs had taken seven wickets at Folkestone in the previous match, I was determined to follow that. I felt if John could perform well there, so could I. When we lost the toss and had to field, I was very disappointed because I fancied us to get a big score and then hoped to try to bowl them out twice. I wanted to put myself under pressure to perform well.'

He did not bowl all that impressively in Warwickshire's first innings. Admittedly conditions were dreadful: it seemed as if a gale was blowing and the advertising boards kept blowing over. Hot drinks were brought out to the players, and there were five stoppages for bad light and rain on the first day. As a bowler who thrives on hard work and loves to settle into a rhythm, Underwood felt frustrated. Dennis Amiss played him particularly well in a fascinating battle between two great technicians, and when Warwickshire were all out on the second morning, Underwood's figures confirmed that he had bowled as meanly as ever – but never looked like running through the side.

By the end of the second day, it was Warwickshire's turn to feel frustrated. The pitch was beginning to deteriorate, with holes appearing in the dry surface, and Kent ought to have fared worse than 293 for 6. Norman Gifford (left-arm spin) and Kevin Kerr (off-breaks) wheeled away for hours, but they could never establish a stranglehold. Young Kerr, who had impressed with his flight and control in his first season, did not do himself justice at all. He had not seen many surfaces like this one in his brief career and never managed to find the requisite accuracy to put the batsmen under pressure. He kept apologizing to his team-mates because he knew he ought to be taking wickets on such a helpful surface. Norman Gifford was unlucky: two close decisions went in favour of Chris

Cowdrey before he got into double figures and, as the day wore on, Gifford just could not break through. After a hard season, the forty-six-year-old captain was understandably tired and he feared the worst: 'The longer I bowled, the more certain I was that Deadly would make us pay the following day. I suppose the burden of expectation got to us, because we knew we should have bowled them out cheaply. Once they got into the lead, anything else was a bonus.'

On the final morning, Kent slogged more precious runs and Cowdrey reached his hundred. The bowling simply was not tight enough: three an over is hopeless on a wearing wicket and the Warwickshire players knew that they were in for an afternoon of stern resistance, with defeat almost certain. The wicket was now a dreadful sight: it was like a golf driving range, with holes appearing every time the ball pitched. It was greyish in colour, and it looked as if there was nothing left to bind the surface. If Underwood could manage to hit the spot consistently, Warwickshire would be in trouble. There was never any doubt that Underwood would be equal to that particular task.

In the Warwickshire dressing-room, the manager David Brown outlined the preferable scenario. The first team had been criticized recently for a lack of backbone, for subsiding gently to defeat. Brown warned there would be none of that this time: Underwood had to be resisted. 'I knew that there was nowhere to go once Deadly had his tail up and that the younger players would have to gain experience in the most practical way. The longer they stayed out there, the better it was for them.' The young openers, Paul Smith and Andy Moles, were sent out with that instruction ringing in their ears.

Underwood took the new ball and bowled the second over of the innings. In the four overs before lunch, Warwickshire made one without loss: they had three hours, plus twenty overs to nego-tiate. Kent could be the only winner with a lead of 95, so it was up to Warwickshire's batsmen to thwart them. It was an unusual task facing their young players, but they acquitted themselves nobly in the circumstances. The first wicket fell in the eighteenth over, when Moles was bowled by Richard Davis. Then the two class players – Amiss and Kallicharran – fell to Underwood, with umpire Whitehead ruling that the ball had hit Amiss on the hand and not the arm. Then Paul Smith was out after thirty-five overs of unyielding defence, and by tea, the score was 37 for 4 off forty-two overs. Smith, a young man of pugnacious approach, had batted out of character for 107 minutes, but he had impressed Underwood: 'He went a long way forward to me, and his long reach helped him smother the ball. For a young lad, I thought he battled away well.'

Geoff Humpage managed to dent the Underwood analysis after tea, with two boundaries from short-pitched deliveries outside the off-stump which positively demanded the treatment – and it is a measure of Underwood's professionalism that he was furious at himself. Humpage enjoyed the duel, kicking away balls pitched on his middle stump, secure in the knowledge that he would not be out lbw because the ball was doing so much. 'I had talked about it to the umpires, and they said that it would need to pitch outside leg-stump to get an lbw decision. So I kept kicking it away off the stumps and Deadly got more and more uptight. I enjoyed the battle.' It could not last – after fifty-seven minutes, Humpage edged one that turned and lifted and first slip took the catch. In the same over, Anton Ferreira played forward, the ball took off, and he fended it off his nose straight up in the air. Twelve minutes later and Asif Din negotiated another exploding shell which threatened his throat and Cowdrey took another catch. Underwood had taken six of the seven wickets and the scent of conquest was in his nostrils.

At least Norman Gifford and Gladstone Small made them work hard for the win. It was a little easier for Gifford: as a left-hander, he was tackling deliveries that came into him, and he simply let the ball hit his pads or hit him high up on the waist. He had faced Underwood in his pomp, when the ball did remarkable things on a wet wicket, so he just trusted to his experience and technique. For an hour he lasted out until, ironically, he fell at the other end. Gladstone Small lingered for thirty-four minutes until he was caught close in, as the ball hit the top of his bat handle when it reared up at his face. 'I stayed away from Deadly's end as long as I could. I played down the line and didn't worry if the ball missed the edge of my bat by a long way. Every ball was on the spot – he just didn't give you the chance to get down the pitch at him, because he was bowling medium-pace leg-breaks at us. Once or twice an over, the ball would fly over your head as you played forward. Now I know why he used to get so many wickets when rain fell on uncovered pitches!'

It was all over at 5.43. In seventy-five minutes, 56 for 4 had become 65 all out, but there was no shame in that. It had taken 462 balls to get them out and 51 of the 76.5 overs were maidens. The fifty had taken 51.3 overs and the innings lasted 236 minutes. Several other county sides would have buckled earlier. One or two decisions had gone against the batsmen, with Chris Cowdrey making enough appeals to satisfy Dr Barnardo. After a time, the umpires were being pressurized into making decisions after a flurry of bat and pad, and it seems they made an error or two – but that is inevitable when a man of Underwood's accuracy can afford men round the bat. Cries of 'catch it!' reverberated throughout the innings and, now and again, the umpires agreed.

Underwood does not feel the wicket was all that unplayable. 'Norman Gifford and I have bowled on far more responsive ones, especially when rain-affected. It looked awful, with all those craters around, but it didn't do as much as they expected. Anton Ferreira got a real pig of a ball, but for the rest, I just relied on bounce to get them to glove it. It plays into my hands when batsmen are just trying to block it out. If Amiss and Kallicharran had stayed in, they had the class to play me into the vacant areas for singles and they might have messed me around.' The senior Warwickshire players disagree, while praising Underwood's bowling. Dennis Amiss said: 'The ball was doing everything. For players brought up in this decade, it was a hell of an experience.' Norman Gifford: 'It was very poor at the end. There was more chance of the arms and gloves being hit, rather than the stumps.' Geoff Humpage: 'You needed a helmet to head the ball away. What can you do when you're looking to play it away off your knee and it threatens your teeth?'

Why did Derek Underwood fare that much better than Norman Gifford? After all, they were both reared in the same generation, when spinners were expected to cash in once the conditions favoured them. Yet Gifford did not run through Kent, despite his good figures. Dennis Amiss has an interesting theory: 'Deadly cuts it more than spins it and that magnificent wrist action gives him that crucial zip. He gets bounce all the time whereas Giffie gets it from his fingers. When your fingers are tired, you can't get as much zip as a man with a great body action like Deadly. Because he goes round the wicket, Deadly relies on a powerful body action to make the ball go across the right-hander. So he's always got a chance of getting good players out. You can never escape him when he bowls round the wicket, because he can also get you caught at bat/pad or straighten one up for an lbw. His quicker one into the blockhole is a great delivery – it's a fast-medium delivery and has always got him surprise wickets.' Geoff Humpage thinks Underwood is a spin bowling version of Richard Hadlee: 'It's all in the body action. He gets right round and follows through as if he means it. Like Hadlee, that final flick of the wrist gets extra bounce and that extra pace destroys you after a time. He never lets up and he brings the best out of you. Batting against Deadly is one of the great challenges for any modern batsman.'

That is the main message to take from this game. All the young Warwickshire players agreed that it was an education to come up against a master craftsman in conditions that favoured him. It was like stepping into a time machine for the likes of Gifford, Amiss and Brown, and they smiled wryly as the youngsters said afterwards, 'So that's what it was like when it rained!' It seems wrong that a great cricketer like Underwood is denied the chance to prosper on rain-affected wickets any more; the decision to cover wickets has hardly unearthed a generation of English bowlers with the wit, variety and technique to bowl out the best batsmen. Let Dennis Amiss have the last word on a man who is in danger of becoming a cricketing anachronism: 'It was marvellous to watch an artist at work, even though we were on the wrong end of it.'

50
Pakistan v. West Indies
FAISALABAD 1986

All over the world, cricket fans pinched themselves at the news: the West Indies beaten at last, and humbled into the bargain. They were beaten for only the second time in thirty-seven Tests, but it was the manner of their defeat that was so astonishing. They were shot out in 127 minutes for their lowest score in Test cricket; even more exotically, the team that espouses the fast bowling juggernaut was undone by the anachronistic mysteries of leg-spin. For once the sledgehammer did not crack the walnut; it was unpicked by the most subtle, intricate form of all bowling.

Abdul Qadir has been the best of the wrist-spinning breed for some years now. That is hardly a fulsome testimony, because there are very few wrist-spinners left in top-class cricket, and Abdul remains the only automatic choice for a Test side. In his previous thirty-eight Tests he had been occasionally frustrating, unpredictably devastating but always fascinating to watch. Few Test players have been able to read his 'googly' with consistent ease (one treasures the baffled reaction of several English batsmen to his wiles in 1982), but a combination of slow wickets, negative captaincy and his own mercurial temperament has hampered Abdul Qadir. Yet there has never been any doubt that on his day he could run through the best of batting sides; that elusive blend of consistency and brilliance has long frustrated cricketers of genius.

One man was not at all surprised by Abdul Qadir's humiliation of the West Indians. At the start of September I visited the Pakistan captain Imran Khan in his Chelsea flat for a BBC radio interview. He was very optimistic about his country's prospects in the forthcoming series. Excessive optimism has never been Imran's cricketing currency, and I asked him why he could be so sure that the West Indies would struggle. After all, the Pakistani batsmen have

PAKISTAN *v* WEST INDIES
(First Test)
At Faisalabad, 24–29 October 1986

PAKISTAN

Mohsin Khan lbw b Marshall	2	– (2) c Haynes b Walsh	40
Mudassar Nazar c Richardson b Marshall	26	– (1) c Haynes b Marshall	2
Rameez Raja lbw b Marshall	0	– c Gray b Patterson	13
Javed Miandad c Dujon b Patterson	1	– (6) c sub (A. L. Logie) b Gray	30
Qasim Omar hit wkt b Gray	3	– lbw b Walsh	48
Saleem Malik retired hurt	21	– (11) not out	3
*Imran Khan c and b Gray	61	– c Harper b Marshall	23
Abdul Qadir c and b Patterson	14	– lbw b Gray	2
†Saleem Yousuf lbw b Gray	0	– (4) c Greenidge b Harper	61
Wasim Akram c Richardson b Gray	0	– (9) st Dujon b Harper	66
Tauseef Ahmed not out	9	– (10) b Walsh	8
B 1, l-b 11, n-b 10	22	B 7, l-b 8, w 2, n-b 15	32
	159		328

1/12 2/12 3/19 4/37 5/37 6/119 7/120 8/120 9/159

1/2 2/19 3/113 4/124 5/208 6/218 7/224 8/258 9/296 10/328

Bowling: First Innings – Marshall 10–2–48–3; Patterson 12–1–38–2; Gray 11.5–3–39–4; Walsh 5–0–22–0. Second Innings – Marshall 26–3–83–2; Patterson 19–3–63–1; Gray 22–4–82–2; Walsh 23–6–49–3; Harper 27.5–9–36–2.

WEST INDIES

C. G. Greenidge lbw b Wasim	10	– lbw b Imran	12
D. L. Haynes lbw b Imran	40	– lbw b Imran	0
R. B. Richardson b Tauseef	54	– c Rameez b Qadir	14
H. A. Gomes c sub (Manzoor Elahi) b Qadir	33	– b Qadir	2
†P. J. L. Dujon c Rameez b Tauseef	0	– (6) lbw b Imran	0
R. A. Harper c Saleem Yousuf b Wasim	28	– (7) c sub (Shoaib) b Qadir	2
M. D. Marshall c Saleem Yousuf b Wasim	5	– (8) c and b Qadir	10
*I.V.A. Richards c Saleem Yousuf b Wasim	33	– (5) c Rameez b Qadir	0
C. A. Walsh lbw b Wasim	4	– (10) b Imran	0
A. H. Gray not out	12	– (9) b Qadir	5
B. P. Patterson lbw b Wasim	0	– not out	6
B 9, l-b 8, n-b 12	29	L-b 2	2
	248		53

1/12 2/103 3/124 4/124 5/178 6/192 7/223 8/243 9/247 10/248

1/5 2/16 3/19 4/19 5/20 6/23 7/36 8/42 9/43 10/53

Bowling: First Innings – Wasim 25–3–91–6; Imran 21–8–32–1; Qadir 15–1–58–1; Tauseef 22–5–50–2. Second Innings – Wasim 3–0–5–0; Imran 13–5–30–4; Qadir 9.3–1–16–6.

Umpires: Khizar Hayat and Mian Aslam.

Pakistan won by 186 runs.

never looked comfortable against high pace, even on their own flat wickets – and no side in cricket history has paraded such an awesome fast bowling line-up. Imran said that he had two bowlers who could do the trick, Wasim Akram and Abdul Qadir. He said that Wasim's left-arm fast bowling would be very difficult to play and added, 'He's an absolute natural, he'll be in the side for years', and that the little leg-spinner was now bowling better than ever. I have always felt that Imran, of all Pakistan's captains, understood Abdul better than anyone (their Lahore background certainly helped) and I made a mental note to keep a close eye on the forthcoming contest. I had little inkling that Imran would be proved right so spectacularly within six weeks.

The omens were not good for Pakistan on the first day of the first Test. The Faisalabad pitch had been re-laid in an attempt to impart extra bounce, but the informed opinion was that the bounce would be dangerously erratic. Such a pitch would be meat and drink to the West Indian fast bowlers and most good judges were not sanguine for Pakistan. Neither were the selectors: they packed the Pakistan side with six specialist batsmen, plus Imran Khan as all-rounder, and played two spinners, Abdul Qadir and the off-spinner Tauseef Ahmed. It did not look cohesive enough to withstand a team that had won its last seven Test series and had not lost a series since 1980 in New Zealand. To all intents and purposes, the West Indies were superhuman: the fittest as well as the best side in the world, with a hunger to carry on their astonishing run of triumphs.

After the first day's play, there seemed little chance of the Caribbean hegemony being threatened. Tony Gray, the Garner clone, had bowled with hostility on his Test debut, backed up by three fast henchmen and there was little resistance. Qasim Omar's dismissal – falling onto his stumps after avoiding a Patterson bouncer – just about summed up the innings. A partnership of 82 by Salim Malik and Imran Khan was the only hint of respectability, and that was ended when Salim's arm was broken by a rising ball from Courtney Walsh. He would be out for at least a month and therefore the series. Imran's heroism should not be forgotten – after Salim's retirement, he dominated a last wicket stand of 39 until he was caught and bowled by Gray. Without the captain's dauntless example it would have been a disaster. English batsmen used to going through the West Indian mangle allowed themselves a wry grin as they heard the details of Pakistan's first innings, and when West Indies closed on 54 for 1, the pattern looked very familiar.

They had a lead of 89 on the first innings, and by the close of the second day two Pakistan wickets had gone for 28. Judging by the way Mudassar Nazar and Ramiz Raja shaped up to the fast bowlers in the last fifty minutes, a couple of front-line batsmen had already lost their nerve. It had been six years since the two sides had met in the Test arena and already the Pakistanis were looking shell-shocked. They had bowled well, though – particularly Wasim Akram. He took the final five wickets, including the last three in one over, and Imran's steadiness helped pull West Indies back from the comfort of 103 for 1, then 223 for 6. There was nothing in it for Abdul Qadir: he went for nearly four an over. Everything pointed to yet another overwhelming victory.

At last, some Pakistani backbone entered the proceedings on the third day. They lost just two wickets in the day, and although progress was painfully slow they did not bend the knee. Mohsin Khan and Salim Yousuf added 94 for the third wicket until Mohsin was caught at mid-wicket, mishooking. It was his first aggressive shot and underlined the need to select the right stroke in the face of such relentless pace and accuracy. Salim hung on for another half an hour until he mistimed a sweep. He had batted for forty-six overs and set his team-mates a great example. Javed Miandad and Qasim Omar followed suit – Javed, still suffering from a fever, took twenty-five minutes to get off the mark and Qasim took ten minutes longer. They lasted to the close when Pakistan led by 94 at 183 for 4, or 5, with Salim Malik not able to bat. It had been a frustrating day for Malcolm Marshall, who was leading the side in the absence of Viv Richards, suffering from a stomach upset. None of the pace bowlers could get much response from the pitch, and the off-spinner Harper found it equally unresponsive. With two days left, the odds still favoured the West Indies but at least Pakistan had displayed overdue resolution.

The events of the fourth day beggar description. It was eventful enough before tea, but after the interval the West Indies collapsed pitifully. For almost ten hours Pakistan defied the might of the fast bowlers, and all the way down the order it was a story of heroism. Javed Miandad, still unwell, batted three hours for 30, Imran Khan, with two stitches in his right index finger, drove fiercely – but the real hero was Salim Malik. When Walsh bowled Tauseef, the crowd and the West Indian players believed that would be the end of the innings, but then Salim walked out to a standing ovation from the 20,000 crowd. His left arm was in a plaster cast from elbow to knuckles. He faced his first ball left-handed, then turned round. Off fourteen balls he pushed three singles, as Walsh and Gray roared in and did their best to frighten him out. At the other end, Wasim Akram was playing brilliantly, hitting cleanly; Marshall suffered the rare experience of being hit over long-on for six and Gray had similar treatment. Marshall and his team began to look increasingly ragged and petulant, and it took Harper to ensnare Wasim off his fifth ball. It was Wasim's highest Test score, and he and his indomitable partner were roared home after adding a vital 32 in forty minutes. West Indies needed 240 to win.

That last-wicket stand was emotionally draining, but what happened next belonged to the realms of fantasy. At tea the West Indies were 7 for 1, with Haynes out lbw, pushing half-forward to Imran. In the ninety-five minutes left for play, Pakistan took another 8 wickets for 36 with Imran's speed and Abdul Qadir's sorcery. Imran trapped Greenidge lbw soon after tea, then Abdul capitalized on the low morale of the West Indians. They looked thoroughly out of sorts as the leg-spinner teased and tormented them. It was a brand of bowling to which many had become unfamiliar – the English county players like Greenidge, Richards, Harper, Marshall, Walsh and Gray hardly ever see it, while Shell Shield cricket normally permits off-spin or slow left arm as an occasional variation from fast bowling. Never leg-spin and googlies. In his second over, Abdul had Gomes and Richards in the space of three balls: the dismissal of Richards, to a blinding catch at forward short leg, was a massive blow to a side relying on the world's finest batsman to get them out of trouble. Yet Richards had not eaten for three days and was in no shape to battle away. When Imran bowled Dujon first ball, the score was 20 for 5 and few could believe the evidence of their own eyes. Harper hung on grimly for six overs until he was taken at second slip, then Richardson was taken at bat/pad. Gray was completely foxed by Abdul Qadir's quicker ball, and then Imran bowled Walsh in the day's last over. Bowling into the rough, Abdul Qadir was virtually unplayable, with 5 for 13 in seven overs. It had been an exhilarating session, all the more so because of its unexpectedness.

The reputation and professionalism of the West Indies side stand so high that some believed that they would hang on for dear life the next day and rely on rain to save the game. There was no miracle: another twenty-five minutes and thirty-two balls were enough, as Marshall gave a return catch to Abdul. It was the lowest total by any Test side in Pakistan and passed the previous West Indies low of 76 against Pakistan in the 1958/9 series. At last a leg-spinner, dismissed as an expensive luxury, had triumphed in the harsh arena of Test cricket. Realists had been saying for years that leg-spin was a hopeless anachronism on wickets that favour the fast bowler, who relies on weak umpiring to let him get away with intimidation on pitches of uneven bounce. No one needed a helmet or arm-guards against this little man, just an excellent technique and enough nerve to play shots. Certainly the pitch helped the leg-spinner, but it had not deteriorated that much over twenty-four hours, when Harper's off-breaks had been so ineffective. Quite simply, the West Indies were not up to the fray; they had been demoralized by the stubborn resistance of the Pakistani batsmen and were not mentally tough enough to fight it out against superb bowling. Now and then they had shown a chink in the armour as they made their triumphal progress across world cricket, but too often a great innings by Richards, Lloyd or Greenidge would pull them round. Despite their impressive attention to detail, their emphasis on supreme fitness, and their remarkable assembly line of fast bowlers, the feeling had lingered that they would crumble if enough pressure was exerted on them. I could never understand why home countries had not prepared slow turners to negate them – especially in England in 1984, where the wickets were dangerously uneven in bounce – and this pitch in Faisalabad seemed exactly the right kind to draw their teeth. It also helps if you can put out two great bowlers against them.

Viv Richards had no complaints about the pitch, nor the umpiring, nor the effects of his stomach upset. It was a pleasant change to hear a losing Test captain accept the fates philosophically. He did hand out this warning to the euphoric Pakistanis: 'One beautiful day does not make a summer.' Within a fortnight, normal service had been resumed as the West Indies bludgeoned their way to an innings win in the second Test – but at least the romantics had enjoyed their day out of the shadows. Faisalabad 1986 remains one in the eye for the pragmatists who say spin bowling has no place in modern Test cricket.

Bibliography

Arlott, John, *Fred* (Coronet, 1974)

Arlott, John, *Jack Hobbs* (John Murray, 1981)

Allen, David Rayvern (ed.), *Arlott on Cricket* (Collins Willow, 1984)

Allen, David Rayvern (ed.), *A Word from Arlott* (Pelham, 1983)

Bailey, Trevor, *Wickets, Catches and the Odd Run* (Collins Willow, 1986)

Bearshaw, Brian, *The Big Hitters* (Queen Anne Press, 1986)

Botham, Ian, *The Incredible Tests* (Sphere, 1983)

Brearley, Mike, *Phoenix from the Ashes* (Allen & Unwin, 1983)

Coldham, J.D., *Northamptonshire Cricket* (Heinemann, 1959)

Duckworth, Leslie, *The Warwickshire History* (Stanley Paul, 1974)

Fingleton, Jack, *The Immortal Victor Trumper* (Collins, 1978)

Frith, David, *England v. Australia* (Collins Willow, 1984)

Frith, David, *My Dear Victorious Stod* (The Cricketer, 1973)

Frith, David, *The Fast Men* (Allen & Unwin, 1982)

Gilligan, A.E.R., *Sussex Cricket* (Chapman & Hall, 1933)

Green, Benny (ed.), *Wisden Book of Obituaries* (Queen Anne Press, 1986)

Haig, Nigel, *Middlesex County Cricket Club* (Middlesex CCC, 1949)

Howat, Gerald, *Walter Hammond* (Allen & Unwin, 1984)

Kilburn, J.M., *A History of Yorkshire Cricket* (Stanley Paul, 1970)

Kynaston, David, *Bobby Abel* (Secker & Warburg, 1982)

Laker, Jim, *A Spell from Laker* (Hamlyn, 1979)

Lewis, Tony, *Playing Days* (Stanley Paul, 1985)

Mailey, Arthur, *10 for 66 and All That* (Sportsman's Book Club, 1959)

Mason, Ronald, *Jack Hobbs* (Hollis and Carter, 1960)

Morgan, J.H., *Glamorgan* (Convoy, 1952)

Parker, Graham, *Gloucestershire Road* (Pelham, 1983)

Roberts, Ron, *Sixty Years of Somerset Cricket* (Westaway, 1952)

Rogerson, Sidney, *Wilfred Rhodes* (Hollis & Carter, 1959)

Ross, Gordon, *The Surrey Story* (Stanley Paul, 1957)

Simmons, Jack, *Flat Jack* (Queen Anne Press, 1986)

Snow, E.E., *Leicestershire Cricket* (Stanley Paul, 1978)

Sutcliffe, Herbert, *For England and Yorkshire* (Edward Arnold, 1931)

Swanton, E.W., *As I Said at the Time* (Collins Willow, 1983)

Swanton, E.W., Plumptree, George and Woodcock, John (eds), *Barclay's World of Cricket* (Collins Willow, 1986)

Thomas, Andrew and Harris, Norman, *Great Moments in Cricket* (Queen Anne Press, 1976)

Williams, Marcus (ed.), *Double Century* (Collins Willow, 1985)

Willis, Bob, *The Captain's Diary* (Collins Willow, 1983)

Willis, Bob, *Lasting the Pace* (Collins Willow, 1985)

The Field

Cricket – A Weekly Record of the Game

Bell's Life in London

Daily Telegraph

The Times

Guardian

Wisden Cricket Monthly

The Cricketer

The Cricket Statistician

Wisden Cricketer's Almanack